CASEBOOKS IN CRITICISM

Edith Wharton's
The House of Mirth

A CASEBOOK

EDITH WHARTON'S
The House of Mirth

◆ ◆ ◆

A CASEBOOK

Edited by
Carol J. Singley

2003

OXFORD
UNIVERSITY PRESS

Oxford New York
Auckland Bangkok Buenos Aires Cape Town Chennai
Dar es Salaam Delhi Hong Kong Istanbul Karachi Kolkata
Kuala Lumpur Madrid Melbourne Mexico City Mumbai Nairobi
São Paulo Shanghai Taipei Tokyo Toronto

Published by Oxford University Press, Inc.
198 Madison Avenue, New York, New York 10016

www.oup.com

Library of Congress Cataloging-in-Publication Data
Edith Wharton's The house of mirth : a casebook / edited by
Carol J. Singley.
p. cm.—(Casebooks in criticism)
Includes bibliographical references.
ISBN 0-19-515602-1; 0-19-515603-X (pbk.)
1. Wharton, Edith, 1862–1937 House of mirth. 2. Social classes in
literature. 3. Single women in literature. I. Singley, Carol J., 1951–
II. Series.
PS3545.H16 H6833 2003
813'.52—dc21 2003001074

1 3 5 7 9 8 6 4 2

Printed in the United States of America
on acid-free paper

Credits

Benstock, Shari. " 'The Word Which Made All Clear': The Silent Close of *The House of Mirth*," in *Famous Last Words: Changes in Gender and Narrative Closure*, ed. Allison Booth. Charlottesville: University of Virginia Press, 1993. 230–58. Reprinted with permission of the University Press of Virginia.

Dimock, Wai Chee. "Debasing Exchange: Edith Wharton's *The House of Mirth*." *PMLA* 100 (October 1985): 783–92. Reprinted by permission of the Modern Language Association of America.

Gair, Christopher. "The Crumbling Structure of 'Appearances': Representation and Authenticity in *The House of Mirth and The Custom of the Country*." *Modern Fiction Studies* 43.2 (1997): 349–73. © Purdue Research Foundation. Reprinted by permission of the Johns Hopkins University Press.

Goldman-Price, Irene C. "The "*Perfect* Jew" and *The House of Mirth*: A Study in Point of View." *Modern Language Studies* 23.2 (spring 1993): 25–36.

Kaplan, Amy. "Crowded Spaces in *The House of Mirth*." *The Social*

Construction of American Realism. Chicago: University of Chicago Press, 1988. 88–103.

Kassanoff, Jennie. "Extinction, Taxidermy, Tableaux Vivants: Staging Race and Class in *The House of Mirth.*" *PMLA* 115 (January 2000): 60–74. Reprinted by permission of the Modern Language Association of America.

Lidoff, Joan. "Another Sleeping Beauty: Narcissism in *The House of Mirth.*" *American Quarterly* 32 (winter 1980): 518–39. © The American Studies Association. Reprinted by permission of the Johns Hopkins University Press.

Merish, Lori. "Engendering Naturalism: Narrative Form and Commodity Spectacle in U.S. Naturalist Fiction." *Novel: A Forum on Fiction* 29 (spring 1996): 319–45. Copyright NOVEL Corp. © 1996. Reprinted with permission.

Showalter, Elaine. "The Death of the Lady (Novelist): Wharton's *House of Mirth.*" *Representations* 9 (winter 1985): 133–49. © 1985 by The Regents of the University of California.

Wagner-Martin, Linda. From *The House of Mirth: A Novel of Admonition.* Twayne's Masterwork Studies. Boston: G. K. Hall, 1990. 1–11; 30–40. Reprinted by permission of the Gale Group.

Wharton, Edith. *A Backward Glance.* New York: Appleton-Century, 1934. 206–8. Reprinted by permission of the Estate of Edith Wharton and the Watkins/Loomis Agency.

Wharton, Edith. Introduction to *The House of Mirth.* Oxford: Oxford University Press, 1936. v–xi. Reprinted by permission of Oxford University Press.

Wolff, Cynthia Griffin. "Lily Bart and the Drama of Femininity." *American Literary History* 6.1 (spring 1994): 71–87. By permission of Oxford University Press.

Contents

Edith Wharton's
The House of Mirth

A CASEBOOK

Introduction

CAROL J. SINGLEY

◆ ◆ ◆

FEW NOVELS OF THE twentieth century pose the question of women and marriage more directly than Edith Wharton's *The House of Mirth.* And few characters compel readers' attention more completely than the beautiful, provocative, and ill-fated Lily Bart. Since the novel was first published in both serial and book form in 1905, readers across the United States have eagerly followed Lily's misadventures and have engaged in vigorous, often passionate debate about her downfall. *The House of Mirth* was an immediate best-seller, earning Edith Wharton high praise and profit. It has been popularly and critically acclaimed ever since. A unique blend of romance, realism, and naturalism, *The House of Mirth* qualifies as a "novel of manners," but it also transcends this narrow classification. It is both a powerful love story and a searing critique of a society so relentlessly materialistic and self-serving that it casually destroys what is most beautiful and blameless within it.

Wharton's brilliance lies in her ability to portray a complex heroine who is capable of making decisions and facing their consequences but who is at the same time vulnerable to an array of internal and external forces that constrict choice. Wharton is particularly sensitive to the role of gender in shaping characters' options. She indicts an early twentieth-century social system that requires women to marry for money, rendering them little more than decorative objects, and she dramatizes the plights of both men and women as they scramble to position themselves socially during a time of tremendous cultural change. The author's second published full-length work of fiction, *The House of Mirth* also marks Wharton's coming of age as a novelist. It remains, along with novels such as *Ethan Frome* (1911), *The Custom of the Country* (1913), *Summer* (1917), and *The Age of Innocence* (1920), a testament to her powers as a great American writer of realism and naturalism.

Edith Wharton sets *The House of Mirth* in New York City, the same upper-class society in which she was raised. Born Edith Jones in 1862 into a privileged world known as Old New York, Wharton could trace her ancestors to seventeenth-century Dutch and Belgian immigrants who settled in lower Manhattan and quietly amassed fortunes from real estate and other investments. She was the third child of a socially prominent couple, George Frederic Jones and Lucretia Rinelander Jones. Because her two brothers were much older than she, Edith was often alone as a child. Provided no formal education, she was tutored by a governess and left on her own to daydream or read surreptitiously in her father's library. She felt close to her father, a quiet, sensitive man who loved poetry but acquiesced in his wife's incessant need for a busy social schedule. She was confused by and eventually alienated from her fashion-conscious mother, who disapproved of her literary ambitions and whose own social aspirations gave rise, it was rumored, to the expression "keeping up with the Joneses."[1] Her parents are possible models in *The House of Mirth* for Lily Bart's beleaguered father and social-climbing mother.

Edith grew up in a tight-knit, insular community in which tradition, business integrity, and good taste were tacitly valued and religiously practiced. Although she would note appreciatively in her memoir, *A Backward Glance*, that her society taught her the importance of good manners and proper English, she found Old New York inhospitable to literature. From an early age, Edith had a passion to "make up" stories,[2] but she received little encouragement from family members, who frowned upon serious intellectual and artistic pursuits of any kind, especially for women. Her parents indulged their daughter's creative ambitions by privately publishing a book of her poems, *Verses*, in 1878, but the young writer otherwise labored alone in her apprenticeship. As was expected of women of her class, she made her social debut—a year early at her mother's insistence—and in 1885 married a man of her social standing. The couple shared an interest in travel but were otherwise incompatible; Wharton remained married to Edward "Teddy" Wharton for twenty-eight years, divorcing him in 1913.

In the 1890s, the decade preceding the publication of *The House of Mirth*, Wharton worked to establish herself as a writer. She endured bouts of illness that included nausea, fatigue, and asthma, which critics ascribe to psychological as well as physical causes.[3] She also traveled extensively, particularly in Europe. She signaled her growing independence from New York and Newport society by building a home in Lenox, Massachusetts, and by continuing to write. She published poems; short stories; two novellas, *The Touchstone* (1900) and *Sanctuary* (1903); a two-volume historical novel set in eighteenth-century Italy, *The Valley of Decision* (1902); and nonfiction, including the co-authored *The Decoration of Houses* (1897), a guide to interior design. Her poems and stories appeared in leading magazines of the day, such as the *Atlantic Monthly, Scribner's, Century*, and *Harper's*, and earned positive reviews.

In September 1903, Wharton began work on the novel that would become *The House of Mirth*, drawing from notes made previously in a donnée book. She abandoned the project during a trip to Europe and took it up again nearly a year later, accepting an invitation from Scribner's for serial publication of the novel beginning in January 1905. Wharton toyed with various titles, including *A Moment's Ornament* and *The Year of the Rose* but settled on *The House of Mirth*. This title, alluding to the biblical book of Ecclesiastes and the vanity of human wishes, underlines the novel's moral as well as social import, a point Wharton emphasized in a 1905 letter to the Reverend Morgan Dix: "*No* novel worth anything can be anything but a novel 'with a purpose,' and if anyone who cared for the moral issue did not see in my work that *I* care for it, I should have no one to blame but myself."[4] She wrote the novel at record speed under strict time constraints. The first installment appeared even before she had devised the ending. Working under pressure proved to be fortuitous; as Wharton writes in *A Backward Glance*, deadlines taught her the "discipline of the daily task" and helped her develop from a "drifting amateur into a professional."[5]

The novel recounts the story of Lily Bart, nearly twenty-nine years old and weary from a decade spent on the marriage circuit. Orphaned and in the care of a wealthy but unsympathetic aunt, Lily cannot solve her perennial problem—a shortage of funds—except by marrying a wealthy man. But Lily is unable or unwilling to marry someone she does not love, and Lawrence Selden, with whom she shares genuine affection, is a committed bachelor. The first book of the two-part novel describes Lily's various bids for marriage; the second book charts her precipitous social and economic decline, including her increasing alienation from family and friends, her attempts to earn a living trimming hats, and her eventual death from an overdose of chloral.

The House of Mirth was an immediate success, astounding publishers and Wharton herself, who, struggling to gain authorial confidence, depreciated her talent in a comment made to a Scribner's senior editor, William Crary Brownell: "*Je rêve d'un aigle, j'accouche d'un colibri*" (I dream of an eagle and give birth to a hummingbird).[6] Two weeks after the book's publication, 40,000 copies of the first printing and 20,000 copies of the second printing had sold out. By the end of 1905, 140,000 copies of the book had been sold. In early 1906, *The House of Mirth* stood at the top of national best-seller lists, ahead of Upton Sinclair's muckraking novel about the meat-packing industry, *The Jungle*.[7] By August of that same year, Wharton had earned from sales of *The House of Mirth* three times the amount of money that the established realist writer William Dean Howells had earned in a year.[8] A French translation of the novel was immediately issued; stage adaptations followed. Readers across the United States reacted emotionally to the news of Lily Bart's death, and a lively debate raged in the *New York Times Saturday Review of Books*, with readers identifying themselves as "Lenox" and "Newport" and arguing about the accuracy of Wharton's depiction of upper-class social life.[9]

It is easy to understand the popularity of *The House of Mirth*. Edith Wharton had reached a middle-class audience eager for insights into glamorous upper-class life, made all the more interesting by her willingness to expose society's flaws. The success of the novel demonstrated Wharton's keen awareness of her readers' tastes, as well as her skill in transforming into fiction the details of elite New York society life that she knew so well. In choosing an upper-class subject matter, however, Wharton was working against the current literary grain. Writers of naturalism, in vogue during the 1890s, often focused on the lower classes to demonstrate the power of internal and external forces to control characters' destinies. Sure that her subject was viable, Wharton protested two critical assumptions about her work at this time: that she was "an echo of Mr. [Henry] James" and that the people she wrote about were "not 'real' because they are not navvies & charwomen." Both views, she added, left her feeling "rather hopeless."[10] After *The House of Mirth* was published, Wharton defended her decision to place a privileged, upper-class character at the center of a naturalistic novel. She continued throughout her career to make Old New York—as well as New England and Europe—the focus of her fiction, always maintaining that it was not the subject matter but the artist's treatment of it that gave a novel or short story its significance.

Readers' sadness and disappointment upon learning that Lily Bart was dead can be understood in terms of the novel's genre. *The House of Mirth* is a romance, that is, a type of women's fiction that tells the story of courtship and marriage. Traditionally, such tales have one of two endings: marriage or death. Narrative conventions insist on the chastity and moral virtue of the heroine, who is rewarded with a felicitous marriage. If virtue is compromised—or even appears to be—the heroine must pay for her deviation from societal norms, and society must be freed from potential contamination by her. Edith Wharton subscribes to the genre of female romance by writing about an eligible maiden who struggles to preserve her reputation and to find a suitable husband, but she shifts narrative focus from the beginning to the end of her heroine's quest. By narrating events at the conclusion of Lily's marital search, Wharton gives her plot a sense of urgency and finality. She also forces readers to confront the fact that Lily's story cannot have a happy ending because she has so few viable options.

Wharton also complicates the romance genre with her complex portrayal of Lily's character. Lily is not the conventionally passive or naïve woman called for in the romance novel. She is a multivalent character, as much modern woman as Victorian lady, whose puzzling, often contradictory actions frustrate readers' attempts to understand or sympathize with her. On the one hand, Lily seems to be a discriminating woman determined to remain in control of her fate. The fact that for ten years she has had ample opportunity to marry but has rejected suitors suggests that she is taking pains to shape the contours of her marital future. Early in the novel, Lawrence Selden notes this deliberateness and credits Lily with the faculty of "calculation [ ]."[11] Readers may also infer that Lily sets high standards, refusing to marry for any reason except love. On the other hand, Lily often makes frivolous or precipitous decisions, and she seems insensitive to the consequences of her actions, even when they are damaging to her. As her friend Carry Fisher comments, Lily "works like a slave preparing the ground and sowing her seed; but the day she ought to be reaping the harvest she over-sleeps herself or goes off on a picnic" (189). Lily has an "insatiable desire to please" others, but she is paradoxically self-absorbed. The narrator notes, for example, about her impulsive gift to Gerty Farish's charity, that Lily "could feel other demands only through her own" (151). Indeed, Lily presents so many faces that at times she seems to have no self at all.[12]

Wharton locates the source of Lily's difficulties not only in her heroine's personality but also in the society that produced her.

Society discourages women like Lily from developing independent identities and grooms them instead to be little more than aesthetic objects or spectacles. Indeed, Wharton constructs her novel as a series of set pieces in which Lily carefully presents constructed images of herself. Conditioned to be valued for her good looks, Lily acquiesces in what Judith Fetterley calls "the temptation to be a beautiful object."[13] In the first scene of the novel, she catches Selden's attention by standing "apart from the crowd," "a figure to arrest even the suburban traveller rushing to his last train" (3, 4). Later that afternoon, en route to the Trenor estate at Bellomont, she contrives to converse with Percy Gryce about Americana, knowing the wealthy bachelor's passion for book collecting, and she similarly intends to impress Gryce with her appearance of piety at Sunday services. Lily performs these functions even though she is loathe to think of Gryce as her husband; success would mean only "that he might ultimately decide to do her the honour of boring her for life" (25).

Lily's elaborate self-constructions culminate in the tableau vivant scene at the Wellington Brys' ball. Dressed as the title figure in Joshua Reynolds's painting *Mrs. Lloyd,* Lily is certain that her audience's enthusiasm is "called forth by herself, and not by the picture she impersonated" (136). Yet, it is not clear where theatrical artifice ends and the "real Lily Bart" begins (135). The scene underlines Lily's creative potential, but also it demonstrates the limits of self-authorship in settings where women are placed on display as spectacles for the voyeuristic approval of males. As Barbara Hochman writes, such a positioning of women promotes dependence rather than independence: "it cannot proceed without an audience."[14] Lily's performance in the tableau vivant scene proves to be more problematic than triumphant. Although she rivets the attention of Lawrence Selden, she also excites the aggressive appetite of Gus Trenor, who later tries to extract sexual favors as repayment for the loan she has accepted from him to pay her ever-mounting bills. Traumatized by Trenor's attempted rape, Lily flees his house late at night and is again seen by onlookers. Lacking the ability to control either her environment or others' interpretations of her actions, Lily can do nothing to salvage her reputation when members of society, including Selden, imagine the worst of her.

Wharton constructs the novel so that the reader often sees Lily from Lawrence Selden's point of view. It is a perspective increasingly suspect and untrustworthy. Although Selden is clearly attracted to Lily, he does not risk his own security to help her. He warns Lily about Bertha Dorset's malicious intentions when she is a guest aboard her yacht but takes no actual steps to save her from social humiliation. He turns away in distaste when he realizes that Lily is registered at a hotel with people he deems disreputable. And he is oblivious to the fact that Lily attempts to protect him, first when she purchases his and Bertha's love letters, and second when she throws these letters into the fire at his apartment. Platonic discourse about the ideals of the "Republic of the Spirit" notwithstanding, Selden is deeply entwined in the society he criticizes. And his notion of freedom from "material accidents" (68) is more easily implemented by men in New York society than by than by women. Lily can little afford, as he can, the luxury of social detachment. As she tells him, "your coat's a little shabby—but who cares? it does n't keep people from asking you to dine" (12). When, in the final scene of the novel, Selden arrives too late at Lily's bedside, the reader realizes not only that Wharton has created a hero of small rather than large proportions but also that Selden is capable of no greater feeling or action. A failure to measure up to romantic ideals is, of course, implicit in Wharton's social realism. However, Selden's inadequacy is also a measure of Wharton's naturalism—of her conviction that everyone, regardless of privilege or wealth, is inexorably subject to forces and circumstances beyond individual control. Selden, Wharton writes, is a bachelor who "had meant to keep free from permanent ties, not from any poverty of feeling, but because, in a different way, he was, as much as Lily, the victim of his environment" (151–52). Like Lily, Selden can be no better than the society that makes him.

Throughout the novel, Wharton alludes to the theories of Charles Darwin and to social and economic philosophies that followers extracted from his work at the end of the nineteenth century. Like many of her generation, Wharton engaged in the ongoing debate over science and religion. In *The House of Mirth*, she writes what elsewhere I have described as "a chronicle of spiritual alienation," describing a world in which traditional Christian values of love and charity are replaced by self-serving, secular practicalities.[15] In such a world, individuals, like organisms, compete against one another and only the fit survive. When Selden gazes at Lily and has the "confused sense that she must have cost a great deal to make, that a great many dull and ugly people must . . . have been sacrificed to produce her," he reflects a popularized form of Darwinism that assumes people and objects are meant to be used, rather than intrinsically valued. He sees Lily only as a "highly specialized" product in an ever-evolving marriage economy (5). Lily herself "had always accepted with philosophic calm the fact that such existences as hers were pedestalled on foundations of obscure humanity" (150). Only when she falls from social grace does she understand the impersonal, brutal nature of such a system. In sacrificing Lily, named for a flower associated with Christian purity and redemption, to gross material interests, Wharton, like many modernists of her day, questions traditional Christianity and the beneficence—even the presence—of God. In *The House of Mirth*, loss leads not to salvation but to tragic waste.

In accordance with Darwinian principles, virtually all of Lily's family and friends neglect or exploit her in order to further their own interests. Ruminating on Lily's beauty, her mother considers only the money that such a beautiful face might attract. With puritanical self-righteousness, her aunt Peniston disinherits her, not to effect Lily's reform but to underline a point. Her smug cousin Grace Stepney, who can well afford to lend Lily money, refuses to do so. Her friend Bertha Dorset becomes her archrival for social position, and even Judy Trenor, who coaches Lily during her brief courtship with Percy Gryce, exacts social favors such as writing invitations in exchange for hospitality. By the end of the novel, Lily is forced into intimate company with women such as Mattie Gormer and Norma Hatch, who use her services without even the pretense of friendship. Only Gerty Farish and Carry

Fisher treat Lily as a true friend, but Carry's modest means and uncertain status as divorcée limit her ability to act on Lily's behalf. Gerty, the most well-meaning of Lily's friends, offers genuine sympathy, but Lily is so conditioned to expect luxury that she is repelled by the "dinginess" of Gerty's impoverished way of life (150). Lily is so unfit for manual labor that she fails at the simple task of millinery.

Wharton offers her heroine a singular form of domestic shelter in Nettie Struther's kitchen, which Lily visits on the day she dies. The scene is reminiscent of those found in sentimental novels by nineteenth-century writers such as Harriet Beecher Stowe, Susan Warner, and Louisa May Alcott, and the encounter between the two women is suggestive of the strength of female bonds and the restorative properties of home and hearth—qualities hailed in nineteenth-century domestic fiction as antidotes to a callous, materialistic world. Once destitute and abandoned by a lover, Nettie seemed to be "one of the superfluous fragments of life destined to be swept prematurely into the social refuse-heap" (313). But Nettie's plight is reversed by the charitable gift that Lily makes to Gerty's women's club; by marriage to a gentle, caring man; and by motherhood. Relaxing in the cozy warmth of Nettie's kitchen, Lily believes this woman "to have reached the central truth of existence" (319). The respite that Lily enjoys in Nettie's home is only temporary, however, and the baby that Lily imagines holding as she drifts into a chloral-induced sleep is pure fantasy. Wharton presents this sentimental vignette ironically; such domestic renovation is impossible in Lily's uncaring world.

If Lily Bart finds herself constrained by circumstance, then Old New York is also under siege. The fluctuations in Lily's personal fortunes parallel upheavals in society as shifting values and behaviors create new patterns of social inclusion and exclusion.[16] *The House of Mirth* reflects the fact that, after the Civil War, the patterned predictability of Wharton's insular society was disrupted as the nation as a whole experienced greater urbanization, industrialization, and commercialization. In New York City, the arrival of thousands of immigrants and a class of newly moneyed industrialists and entrepreneurs—the nouveau riche—altered

Old New York's social demography. Born into privilege, Lily struggles to adapt to an altered social landscape in which her established assets—beauty and status—are no match for her mounting social and financial debts. Without either a wealthy husband or funds of her own, Lily can only descend the social ladder, in contrast to the newly wealthy, who only rise.

Wharton foregrounds the tension between Old New Yorkers and affluent arrivistes in her depiction of the relationship between Lily Bart and Simon Rosedale. Excluded because he is Jewish and because society abhors the acquisitive business practices that they associate with Jews, Rosedale seems to embody the invasive qualities that Old New York society most fears.[17] Yet, Wharton's portrayal of this shrewd businessman is ambiguous and complex. Lily follows the prejudices of her society in thinking Rosedale unattractive and uncultured, but he is her most attentive suitor. Whereas many characters avoid Lily, Rosedale is the only person to offer sympathy when she loses social currency and is reduced to poverty. The reader of *The House of Mirth*—and, eventually, even Lily herself—is not insensible to this kindness. Rosedale represents, then, not only Wharton's rallying cry to the elite about the dangers of infiltration by those deemed socially undesirable but also her alarm over a more fundamental loss of values in society at large.

Lily searches throughout the novel for a welcoming home, but her pursuits lead only—as the allusion to Ecclesiastes in the novel's title suggests—to a house of mirth and a house of mourning. The word "house" implies permanence, the word "home" warmth and care; the fact that throughout the novel Lily is in ceaseless motion, carried by every manner of conveyance to temporary, often inhospitable shelters, communicates Wharton's concern about the loss of stability and the deterioration of human relations in modern life.[18] Early on, Lily describes her need for care and intimacy, telling Selden, "what I want is a friend who won't be afraid to say disagreeable [things] when I need them. Sometimes I have fancied you might be that friend" (9). Later, when she flees the Trenor home after Gus's assault, she feels "alone in a place of darkness and pollution.—Alone!" (148). By the end of the novel, Lily sits at her desk and laments a depleted checkbook, but she is aware of an inner poverty more devastating than any monetary one: "it was the clutch of solitude at her heart, the sense of being swept like a stray uprooted growth down the heedless current of the years." As Lily reviews her life, including tutelage by parents who were similarly "blown hither and thither on every wind of fashion," she realizes "that there had never been a time when she had had any real relation to life" (319). She remains alone, disconnected from herself and others, too listless to monitor or even care about the possibly lethal effects of the sleep-inducing drug she takes to soothe her overwrought nerves.

We can see in Lily Bart's rootlessness Wharton's growing misgivings as the nation set its course for the twentieth century. The emphasis on materialism and the accelerated pace of modern life threatened not only essential connections among people but also the foundations on which those associations are based. *The House of Mirth* is one of the first novels of the twentieth century to demonstrate how this modernist sense of dislocation and fragmentation can lead to an individual's apathy, even death. Wharton was to pursue this theme of personal and social disintegration in varying ways in much of her fiction. For example, in *The Custom of the Country*, she creates Lily's counterpart, the ruthless Undine Spragg, who succeeds where Lily fails in acquiring husbands and money but who, in the process, is stripped of every caring emotion. In novels such as *Ethan Frome*, *Summer*, and *The Age of Innocence*, Wharton explores the sense of alienation and helplessness that arises when characters cannot escape their stifling social environments. In the Pulitzer Prize–winning *Age of Innocence*, she offers another answer to Lily Bart, portraying Ellen Olenska as a woman who is capable of beauty, passion, intelligence, *and* autonomy but who is unable to find personal fulfillment except in settings outside the United States. During the 1920s, in such novels as *The Mother's Recompense* (1925), *Twilight Sleep* (1927), and *The Children* (1928), Wharton focuses on the failure of modern institutions, especially the family, to nurture the individual.

Just before taking an overdose of chloral, Lily reflects on what is missing from her life. She longs "for a spot of earth . . . dearer to her than another," for "grave endearing traditions, to which the heart could revert and from which it could draw strength" (319). In Wharton's articulation of Lily's ailment we also find her remedy. Although Lily fails to respond to society's call to adapt or perish, Wharton herself drew on a multitude of resources in order to flourish personally and professionally. The publication of *The House of Mirth* in 1905 marked the beginning of the major phase of her writing, a productive period that extended to the publication of *The Age of Innocence* in 1920. Until her death in 1937, Wharton continued along her chosen path, earning acclaim as a novelist and using her earnings to create beautiful homes and gardens in the United States and abroad. In contrast to Lily, she cultivated an intimate circle of friends who shared her values and interests; experienced the passion of a midlife love affair; and traveled extensively, feeling at home wherever she went. Well rewarded for her efforts, she died peacefully in her home, surrounded by friends and the domestic harmony that she had created. Viewed in relation to Wharton's life and work as a whole, the narrative of Lily's failure is but a prelude to the successful striving and fulfillment that Wharton achieved for herself and envisioned for some of her heroines.

SINCE ITS FIRST APPEARANCE, *The House of Mirth* has inspired lively commentary from readers and critics. The essays in this volume, all previously published, reflect the rich development of ideas about Wharton and the novel during the last two decades of the twentieth century. They represent a wide range of critical methodologies—from formal analyses to interpretations that emphasize biographical, feminist, psychological, materialist, new historicist, and cultural studies approaches—and they reflect a broad spectrum of perspectives about Lily Bart and her New York society. Many of the essays included in this collection engage in dialogue with one another, demonstrating how the process of literary criticism leads not only to fresh insights but also to new questions. Considered as a whole, the essays attest to the continuing importance of *The House of Mirth* in the American literary canon and to the importance of Edith Wharton in American letters.

The volume opens with two selections by Edith Wharton. The first is drawn from her autobiography, *A Backward Glance*, published in 1934. In this passage, Wharton describes her theory of fiction and details the circumstances that surrounded the composition of *The House of Mirth*. Despite being a relative novice when she wrote the novel, Wharton was committed to "us[ing] the material closest to hand": that of the upper-class New York society in which she was born and raised. Although literary naturalism favored fiction focused on the commonplace—on what Wharton calls "the man with the dinner pail" (27)—she argues that literary merit depends not so much on the subject matter as on the author's treatment of it, "how deeply he is able to see *into* it." Wharton also insists on the moral as well as social dimensions of her art. How can a novelist give "a society of irresponsible pleasure-seekers" "any deeper bearing than the people composing such a society could guess?" she asks. "A frivolous society can acquire dramatic significance only through what its frivolity destroys. . . . The answer . . . was my heroine, Lily Bart" (28). Wharton gained immense satisfaction and self-confidence from completing her first best-seller, *The House of Mirth*, in a short period of time in order to meet contract deadlines.

The second passage is an introduction that Wharton wrote for a 1936 edition of *The House of Mirth*, published in the World's Classics series by Oxford University Press. Wharton discusses what "dates" art and what gives it lasting value (34). She notes that much has changed in the thirty years since she wrote the novel, when the "venial lapses" of "a young girl who rouged, smoked, ran into debt, borrowed money, gambled, and—crowning horror! went home with a bachelor friend to take tea in his flat" "loomed gigantically" (36). But she also defends a novelist's need to depict in detail the manners and mores of a specific time and place, arguing that "everything dates in a work of art, and should do so." Beyond the superficial attributes of a novel lies its "essential soul," a view of unchanging human nature that endures despite shifting winds of fashion (34). Although she wrote about insignificant people in a now outmoded social world, "the book still lives," she affirms (33). Wharton's "self-reconsideration," as Frederick Wegener has called it,[19] also includes an observation about the difficulties she faced from members of her own class who were outraged by her exposure of them and who futilely hoped that both the novel and its misguided author would "soon be forgotten" (36).

The first critical essay in the collection is Elaine Showalter's "The Death of the Lady (Novelist): Wharton's *House of Mirth*," first published in 1985. Showalter compares *The House of Mirth* with a novel of the same time period, Kate Chopin's *The Awakening*, and defines the literary tradition from which both novels evolve. She also discusses *The House of Mirth* in relation to Edith Wharton's personal and professional development. As Showalter explains, *The House of Mirth* is part of an emergent genre at the turn of the twentieth century that she terms "the novel of the woman of thirty" (39). Lily's crisis of maturation is situated at a moment of historical transition from a nineteenth-century world marked by sisterly and maternal bonds to a modernist world of male and female interactions affected by women's increased mobility, education, and participation in public realms. Whereas some female writers grieved for a "lost Paradise" (41) of women's culture, others, such as Wharton, bravely explored new options for men and women as they broke traditional boundaries that defined gender, marriage, and work. Wharton unsentimentally portrays her heroine Lily Bart as a "Perfect Lady" (46) who lacks outlets for her creative energies. However, in designing Lily's defeat and death, Wharton also gives birth to herself as an artist who can rise above her own ladylike training to become a professional writer. *The House of Mirth* marks Wharton's transition from amateur to professional writer and demonstrates her ability to merge the female and male sides of her lineage into mature fiction that deals seriously with changing relationships between men and women.

Wai Chee Dimock shifts the terms of discussion about Lily Bart's personal and social crisis from the arena of marriage to that of the market in her essay, "Debasing Exchange: Edith Wharton's *The House of Mirth*," also published in 1985. Citing the brutal scene in which Gus Trenor pressures Lily sexually for repayment of his loan to her, Dimock argues for the centrality of exchange rather than of sex in the novel. In her detailed analysis, she delineates the power of the marketplace to reproduce itself at all levels of society. The logic of a market economy permeates New York society and dehumanizes its members, especially Lily, who, although she protests such an "ethos of exchange" (64), cannot transcend her culture's crass materiality. As a result, Lily pays disproportionately to what she owes, finally paying with her life. Dimock notes that Wharton gestures toward the possibility of transcendence over base circumstances with the final domestic scene in Nettie Struther's kitchen, but the novel concludes that such romantic idealism is impossible to sustain given the economic realities of early twentieth-century American society.

Edith Wharton is widely acknowledged as one of the United States's finest realistic writers. Amy Kaplan, in her essay "Crowded Spaces in *The House of Mirth*" first published in 1988, explores the social nature of Wharton's literary realism. Noting Wharton's depiction of Lily Bart as a character refined in appearance and sensibility, set amid scenes of elite luxury, Kaplan reads *The House of Mirth* as a critique of Howellsian realism, which advocated depictions of the commonplace. Realism in *The House of Mirth*, she argues, explores relations between two conflicting meanings of society: the intimate, exclusive realm of Old New York and the impersonal network of institutions that increasingly bind individuals to one another. Wharton's fin-de-siècle novel appeared at a time when both meanings were undergoing social change, when shifting social and economic hierarchies led classes to encounter and clash with one another. *The House of Mirth* specifically maps a social terrain in which the male and the female realms of work and marriage are interconnected and mediated through spectatorship, with the elite classes struggling to manage and protect themselves from the "gaping mob" (88).

Linda Wagner-Martin, in a selection drawn from her book, "*The House of Mirth*: A Novel of Admonition" (1990), provides social and literary contexts for understanding *The House of Mirth* by describing the novel's success and illuminating its structure. She explains how the figure of the New Woman, a harbinger of change in the early twentieth century, shaped Wharton's conception of Lily Bart, allowing her to criticize the reigning nineteenth-century cult of True Womanhood, which insisted on images of women as self-sacrificing, impressionable, and fragile. The novel's astounding commercial success, Wagner-Martin suggests, resulted from Wharton's choice of strategies that appeased readers hostile to the New Woman: a seemingly objective point of view that shows all sides of Lily's personality and an ambiguous ending that leaves the important questions of Lily's death unanswered. The novel's two-part structure and shifting narrative perspectives, she argues, reveal the insufficiency of Selden's point of view and love for Lily. Aware of her audience, Wharton ingeniously constructs the final scene, in which Selden appears at Lily's bedside, so that readers can choose to view the novel either as a conventional "marriage novel" or as a critique of this genre.

The ending of *The House of Mirth* is also the focus of Shari Benstock's 1993 essay " 'The Word Which Made All Clear': The Silent Close of *The House of Mirth*." Benstock recounts readers' shocked responses to news of Lily Bart's death and the ensuing debate that raged about the meaning of the novel. Many readers considered the ending too brutal; others judged Lily as deserving of death; and some complained that Wharton's characterizations of Lily and her society were too shallow. Benstock argues that, by withholding the word that might have passed between Lily and Selden, Wharton "opened a textual space quickly filled by readers and reviewers" (134). More important, Wharton's shift in the final chapter from omniscient narration to free indirect discourse—a technique that denies readers access to Lily's dying thoughts—positions the novel as psychological realism at the brink of modernism. A novelist of character who understood the tensions between societal and personal desire, Wharton never separates her heroine from her social—and moral—context. Benstock declares Wharton an innovative novelist, distinct from Henry James, with whom she is often compared, who is able to bridge ethical and aesthetic concerns.

In her 1993 essay "The *"Perfect* Jew" and *The House of Mirth*: A

Study in Point of View," Irene C. Goldman-Price analyzes the character of Simon Rosedale in order to explain Wharton's complex portrayal of Jewishness and the prevailing anti-Semitic attitudes in the late nineteenth century. Noting patterns of Jewish immigration to the United States and the socially limited interactions between Jews and members of Wharton's Anglo-Dutch society, Goldman explains how difference came to be understood not only as religious but also as cultural and racial. *The House of Mirth* reflects the dominant social belief, expressed by writers such as Hippolyte Taine and William Lecky, that American democracy derived from and depended upon Aryan superiority. Wharton participates in race-typing, depicting Rosedale as physically unattractive and socially and financially aggressive. However, the "complicated irony" (165) of the novel is that, despite Rosedale's offenses against taste, he is a fully drawn character, the only one to demonstrate honesty, basic humanity, and love for Lily. Through her portrayal of Rosedale, Wharton illuminates various, often conflicting layers of social hypocrisy in Wharton's New York society.

Virtually every critic of *The House of Mirth* wrestles in some way with Wharton's portrayal of her heroine, Lily Bart, and with the novel's central question: "Why must Lily die?" In her 1980 essay "Another Sleeping Beauty: Narcissism in *The House of Mirth*," Joan Lidoff argues that, although Lily is destroyed by "the tyranny of social manners," the novel's social realism is controlled by a "deeper underlying dynamic." Citing the form of the romance in which the hero reclaims divided aspects of himself to achieve new personal and social integration, Lidoff declares the novel "primarily a romance of identity" (182). Her psychoanalytic study positions Lily in an unbounded fantasy in which every alternative becomes an impossible one. Noting myriad fairy-tale motifs in the novel, Lidoff argues that Lily's social failure results from her inability to develop past an infantile stage of neediness and narcissism. Lily's arrested development points to a similarly delayed emotional maturation in Wharton; she had not yet integrated the competing demands of sexuality and authorial assertiveness when she wrote the novel. Unable to imagine a fully mature adult capable of tragic stature, Wharton could only ennoble her heroine as a suffering victim.

In her essay "Lily Bart and the Drama of Femininity" (1994), Cynthia Griffin Wolff turns to the visual arts to explain Lily's spectacular failure, in particular to Wharton's extensive knowledge of the theater. During the years that Wharton conceived and wrote *The House of Mirth*, she was intimately involved with drama; from 1900 to 1902, for example, she worked on four plays. Wolff notes parallels between *The House of Mirth* and the well-made play, a popular Edwardian form of drama with which New York theatergoers were well acquainted. Wharton borrows conventional plot elements from the five-act well-made play, including secrets, often in the form of letters; reversals of fortune; and endings in which virtue triumphs. Two scenes mark Wharton's departure from convention, however: Selden fails to notice when Lily throws his letters into the fire, and Lily cannot permanently avail herself of the cozy domesticity experienced at Nettie Struther's home. Stock dramatic conventions, Wolff argues, left Wharton "no story adequate for the construction of [Lily's] adult identity" (216). Lily's death underlines Wharton's critique of the limited roles available to women.

Lori Merish also explores the importance of gender in her 1996 essay "Engendering Naturalism: Narrative Form and Commodity Spectacle in U.S. Naturalist Fiction." Noting parallels between Theodore Dreiser's novel *Sister Carrie* and Wharton's *The House of Mirth*, Merish explains how a newly emerged consumer culture both affords and limits women's choices. In both novels, we witness "the making of the modern American consumer whose 'civilized' desires constituted a salient marker of national identity" in the late nineteenth century (231). Lily, like Carrie, is filled with desire, but she is also commodified, or framed, by male characters' desire for her. Naturalism is gendered, Merish argues, because it transforms the female consumer quite literally into the things she desires, and it subordinates such objects to the power of masculine observation. Selden's social invisibility, in contrast to Lily's conspicuousness, signals his escape from pervasive commodification and marks his power—voyeuristic, social, economic—over her. Wharton expresses Lily's subordination to such power formally as well as thematically: she constructs the point of view so that readers collude with Selden in viewing Lily as an object of consumption.

Christopher Gair, in his 1997 essay "The Crumbling Structure of 'Appearances': Representation and Authenticity in *The House of Mirth* and *The Custom of the Country*," discusses Wharton's representation of relationships among individual, ethnic, and national identities. He argues that throughout the novel "characters attempt to define 'self' and 'culture' as stable constructs in the face of overwhelming evidence to the contrary" (272). He shows how older generations of Americans repeatedly express anxieties about a newer group of invaders, and how Lily's sense of "inherited value" (287) ill prepares her for a more fluid society. Gair points specifically to changes in New York City architecture in the closing decades of the nineteenth century, noting that increasingly blurred distinctions between private and public spheres transformed the role of leisure-class women. New economic forces and a machine-age culture similarly made sought-after permanence impossible. Citing examples from Wharton's *The House of Mirth* and *The Custom of the Country*, as well as from Henry James's *The American Scene*, Gair argues that a transformed cityscape unsettled identities, creating a "Reservation" (277) mentality among the elite classes that foretold their doom.

The volume concludes with Jennie A. Kassanoff's essay, "Extinction, Taxidermy, Tableaux Vivants: Staging Race and Class in *The House of Mirth*," published in 2000. Kassanoff's argument interweaves strands of race, class, and gender, showing how Wharton's depiction of Lily's whiteness becomes an essentialist answer to cultural vulnerabilities experienced by members of the New York upper class. In dialogue with racial questions of her day, Wharton adopts a pliant definition of race—as nature, culture, and spirit—to sound the alarm over a disappearing American patriciate. Kassanoff draws on other writings by Wharton—specifically her book on interior design, *The Decoration of Houses*, and an unfinished novel in typescript, "Disintegration"—as well as on contemporary scientific and cultural writings to make the case that Lily Bart, a racial icon, embodies the "apotheosis, sacrifice, and extinction" (320) of whiteness.

As the range of topics addressed in these summaries demonstrates, readers continue to be intrigued by the complexity of Lily Bart's character and by the conflicting demands made upon her by society. A consummate stylist, a genius of plot and characterization, and an astute critic of her times, Wharton manages in *The House of Mirth* not only to articulate women's challenges at the beginning of the twentieth century but also to confront the issues that faced both genders as they negotiated a shifting social and economic terrain. At the same time as she dissects society's problems, Edith Wharton affords readers all the aesthetic pleasures associated with novel-reading. The essays in this collection suggest how, in a variety of ways, she rewards the many forms of critical inquiry that her fiction invites.

Notes

1. Shari Benstock, *No Gifts from Chance: A Biography of Edith Wharton* (New York: Scribner's, 1994), 26.
2. Edith Wharton, *A Backward Glance* (New York: Scribner's, 1934), 33.
3. See critical biographies by Cynthia Griffin Wolff, *A Feast of Words: The Triumph of Edith Wharton* (New York: Oxford University Press; repr., Reading, Mass.: Addison-Wesley, 1995), 23, 51–53; R. W. B. Lewis, *Edith Wharton: A Biography* (New York: Harper and Row, 1975), 122–28; and Benstock, *No Gifts from Chance*, 78–123.
4. Edith Wharton to Dr. Morgan Dix, 5 December 1905. *The Letters of Edith Wharton*, ed. R. W. B. Lewis and Nancy Lewis (New York: Scribner's, 1988), 98–99.
5. Wharton, *Backward Glance*, 208–9.
6. Edith Wharton to William Crary Brownell, 5 August 1905. *Letters*, ed. Lewis and Lewis, 95.
7. Benstock, *No Gifts from Chance*, 150.
8. Ibid., 154.
9. For reviews of the novel, see *Edith Wharton: The Contemporary Reviews*, ed. James W. Tuttleton, Kristin O. Lauer, Margaret P. Murray (Cambridge: Cambridge University Press, 1992).

10. Edith Wharton to William Crary Brownell, 25 June 1904. *Letters*, ed. Lewis and Lewis, 91.

11. Edith Wharton, *The House of Mirth*. Intro. Cynthia Griffin Wolff (New York: Penguin, 1985), 6. Subsequent citations appear parenthetically in the text.

12. For psychological interpretations of Lily's character, see also Clare Colquitt, "Succumbing to the 'Literary Style': Arrested Desire in *The House of Mirth*," *Women's Studies: An Interdisciplinary Journal* 20.2 (1991): 153–62, and Kathy Fedorko, *Gender and the Gothic in the Fiction of Edith Wharton* (Tuscaloosa: University of Alabama Press, 1995). Colquitt notes Lily's "inability to come to terms . . . [with] sexual passion" (155), and Fedorko views Lily's "tenuous sense of self" as a Gothic struggle for female sexuality and autonomy against male attempts to suppress them (32).

13. Judith Fetterley, "The Temptation to Be a Beautiful Object: Double Standard and Double Bind in *The House of Mirth*," *Studies in American Fiction* 5 (1997): 199–211.

14. Barbara Hochman, "The Rewards of Representation: Edith Wharton, Lily Bart, and the Writer/Reader Interchange," *Novel: A Forum on Fiction* 24 (1991): 148. See also Ruth Yeazell, who notes that "few fictional heroines have been as consistently under observation as Lily Bart" (15). For further discussion of Lily's efforts to become an author of her own life, see Candace Waid, *Edith Wharton's Letters from the Underworld* (Chapel Hill: University of North Carolina, 1991), 15–51.

15. Carol J. Singley, *Edith Wharton: Matters of Mind and Spirit* (Cambridge: Cambridge University Press, 1995), 86. On religious and moral dimensions of Wharton's art, also see the early work of Marilyn Lyde, *Edith Wharton: Convention and Morality in the Work of a Novelist* (Norman: University of Oklahoma Press, 1959).

16. See Clare Preston, who analyzes social change in Wharton's fiction in light of sociological, anthropological, and evolutionary theories: Preston, *Edith Wharton's Social Register* (London: Macmillan, 2000).

17. On racial stereotyping in *The House of Mirth* and other fiction, see Elizabeth Ammons, who writes in "Edith Wharton and the Issue of Race" that Wharton "lived at a time and led her life in such a way that racial difference was an inescapable part of life" (*The Cambridge Companion to Edith Wharton*, ed. Millicent Bell [Cambridge: Cambridge University Press, 1995], 68). See also Dale Bauer, *Edith Wharton's Brave New Politics* (Madison: University of Wisconsin Press, 1994), 60–62, 150–52; and Christian Riegel, "Rosedale and Anti-Semitism in *The House of Mirth*," *Studies in American Fiction* 20.2 (1992): 219–24.

18. On twentieth-century travel and dislocation in *The House of Mirth* and other novels, see Nancy Bentley, "Wharton, Travel, and Modernity," in *The Historical Guide to Edith Wharton*, ed. Carol J. Singley (New York: Oxford University Press, 2002), 147–80.

19. Frederick Wegener, ed., *The Uncollected Critical Writings* (Princeton, N.J.: Princeton University Press, 1996), 257.

A Backward Glance

EDITH WHARTON

◆ ◆ ◆

FATE HAD PLANTED me in New York, and my instinct as a story-teller counselled me to use the material nearest to hand, and most familiarly my own. Novelists of my generation must have noticed, in recent years, as one of the unforeseen results of "crowd-mentality" and standardizing, that the modern critic requires every novelist to treat the same kind of subject, and relegates to insignificance the author who declines to conform. At present the demand is that only the man with the dinner pail shall be deemed worthy of attention, and fiction is classed according to its degree of conformity to this rule.

There could be no greater critical ineptitude than to judge a novel according to *what it ought to have been about.* The bigger the imagination, the more powerful the intellectual equipment, the more different subjects will come within the novelist's reach; and Balzac spread his net over nearly every class and situation in the French social system. As a matter of fact, there are but two essential rules: one, that the novelist should deal only with what is within his reach, literally or figuratively (in most cases the two are synonymous), and the other that the value of a subject depends almost wholly on what the author sees in it, and how deeply he is able to see *into* it. Almost—but not quite; for there are certain subjects too shallow to yield anything to the most searching gaze. I had always felt this, and now my problem was how to make use of a subject—fashionable New York—which, of all others, seemed most completely to fall within the condemned category. There it was before me, in all its flatness and futility, asking to be dealt with as the theme most available to my hand, since I had been steeped in it from infancy, and should not have to get it up out of note-books and encyclopaedias—and yet!

The problem was how to extract from such a subject the typical human significance which is the story-teller's reason for telling one story rather than another. In what aspect could a society of irresponsible pleasure-seekers be said to have, on the "old woe of the world," any deeper bearing than the people composing such a society could guess? The answer was that a frivolous society can acquire dramatic significance only through what its frivolity destroys. Its tragic implication lies in its power of debasing people and ideals. The answer, in short, was my heroine, Lily Bart.

Once I had understood that, the tale rushed on toward its climax. I already had definite ideas as to how any given subject should be viewed, and from what angle approached; my trouble was that the story kept drawing into its web so many subordinate themes that to show their organic connection with the main issue, yet keep them from crowding to the front, was a heavy task for a beginner. The novel was already promised to *Scribner's Magazine*, but no date had been fixed for its delivery, and between my critical dissatisfaction with the work, and the distractions of a busy and hospitable life, full of friends and travel, reading and gardening, I had let the months drift by without really tackling my subject. And then, one day, Mr. Burlingame came to my rescue by asking me to come to his. A novel which was to have preceded mine in the magazine could not be ready in time, and I was asked to replace it. The first chapters of my tale would have to appear almost at once, and it must be completed within four or five months! I have always been a slow worker, and was then a very inexperienced one, and I was to be put to the severest test to which a novelist can be subjected: my novel was to be exposed to public comment before I had worked it out to its climax. What that climax was to be I had known before I began. My last page is always latent in my first; but the intervening windings of the way become clear only as I write, and now I was asked to gallop over them before I had even traced them out! I had expected to devote another year or eighteen months to the task, instead of which I was asked to be ready within six months; and nothing short of "the hand of God" must be suffered to interrupt my labours, since my first chapters would already be in print!

I hesitated for a day, and then accepted, and buckled down to my job; and of all the friendly turns that Mr. Burlingame ever did me, his exacting this effort was undoubtedly the most helpful. Not only did it give me what I most lacked—self-confidence—but it bent me to the discipline of the daily task, that inscrutable "inspiration of the writing table" which Baudelaire, most untrammelled and nerve-racked of geniuses, proclaimed as insistently as Trollope. When the first chapters appeared I had written hardly fifty thousand words; but I kept at it, and finished and delivered my novel on time.

It was good to be turned from a drifting amateur into a professional; but that was nothing compared to the effect on my imagination of systematic daily effort. I was really like Saul the son of Kish, who went out to find an ass, and came back with a kingdom: the kingdom of mastery over my tools. When the book was done I remember saying to myself: "I don't yet know how to write a novel; *but I know how to find out how to.*"

Introduction to the 1936 Edition of *The House of Mirth*

EDITH WHARTON

◆ ◆ ◆

I

It seems like going back to the Pharaohs to try to re-enter the New York world in which *The House of Mirth* originated. The book was written only thirty years ago, and the circle I described in it was that in which I had lived since my eleventh year, and which, in all essentials, had remained unchanged in the interval between my childhood and the writing of the book.

It is given to some novelists, even though they continue to ply their craft beyond middle age, to retain to the end an audience familiar with the life their tales depict, and still to a great extent leading that life. Thackeray and Balzac, for instance, were spared the difficulty of having to readjust themselves to any marked modification in the point of view and the social habits of their readers: whereas in Trollope's latest novels one feels the effort, remarkable if not always successful, of a painter of social life to adapt his vision and its expression to conditions so abruptly modified that the resplendent Duke of Omnium of Framley Parsonage would have seemed an almost legendary figure to the society described in *The Way We Live Now*, and *The American Senator*.

Trollope's difficulty, however, was as nothing compared with that of the novelist of manners whose first tales go back to the eighteen-nineties, and who is asked to deal with one of them from the formidable vantage-ground of 1935. To find an analogy, it would be necessary to imagine a French novelist of manners the curve of whose work should bestride the cataclysmic period from the execution of Louis XVI to the battle of Waterloo. Out of the savage crimes and senseless destruction of those brief years a new world was born, differing as radically from the old world which it destroyed as that strange amalgam of new forces that grew out of the fall of the Roman empire differed from the civilization it overthrew; and great must have been the difficulties of the humble story-teller seeking to reconstruct the setting of his tales from the fragments of a shattered world. It is easy to see why Stendhal dealt with, and dismissed, the battle of Waterloo in the first pages of *La Chartreuse de Parme*, barely suffering his hero to skirt its periphery before hurrying him on to a world as yet unaffected by such convulsions!

It may seem slightly out of scale to invoke the cosmos in dealing with the fortunes of a social chronicler; but when there is anything whatever below the surface in the novelist's art, that something can be only the social foundation on which his fable is built; and when that foundation totters, and is swallowed up in a great world-convulsion, the poor story-teller's structural problem is a hard one. No wonder that Benjamin Constant, and Goethe in later life, hung their creations in the void, and that, for instance, all the furniture, dresses, manners, and customs which make the first volume of *Wilhelm Meister* so magically real, have vanished from its sequel, and from the *Wahlverwandschaften*!

II

When I wrote *The House of Mirth* I held, without knowing it, two trumps in my hand. One was the fact that New York society in the nineties was a field as yet unexploited by any novelist who had grown up in that little hot-house of traditions and conventions; and the other, that as yet these traditions and conventions were unassailed, and tacitly regarded as unassailable.

Why had no one written a novel of New York society? The answer is fairly obvious—most people thought it offered nothing worth writing about. I was very nearly of the same mind; yet I had always felt that the field might prove to be a rich one for any writer with imagination enough to penetrate below the surface.

I remember once saying to Henry James, in reference to a novel of the type that used euphemistically to be called "unpleasant": "You know, I was rather disappointed; that book wasn't nearly as bad as I expected"; to which he replied, with his incomparable twinkle: "Ah, my dear, the abysses are all so shallow."

Well, so they are; but at least they are always there, and the novelist who has the patience to dip down into them will find that below a certain depth, whatever his subject, there is almost always "stuff o' the conscience" to work in. That is why, on reflection, I was not afraid of the poverty of my subject, but proceeded to attack it with the first fine careless valour of the inexperienced. And the subsequent career of the book would seem to justify my audacity; for, in spite of the fact that I wrote about totally insignificant people, and "dated" them by an elaborate stage-setting of manners, furniture and costume, the book still lives, and has now attained the honour of figuring on the list of the Oxford University Press.

The fact is that Nature, always wasteful, and apparently compelled to create dozens of stupid people in order to produce a single genius, seems to reverse the process in manufacturing the shallow and the idle. Such groups always rest on an underpinning of wasted human possibilities; and it seemed to me that the fate of the persons embodying these possibilities ought to redeem my subject from insignificance. This is the key to *The House of Mirth*, and its meaning; and I believe the book has owed its success, from the first, as much to my picture of the slow disintegration of Lily Bart as to the details of the "conversation piece" of which she forms the central figure.

Not that I consider the details in question without their value in giving substance and reality to the novelist's vision. Some readers may still recall Ruskin's savage invective against the school of painters who first substituted "drapery" for real clothes, with their buttons, tags and tucks, under the erroneous impression that vague folds of paint would "date" a picture less than a bustle or leg-o'-mutton sleeves. Alas, the lapse of time was to prove that they date it far more; and a practised eye can easily tell exactly to what year of the eighties or nineties the professional beauties painted or photographed in "drapery" owe their dateless commemoration.

Of course bustles and leg-o'-mutton sleeves date! And what is more, they need not even be described by the novelist in order to figure in his pages as vividly as in contemporary portraiture. Everything dates in a work of art, and should do so; and to situate a picture or a novel firmly where it belongs in the unrolling social picture is to help it draw vitality from the soil it grew in. Jane Austen did not have to describe the attire of her shawled and ruffled heroines, nor the tight trousers and high stocks of their suitors; to bring them before us in their habit as they lived she had only to make her characters speak, move, behave, as people so clothed were in the habit of doing, instead of making them talk "drapery," after the manner of most heroes of fiction in her day.

Obviously, however, the other, and supreme, preservative of fiction is whatever of unchanging human nature the novelist has contrived to bring to life beneath the passing fripperies of clothes and custom. The essential soul is always there, under whatever disguise; and the story-teller's most necessary gift is that of making its presence felt, and of discerning just how far it is modified and distorted by the shifting fashions of the hour.

III

In my volume of reminiscences, *A Backward Glance*, I analysed, to the best of my ability, the origin of *The House of Mirth*, as viewed from what may be called the subjective side: the germination of the tale in the author's mind, and the reasons for its unfolding in the particular way it did. Here, on the contrary, I should like to try to describe what happened to it when it entered other people's minds; for the strangest, and not the least interesting, adventure of any work of the imagination is the inevitable distortion it undergoes in passing from the mind of the writer to that of his readers. It was Mr. Kipling, I think, who cited as an extreme example of this curious transposition of values the fact that *Gulliver's Travels*, intended by its author to be the most savage of social satires, has long since settled down comfortably by the nursery fire as a wonder-tale for children; and the same kind of transposition, though on a less startling scale, happens to every novel which attempts to go a little below the surface of life.

At the time of writing *The House of Mirth* I had too little literary experience to have taken note of this curious phenomenon, and great was my astonishment when the story which I had conceived as a simple and fairly moving domestic tragedy, was received with a loud cry of rejection and reprobation! The cry, to be sure, was not a general one; but the quarter from which it came made it peculiarly audible to me, for it proceeded from the very group among whom I had lived my life and situated my story. If I had been an older hand at my trade, this would not have surprised me; for the attitude of the fashionable world towards those who try to catch its likeness has invariably been one of surprise and resentment. One of the most acutely observed scenes in Proust's *A la recherche du temps perdu* is that in which the old Marquise de Villeparisis says to the young Marcel: "But do you really consider Châteaubriand a genius? Why, he was an intimate friend of my grandfather's, *et c'était de la très petite noblesse.*" My society critics took the opposite attitude, but one based on the same anthropomorphic conception of the work of fiction as something after all half real and half alive—like a frightened child's idea of the terrifying stone water-gods glimpsed through the mist of gushing fountains.

This supposed picture of their little circle, secure behind its high stockade of convention, alarmed and disturbed the rulers of Old New York. If the book had been the work of an outsider, of some barbarian reduced to guessing at what went on behind the stockade, they would not so much have minded—might have laughed over its absurdities, or, more probably, not even have heard of its existence. But here was a tale written by one of themselves, a tale deliberately slandering and defiling their most sacred institutions and some of the most deeply revered members of the clan! And what picture did the writer offer to their horrified eyes? That of a young girl of their world who rouged, smoked, ran into debt, borrowed money, gambled, and—crowning horror!—went home with a bachelor friend to take tea in his flat! And I was not only asking the outer world to believe that such creatures were tolerated in New York society, but actually presenting this unhappy specimen as my heroine! And the people who surrounded her—dreadful caricatures of this or that cousin or uncle or aunt (for of course my characters were all immediately labelled, and some of them wore at least three different labels)—well, it was all so painful and surprising and unaccountable that the best way, perhaps, was not to allude to the book in the presence of its misguided author, but firmly to ignore the fact that she had committed this deplorable blunder; a blunder which, like the book itself, would doubtless soon be forgotten.

IV

Less than twenty years later, if I had offered the same story to the same readers as a study in social corruption, they would have smiled instead of shuddering, and have wondered why I had chosen the tame and blameless Lily Bart as a victim of avenging moral forces. I was certainly lucky in introducing her to the public at a moment when her venial lapses loomed gigantically against a sulphurous background; and looking back on her now, from the superior eminence of a world in which facilities for divorce and remarriage have kept pace with all the other modern devices for annihilating time and space, it seems incredible that the early success of *The House of Mirth* should in some measure have been one of scandal! But so it was, to my own amusement, and to the immense satisfaction of my publishers. Ah, golden days for the novelist were those in which a lovely girl could besmirch her reputation by taking tea between trains at a bachelor's flat! Thanks to this daring expedient, I had no reason for envying Octave Feuillet, who, years earlier, and perhaps as unwittingly, had achieved the same success by causing his hero (in *Le Roman d'un jeune homme pauvre*) to leap at the peril of his life from the top of a ruined tower, in order to shield the honour of a young lady with whom he had been accidentally shut up in that romantic trap! But I sometimes wonder if the novelists of the present day, so put to it to find new horrors in the domestic circle, do not envy *me*—if the brilliant leaders of the new fiction do not now and then sit down and wipe their dripping brows, and say to themselves: "Ah, how easy it must have been to tell a story when the mere appearance of lapsing from conventional rules of conduct caused far more scandal than we can produce after searching the medical encyclopaedias and the confessional manuals of eminent theologians for every known form of human perversity."

Yes—it was certainly easier; for the abysses, which were always so shallow, have grown even more so, now that they are on the itinerary of all the luxury-cruisers.

The Death of the Lady (Novelist)

Wharton's House of Mirth

ELAINE SHOWALTER

◆ ◆ ◆

> The lady is almost the only picturesque survival in a social order which tends less and less to tolerate the exceptional. Her history is distinct from that of woman though sometimes advancing by means of it, as a railway may help itself from one point to another by leasing an independent line. At all striking periods of social development her status has its significance. In the age-long war between men and women, she is a hostage in the enemy's camp. Her fortunes do not rise and fall with those of women but with those of men.
>
> —Emily James Putnam, *The Lady* (1910)

> Perfection is terrible, it cannot have children.
>
> —Sylvia Plath, "The Munich Mannequins"

AT THE BEGINNING OF Edith Wharton's first great novel, *The House of Mirth* (1905), the heroine, Lily Bart, is twenty-nine, the dazzlingly well-preserved veteran of eleven years in the New York marriage market. By the end of the novel, she is past thirty and dead of an overdose of chloral. Like Edna Pontellier, Kate Chopin's heroine in *The Awakening* (1899), who celebrates her twenty-ninth birthday by taking a lover, Lily Bart belongs to a genre we might call "the novel of the woman of thirty," a genre that emerged appropriately enough in American women's literature at the turn of the century. These novels pose the problem of female maturation in narrative terms: What can happen to the heroine as she grows up? What plots, transformations, and endings are imaginable for her? Is she capable of change at all? As the nineteenth-century feminist activist and novelist Elizabeth Oakes Smith noted in her diary, "How few women have any history after the age of thirty!"[1]

Telling the history of women past thirty was part of the challenge Wharton faced as a writer looking to the twentieth century. The threshold of thirty established for women by nineteenth-century conventions of "girlhood" and marriageability continued in the twentieth century as a psychological observation about the formation of feminine identity. While Wharton's ideas about personality were shaped by Darwinian rather than by Freudian determinants, she shared Freud's pessimism about the difficulties of change for women. In his essay "Femininity," for example, Freud lamented the way that women's psyches and personalities became fixed by the time they were thirty. While a thirty-year-old man "strikes us as a youthful, somewhat unformed individual, whom we expect to make powerful use of the possibilities for development opened up to him by analysis," Freud wrote, a woman of thirty "often frightens us by her psychical rigidity and unchangeability. Her libido has taken up fixed positions and seems incapable of exchanging them for others."[2] From Wharton's perspective, Lily Bart is locked into fixed positions that are social and economic as well as products of the libido. Her inability to exchange these positions for others constitutes an impasse in the age, as well as the individual.

Wharton situates Lily Bart's crisis of adulthood in the contexts of a larger historical shift. We meet her first in Grand Central Station, "in the act of transition between one and another of the country houses that disputed her presence at the close of the Newport season," and indeed *The House of Mirth* is a pivotal text in the historical transition from one house of American women's fiction to another, from the homosocial women's culture and literature of the nineteenth century to the heterosexual fiction of modernism.[3] Like Edna Pontellier, Lily is stranded between two worlds of female experience: the intense female friendships and mother-daughter bonds characteristic of nineteenth-century American women's culture, which Carroll Smith-Rosenberg has called "the female world of love and ritual," and the dissolution of these single-sex relationships in the interests of more intimate friendships between women and men that was part of the gender crisis of the turn of the century.[4] Between 1880 and 1910, patterns of gender behavior and relationship were being redefined. As early as the 1880s, relationships between mothers and daughters became strained as daughters pressed for education, work, mobility, sexual autonomy, and power outside the female sphere. Heroines sought friendship from male classmates and companions, as well as within their single-sex communities.[5]

These historical and social changes in women's roles had effects on women's writing as well. Pre–Civil War American women's fiction, variously described as "woman's fiction," "literary domesticity," or "the sentimental novel," celebrated female solidarity and revised patriarchal institutions, especially Christianity, in feminist and matriarchal terms.[6] Its plots were characterized by warmth, intense sisterly feeling, and a sacramental view of motherhood. As these "bonds of womanhood," in Nancy Cott's term, were being dissolved by cultural pressures toward heterosexual relationships, women's plots changed as well. In 1851, for example, Susan Warner's best-selling novel *The Wide, Wide World* tearfully recounted the history of a girl painfully separated from her mother.[7] But, in 1882, in Warner's artistically superior but less-celebrated *Diana*, we are given an astringent and startling modern analysis of the psychological warfare between mother and daughter and the mother's fierce efforts to thwart her daughter's romance. As women's culture came under attack, so too its survivors clung desperately to the past, seeing men as the interlopers in their idyllic community. While some women writers of this generation championed the New Woman, others of the older generation grieved for the passing of the "lost Paradise" of women's culture. In their fiction, male invaders are met with hostility, and the struggle between female generations is sometimes murderous. By the century's end, as Josephine Donovan explains, "the woman-centered, matriarchal world of the Victorians is in its last throes. The preindustrial values of that world, female identified and ecologically holistic, are going down to defeat before the imperialism of masculine technology and patriarchal institutions."[8]

The writers and feminist thinkers of Wharton's transitional generation, Elizabeth Ammons has noted, wrote "about troubled and troubling young women who were not always loved by their American readers." This literature, Ammons points out, "consistently focused on two issues: marriage and work."[9] Seeing marriage as a form of work, a woman's job, it also raises the question of work and especially of creativity. The fiction of this transitional phase in women's history and women's writing is characterized by unhappy endings, as novelists struggled with the problem of going beyond the allowable limits and breaking through the available histories and stories for women.

Unlike some other heroines of the fiction of this transitional phase, Lily Bart is neither the educated, socially conscious, rebellious New Woman nor the androgynous artist who finds meaning for her life in solitude and creativity, nor the old woman fiercely clinging to the past whom we so often see as the heroine of the post–Civil War local colorists.[10] Her skills and morality are those of the Perfect Lady. In every crisis she rises magnificently to the occasion, as we see when Bertha insults her, her aunt disinherits her, Rosedale rejects her. Lawrence Selden, the would-be New Man to whom she turns for friendship and faith, criticizes Lily for being " 'perfect' to everyone"; but he demands an even further moral perfection that she can finally satisfy only by dying. Lily's uniqueness, the emphasis Wharton gives to her lonely pursuit of ladylike manners in the midst of vulgarity, boorishness, and malice, makes us feel that she is somehow the *last* lady in New York, what Louis Auchincloss calls the "lone and solitary" survivor of a bygone age.[11]

I would argue, however, that Wharton refuses to sentimentalize Lily's position but rather, through associating it with her own limitations as the Perfect Lady Novelist, makes us aware of the cramped possibilities of the lady whose creative roles are defined and controlled by men. Lily's plight has a parallel in Wharton's career as the elegant scribe of upper-class New York society, the novelist of manners and decor. Cynthia Griffin Wolff calls *The House of Mirth* Wharton's "first Kunstlerroman," and, in important ways, I would agree, Wharton's *House of Mirth* is also a fictional house of birth for the woman artist. Wolff points out that *The House of Mirth* is both a critique of the artistic representation of women—the transformation of women into beautiful objects of male aesthetic appreciation—and a satiric analysis of the artistic traditions that "had evolved no conventions designed to render a woman as the maker of beauty, no language of feminine growth and mastery." In her powerful analysis of Lily Bart's disintegration, Wharton "could turn her fury upon a world which had enjoined women to spend their artistic inclinations entirely upon a display of self. Not the woman as productive artist, but the woman as self-creating artistic object—that is the significance of the brilliant and complex characterization of Lily Bart."[12] In deciding that a Lily cannot survive, that the lady must die to make way for the modern woman who will work, love, and give birth, Wharton was also signaling her own rebirth as the artist who would describe the sensual worlds of *The Reef, Summer*, and *The Age of Innocence* and who would create the language of feminine growth and mastery in her own work.

We are repeatedly reminded of the absence of this language in the world of *The House of Mirth* by Lily's ladylike self-silencing, her inability to rise above the "word-play and evasion" (494) that restrict her conversations with Selden and to tell her own story. Lily's inability to speak for herself is a muteness that Wharton associated with her own social background, a decorum of self-restraint she had to overcome in order to become a novelist. In one sense, Lily's search for a suitable husband is an effort to be "spoken for," to be suitably articulated and defined in the social arena. Instead, she has the opposite fate: she is "spoken of" by men, and, as Lily herself observes, "The truth about any girl is that once she's talked about, she's done for, and the more she explains her case the worse it looks" (364). To become the object of male discourse is almost as bad as to become the victim of male lust; "It was horrible of a young girl to let herself be talked about," Mrs. Peniston reflects in agitation. "However unfounded the charges against her, she must be to blame for their having been made" (205).

Whenever Lily defies routine, the male scandalmongers are there to recycle her for their own profit. After the tableaux vivants, her performance and her relationship with Gus Trenor are so racily described in *Town Talk* that Jack Stepney is perturbed, although the elderly rake Ned Van Alstyne, "stroking his mustache to hide the smile behind it," comments that he had "heard the stories before" (254). When Bertha Dorset announces that Lily is not returning to the yacht, the scene is witnessed by Dabham, the society columnist of "Riviera Notes," whose "little eyes," Selden fears, "were like tentacles thrown out to catch the floating intimations with which . . . the air at moments seemed thick" (347). These men can rewrite the story of Lily's life, as they can also enjoy the spectacle of her beauty and suffering.

Although Lily has a "passionate desire" to tell the truth about herself to Selden, she can only hint, can speak only in parables he is totally unable to comprehend. Even the body language of her tears, her emaciation, and her renunciatory gestures are lost on him. On her deathbed, as she is drifting into unconsciousness, Lily is still struggling with the effort to speak: "She said to herself that there was something she must tell Selden, some word she had found that should make life clear between them. She tried to repeat the word, which lingered vague and luminous on the far edge of thought. . . . If she could only remember it and say it to him, she felt that everything would be well" (522). Yet she dies with this word of self-definition on her lips, not the bride of a loving communication but rather the still-unravished bride of quietness. After her death, Selden kneels and bends over her dead body on the bed, like Dracula or little Dabham, "draining their last moment to its lees" (as he has earlier led Gerty on, "draining her inmost thoughts"), "and in the silence there passed between them the word which made all clear" (533). This word, Susan Gubar argues, "is Lily's dead body; for she is now converted completely into a script for his edification, a text not unlike the letters and checks she has left behind to vindicate her life. . . . Lily's history, then, illustrates the terrors not of the word made flesh, but of the flesh made word. In this respect, she illuminates the problems Wharton must have faced in her own efforts to create rather than be created."[13]

Among the issues the novel raises is the question of writing itself, both in terms of female creativity and in terms of a relationship to literary traditions. Whereas mid-nineteenth-century American women writers, unlike their English and European counterparts, had explicitly and in their writing styles rejected a male literary tradition that seemed totally alien to their culture, Wharton's generation of women writers, who defined themselves as artists, were working out their relationship to both the male and female literary heritage. *The House of Mirth* revises both male and female precursors, as Wharton explores not only the changing worlds of women but also the transformed and equally limiting worlds of men. In a number of striking respects, *The House of Mirth* goes back to adapt the characteristic plot of mid-nineteenth-century "woman's fiction" and to render it ironic by situating it in the postmatriarchal city of sexual commerce: This plot, as Nina Baym has established, concerned "a young girl who is deprived of the supports she had rightly or wrongly depended on to sustain her throughout life and is faced with the necessity of winning her own way in the world." Despite hardships and trials, the heroine overcomes all obstacles through her "intelligence, will, resourcefulness, and courage." Although she marries, as an indication that her progress toward female maturity has been completed, marriage is not really the goal of this heroine's ordeal, and men are less important to her emotional life than women.[14]

Lily Bart's story alludes to but subverts these sentimental conventions of nineteenth-century women's literature, conventions that dozens of female best-sellers had made familiar. Lily has certainly been deprived of the financial and emotional supports she has been raised to expect and has been even more seriously deprived of the environment for the skills in which she has been trained. First of all, Wharton puts the question of youth itself into question. At twenty-nine, Lily sees eligible "girlhood" slipping into spinsterdom and faces the impending destruction of her beauty by the physical encroachments of adulthood—not simply the aging process, but also anxiety, sexuality, and serious work. Second, in contrast to the emotionally intense relationships among mothers, daughters, sisters, and friends in most nineteenth-century women's writing, women's relationships in *The House of Mirth* are distant, formal, competitive, even hostile. Selden deplores "the cruelty of women to their kind" (352). Lily feels no loving ties to the women around her; in her moment of crisis "she had no heart to lean on" (240). Her mother is dead and unmourned; "Her relation with her aunt was as superficial as that of chance lodgers who pass on the stairs" (240). Her treatment of her cousin Grace Stepney is insensitive and distant, and Grace is bitterly jealous of her success. Lily sees and treats other women as her allies, rivals, or inferiors in the social competition; she is no different from the "best friends" she describes to Selden as those women who "use me or abuse me; but . . . don't care a straw what happens to me" (13).

Whereas childbirth and maternity are the emotional and spiritual centers of the nineteenth-century female world, in *The House of Mirth* they have been banished to the margins. Childbirth seems to be one of the dingier attributes of the working class; the Perfect Lady cannot mar her body or betray her sexuality in giving birth. There are scarcely any children occupying the Fifth Avenue mansions and country cottages of Lily's friends. (Judy and Gus Trenor have two teenage daughters, briefly glimpsed, but not in their mother's company. Judy refers to them only once as having to be sent out of the room because of a guest's spicy stories.)

And, whereas the heroine of women's fiction triumphs in every crisis, confounds her enemies, and wins over curmudgeons and reforms rakes, Lily is continually defeated. The aunt who should come to her rescue disinherits her; Bertha Dorset, the woman friend who should shelter her, throws her out in order to protect her own reputation; the man who should have faith in her cannot trust her long enough to overcome his own emotional fastidiousness. With stark fatalism, rather than with the optimism of woman's fiction, Wharton takes Lily from the heights to her death. As Edmund Wilson first noted in his 1937 essay "Justice to Edith Wharton," Wharton "was much haunted by the myth of the Eumenides; and she had developed her own deadly version of the working of the Aeschylean necessity. . . . She was as pessimistic as Hardy or Maupassant."[15] Indeed, Lily's relentless fall suggests the motto of Hardy's *Tess of the D'Urbervilles*: "The Woman Pays." Despite being poor, in debt, disinherited, an outsider in a world of financiers and market manipulators, speculators and collectors, Lily is the one who must pay again and again for each moment of inattention, self-indulgence, or rebellion. "Why must a girl pay so dearly for her least escape from routine?" she thinks after her ill-timed meeting with Rosedale outside Selden's apartment. But, while Tess pays with her life for a real fall, Lily pays only for the appearance of one, for her inability to explain or defend herself.

In other respects, many details of the novel allude to an American female literary tradition. As Cynthia Griffin Wolff has shown, the name "Lily" referred to a central motif of art nouveau: the representation of female purity as lilies adapted from Japanese art themes, "Easter lilies, tiger lilies, water lilies, liquescent calla lilies, fluttering clusters of lily-of-the-valley."[16] It was also a name with a special history in nineteenth-century women's writing. Amelia Bloomer's temperance and women's rights journal of the 1850s was called *The Lily*, to represent, as the first issue announced, "sweetness and purity."[17] In women's local-color fiction, "Lily" was a recurring name for sexually attractive and adventurous younger women, as opposed to women of the older generation more bound to sisterly and communal relationships. In Mary Wilkins Freeman's most famous story, "A New England Nun," Lily Dyer is the blooming girl to whom the cloistered Louisa Ellis thankfully yields her red-faced suitor. In Freeman's later "Old Woman Magoun," "Lily" represents the feminine spirit of the new century, a sexuality terrifying to the old women who guard the female sanctuaries of the past. In this stark and terrifying story, Old Woman Magoun has managed to keep her pretty fourteen-year-old granddaughter, Lily, a child within a strictly female community; but when it becomes clear that she will lose the orphaned girl both to adolescence and to the predatory sexuality of the male world, the grandmother poisons her.[18]

Furthermore, Wharton's pairing of Lily Bart with her nemesis, Bertha Dorset, echoes the pairing of Berthas and Lilys in an earlier feminist text: Elizabeth Oakes Smith's *Bertha and Lily* (1854). Oakes Smith's novel describes the relationship of a mother (Bertha) and her illegitimate daughter (Lily). While the erring Bertha's life has been painful and limited, Lily's future is presented as radiantly hopeful: "She will be an artist, an orator, a ruler . . . just as her faculties impel." Lily seems to represent the possibilities of the creative buried self Oakes Smith felt in her own stifled career.[19]

Constance Cary Harrison's *The Anglomaniacs* (1890), a successful novel of the fin de siècle set in the same upper-class New York milieu as *The House of Mirth*, also has a heroine named Lily, a young heiress who is pressured to marry a titled Englishman she does not love in order to satisfy her mother's social ambitions. Like Lily Bart, Lily Floyd-Curtis has the graceful figure of a "wood-nymph," socializes with a sensitive bachelor friend who lives "in the Benedick with his violincello," and attends a charity ball where the dinner table is set to represent a Veronese painting and she herself is dressed as a Venetian princess.[20]

Wharton is ironically aware of the way that Lily Bart becomes the object of male myths and fantasies, like that of the wood nymph, that must be revised from the woman's perspective. Selden insists on seeing her as a "captured dryad subdued to the conventions of the drawing-room," yet the image of the dryad is as much one of these drawing-room conventions as that of the woman of fashion. Indeed, Lily, as Wharton tells us, "had no real intimacy with nature, but she had a passion for the appropriate" (19, 101). For her role in the tableaux vivants. Lily chooses to represent the figure of Sir Joshua Reynolds's *Mrs. Lloyd*, in a draped gown that revealed "long dryad-like curves that swept upwards from her poised foot to her lifted arm" (217). Selden is enraptured by her performance, finding the authentic Lily in the scene; but it is rather the carefully constructed Lily of his desire that he sees. The "streak of sylvan freedom" he perceives in her is rather what he would make of her, and we are reminded that Ezra Pound at this same period was imposing the title "Dryad" on the equally plastic H. D.[21]

The myth of Tarpeia was another case of differing male and female interpretations. Simon Rosedale tells it in garbled form to Lily when he comes to propose to her: "There was a girl in some history book who wanted gold shields or something, and the fellows threw 'em at her, and she was crushed under 'em; they killed her" (284). Tarpeia, the Roman who betrayed her city to the Sabines by opening the Capitoline citadel in exchange for gold bracelets and was crushed by the shields of the invading Sabine army, was also the subject of Louise Guiney's well-known poem of the 1890s that dramatized the paradox of a woman's being condemned by her society for the mercenary and narcissistic values it has encouraged.[22]

Wharton's major revision of a male text, as those critics not obsessed with her alleged apprenticeship to Henry James have noted, was with relation to Oscar Wilde's *Picture of Dorian Gray* (1890). Lily's picture is in one sense her mirror, but it is more fully her realization of the ways in which her society has deformed her. In contrast to Dorian Gray's portrait, Lily's monster in the mirror is not one whose perfect complexion has been marred by lines of worry, shame, or guilt but rather a woman with a "hard, brilliant" surface (191). In the aftershock of her encounter with Gus Trenor in his empty house, Lily recognizes "two selves in her, the one she had always known, and a new abhorrent being to which it found itself chained" (238). As she tells Gerty, this self seems like a "disfigurement," a "hideous change" that has come to her while she slept, a moral ugliness that she cannot bear to contemplate (265).

Some feminist critics have argued that this "stranger" in Lily, this second and abhorrent self, is the female personality produced by a patriarchal society and a capitalist economy. As Elizabeth Ammons notes, "the system is designed to keep women in divisive and relentless competition" for the money and favor controlled by men. "Forbidden to aggress on each other directly, or aggress on men at all, women prey on each other—stealing reputations, opportunities, male admirers—all to parlay or retain status and financial security in a world arranged by men to keep women suppliant and therefore subordinate." Women employ, exploit, and cheat each other as coldbloodedly as their Wall Street husbands carry out deals, but "by nature" women "feel no necessity to harm each other."[23]

Yet, the nature of both men and women is in question in the novel, rather than given. It is often overlooked that Wharton develops a full cast of male characters in *The House of Mirth*, whose dilemmas parallel those of the women. As historians now recognize, the period 1880–1920 redefined gender identity for American men as well as for American women. Among the characteristics of progressivism and of the masculinity crisis was the increased specialization of men as workers marginal to the family and culture: "According to the capitalistic ethos, men were expected to promote industry and commerce, which they did in abundance, often spending long hours at the office, the plant, or in the fields and forests. With their energies spent, they came home too weary and worn to devote much time and interest to family or friends."[24]

Wharton's critique of the marriage system is not limited to the economic dependency of women but also extends to consider the loneliness, dehumanization, and anxiety of men. Lily's father, a shadowy figure in the prehistory of the novel, establishes the theme of the marginal man. This "neutral-tinted father, who filled an intermediate space between the butler and the man who came to wind the clocks," is a dim and pathetic fixture of Lily's scant childhood memories (45). "Effaced and silent," patient and stooping, he is an exhausted witness to the stresses his society places on men. Even on vacation at Newport or Southampton, "it seemed to tire him to rest, and he would sit for hours staring at the sea-line from a quiet corner of the verandah, while the clatter of his wife's existence went on unheeded a few feet off" (45–46). Mr. Bart does not so much die as get discarded; to his wife, once he had lost his fortune "he had become extinct," and she sits at his deathbed "with the provisional air of a traveller who waits for a belated train to start" (51). Unable to love her father, to feel more for him than a frightened pity, or to mourn him, Lily nonetheless comes to identify with him in her own trial, recalling his sleepless nights in the midst of her own and feeling suddenly "how he must have suffered, lying alone with his thoughts" (266).

The story of Mr. Bart, who in his enigmatic solitude and marginality here strongly resembles Mr. Bartleby, lingers in our consciousness as we read *The House of Mirth*, coloring our impression of even the crudest male characters. If Gus Trenor is beefy and stupid, he is nonetheless repeatedly used by the women in the book, and there is some justice in the words, if not the tone, of his complaint to Lily: "I didn't begin this business—kept out of the way, and left the track clear for the other chaps, till you rummaged me out and set to work to make an ass of me—and an easy job you had of it, too" (234). To Lily, we have seen earlier, Trenor is merely "a coarse dull man . . . a mere supernumerary in the costly show for which his money paid; surely, to a clever girl, it would be easy to hold him by his vanity, and so keep the obligation on his side" (137). Lily repays her financial debt to Trenor, but never her human one.

If women in this system harm each other, they also do an extraordinary amount of harm to men. It's hard not to feel a sympathy for shy Percy Gryce when Lily sets out to appeal to his vanity and thus to make an ass of *him*: "She resolved so to identify herself with her husband's vanity that to gratify her wishes would be to him the most exquisite form of self-indulgence" (78). Despite the loss to Lily, we must feel that Gryce is better off with even the "youngest, dumpiest, dullest" of the Van Osburgh daughters (146).

Edmund Wilson described the typical masculine figure in Edith Wharton's fiction between 1905 and 1920 as "a man set apart from his neighbours by education, intellect, and feeling, but lacking the force or the courage either to impose himself or to get away."[25] Selden is obviously such a figure, a man who seems initially to be much freer than Lily but who is revealed to be even more inflexible. His failed effort to define himself as the New Man parallels Lily's futile effort to become a New Woman; "In a different way," as Wharton points out, "he was, as much as Lily, the victim of his environment" (245). Selden's limitations are perhaps those of the New Man in every period of gender crisis. Cautious about making a commitment, successful and energetic in his law practice, fond of travel, taking enormous pleasure in his Manhattan apartment with its "pleasantly faded Turkey rug," its carefully chosen collectibles, and its opportunities for intimate entertaining, Selden lacks only jogging shoes and a copy of *The Color Purple* on his coffee table to fit into the culture of the 1980s.

Real change, Wharton shows us in the novel, must come from outside the dominant class structures. Thus, the figure of Simon Rosedale, the Jewish financier making it big on Wall Street, takes on increasing importance as the novel develops. He plays one of the main roles in the triangle with Lily and Selden, and while Selden asserts too late that he has faith in Lily, Rosedale demonstrates his faith by coming to see her in her dingy exile and by offering her money to start again. Rosedale's style is certainly not that of the Perfect Gentleman, and even to the last Lily's ladyhood cannot quite accept him: "Little by little, circumstances were breaking down her dislike for Rosedale. The dislike, indeed, still subsisted; but it was penetrated here and there by the perception of mitigating qualities in him: of a certain gross kindliness, a rather helpless fidelity of sentiment, which seemed to be struggling through the surface of his material ambitions" (485). In order to break out of the social cage, Lily must make compromises with elegance, compromises that ultimately are beyond her scope. But Rosedale, the only man in the novel who likes children (we see him through Lily's eyes "kneeling domestically on the drawing room hearth" with Carry Fisher's little girl [401]), offers the hope of continuity, rootedness, and relatedness that Lily finally comes to see as the central meaning of life.

Lily's changing perceptions of Rosedale are a parallel to the most radical theme in the novel: her growing awareness and finally her merger with a community of working women. With each step downward, each removal to a smaller room, Lily's life becomes more enmeshed with this community, and she sees it in more positive terms. We see her first as an exceptional figure, silhouetted against a backdrop of anonymous female drones in Grand Central Station, "sallow-faced girls in preposterous hats and flat-chested women struggling with paper bundles and palm-leaf fans" (5). For the observant Selden, the contrast to "the herd" only brings out Lily's high gloss: "The dinginess, the crudity of this average section of womanhood made him feel how specialized she was" (6).

The crudest of these women is the charwoman, Mrs. Haffen, whose appearance frames the first part of the novel as that of the typist Nettie Struther frames the end. Leaving Selden's apartment, Lily encounters this woman scrubbing the stairs, stout, with "clenched red fists . . . a broad, sallow face, slightly pitted with smallpox, and the straw-coloured hair through which her scalp shone unpleasantly" (20). In her hardness, ugliness, poverty, and age, Mrs. Haffen is the monstrous specter of everything Lily most dreads, the very heart of dinginess. Trying to make money out of Bertha Dorset's love letters, she also embodies the moral corruption Lily has come to fear in herself, the willingness to sacrifice all sense of value to the need to survive.

Lily's gradual and painful realization that her status as a lady does not exempt her from the sufferings of womanhood is conveyed through her perceptions of her own body as its exquisite ornamentality begins to decline. Her luxuriant hair begins to thin, as Carry Fisher notices (404); her radiant complexion too will become "dull and colourless" in the millinery workshop (455). In the beginning, she is one of the lilies of the field, who neither toils nor spins, nor, certainly, scrubs; her hands are not the "clenched red fists" of anger, labor, rebellion, but art objects "polished as a bit of old ivory" (10). Yet, in her confrontation with Gus Trenor, Lily is suddenly aware that these lovely hands are also "helpless" and "useless" (237). Lily has had fantasies of her hands as creative and artistic, dreaming of a fashionable shop in which "subordinate fingers, blunt, grey, needle-pricked fingers" would do all the hard work, while her delicate fingers added the distinctive finishing touch (456–57). In reality, she learns, her "untutored fingers" are blundering and clumsy; like the hands of the working women, her hands too have "been formed from childhood for their special work," the work of decoration and display, and they can never compete in the workaday world (477). When Selden sees her for the last time in his apartment, noting "how thin her hands looked" against the fire, it is as if they are fading and disappearing, vestigial appendages useless to her solitary existence (501).

At the center of Lily's awakening to her kinship with other women is Gerty Farish's Working Girls' Club. Gerty works with a charitable association trying "to provide comfortable lodgings, with a reading-room and other modest distractions, where young women of the class employed in down-town offices might find a home when out of work, or in need of a rest" (179).[26] Visiting this club as Lady Bountiful, Lily nonetheless makes the first imaginative identification between herself and the working girls, "young girls, like herself, some perhaps pretty, some not without a trace of her finer sensibilities. She pictured herself leading such a life as theirs—a life in which achievement seemed as squalid as failure—and the vision made her shudder sympathetically" (179).

Yet when she "joins the working classes," Lily also sees "the fragmentary and distorted image of the world she had lived in, reflected in the mirror of the working-girls' minds" (461). They idealize the society women whose hats they trim. Lily. Bart herself has become a kind of romantic heroine for Nettie Struther, the working girl she meets in Bryant Park on her return from Selden's apartment. Nettie has followed Lily's social career in the newspapers, reading about her dresses, thinking of her as "being so high up, where everything was just grand" (505). She has named her baby daughter "Marry Ant'nette" because an actress playing the queen reminded her of Lily. Their encounter is the strongest moment of female kinship in the novel, as Lily also sees herself mirrored in Nettie and her baby and recognizes that Nettie's achievement is far beyond any she has previously conceived for herself.

Nettie is a typist who has had an unhappy affair with a man from a higher social class, a man who promised to marry her but deserted her. (Margaret McDowell, one of Wharton's critics, leaps to the false conclusion that Nettie has been a prostitute.)[27] Although Nettie felt that her life was over, she was given the chance to begin again by a man who had known her from childhood, knew that she had been seduced, and loved her enough to marry her anyway. There is even an ambiguity about the paternity of the child; Nettie may have been pregnant when George married her. This testament of male faith and female courage stands in sharp contrast to Selden's caution and Lily's despair.

The scene between the two women is unique in *The House of Mirth* for its intimacy and openness (Lily too tells Nettie that she is unhappy and in trouble), for its setting in the warm kitchen (the ritual center of much nineteenth-century woman's fiction), for the presence of the baby, and for its acknowledgment of physical needs. In holding Nettie's baby, the untouchable Lily gives in at last to her longing for touch. Holding the baby, she is also being held, expressing her own hunger for physical bonding: "As she continued to hold it the weight increased, sinking deeper, and penetrating her with a strange sense of weakness, as though the child entered into her and became a part of herself" (510).

Some feminist critics, however, have tended to see the images of the mother and child in this scene, and in Lily's deathbed hallucination of holding the infant, as sentimental and regressive. Patricia M. Spacks, for example, criticizes Lily's "escapist fantasy of motherhood."[28] Cynthia Griffin Wolff maintains that the scene with Nettie "gives poignant evidence of Lily's inability to conceive of herself in any other way than as the object of aesthetic attention," that she is once again self-consciously arranging herself in a tableau vivant for Nettie's admiration. Wolff also argues that in her death Lily is relinquishing her "difficult pretenses to adulthood." Thus, in Wolff's view, the extraordinary passage in which Lily, as she is succumbing to the drug, feels "Nettie Struther's child . . . lying on her arm . . . felt the pressure of its little head against her shoulder" is a sign of Lily's own retreat into the safety of infantilization.[29]

It seems to me, however, that this hallucination speaks rather for Lily's awakened sense of loving solidarity and community, for the vision she has had of Nettie's life as representing "the central truth of existence" (517). That Nettie should be the last person to see Lily alive and that Gerty should be the first to discover her death suggests that Lily's death is an acknowledgment of their greater strength. Doing justice to Lily Bart requires that we see how far she has come, even in her death. Unlike the infantilized Edna Pontellier, who never awakens to the dimensions of her social world, who never sees how the labor of the mulatto and black women around her makes her narcissistic existence possible, Lily is a genuinely awakened woman, who fully recognizes her own position in the community of women workers. Whereas Edna's awakening is early, easy, and incomplete and brings a warm liquid sense of satisfaction, Lily's enlightenment is gradual and agonizing: "It was as though a great blaze of electric light had been turned on in her head. . . . She had not imagined that such a multiplication of wakefulness was possible; her whole past was re-enacting itself at a hundred different points of consciousness" (520). Although her awakening proves unendurable, she really tries to overcome rejection, failure, and the knowledge of her own shortcomings. *The House of Mirth* ends not only with a death but with the vision of a new world of female solidarity, a world in which women like Gerty Farish and Nettie Struther will struggle hopefully and courageously. Lily dies—the lady dies—so that these women may live and grow. As Elizabeth Ammons observes, "In the arms of the ornamental, leisure-class Lily lies the working-class infant female, whose vitality succors the dying woman. In that union of the leisure and working classes lies a new hope—the New Woman that Wharton would bring to mature life in her next novel."[30]

For Edith Wharton as novelist, then, *The House of Mirth* also marked a transition to a new kind of fiction. Like Lily Bart, Wharton had retreated from touch, from community, from awakenings to her own sexuality and anger. While the standard pattern for nineteenth-century American women writers was a strong allegiance to the maternal line and the female community, Wharton belonged to the more troubled and more gifted countertradition of women writers who were torn between the literary world of their fathers and the wordless sensual world of their mothers. These two lines of inheritance are generally represented in the literary history of American women writers by the spatial images of the father's library and the mother's garden. Like Margaret Fuller, Edith Wharton felt that "the kingdom of her father's library" was the intellectual center of her development. But, unlike Fuller, she did not have the childhood alternative of her mother's garden—a space of sensuality, warmth, and openness. Instead, Lucretia Wharton was a chilly woman who censored her daughter's reading, denied her writing paper (as a child Wharton was "driven to begging for the wrappings of the parcels delivered at the house"), withheld physical affection, and met her literary efforts with "icy disapproval."[31]

Nonetheless, in her literary memoir, *A Backward Glance*, Wharton called her writing a "secret garden," echoing the title of Frances Hodgson Burnett's popular novel for girls.[32] The connection with maternal space (in Burnett's novel it is the dead mother's garden, lost and overgrown) may have come from her sense of writing as a forbidden joy. From childhood Wharton was possessed with what she called the "ecstasy" of "making up," almost a form of illicit sexual indulgence: "The call came regularly and imperiously and . . . I would struggle against it conscientiously."[33]

The House of Mirth marks the point at which Wharton found herself able to give in to her creative jouissance, to assert her creative power as a woman artist, and to merge the male and female sides of her lineage into a mature fiction that could deal seriously with the sexual relationships of men and women in a modern society. Writing *The House of Mirth* had important professional, literary, and psychological consequences for Wharton's career, and it is clear that she herself thought of it as a turning point in her life as a writer. In her autobiography, Wharton described the process of writing *The House of Mirth* as a serial for *Scribner's Magazine* as one that taught her the work of writing, that transformed her "from a drifting amateur into a professional." Because she had agreed to complete the book within five months, Wharton was forced to exchange the leisurely rhythms of the lady novelist's routine, with its manifold "distractions of a busy and hospitable life, full of friends and travel, reading and gardening," for the "discipline of the daily task." The necessity for "systematic daily effort" also redefined and excused the pleasures of "making up" as part of her process of gaining "mastery over my tools."[34]

Under the pressures of the deadline, Wharton also made tough choices about her narrative, choices that reflected her own transition to a more serious artistic professionalism, craftsmanship, and control. In choosing to have Lily die, Wharton was judging and rejecting the infantile aspects of her own self, the part that lacked confidence as a working writer, that longed for the escapism of the lady's world and feared the sexual consequences of creating rather than becoming art. Second, Wharton mastered her emotional conflicts as material for art, learning through the process that anger and other strong emotions, including sexual desire, could be safely expressed.[35] The death of the lady is thus also the death of the lady novelist, the dutiful daughter who struggles to subdue her most powerful imaginative impulses. If Lily Bart, unable to change, gives way to the presence of a new generation of women, Edith Wharton survives the crisis of maturation at the turn of the century and becomes one of our American precursors of a literary history of female mastery and growth.

Notes

1. Joy Wittenburg, "Excerpts from the Diary of Elizabeth Oakes Smith." *Signs* 9 (1984): 537. The diary covers the year 1861.

2. Sigmund Freud. "Femininity," in *The Standard Edition of the Complete Psychological Works of Sigmund Freud*, ed. and trans. James Strachey (London: Hogarth Press, 1964) 22: 112–35.

3. *The House of Mirth* (New York: Scribner's, 1905), 3. All further references to this work will be included parenthetically in the text.

4. Carroll Smith-Rosenberg's influential essay, "The Female World of Love and Ritual: Relations between Women in Nineteenth-Century America," appeared in the first issue of the feminist journal *Signs* 1 (1975): 1–30. Along with Nancy F. Cott's *The Bonds of Womanhood: "Woman's Sphere" in New England, 1780–1833* (New Haven: Yale University Press, 1977), Smith-Rosenberg's work defined a woman's culture of intimate emotional re-

lationships, social conventions, and female rituals, "supported and paralleled by severe social restrictions on intimacy between young men and women" (9).

5. The breakdown in women's culture at the turn of the century has been the subject of extensive recent study by feminist social historians. In a symposium on the problem of "women's culture," Carroll Smith-Rosenberg noted that by the 1870s and 1880s, "as role options expanded for daughters . . . mothers and other older women frequently acted to thwart their daughters' new role aspirations." The period 1890 to 1920, she argues, "saw a concerted male attack upon the legitimacy of this world of female identification and solidarity, an attack abetted by economic and demographic changes which undermined female institutional structures." See "Politics and Culture in Women's History: A Symposium," *Feminist Studies* 6 (1980): 59, 63. Other important work on this period of gender crisis includes Nancy Sahli, "Smashing: Women's Relationships before the Fall," *Chrysalis* 8 (1979): 17–27; Lillian Faderman, *Surpassing the Love of Men: Romantic Friendships and Love between Women from the Renaissance to the Present* (New York: Morrow, 1981); and Martha Vicious, "Sexuality and Power: A Review of Current Work on the History of Sexuality," *Feminist Studies* 8 (1982): 133–56.

6. See Nina Baym, *Woman's Fiction: A Guide to Novels by and about Women in America, 1820–1870* (Ithaca: Cornell University Press, 1978); Mary Kelley, *Private Women, Public Stage: Literary Domesticity in Nineteenth-Century America* (New York: Oxford University Press, 1984); and Ann Douglas, *The Feminization of American Culture* (New York: Avon, 1977).

7. For two different feminist accounts of *The Wide, Wide World* see Baym, *Woman's Fiction*, 143–50, and Jane Tompkins, "The Other American Renaissance," in *The American Renaissance Reconsidered: Selected Papers from the English Institute, 1982–83*, ed. Walter Benn Michaels and Donald Pease (Baltimore: John Hopkins University Press, 1984).

8. Josephine Donovan, *New England Local Color Literature: A Woman's Tradition* (New York: Ungar, 1983), 119.

9. Elizabeth Ammons, *Edith Wharton's Argument with America* (Athens: University of Georgia Press, 1980), 27. Ammons sees this literature as influenced by such contemporary studies of the economics of marriage as Charlotte Perkins Gilman's *Women and Economics* (1898) and Thorstein Veblen's *The Theory of the Leisure Class* (1899).

10. For discussions of these other transitional heroines of women's fiction, see Grace Stewart, *A New Mythos: The Novel of the Artist as Heroine,*

1877–1977 (Montreal: Eden Press Women's Publications, 1981); and Ann Douglas, "The Literature of Impoverishment: The Women Local Colorists in America, 1865–1914," *Women's Studies* 1 (1972): 3–45.

11. "Edith Wharton and Her New Yorks," in *Edith Wharton: A Collection of Critical Essays*, ed. Irving Howe (Englewood Cliffs, N.J.: Prentice Hall, 1962), 36.

12. Cynthia Griffin Wolff, *A Feast of Words: The Triumph of Edith Wharton* (New York: Oxford University Press, 1977), 11.

13. Susan Gubar, "The 'Blank Page' and Female Creativity," in *Writing and Sexual Difference*, ed. Elizabeth Abel (Chicago: University of Chicago, 1982), 81.

14. See Baym, *Woman's Fiction*, 11–12, 23, 39.

15. Edmund Wilson, "Justice to Edith Wharton," in *Edith Wharton: A Collection of Critical Essays*, ed. Howe, 20.

16. See Wolff, *A Feast of Words*, 114–15. Wolff also notes that Wharton herself was called "Lily" as a girl (110).

17. On *The Lily*, see D. C. Bloomer, *Life and Writings of Amelia Bloomer* (Boston: Arena Publishing, 1895), 41–43.

18. Mary Wilkins Freeman repeatedly used the name "Lily" for the younger woman in a generational transition from women's culture to New Womanhood; see also Lily Almy and Aunt Fidelia in "A Patient Waiter." The best recent collection of Freeman's work is *Selected Stories of Mary Wilkins Freeman*, ed. Marjorie Pryse (New York: Norton, 1983).

19. I am indebted for these details to Katy Birckmayer, "A Critical Introduction to *Bertha and Lily*" (unpublished paper, Rutgers University, 1984).

20. Constance C. Harrison, *The Anglomaniacs* (New York: Arno, 1977) was reprinted with a short introduction by Elizabeth Hardwick in her series of neglected American women's writing.

21. On H. D. as "Dryad" and on her fashionable "Greekness," see Barbara Guest, *Herself Defined: The Poet H. D. and Her World* (New York: Quill, 1984), 33ff.

22. See Sheila A. Tully, "Heroic Failures and the Literary Career of Louise Imogen Guiney," *American Transcendental Quarterly*, no. 47–48 (summer–fall 1980): 178. Cheryl Walker calls Guiney "the most interesting of the turn-of-the-century [women] poets"; she sees a commentary on the ambitions and passions of the New Woman in the final words of Guiney's "Tarpeia": "O you that aspire! / Tarpeia the traitor had fill of her woman's desire." See *The Nightingale's Burden: Women Poets and American Culture before 1900* (Bloomington: Indiana University Press, 1982), 130–33.

23. Ammons, *Edith Wharton's Argument with America*, 39.

24. Joe L. Dubbert, "Progressivism and the Masculinity Crisis," in *The American Man*, ed. Elizabeth H. Pleck and Joseph H. Pleck (Englewood Cliffs, N.J.: Prentice Hall, 1980), 307.

25. Wilson, "Justice to Edith Wharton," 26–27.

26. Elizabeth Ammons points out that Wharton's contemporary readers would have been familiar with the institution of the Working Girls' Club; Wharton's sister-in-law Mary Cadwallader Jones had even written about these clubs in *The Woman's Book* (1894). See *Edith Wharton's Argument with America*, 40–41. A book published the same year as *The House of Mirth*, Dorothy Richardson's *The Long Day: The Story of a New York Working Girl* (1905; reprinted in *Women at Work*, ed. William L. O'Neill [Chicago: Quandrangle, 1972], 3–303), discusses the relationships between factory girls and the leisured ladies who offered them charity and also became the subjects of their fantasies. According to Richardson, working girls even adopted the names of society heroines from the newspapers and from romantic novels.

27. Margaret McDowell, *Edith Wharton* (Boston: Twayne, 1976), 44–45.

28. Patricia Meyer Spacks, *The Female Imagination* (New York: Knopf, 1975), 241.

29. Wolff, *A Feast of Words*, 130–31. Wolff maintains that Lily's feelings are primarily narcissistic, whereas I read the conclusion of the novel as a demonstration of her reawakened emotional capacities.

30. Ammons, *Edith Wharton's Argument with America*, 43.

31. See Wolff, *A Feast of Words*, 31, 46–47.

32. Edith Wharton, *A Backward Glance* (New York: Scribner's, 1962), chap. 9. Marilyn French, who notes the reference to Burnett, argues that Wharton's writing always remained secretive and in some sense illegitimate. "Introduction," *The House of Mirth* (New York, 1981), xii.

33. Wharton, *A Backward Glance*, 35.

34. Ibid., 207–9.

35. See Wolff, *A Feast of Words*, 134–38. Wolff calls *The House of Mirth* a "momentous novel."

Debasing Exchange

Edith Wharton's The House of Mirth

WAI CHEE DIMOCK

◆ ◆ ◆

> ". . . you got reckless—thought you could turn me inside out and chuck me in the gutter like an empty purse. But, by gad, that ain't playing fair: that's dodging the rules of the game. Of course I know now what you wanted—it wasn't my beautiful eyes you were after—but I tell you what, Miss Lily, you've got to pay up for making me think so." . . .
>
> "Pay up?" she faltered. "Do you mean that I owe you money?"
>
> He laughed again. "Oh, I'm not asking for payment in kind. But there's such a thing as fair play—and interest on one's money—and hang me if I've had as much as a look from you—"
>
> —Wharton, *House of Mirth*, 145–46

THE MOST BRUTAL moment in *The House of Mirth* dramatizes not so much the centrality of sex as the centrality of exchange. Sexual favors are what Gus Trenor wants, but his demands are steeped in—and legitimated by—the language of the marketplace, the language of traded benefits and reciprocal obligations. Odious as it may seem, Trenor's speech merely asserts what everyone assumes. "Investments" and "returns," "interests" and "payments": these words animate and possess Wharton's characters, even in their world of conspicuous leisure. The power of the marketplace, then, resides not in its presence, which is only marginal in *The House of Mirth*, but in its ability to reproduce itself, in its ability to assimilate everything else into its domain. As a controlling logic, a mode of human conduct and human association, the marketplace is everywhere and nowhere, ubiquitous and invisible. Under its shadow even the most private affairs take on the essence of business transactions, for the realm of human relations is fully contained within an all-encompassing business ethic. Some characters—Trenor and Rosedale, for instance—obviously speak the voice of the marketplace, but even those who hold themselves aloof (as Lawrence Selden does) turn out to be more susceptible than they think.

Of all the characters, Lily Bart has the most puzzling and contradictory relation to the marketplace. A self-acknowledged "human merchandise" (256), she is busy marketing herself throughout most of the book, worried only about the price she would fetch. She tries to induce Percy Gryce to purchase her, and if she had succeeded she would have been "to him what his Americana had hitherto been, the one possession in which he took sufficient pride to spend money on it" (49). Much later, as she forces herself to accept Rosedale's attentions, she consoles herself by calculating "the price he would have to pay" (253). Lily is clearly caught up in the ethos of exchange. And yet, her repeated and sometimes intentional failure to find a buyer, her ultimate refusal to realize her "asset" (34)—as her mother designates her beauty—makes her something of a rebel. She is not much of a rebel, of course, and that is precisely the point. For Lily's "rebellion," in its very feebleness and limitation, attests to the frightening power of the marketplace. It attests as well to Wharton's own politics, to her bleakness of vision in the face of a totalizing system she finds at once detestable and inevitable.

The persistent talk of "cost" and "payment" in *The House of Mirth* raises the question of *currency*. How does one compute the "cost" of an action, what constitutes a "debt," and in what form must "payments" be made? Money, the standard medium of exchange, is not the only currency in circulation. Trenor clearly does not wish to be paid back with a check. In fact, "payment in kind" is never expected in transactions in the social marketplace, and this unspoken rule makes for a plethora of business opportunities. A "society" dinner, for instance, is worth its weight in gold. Since the likes of Rosedale habitually "giv[e] away a half-a-million tip for a dinner" (82), Jack Stepney regularly "pay[s] his debts in dinner invitations" (16). Others—even those who protest—eventually follow Stepney's example, for the simple reason that Rosedale is "placing Wall Street under obligations which only Fifth Avenue could repay" (240). There are other expenses, other debts, and other means of payment, as well. Lily's visit to Selden's bachelor apartment is a "luxury" that is "going to cost her rather more than she could afford" (15). Still, she might have "purchased [Rosedale's] silence" if she had only allowed him to take her to the train station, since "to be seen walking down the platform at the crowded afternoon hour in the company of Miss Lily Bart would have been money in his pocket" (15). Business, in the social world, operates by what we might call the commodification of social intercourse.[1] Everything has a price, must be paid for, just as—on the opposite end—everything can be made to "count as" money, to be dealt out and accepted in lieu of cash. Dispensed in this manner, social gestures lose their initial character and figure only as exchange values: the dinner invitations, for Stepney and Rosedale, presumably have no meaning except as surrogate cash payments. A social world predicated on business ethics is an essentially reductive world, and the power of money lies not so much in its pristine form as in its claim as a model, in its ability to define other things in its own image.[2] The fluidity of currencies in *The House of Mirth*, the apparently endless business possibilities, attests to the reduction of human experienees experiences to abstract equivalents for exchange (see Marx 35–93; chs. 1–2).

The principle of exchange, the idea that one has to "pay" for what one gets, lays claim to a kind of quid pro quo justice, and it is this justice, this "fair play," that Trenor demands from Lily. What he does not (or chooses not to) recognize is that what he calls "fair" is by no means self-evident and certainly not computable on an absolute scale. The problem stems, of course, from the rate of exchange, from the way prices are fixed. After all, why should a single dinner cost Rosedale a tip worth half a million (why not a quarter of a million, or a million)? And, for that matter, why should a ride in the park *not* be sufficient "payment" for the money Lily owes Trenor? In both instances, the "price" for the received benefit could easily have been otherwise, since the rate of exchange is altogether variable, altogether an artificial stipulation. In other words, two items might be yoked in one equation, pronounced of equal worth, but their "equality" will always remain imputed rather than inherent. Prices will remain arbitrary as long as the exchange rests on a negotiated parity between the exchange items—negotiated according to the bargaining powers of the contracting parties. Not everyone pays a half million dollars for a dinner invitation. Some pay nothing at all. The manipulatable rate of exchange makes it a treacherous model for "fair play." Lily "owes" Trenor the payment that he now demands only according to his rate of exchange—not hers—and his ability to set the rate and impose it on Lily says nothing about fairness, only something about power.

Power in *The House of Mirth*, many critics have suggested, is patriarchical.[3] They are right, no doubt, about the basis for power, insofar as power is economic and insofar as money making is a male prerogative, but the actual wielders of power in the book are often not men but women. On the whole, Wharton is interested less in the etiology of power than in the way power comports itself, in the mode and manner of its workings. She is most interested, that is to say, in the mediated and socialized forms of power, power that women do enjoy and that they use skillfully and sometimes brutally. Within the orbits of exchange, power resides in the ability to define the terms of exchange, to make one thing "equal" to another. That privilege belongs, obviously, to only one of the partners, and this intrinsic inequity gives the lie to Trenor's notion of fairness. A presumed model of justice and mutuality, exchange really grows out of an imbalance of power, which it in turn reconstitutes. Its "fair play" is in fact a fiction masking a deeper reality of unfairness, for the rate of exchange is no more than a tautological reflection of the inequity that is the condition as well as the result of its operations.

Nowhere is the injustice of exchange more clearly demonstrated than on board the *Sabrina*. Lily's presence on the yacht is, as everyone recognizes, simply a business arrangement. "We all know that's what Bertha brought her abroad for," Carry Fisher observes. "When Bertha wants to have a good time, she has to provide occupation for George . . . and of course Lily's present business is to keep him blind" (189–90). Afterward, Lily seems to realize this fact equally well: "That was what she was 'there for': it was the price she had chosen to pay for three months of luxury and freedom from care" (227). But the "price" turns out to be steeper than Lily thinks, for she pays eventually with her good name and, indirectly, with her aunt's inheritance. The luxurious yacht cruise is a rotten deal for Lily, but it remains a "deal." And, without deviating from the model of exchange, Bertha has managed to get her money's worth from Lily; she has simply managed to get away with a good bargain. Like Trenor, Bertha has come up with a rate of exchange to suit herself; unlike Trenor, she is eminently successful in exacting payments from Lily. Thanks to her adroit management, the reconciliation with her husband is "effected at [Lily's] expense" (243). Bertha has got everything she wants without any significant expenditure. This feat is all the more remarkable because—if the logic of exchange were to be faithfully followed—she ought to have paid a heavy price for her affair with Ned Silverton. But Bertha, in her "cold determination to escape [the] consequences" of her actions, has raised nonpayment to an art.

Bertha's success summarizes the contradiction that energizes and sustains the system of exchange. The art of nonpayment requires, after all, the most brazen sort of doublethink. The principle that enables Bertha to collect payments from Lily is the same principle that enables her to shrug off her own debts, and Bertha's ability to master that contradiction entitles her to her considerable rewards. For doublethink is the very essence of the exchange system, a system in which use and abuse are the same thing, in which legislations violate and violations legislate, in which, to play by the rules, one must break the rules. Doublethink explains why a system based on exchange should have nonpayment as its secret motto.

"The hatred of expenditure," Georges Bataille has written, "is the raison d'être of and the justification for the bourgeoisie" (73). Bertha Dorset's bold miserliness—her absolute refusal to "pay"—is therefore only the extreme and ruthless version of a prevailing stinginess, observable in duller and stodgier persons. A case in point is Mrs. Peniston, Lily's aunt. She is quite willing to give her niece room and board and occasional checks for clothes in return for "the reward to which disinterestedness is entitled" (36). But she is loath to give anything else. "When I offered you a home, I didn't undertake to pay your gambling debts," she informs Lily (172). Apparently she is not ready for other kinds of expenditure, either. When Lily intimates that she has "had worries," Mrs. Peniston "shut[s] her lips with the snap of a purse closing against a beggar" (170). Obviously no spendthrift, emotional or otherwise, Mrs. Peniston manages her affections economically and keeps her obligations minimal. Both her generosity and her forbearance have limits, which Lily in time exceeds. Mrs. Peniston has not bargained for the troubles Lily gets into, and she "recognize[s] no obligation" to help (172). But she is quick to detect any breach of contract on Lily's side and to retaliate accordingly. Nothing can be more logical than her eventual decision to disinherit her niece. Since Lily has failed to meet her obligations, Mrs. Peniston sees no reason to meet *hers*. If there is something hard and mechanical in the aunt's moral accounting, it is no more than what is considered "just" (222) among those who stick to business principles. Mrs. Peniston is not alone in turning away from Lily. Her conditional affection parodies that of another character. In the same chapter in which Lily looks in vain to her aunt for help, she also waits in vain for Lawrence Selden to come to her (ch. 15).

Selden has other things in common with Lily's aunt aside from their shared abandonment of Lily. Like Mrs. Peniston, who chooses to be a "looker-on" in life (120), Selden relishes his "spectatorship" and "indolent amusement" (8). In the opening scene, we find him amused in just this way: he is "divert[ed]" by Lily, "enjoy[ing]" her "as a spectator" (4) "with a purely impersonal enjoyment" (10). Unlike Mrs. Peniston, however, Selden does not always remain a spectator.[4] He has had his share of action (an affair with Bertha Dorset, for instance), and even in his indolent enjoyment of Lily he is not without other intentions. For Selden also happens to be a connoisseur, an investor in aesthetic objects, a man equipped with the "lingering, appraising, inventorial mind of the experienced collector" (Wolff 12). Selden collects, Wharton explains, "as much as a man may who has no money to spend"; now and then he "pick[s] up something in the rubbish heap, and [he goes] and look[s] on at the big sales" (10). Selden remains a spectator when he cannot afford to buy, but he is not averse to pocketing little tidbits when they can be had for a small price. The investor picks up where the spectator leaves off, and, in making the most of his resources, in getting the most from exchange, Selden shows more speculative instinct than he would like to admit.

"Speculation" is precisely what draws Selden to Lily. "[H]e could never see her without a faint movement of interest," we learn as soon as the novel opens; "it was characteristic of her that she always roused speculation" (3). Selden is "interest[ed]" in Lily—curious about what she will do—but he is "interested" also in another sense, as every investor would be in an eminently collect ible item. To be sure, Selden is not half as crude as the others: while they notice Lily's "outline" (138), he admires the "modelling of her little ear, the crisp upward wave of her hair," "the thick planting of her straight black lashes" (5), and "her hand, polished as a bit of old ivory, with its slender pink nails" (7).[5] Lily would have been a valuable acquisition, and Selden knows it. "Ah, well, there must be plenty of capital on the look-out for such an investment" (12), he muses as they discuss her marriage prospects. Selden himself, apparently, has no such "capital" to "invest" and chooses simply to look on. His "admiring spectatorship" (68) costs him nothing, involves "no risks" (74), and allows him to enjoy the goods without the responsibility of paying for them.

Why does Selden not invest in Lily? On the face of it, he cannot afford to: he has "nothing to give" her (72). That is true as far as money goes, but money is not the only asset in Selden's portfolio, nor does he always count himself indigent. What holds him back, indeed, is not so much the thought of having "nothing to give" as the thought of what he might have to lose. And Selden stands to lose a great deal. His currency is not money, of course, but spiritual stocks, and in this currency he has been saving and hoarding for so long that he is afraid there might be "a chance of his having to pay up" (151). If he has so far kept his riches to himself, he has done so "not from any poverty of feeling" (151) but from a conscious sense of his accumulated wealth and from a determination to safeguard that wealth. Lily now presents him with an opportunity to "invest," and the question for Selden is whether she can be trusted with his emotional capital, whether he can "stake his faith" on her (320). The quandary he faces is not unlike that of his friends on the stock exchange, and the way he settles the question puts him in good company, which is to say, the company of the nonpayers, the company of Mrs. Peniston and Bertha Dorset.[6]

Selden is loath to part with his assets in the hazardous business of exchange. This self-serving conservatism comes through most vividly in a seemingly jesting moment between him and Lily:

> "Do you want to marry me?" she asked.
> He broke into a laugh. "No, I don't want to—but perhaps I should if you did!" (73)

Never is romance so unpassionate, so bluntly contractual. "Perhaps I should if you did"—the niggardly proposition epitomizes Selden's love for Lily. He will not propose to her until he knows that she will accept him; indeed, he will not love her until he knows that she will love him in return, until he can be "as sure of her surrender as of his own" (153). Short of this assurance—and all through the book Selden is never completely sure—he will not part with his spiritual capital; he will not take "risks" with it. For Selden, love is a form of exchange, and he will hear of nothing but profits.

The discipline of business determines which of the two roles, spectator or investor, Selden chooses to play. The spectator turns into the investor at the point where returns are guaranteed. These, then, are the two faces of the speculator—for Selden is no less business-minded when he "looks on" than when he "picks up" a find—and their equal congeniality enables him to perform some heady emotional flip-flops. As a spectator Selden remains cynically amused by Lily; as an investor he seeks to acquire her hand. Disparate as these sentiments may seem, for Selden they are both "options," to be taken up or put aside at will, and he trades options with daunting facility. Meeting him for the first time after Bellomont, Lily is struck by his having "gone back without an effort to the footing on which they had stood before their last talk together" (94). But such adaptability is to be expected from someone who computes his love as if it were on a balance sheet, "proportion[ing]" his expenditure to anticipated returns (307). Selden's "speculation" is the sort that will brook no risks (and certainly no losses), and Lily is simply not a sound enough investment for him. The sight of her emerging late at night from the Trenor house shatters his slim confidence, and Selden is quick to pull out. When they meet again, he has once more become a spectator. In Monte Carlo, he can "give his admiration the freer play because so little personal feeling remained in it" (216), and he sticks to this convenient role all through Lily's subsequent troubles.

Still, the investor in Selden is not quite willing to give up. As the book closes, he is ready to make another move, to trust once again to his "sense of adventure" (324). Of course, he arrives just a few hours too late for the adventure to take off, but even that unfortunate fact has no meaning for him except as a "loss" to himself. Faced with Lily's death, he will only "accuse himself for having failed to reach the height of his opportunity" (329). Selden does not seem aware of his responsibility—of his complicity—in her death. Like Mrs. Peniston, he "recognize[s] no obligation" toward Lily's welfare and accords himself no blame for her demise. Indeed, the worst thing that Selden can say about himself is that he has not been enterprising enough, that he has missed his "opportunity." And so he remains, to the end, a closet speculator. Selden's lament is one that Rosedale would have understood and might even have made himself. The "republic of the spirit" turns out to be less a republic than a refined replica of the social marketplace, of which Selden is a full participating member.[7]

Selden is a "negative hero," then, as Wharton herself admits, not a high-minded dissident but very much "one of them" (73).[8] Like the others, he too exudes a cold stinginess, a desire for acquisition without risk and without expenditure. It is not Selden but Lily, the woman he tutors and scolds, who comes closest to breaking away from the rules and premises of the marketplace. Lily is also, of course, the only one who pays routinely and scrupulously, and often with currency she can little afford. "You think we live on the rich, rather than with them," Lily observes to Gerty, "and so we do, in a sense—but it's a privilege we have to pay for!" (266). She is right. It is no accident that the one who pays most regularly is also the one with the scantest means, for nonpayment, as we have seen, is a privilege of the powerful, those who fix the rate of exchange. Lily is therefore the obverse of, and the needed complement to, three characters: Bertha Dorset, who avoids paying by making others foot the bill; Mrs. Peniston, who scrimps on her obligations; and Lawrence Selden, who pulls out when the deal seems overly risky. "Paying" is Lily's habitual way of being, and she is at it almost as soon as the book opens. It is she, not Selden, who has to "pay so dearly for" her visit to his apartment (15). Lily goes on to pay for her stay at Bellomont by performing "social drudgery" for Mrs. Trenor (39), as well as by incurring gambling debts. She pays for her momentary truancy from Percy Gryce. She pays Trenor, though not to his satisfaction. She pays Bertha for the cruise on the *Sabrina*, just as she pays Norma Hatch for her brief stay at the Emporium Hotel. And she pays, finally, for those extravagant sentiments she permits herself to feel toward Selden.[9]

Lily's dutiful payments are altogether in keeping with the principle of exchange. She is merely doing what the system requires of her, what she is supposed to. And yet—such is the irony of exchange—it is precisely this strict compliance that marks her as a deviant. Lily is working, after all, within a system in which nonpayment is the norm, in which violation is the only mode of conformity. She is penalized, then, not for breaking the rules but for observing them.[10] This sort of absurdity is the logic of nightmare, but it is just this absurd logic that makes the exchange system work. In its disfiguring light Lily's "rebellion" takes on the correspondingly absurd form of playing by the rules, of rebellion by submission.

Lily's paradoxical conformity and deviance come across most clearly in her dealings with Trenor. Having taken almost nine thousand dollars from him and finding her obligation "not the sort . . . one could remain under" (292), she proceeds to settle her debt as soon as she receives her aunt's legacy—a decision that "cleans [her] out altogether," as Rosedale rather indelicately puts it (292). In repaying Trenor, Lily is indeed complying with the rules of exchange, but she is also challenging the very basis of exchange. Trenor never expects to be paid back in quite this way. "Payment in kind," the most primitive form of barter economy, has no place in a highly developed social marketplace, which trades on the putative equivalence between disparate entities. By paying back the exact monetary amount, by equating nine thousand dollars with nine thousand dollars, Lily at once obeys the principle of exchange and reduces it to tautology. Her nine-thousand-dollar debt is now just that: a nine-thousand-dollar debt, not some ill-defined and possibly limitless obligation. In other words, by making money its own equivalent, Lily reduces it to its own terms and defies its purchasing power. She has understood what it means to live under the "intolerable obligation" of an all-consuming system of exchange, and she now tries to exorcise its influence by facing up to what she owes—in all the crudeness and brutality of its cash amount—just to rescue from its dominion the other strands of her life. What appears as a gesture of submission turns out to be a gesture of defiance, for by adhering literally to the terms of exchange Lily turns the system on its head. And yet, as every reader must recognize, defiance of this sort is ultimately unavailing. The exchange system can easily accommodate rebellion like Lily's: Trenor, no doubt, will take the money and even circulate it anew. Lily's action hurts no one but herself. It remains a challenge to the exchange system in spirit but not in fact.

When Lily returns the money, her rebellion by submission assumes its final and characteristically self-defeating form, the only form it is permitted to take within the exchange system. We see the beginning of that pattern in her earlier and grateful refusal of the "plain business arrangement" Rosedale offers her. What Rosedale proposes is this:

> "Well, I'll lend you the money to pay Trenor; and I won't—I—see here, don't take me up till I've finished. What I mean is, it'll be a plain business arrangement, such as one man would make with another. Now, what have you got to say against that?"
>
> Lily's blush deepened to a glow in which humiliation and gratitude were mingled, and both sentiments revealed themselves in the unexpected gentleness of her reply.
>
> "Only this: that it is exactly what Gus Trenor proposed; and that I can never again be sure of understanding the plainest business arrangement." Then, realizing that this answer contained a germ of injustice, she added, even more kindly: "Not that I don't appreciate your kindness—that I'm not grateful for it. But a business arrangement between us would in any case be impossible, because I shall have no security to give when my debt to Gus Trenor has been paid." (299)

This reply is surely an impressive statement from someone who, not so long ago, believed that "her modest investments were to be mysteriously multiplied" with Trenor's help (85). Lily has since found out what even "the simplest business arrangement" entails, and on this occasion she is careful to keep "business" to its strictest possible definition. She is in fact blunter, more matter-of-fact than Rosedale himself, but, by being so implacably businesslike, Lily paradoxically obstructs, rather than facilitates, business opportunities. By insisting on money as the only legitimate currency, she limits the field of action as well as the available material for exchange. There is something heroic in her refusal to accept money when she knows she has no money to give in return, and yet such principles are surely suicidal, when the point of exchange is to get and not to give. What is honorable from a moral point of view is plain foolishness within the context of the marketplace.[11] Like her decision to return Trenor's money, Lily's rejection of Rosedale's loan leaves the exchange system intact and hurts only herself. Where the marketplace is everywhere, in refusing to do business Lily is perhaps also refusing to live—an implication Wharton takes up at the end.

Meanwhile, Lily is left to commit two more business errors. The more serious one (from a practical point of view) concerns the disposition of Bertha's letters. These are valuable assets, and Rosedale, the consummate businessman, has no doubt about how Lily should use them. "The wonder to me is that you've waited so long to get square with that woman, when you've had he power in your hands," he declares (257). After all, Bertha had saved her own skin "at Lily's expense," she "owes" Lily, and nothing would be more natural than an attempt to right the balance. Of course, there are different ways of "getting even" (258). Going to Bertha's husband with proof of her infidelity could be one way, but from a "purely business view of the question" Rosedale does not recommend this method, since "in a deal like that, nobody comes out with perfectly clean hands" (258). He has a much better "deal" in mind. Lily is to use the letters not to destroy Bertha but to cow her, to "get [her] into line" (259). Unlike the other deal, a risky business, this one is guaranteed to work:

> [Rosedale's plan] reduced the transaction to a private understanding, of which no third person need have the remotest hint. Put by Rosedale in terms of business-like give-and-take, this understanding took on the harmless air of a mutual accommodation, like a transfer of property or a revision of boundary lines. It certainly simplified life to view it as a perpetual adjustment, a play of party politics, in which every con-

> cession had the recognized equivalent; Lily's tired mind was fascinated by this escape from fluctuating ethical estimates into a region of concrete weights and measures. (259)

Properly managed, even revenge can become a form of exchange. And in the hands of Rosedale, exchange will be very good business indeed—completely without risk, with profits guaranteed.[12] Lily's grievances are to be paid back with "recognized equivalent[s]"; they are to count as credits with which to exact payment (and indeed interest) from the offending party. The past wrongs are to be set right by a little "adjustment" between the two women in the form of a "private transaction," a "transfer of property," from which Lily is to be—for once—the receiving rather than the paying party.

Lily has not always been averse to righting her balance. Much earlier, when she was contemplating marriage to Percy Gryce, she had looked forward to the "old scores she would pay off as well as old benefits she could return" (49). Still, she cannot bring herself to use Bertha's letters. Even though Rosedale will not carry her unless she is "reconciled" with Bertha and "rehabilitated" in society and even though marriage is her only remaining hope, Lily cannot carry out the "private transaction" he has so plainly laid out. To strike a deal with Bertha, Lily is required not only to "trade on [Selden's] name and profit by a secret from his past" (304) but to "trade on" and "profit by" her past wrongs. Rosedale's method represents the ultimate commodification of experience, the reduction and quantification of moral outrage into "concrete weights and measures" for exchange. Lily cannot do it. This, too, is a business opportunity she must reject. If she refuses to pay her debts with surrogate money, she also refuses to "cash in" on her injuries. Since she will not make Bertha "pay back" what Bertha "owes" her, she must leave the imbalance between herself and Bertha unredressed. What Lily is rejecting is not so much the idea of revenge as the degradation of revenge in the arena of exchange.[13]

As Lily leaves Selden's apartment, she quietly slides the packet of letters into the fire. Rosedale would have been horrified. Her last "asset" is now destroyed and, with it, any hope of rehabilitation. But Lily has not planned to burn the letters—she does so on the spur of the moment—and her sudden decision probably has something to do with another mistake she makes during the same visit, the mistake of indulging in "the passion of her soul" (309). Hardly anyone else in the book has been guilty of this mistake, and it becomes all the more startling against the background of Selden's tepid civilities. He offers her tea—"that amount of hospitality at my command," he tells her. Lily sees that "her presence [is] becoming an embarrassment to him," she notices his "light tone" and his all-too-evident "linger[ing] in the conventional outskirts of word-play and evasion" (305–06). But his demeanor no longer holds her back; for once she can accept the disparity between her sentiments and his.[14] In Wharton's wonderful phrase, Lily has "passed beyond the phase of well-bred reciprocity, in which every demonstration must be scrupulously proportioned to the emotion it elicits" (307). In destroying Bertha's letters, she is offering Selden a great deal more than he has offered her or will ever offer her. But Lily no longer weighs and "proportion[s]" her feelings; she is no longer deterred by thoughts of "profits" and "returns." As she throws away her love in an act of wanton expenditure, she is making what is perhaps her most eloquent protest against the ethics of exchange.

And yet, this protest, like her other ones, is ultimately futile, ultimately contained, absorbed, and exploited by the very system against which it is directed. The exchange system has room for money foolishly returned and loans foolishly refused, just as it has room for sentiments foolishly indulged in. Far from being a threat to the system, Lily's gesture of defiance merely recapitulates its assignation—merely reaffirms its sovereignty—for in giving Selden more than she gets from him, Lily is simply reverting to her customary role within the exchange system: her role as the one who "pays."

Even more ironically, Lily's extraordinary expenditure, like her previous ones, is not valued by those who benefit from it; it literally goes unnoticed. For a man who prides himself on his spectatorship, Selden is surprisingly blind to the moral drama unfolding before his very eyes. "When she rose, he fancied that he saw her draw something from her dress and drop it into the fire; but he hardly noticed the gesture at the time" (310). The gesture will never be noticed; it is not meant to be. Lily's delicacy of feeling, her rectitude and generosity—all these are lost on Selden. They will always be unrecognized, unrewarded even by his gratitude. But that, too, is only to be expected. For the nobility of her action surely lies in its fruitlessness, in its utter lack of material consequence, in its erasure from history.

With her death, Lily's moral triumph evaporates as if it had never taken place. In the last chapter of *The House of Mirth*, Wharton presents us with the spectacle of Selden rummaging through Lily's papers, fretting over the check made out to Trenor, feeling sorry for himself—and remaining, all the while, abysmally ignorant of what she has done for his sake. Wharton could not have written a stronger or more bitter commentary on the loneliness and futility of Lily's "rebellion." But even if her secret had somehow been revealed, it would have made no sense to her friends. They would have dismissed it as a species of folly. Private morality is finally defenseless against an exchange system that dissolves the language of morality into its own harsh, brassy parlance. Within this totalizing system, moral rectitude simply counts as another exchange value, another commodity—and an insanely expensive one, as it turns out.[15] For this ultimate luxury Lily pays with her life. Her few moments of moral triumph, translated into the idiom of the marketplace, merely figure as moments of ill-advised improvidence, altogether in keeping with her lifelong habit of spending "more than she could afford" (15). Morality, in *The House of Mirth*, provides no transcendent language, no alternative way of being, but feeds directly into the mechanisms of the marketplace. Lily's rebellion, which appeals to and presupposes a transcendent moral order, is doomed for that very reason.[16]

"A frivolous society can acquire dramatic significance only through what its frivolity destroys. Its tragic implication lies in its power of debasing people and ideas," Wharton once said about *The House of Mirth* (*Backward* 207). Such debasement and destructiveness she conveys with devastating clarity. Her difficulty arises only when she is confronted with the need to imagine an alternative to the exchange system, a positive ideal to complement her ringing critique. To do so, Wharton can only invoke an absent ideal—something that it has never been Lily's privilege to experience:

> And as [Lily] looked back she saw that there had never been a time when she had had any relation to life. Her parents too had been rootless, blown hither and thither on every wind of fashion, without any personal existence to shelter them from its shifting gusts. She herself had grown up without any one spot of earth being dearer to her than another: there was no centre of early pieties, of grave endearing traditions, to which her heart could revert and from which it could draw strength for itself and tenderness for others. In whatever form a slowly-accumulated past lives in the blood--whether in the concrete image of the old house stored with visual memories, or in the conception of the house not built with hands, but made up of inherited passions and loyalties--it had the same power of broadening and deepening the individual existence, of attaching it by mysterious links of kinship to all the mighty sum of human striving. (319)

Wharton's image of the sanctified ancestral home, like the house of custom and ceremony Yeats prays for, is a quintessentially aristocratic ideal. As metaphor and as fact, the ancestral house stands aloof, in all its feudal strength, from the contemporary world of commodities, the world of "the wares / Peddled in the thoroughfares."[17] It is Wharton's fantasy of a transcendent order, for an organic life based on "blood" and "root[s]" is indeed antithetical to the mechanical exchange of capitalism. Wharton's critique of the marketplace is essentially an aristocratic critique, a critique from the standpoint of "early pieties," "grave endearing traditions," and "inherited passions and loyalties." And yet, even as she articulates her ideal, she sees that it does not exist, will not exist, and indeed has never existed, either in her own experience or in Lily's. The ideal is declared impossible even as it is invoked. The ancestral home is no alternative to the commodified "house of mirth," irrevocably present and here to stay.

Still, Wharton is not quite willing to give up the idea of transcendence. She finally compromises, ingeniously if not altogether convincingly, by grafting her ideal on a lower social order, the working class.[18] The fantasized ancestral house does appear in the book after all, if only in the modernized and modified form of a working-class tenement. And to the occupant of this humble habitation, Nettie Struther, Wharton entrusts her vision of a life antithetical to the one she condemns. It is in Nettie's kitchen that Lily catches her "first glimpse of the continuity of life." She sees in Nettie someone who seems "to have reached the central truth of existence" (319). It is not clear how Nettie accomplishes that feat (aside from her good fortune in having found a trusting husband); nor is it clear how her haphazard life as a wage laborer can withstand the ravages of the marketplace. As an ideal, Nettie remains curiously unsubstantiated, curiously unexamined: Wharton seems to have suspended her ironic incisiveness, her withering sense of all that entraps and compromises the human spirit. She does not look more closely at Nettie, one suspects, because she cannot afford to. Wharton is not completely persuaded by the virtues of the working class, nor is she altogether sympathetic to their causes. Even though she looks instinctively to the "poor little working girl" (319) in her search for a redemptive figure, she sees Nettie less as the representative of the working class than as the embodiment of a private ideal—Wharton's ideal. Nettie, then, is to be *from* the working class but not too militantly, not too clamorously *of* it.[19] To be all that Wharton wants her to be, Nettie must be abstracted from the all-contaminating exchange system. She must be romanticized and, to some extent, insulated—transported, in short, from the social realm into another realm, what we might call the realm of nature, a realm Wharton metaphorically invokes. Nettie's makeshift tenement, Wharton would have us believe, has "the frail, audacious permanence of a bird's nest built on the edge of a cliff" (320). As an organic force, a principle of tenacity and continuity, Nettie takes her place within the "permanence" of natural history, at once more primitive and (Wharton hopes) more enduring than the exchange system.

A "naturalized" working class represents Wharton's best hope for an organic life beyond the marketplace. It is the only romanticism she permits herself in the book, but even this ideal is not always easy to sustain. On a number of occasions—most particularly when Nettie expresses her innocent hope that her daughter ("Marry Anto'nette") will grow up to be just like Lily—we see the corrosive vision of the ironist subverting the "alternative" she has so painstakingly set up. The book is fueled, then, by an almost exclusively critical energy directed at the marketplace Wharton disdains. She can only confusedly gesture toward a redeeming alternative: for her, the house of mirth has no exit.

Notes

1. Most recent critics have related commodification to gender issues. See Montgomery 897; Ammons 33; and Wershoven 56. But women are hardly the only ones turned into commodities; indeed, the entire fabric of social intercourse is, in my view, commodified.

2. Trilling observes that "*The House of Mirth* is always and passionately a money story" (122). While agreeing with her assessment, I would argue that the power of money lies not so much in its crude form—in a bank account, for example—as in its ability to engender a certain way of being.

3. This assumption informs some of the best criticism on *The House of Mirth*. See, for instance, Fetterley's article and Wolff 109–33.

4. For an interesting discussion of spectatorship as a product of commodity culture, see Agnew.

5. No less than the other men, Selden "objectifies" Lily in his aesthetic appreciation—a point several critics have made. See, for instance. Wolff 120–33 and Wershoven 46.

6. Wharton does not seem to differentiate the various modes of activity within the marketplace. She does not, for instance, distinguish between speculation and production or between finance capital and industrial capital; she assigns them a single label: "business." In this regard she is considerably less sophisticated than some of her contemporaries—Dreiser, for instance—who discriminate among different kinds of business, as well as different kinds of businessmen (see, e.g., Michaels).

7. Wolff also sees the last chapter as an ironic commentary on Selden. While she emphasizes Selden's "bathetic sentimentality" (132–33), I emphasize his business-mindedness.

8. Wharton referred to Selden as a "negative hero" in a letter to Sara Norton, 26 Oct. 1906. Wharton Archives, Beinecke Library, Yale University, New Haven, Conn., quoted in Wolff 111.

9. Lily's conscientious bookkeeping is imaged in two parallel scenes—one at the beginning of the novel and the other at the end—in which she anxiously pores over her checkbook. She is the only character caught in that activity.

10. In another context, Fetterley has written that "Lily can be what she is supposed to be only at the cost of being what she is supposed to be" (208). Fetterley is speaking of the "double standard and double bind" inherent in the aesthetic feminine ideal to which Lily is subjected, but the same absurd logic applies to her role in the exchange system.

11. Davidson has noted that Lily's "finer sensibilities prove to be a definite liability" (10). Those "finer sensibilities" prove to be especially damaging, I would argue, when they prevent Lily from achieving the doublethink essential to exchange.

12. That point seems to have struck Lily, as well. For her, "the essential baseness of the act lay in its freedom from risk" (260).

13. In emphasizing Lily's moral stance, I am departing implicitly from Wolff's characterization of Lily as someone whose "sense of 'self' is confirmed only when she elicits reactions from others" and who otherwise suffers from an "inner emptiness" (128). The scruples Lily feels toward the end of the book could not have come from anyone else. No one else is making decisions like hers, and no one expects her to make them.

14. The peculiar poignancy of this scene might have something to do with Wharton's own memory of "her disappointment at the word not spoken" during her early romance with Walter Berry. Since Wharton herself was known as "Lily" during her Newport days, and since at least one of her acquaintances—Winthrop Chanler—recognized "Walter Berry [as] the hero" of *The House of Mirth*, the biographical interest of the scene is more than negligible. See Lewis 48–50, 153.

15. Wharton, Howe writes, "believed [that] what the heart desires brings with it a price—and often an exorbitant price," and he suggests that she would have responded with "sardonic pleasure" to these lines by Auden: "Every farthing of the cost / All the bitter stars foretell / Shall be paid" (Howe 18). He does not, however, fully examine why Wharton thought that everything should have a price.

16. An opposing view is that Lily's moral insight is her ultimate vindication. See Wershoven 42, 58 and McDowell 43–44. I differ from these critics in seeing morality in *The House of Mirth* not as an autonomous or transcendent order but as a subordinate part of the exchange system.

17. In "A Prayer for My Daughter," Yeats, like Wharton, images a house sanctified against the corruption of the marketplace:

> And may her bridegroom bring her to a house
> Where all's accustomed, ceremonious;
> For arrogance and hatred are the wares
> Peddled in the thoroughfares.
> How but in custom and in ceremony
> Are innocence and beauty born?
> Ceremony's a name for the rich horn,
> And custom for the spreading laurel tree.

18. Wharton seems to pit the bourgeoisie against both the aristocracy and the working class. While her assumption is never articulated, it nevertheless makes her something of an involuntary Marxist in her vision of history.

19. Trilling makes the interesting observation that Wharton's "commitment to the democratic principle, if it can be said to have existed at all, existed only in a much transmogrified form" (114).

Works Cited

Agnew, Jean-Christophe. "The Consuming Vision of Henry James." *The Culture of Consumption: Critical Essays in American History, 1880–1980*, ed. Richard Wightman Fox and T. J. Jackson Lears. New York: Pantheon, 1983. 65–100.

Ammons, Elizabeth. *Edith Wharton's Argument with America*. Athens: University of Georgia Press, 1980.

Bataille, Georges. "The Notion of Expenditure," trans. Allan Stoeki. *Raritan Review* 3 (1984): 62–79.

Davidson, Cathy N. "Kept Women in *The House of Mirth*." Markham Review 9 (1979): 10–13.

Fetterley, Judith. " 'The Temptation to Be a Beautiful Object': Double Standard and Double Bind in *The House of Mirth*." *Studies in American Fiction* 5 (1977): 199–211.

Howe, Irving. "Introduction: The Achievement of Edith Wharton." *Edith Wharton: A Collection of Critical Essays*, ed. Howe. Englewood Cliffs N.J.: Prentice, 1962. 1–18.

Lewis, R. W. B. *Edith Wharton: A Biography*. New York: Harper, 1975.

Marx, Karl. *Capital*, trans. Samuel Moore and Edward Aveling. New York: International, 1967.

McDowell, Margaret. *Edith Wharton*. Boston: Twayne, 1976.

Michaels, Walter Benn. "Dreiser's *Financier*: The Man of Business as a Man of Letters." *American Realism: New Essays*, ed. Eric J. Sundquist. Baltimore: Johns Hopkins University Press, 1982. 278–95.

Montgomery, Judith H. "American Galatea." *College English* 32 (1971): 890–99.

Trilling, Diana. "*The House of Mirth* Revisited." *American Scholar* 32 (1962–1963): 113–26.

Wershoven, Carol. *The Female Intruder in the Novels of Edith Wharton*. London: Associated University Press, 1982.

Wharton, Edith. *A Backward Glance*. 1933. New York: Scribner's, 1964.

———. *The House of Mirth*. 1905. New York: Scribner's, 1933.

Wolff, Cynthia Griffin. *A Feast of Words: The Triumph of Edith Wharton*. New York: Oxford University Press, 1977.

Crowded Spaces in *The House of Mirth*

AMY KAPLAN

◆ ◆ ◆

THE HOUSE OF MIRTH opens in a crowded train station when Selden glimpses Lily Bart in the midst of the afternoon rush. In the "act of transition between one and another of the country-houses," the main character does not first appear ensconced in one of their interiors along with the other ladies of her class.[1] Instead, she stands out as a "highly specialized" product against a throng of "sallow-faced girls in preposterous hats and flat-chested women struggling with paper bundles and palm-leaf fans" (5). Although Lily remains "apart from the crowd," her relation to that crowd is enigmatic. On the one hand, it forms a background that outlines her brilliance: "her vivid head, relieved against the dull tints of the crowd, made her more conspicuous than in a ball-room" (4). On the other hand, the passers-by constitute an audience of spectators, "who lingered to look; for Miss Bart was a figure to arrest even the suburban traveller rushing to his last train" (4). As a privileged onlooker, Selden engages in "speculation" about Lily's relation to her setting, with a "confused sense that she must have cost a great deal to make, that a great many dull and ugly people must, in some mysterious way, have been sacrificed to produce her" (5). By introducing the main character through Selden's confusion, the narrative introduces itself as a more accurate "speculation," a promise to clarify the mystery of Lily's production by computing her cost, by unfolding the relation between the veiled figure of the lady and the crowd that surrounds her.

The opening scene describes Lily Bart in precisely those idealistic terms which Howells dismissed as unrealistic: artificial, polished, painted, and covered with a "fine glaze," she appears behind a veil, like a mysterious heroine of a romantic novel. Howells's aesthetic of the common, in contrast, advocates representing the members of the crowd, who exhibit for Selden "the dinginess, the crudity of this average section of womanhood" (5). The lady indeed represents all that is uncommon and superfluous, useless and rarefied, as far away from the financial world of the businessmen of her own class as from the working world of the lower-class women. Epitomizing the unreal qualities of modern life, the lady of leisure seems a most inappropriate subject matter according to the producer ethos underlying Howells's theory of realism, to which Wharton herself subscribed. Yet, Wharton's opening scene can be read as a critique of Howellsian realism by posing the figure of Lily at center stage and then decentering her by revealing her social production. Just as Selden first views. Lily against the crowd of average women rushing through the station, the reader approaches the coming scenes of upper-class luxury and intimacy against a crowded society in flux.

Realism in *The House of Mirth* explores the relation between two conflicting meanings of "society": as the exclusive realm of the elite, whose members are known or knowable to one another, and as the inclusive, yet impersonal, network of civic, political, and cultural institutions, in which the connections between members are binding, yet elusive. Wharton poses this conflict at a time when both meanings were undergoing radical change as the rapid growth of wealth destabilized the upper classes and the increasing interdependence yet stratification of society as a whole made its inner workings and interconnections all but invisible.

The House of Mirth represents high society as a predominantly female realm, whose relation to the hidden male arena of business and to the equally shadowy world of working women must be charted by the narrative, with Lily deployed as a scout. The novel maps a social terrain where these realms become increasingly interconnected not only through the relations of work and marriage but through the mediation of spectatorship. Wharton's realistic narrative as well becomes enmeshed in producing the spectacle of the unreal world it strives to unveil.

ALTHOUGH THE NARRATIVE OF *The House of Mirth* is tightly structured around Lily's progression from one enclosed interior to the next, the interstices of the novel are filled with crowds. Throngs of newcomers cram the entrance to the "charmed circle" of high society, while packs of onlookers lurk around its edges to peer inside. In contrast to Mrs. Peniston's empty house, built upon inherited wealth and rigid decorum, the social set in which Lily circulates is presented as "a crowded selfish world of pleasure." At its center stands the guest-filled home of Judy Trenor, who "seemed to exist only as a hostess, not so much from any exaggerated instinct of hospitality as because she could not sustain life except in a crowd" (41). Her own identity, like that of the other characters in the novel, depends upon the very crowd she dominates. Trenor's identity as hostess stems neither from kindness to strangers nor from the rituals among an established community but from her power to control the crowd by regulating the influx of newcomers.

Haunting the outskirts of the Trenor's social world is a more amorphous and threatening crowd. What Lily sees at first as "the charmed circle about which all her desires revolved" (50) later appears to her as a "great gilt cage" in which its members "were all huddled for the mob to gape at" (56). Although the members of this "charmed circle" draw its boundaries through their power of exclusion, through "the force of negation which eliminated everything beyond their own range of perception" (49), they paradoxically thrive on being recognized by those they negate. To legitimate their privilege, the upper class cannot afford to seclude itself in a private sphere but depends upon displaying itself before the gaping mob. Such publicity must simultaneously appeal to the crowd by arousing its desire to belong and control that crowd by maintaining an inviolate boundary between actors and audience. High society in *The House of Mirth* is threatened less by the parvenus that enter it, as is commonly assumed, than by its need to turn the rest of society into an audience. If the demands of the urban poor threaten to disrupt the middle-class community in *A Hazard of New Fortunes*, the gaping mob in *The House of Mirth* threatens the power of the elite by entrapping them in its gaze, in their own dependence upon publicity.

One of Wharton's recurring narrative strategies is to give material substance to those threats which first appear in the text as figures of speech. The specter of the "gaping mob," for example, materializes during the first major social gathering of the novel, the wedding between Lily's cousin, Jack Stepney, and Miss Van Osburgh, another member of New York's older elite. The ritual of the wedding has the dual function of consolidating class unity and staging a gala spectacle for a mass audience. Although the ceremony takes place outside the crowded city, in "the village church near the paternal estate on the Hudson," it is performed against a background of voyeuristic crowds clamoring for a glimpse: "It was the 'simple country wedding' to which guests are conveyed in special trains, and from which the hordes of the uninvited have to be fended off by the intervention of the police" (88). Not entirely excluded, the hordes gain a channeled entry in the form of the press, whose representatives "were threading their way, note-book in hand, through the labyrinth of wedding presents, and the agent of a cinematograph syndicate was setting up his apparatus at the church-door" (89). In the role of mediator, the press, on the one hand, represents elite society by making it visible to the classes beneath them. On the other hand, the press represents these classes as mobs or hordes and attempts both to arouse and contain their desire to enter a world they must serve as spectators.

Articulating the spectacular nature of this upper-class ritual, Lily imagines trading her place as "casual spectator" for the role of the "mystically veiled figure occupying the center of attention" (89). Lily's contradictory self-image encapsulates that of her class, which to maintain its power as the center of attention must also remain mystically veiled. The combination of conspicuousness and elusiveness empowers the elite as the center of desire by simultaneously attracting the notice of the audience beneath them and keeping that audience at bay.

The upper-class woman plays a central role in this pageant. While the press displays the wedding presents to the gaping mob, those same presents stir the envy of the inner coterie. As spectator, Lily is especially struck by the bride's jewels, whose "precious tints [were] enhanced and deepened by the varied art of their setting." Lily identifies not only with the mystically veiled figure of the bride but with the fully exposed objects, the jewels: "More completely than any other expression of wealth, they symbolized the life she longed to lead, the life of fastidious aloofness and refinement in which every detail should have the finish of a jewel, and the whole form a harmonious setting to her own jewel-like rareness" (91). Lily's desire for aloofness depends upon her attachment to the setting from which she wishes to be distinguished. Throughout the novel, Lily's identity is described in relation to a background against which she can outline herself, or a mirror in which she can be viewed. Yet each attempt to ignore that dependence contributes to her further decline.

The narrative of Lily's descent can be traced through her relation to the mirror, from the one in Selden's apartment in which he sees her as "a captured dryad subdued to the conventions of the drawing-room" (12), to Mrs. Bry's admiration, which "was a mirror in which Lily's self-complacency recovered its lost outline" (114), to Gerty's mirror, which reflects Lily's "disfigurement," to the "blank surface of the toilet-mirror" in her death room (327). Lily's reliance on mirrors and settings for her identity has been viewed as either a weakness of moral character or an indication of her plight as a woman who exists passively as a beautiful object rather than acting in the world.[2] Yet this dependence also shows [how the lady of leisure becomes emblematic of her class.] Just as she can achieve an identity only from the gaze of those around her, the class she represents depends not only on the subservience but on the spectatorship of the crowds around it.

Wharton has long been seen to chronicle the rapid succession of New York's established elite by succesive waves of parvenus, who supplanted inherited wealth with industrial fortunes and traditional values with conspicuous consumption. *The House of Mirth*, however, shows that the dazzling ascendancy of new money did more than alter the demographic composition of New York's elite. The representation of this class and of its relation to other classes underwent fundamental transformations as "members of old and new money emerged into the public social life in a grand way."[3] The New York "old guard"—itself only as old as the merger of antebellum Knickerbockers with post–Civil War industrial fortunes—formulated rituals and rules of polite behavior designed to consolidate their class interests and regulate the admission of newcomers. Both their lack of stability and their attempt to achieve it was epitomized by the Astor Four Hundred Club, a grouping based on the notion that a select number of individuals could be designated as the upper crust of society. Their social gatherings took place in the formalized privacy of the dining room at home, or the equally circumscribed space of the elaborate formal ball.[4]

When the huge influx of wealth turned New York into the finance and trust center of the country in the late nineteenth century, the older families lost their authority to control the admission to an elite coterie. With fewer guarantees of social status, the wealthy focused more on competing for power with one another than on acknowledging their common interests. If the old guard had tried to cement its membership through exclusive rituals in a private setting, both new and old money now competed for status through extravagant public spectacles.[5] Rather than adhere to formal rules of etiquette to prove their worthiness to enter the upper echelon, the newer elites tried to outdo one another in innovative and often outlandish performances, staged as much for one another as for the masses beneath them. The change in upper-class leisure from private functions to public displays was reflected in the social geography of the city, with the building of palatial hotels and restaurants. These monuments served the double purpose of a meeting ground and competitive arena for the expanding elite and an advertisement purveying their luxury and power to the masses. Social life was thus gradually moving out of the private dining hall and exclusive ball of the Astor Four Hundred Club to the public stage of the hotel and restaurant, where anyone with wealth could come to see and be seen.[6]

In New York City, the struggle for economic power on Wall Street was manifest less in the political and civic arena (where it went on, for example, in Boston) than in the social realm of Fifth Avenue, a sphere dominated by women. Whereas Thorstein Veblen analyzed the conspicuous consumption that turned the lady of leisure into an ornamental display of her husband's power as an outdated vestige of barbaric customs, Wharton presented this role as pivotal in new modes of representing class power. Visitors to the United States in the 1890s and in the first decade of the twentieth century often commented on the female domination of a social scene vacated by men who were busy building economic empires. To Henry James and Paul Bourget, both friends of Wharton's, this division constituted "*the* feature of the social scene" of American life.[7] Wharton, however, takes this observation further to explore the hidden connections between these bifurcated realms. For the lady of leisure, domesticity was subordinated to publicity as the home became a stage setting for the gala social events orchestrated and acted out by women. The upper-class home functioned less as a private haven from the competition of the marketplace than as the public stage for that competition. Indeed, the meaning of public and private underwent an interesting reversal. In *The House of Mirth* it is the dealings of the business world which seem private and unspeakable, while the cultural work of women dominates the public scene. The women of this group have a dual role: to display the wealth and social power of their husbands and to conceal the source of this power.

Thus, Wharton does not simply chart the breakdown of the traditions of the old guard and the rootlessness of the new; rather, she participates in changing forms of representing class power.

The wedding scene in *The House of Mirth* stands at the crossroads of this transformation. On the one hand, the wedding takes place in the privacy of "the paternal estate" between members of the old guard with the traditional function of assuring their future through kinship. On the other hand, the wedding has a circus-like quality in that it is performed for a mass audience excluded from participation. The wedding, furthermore, challenges the traditional social and literary meaning of domesticity. Lily Bart longs to be the bride, not because this status promises to remove her to a secure domestic retreat but because of the power it would afford her to star in the public eye. By having Lily miss her chance to play this role in the beginning of the novel, Wharton rejects marriage as the narrative teleology of the domestic novel and implicitly calls attention to her own narrative as realistic.

The narration of Lily's fall away from the center of the older elite traces the rise not only of the nouveau riche but of new modes of upper-class leisure and self-representation. Whereas the Osborn wedding still maintains the sanction of a traditional ritual, the next major gathering in the novel, the Wellington tableaux vivants, has a purely theatrical function. The Brys stage this gala event to break into high society in a grand way, not by conforming to its preexisting rules but by redefining its terms of pleasure and leisure. The tableaux vivants enact imitations of famous old paintings, with fashionable ladies costumed as the main characters. Since the sixteenth century, oil paintings have had a double significance as property: not only are they owned as valuable possessions, but also they represent in tangible and tactile detail those objects that the owner has the wealth to possess.[8] In addition to displaying the owner-spectator's power in the present, their solidity promises a permanent record of his image for the future. The Brys' tableaux vivants invert the way painting functions as a representation of social status by harnessing the cutural authority of the artistic tradition while transcribing it in a new context. Rather than buy paintings that represent the things they own, they spend money to imitate the art of the past. They hire a "distinguished portrait painter" not to paint a lasting portrait of themselves but to direct a show. If oil paintings are valued for their realism, for their tangible and lasting properties, the tableaux vivants advertise the ability of the Brys to copy the real thing and to perform it as something unreal and fleeting. They turn art into performance. These performances are not paeans to property and ownership, they flaunt the power of conspicuous consumption, the power to spend money for its own sake. Instead of buying unique and enduring works of art, the Brys spend money to deny the material reality of objects and treat art merely as a means of producing "spectacular effects."[9]

The Brys' newly built mansion has the same effect as their evening entertainment. As opposed to a private setting for domesticity, the house is constructed for public display and is self-consciously built as a stage: "the air of improvisation was in fact so strikingly present; so recent, so rapidly evoked was the whole *mise-en-scène* that one had to touch the marble columns to learn they were not of cardboard, to seat one's self in one of the damask-and-gold armchairs to be sure it was not painted against the wall" (133). In contrast to the older homes of Mrs. Peniston and Percy Gryce, which impose themselves on the spectator with their mausoleum-like solidity, the Brys' mansion flaunts its newness and improvised quality.

Although the performance of the tableaux vivants may appear as the antithesis of the activities of collecting and connoisseurship in the novel, it is the logical culmination of the collector's ethos. A member of the older elite, Percy Gryce, collects Americana for its "mere rarity," but his collection denies the historical content of the documents just as the tableaux vivants deny the historicity of the art of the past. While Gryce shuns the conspicuousness which the Brys court, his Americana collection has the exchange value for him less of money than of personal publicity: "Anxious as he was to avoid personal notice, he took, in the printed mention of his name, a pleasure so exquisite and excessive that it seemed a compensation for his shrinking from publicity" (21). The collection, which he inherited from his father, serves as a mirror which allows him "to regard himself as figuring prominently in the public eye" (21). Gryce's modest collection has the same purpose as the more voracious acquisition of Rosedale, who catches the "envious attention" of those who formerly shunned him by "buying the newly furnished house of one of the victims of the crash, who in the space of twelve short months, had made the same number of millions, built a house on Fifth Avenue, filled a picture gallery with old masters, entertained all New York in it, and been smuggled out of the country between a trained nurse and doctor while his creditors mounted guard over the old masters and his guests explained to each other that they had dined with him only because they wanted to see the pictures" (122). Rather than accumulate art objects piece by piece, Rosedale acquires a whole collection at once; the value of the collection lies in the fact that he has taken over what someone else has lost, not in the objects themselves. Although Rosedale prides himself on being less aggressive and obvious than the Brys in his social ascent, his acquisition of real "old masters" has the same effect as the Brys' performance of the imitation, that of producing publicity for the social power of the owner.

Although the Brys present their tableaux vivants to an exclusive party of invited guests, "to attack society collectively," they stage their entertainment for a broader audience, for the larger crowd of the gaping mob. The next evening finds *Town Talk* full of innuendos about Lily's role in the performance, and her cousin, Mr. Ned Van Alstyne, claims to have read about her in "the dirty papers" (158). *Town Talk* is an obvious parody of New York's *Town Topics*, a popular society magazine and scandal sheet. Although originally published for the inner circle of "gentle folk," the magazine began to appeal to a wider readership as its circulation passed fifty thousand in the 1890s.[10] The popular press has a function similar to that of the collection of high art; both reflect to the elite their own sense of importance in the eyes of others. If they invite their peers into their mansions to view enviously their art collections and entertainments, they depend upon the press to invite outsiders to participate vicariously in the same events.

As all social interaction in *The House of Mirth* becomes more staged and theatrical, the novel becomes more crowded with references to the media, to popular forms of representing the wealthy classes. The opening scene of book 2 parallels that of book 1 and demonstrates this progressive theatricalization of social intercourse. Book 2 opens in a public space that does not have the functionality of the train station but serves self-consciously as "sublime stage setting" (183). Both scenes are framed by the observations of Selden, "who began to feel the renewed zest of spectatorship that is the solace of those who take an objective interest in life" (184). Yet, rather than stare at Lily, who seems caught unaware in Grand Central Station, Selden notices a "consciously conspicuous group of people" who

> advanced to the middle front and stood before Selden with the air of chief performers gathered together by the exigencies of the final effect. Their appearance confirmed the impression that the show had been staged regardless of expense, and emphasized its resemblance to one of those "costume-plays" in which the protagonists walk through the passions without displacing a drapery. The ladies stood in unrelated attitudes calculated to isolate their effects, and the men hung about them as irrelevantly as stage heroes whose tailors are named in the program. (184)

In this scene, high society imitates the costume play, itself a theatrical form which imitated the manners of the wealthy. The copy and the original become indistinguishable, just as spectators and actors become inseparable when "it was Selden himself who unwittingly fused the group by arresting the attention of one of its members."

Selden is not the only spectator-participant in the scene; he is rivaled by the presence of "that horrid little Dabham who does 'Society Notes from the Riviera' " (199). In the figure of Dabham, the gaping mob becomes ever more concrete. He gains entrance into closed circles that others merely glimpse from the outside. The next day, the same group chooses a restaurant which "was crowded with persons mainly gathered there for the purpose of spectatorship, and accurately posted as to the names and the faces of the celebrities they had come to see" (216). It is Dabham's job both to keep the crowds posted and to provide those on the inside with the measure of their success. Lily Bart feels reinstated in her position in "high company" by "making her own ascendancy felt there so that she found herself figuring once more as the 'beautiful Miss Bart' in the interesting journal devoted to recording the least movements of her cosmopolitan companions" (196). Securing her identity in such a setting, Lily manages to "throw into the extreme background of memory the prosaic and sordid difficulties from which she had escaped" (196).

As the tone here indicates, the narrator disapproves of the theatricality of this setting, which erases all traces of the past in the beam of the moment's publicity. She blatantly criticizes "the strident setting of the restaurant, in which their table seemed set apart in a special glare of publicity," a setting in which the presence "of little Dabham of the 'Riviera Notes' emphasized the ideals of a world where conspicuousness passed for distinction and the society column had become the roll of fame" (215). The intrusive narrative moralizing indicates particular discomfort with the presence of Dabham, whose "little eyes were like tentacles thrown out to catch the floating intimations with which, to Selden, the air at moments seemed thick" (215). Dabham is a subject for scorn not simply because of his sordid voyeurism but, more important, because of the similarity between his role and that of the author. Like the gossip columnist, the novelist takes us "behind the scenes" into the interior of *The House of Mirth* to reveal the nuances and intimations of an otherwise inaccessible elite circle. Expressing her own discomfort with capitalizing on such privileged knowledge, she concludes the description of the dinner's finale by suggesting that "the whole scene had touches of intimacy worth their weight in gold to the watchful pen of Mr. Dabham" (216). How is this pen distinguished from that of the novelist using the same material?

To make this distinction, Wharton poses Selden as a model for the realist who has one foot in the gilded cage but still seems to keep the other outside by the power of detached, objective observation. He acts as a policeman monitoring Dabham, who "suddenly became the center of Selden's scrutiny." Yet, precisely in this position as spectator of the spectator—watching over Dabham—Selden loses his objective status and participates in the same game of publicity and spectatorship that everyone else takes part in. His own complicity can be seen in his response to the crisis when Bertha Dorset publicly forbids Lily to return to the yacht. Rather than defend Lily in public, he "was mainly conscious of a longing to grip Dabham by the collar and fling him out into the street" (217). Selden accepts Dabham's terms that what is staged for public exposure takes precedence over any other narrative of events. There is no distinction, just as no difference exists between the costume play and the drawing room. At key junctures in the novel, Selden is seduced by the immediacy of the spectacle and cannot understand the countervailing evidence. Despite—or because of—his air of detachment, Selden participates fully in the social world in which conspicuousness turns effortlessly into notoriety and Bertha Dorset can replay Lily's reinstatement as banishment.

When Lily returns to New York, she makes no attempt to prepare an alternative story to that initiated by Bertha and circulated by Dabham and his colleagues. In reply to Gerty's request for the truth, she explains, "it's a great deal easier to believe Bertha Dorset's story than mine, because she has a big house and an opera box and it's convenient to be on good terms with her" (225). Throughout the novel, narration is impotent against the power of vision, not necessarily because sight is more accurate than stories but because spectacles are staged by the wealthy and powerful. In Mrs. Peniston's outdated social world, she is horrified to learn that Lily has made herself "conspicuous," and she refuses to speak to Lily because it would be as "unwarrantable as a spectator's suddenly joining in a game" (128). If Mrs. Peniston were to confront her, however, Lily would probably be incapable of telling her own story, "as she was of more service as a listener than as a narrator" (108). Lily tries to counter her conspicuousness not with narrative but instead with more conspicuousness in the right setting, until she reaches the point where she avoids being seen at all. Rosedale articulates this powerlessness of narrative when he proposes to marry Lily on the condition that she regain power over Bertha. Although Rosedale does not believe the stories about Lily, he claims that the truth or falsity of stories matters only in novels, "but I'm certain it don't matter in real life" (256). He goes on to show that in real life what matters is the balance of power demonstrated solely by the visible. The impotence of narrative in *The House of Mirth* poses a peculiar dilemma for the realist, who sets herself up as the teller of truth rather than as the spectator or producer of scenes. Yet she thereby aligns herself with a position of social impotence not unlike that in which Lily finds herself.

Upon returning to New York, only to face her disinheritance, Lily enters the new social milieu of the Gormer family. After painstakingly mounting the social ladder according to the rules, they prefer to "strike out on their own: what they want is to have a good time and to have it their own way" (233). Despite their initial success at social climbing, "they decided that the whole business bored them and that what they wanted was a crowd they could really feel at home with" (232). Indeed, their notion of domesticity depends on effacing the difference between the crowd and the home, between spectators and performers. Instead of staging a major social event, as the Brys do, they "start a sort of continuous performance of their own, a kind of social Coney Island, where everybody is welcome who can make noise enough" (233). In contrast to the Brys, they do not rely on the authority of tradition by imitating the old masters; instead, they invoke the authority of novelty. They enact a new kind of upper-class leisure in which "ridiculing ritual substituted fun for formality. The search for sensation replaced the continuity of tradition which held the old guard together."[11] Instead of assembling an exclusive guest list of old names, the Gormers invite glamorous outsiders—actresses, artists, and celebrities, "everyone who's jolly and makes a row."

Among the Gormer set, Lily's former social disgrace only brands her "the heroine of a queer episode" as they accept her just like the others into the "easy promiscuity of their lives." In this group, Lily gains "the odd sense of having been caught up into the crowd as carelessly as a passenger is gathered in by the express train" (233). Echoing the first scene, the change in Lily's status is marked by her membership in the crowd, rather than by her capacity to stand above it. The metaphor of being swept along is realized when she agrees to participate in the Gormers' motoring trip to Alaska. Despite the social distance she has traveled and the fact that "the Gormer *milieu* represented a social outskirt which Lily had always fastidiously avoided," it strikes her, "now that she was in it, as only a flamboyant copy of her own world, a caricature approximating the real thing as the 'society play' approaches the manners of the drawing-room" (234). Yet, as Lily descends the social scale, she finds that the copy and the real thing become indistinguishable. The caricature of the Gormers easily turns into the real thing when Bertha enlists Gormer in her campaign against Lily. "The real thing" thus is not the inimitable manners of the older elite but the "impregnable bank-account" which underlies the authority that sets standards against which imitators appear as caricatures.

As Lily descends the social scale, she visits regions which seem more and more unreal because of their distance from the center of her old world yet strangely interconnected with that world. After being snubbed by the Gormers, Lily becomes the "secretary for a western divorced ingenue," Mrs. Norma Hatch, who inhabits "the world of the fashionable New York hotel, a world over-heated, over-upholstered, and over-fitted with mechanical applicances for the gratification of fantastic requirements" (274). Mrs. Hatch's hotel life exemplifies what James called "the sense of promiscuity which manages to be at the same time an inordinate untempered monotony."[12] Promiscuity refers not to sexual excess but to the older meaning of an indiscriminate and disorderly mixture of varied elements. The unreality of the hotel world is characterized by the lack of acknowledged distinctions and boundaries. Even more distant than the popular amusements of Coney Island, Norma Hatch's "habits were marked by an Oriental indolence and disorder peculiarly trying to her companion. Mrs. Hatch and her friends seemed to float together outside the bounds of time and space. No definite hours were kept; no fixed obligations existed" (275). This lack of boundaries extends to people as well, as Mrs. Hatch makes no distinctions among her peers, her manicurists, her society friends, and her doctors. To Lily, the lack of distinction in time and social place makes the people seem to have "no more real existence than the poet's shades in limbo" (274). The hotel seems to allow the gaping mob to enter in a controlled form, in the technological "blaze of electric light." Rather than appear in the elite column of the society pages, Mrs. Hatch makes her social debut in the photographs of the "Sunday Supplement." Like the hotel, the Sunday Supplement represents a step closer to the gaping mob. Begun in the 1890s with the boom in mass-circulation newspapers, these illustrated supplements represented a new form of celebrity. Mrs. Hatch aspired to be a member of the world she read about, as she "swam in a haze of indeterminate enthusiasms, of aspirations culled from the stage, the newspapers, the fashion-journals, and a gaudy world of sport still more completely beyond her companion's ken" (277).

If Mrs. Hatch's world seems unreal to Lily, the most shocking aspect of it is the intersection with "her own circle," when she meets the sons of the oldest and most respectable New York families. Indeed, the social life of upper-class young men in this period was bifurcated between allegiance to the proprieties of their own sphere and their freedom to frequent the new after-dinner clubs and hotels, "when released from the official social routine" (276).[13] The appearance of these young men gave Lily "the odd sense of being behind the social tapestry, on the side where the threads were knotted and the loose ends hung" (276). Throughout the novel, wealth means having the power to hide these loose ends, to render invisible the work on which one's existence depends. Lily herself has a horror of cleaning smells and of the sight of rumpled dresses the morning after a party because these sensations attest both to her dependence on those beneath her and her own proximity to a sphere of servitude. She finds one of the worst aspects of life in the boardinghouse to be the smell of cooking that seeps into her room, the absence of boundaries that keep out of sight her own means of subsistence. The luxury of the world which Lily leaves behind depends on keeping the "machinery" of its production "so carefully concealed that one scene flows into another without perceptible agency" (301).

If the hotel of Norma Hatch yields Lily a glimpse of this agency behind the social tapestry, the next chapter finds her literally working there, the place "where threads were knotted and the loose ends hung." By taking a job at the milliner's, Lily finds herself creating the setting against which she had formerly displayed herself. She is driven to the job by her attempt to turn her only talent, that of producing herself as an ornament, into a marketable skill. Rather than play the role of model, the image of the consumer of these goods, she attempts to step over the line into that world of production which so horrifies her.

Lily's work at the milliner's returns to the opening question of her relation to the average working women of the crowd by thrusting her among them. These women have a double-edged relation to the society women above them: their labor produces the setting that creates the conspicuousness of upper-class leisure, and they become an audience that watches the same setting they produce. For Lily, the strangest aspect of working in the milliner's shop is hearing the names of her former peers, "seeing the fragmentary and distorted image of the world she had lived in reflected in the mirror of the working-girls' minds. She had never before suspected the mixture of insatiable curiosity and contemptuous freedom with which she and her kind were discussed in this underworld of toilers who lived on their vanity and self-indulgence" (286). The working girls are members of the gaping mob, who provide not only the labor but the mirror in which upper-class ladies must reflect their own identity. This relation reverses the direction taken by Gerty Farish in her working-girl clubs. Reformers like Gerty assume a one-way mirror, in which they visit the lives of the poor in order to uplift them. The working girls are scrutinized by charitable ladies who expect in turn a passive gratitude and admiration, not a radical scrutiny in kind.

Thus, in answer to the opening question of Lily's relation to the crowd, the price of making Lily is both the work of women who produce her and the cost of their spectatorship, which sustains her. The narrative charts a social world in which class segmentation is highly spatialized, clearly marked in *The House of Mirth* by the spatial coordinates of Lily's descent as she moves down the social scale through very different interiors, from her aunt's inherited mansion, to the country home of the Trenors, to the boardinghouse. These rigid boundaries, however, are penetrated through the relations of spectatorship and voyeurism. In *The House of Mirth*, class stratification is not trascended by the common interests of domesticity, as it is for Howells. Instead, both the bond between classes and their hierarchical difference depend on conspicuousness. At the end of the novel, the working girl Nettie Struther seems to represent a Howellsian solution of domesticity to Lily's wasted life, but Nellie's relation to Lily is mediated through spectatorship, as well. She follows Lily's career in the newspaper and tells Lily that she talked over with her husband "what you were doing and read descriptions of the dresses you wore" (314). If Lily first visits Nettie through the channel of the girls' club and the work of charity, Nettie follows Lily through the channel of the mass media. In addition, she names her baby after a character in a popular play, the French queen "Marry Anto'nette," who reminded her of Lily. Through her values of domesticity and productivity, Nettie may appear as an example of "real life" unavailable to Lily. Yet, Nettie's life also becomes a parody of its own imitation of upper-class life, as she becomes a domesticated version of the gaping mob.

Throughout the novel, the gaping mob both defines and threatens the upper class, which depends on the mob's admiration and its exclusion. Lily similarly depends on the mirror of the gaping mob to maintain her identity. When she loses this mirror, she loses a self. At the end of the novel, Lily kills herself to avoid a mirrorless future in which time itself suddenly faces her as "a shrieking mob" (322).

The gaping mob does more than play the role of a passive audience in *The House of Mirth*. Its threatening quality emerges in the first scene in the figure of the charwoman scrubbing the stairs and blocking the hall as Lily leaves Selden's apartment. Although Lily explains away her "persistent gaze" by imagining "the poor thing" to be "probably dazzled," she is visibly upset by the stare of the charwoman, who later turns her vision into a source of considerable power that shapes the trajectory of Lily's career. As a cleaning woman, she has access to Selden's wastepaper basket, from which she retrieves Bertha's love letters. Mrs. Haffen resurfaces with the letters for sale almost as a confirmation of Lily's own fears of falling into a "future of servitude" at the same moment she resents the smells and sights of the women cleaning her aunt's house, "as though she thought a house ought to keep clean of itself" (102). These retrieved letters, whose contents are never directly revealed, become a central medium for exchange throughout the novel. As writing, they form a kind of circuit which intertwines class and character in the novel—from Bertha to Selden to Mrs. Haffen to Lily, who purchases them fully aware of their exchange value, their power to reinstate her in her social circle.[14]

The exchange of letters thus offers an alternative narrative to the plot of decline which Lily follows. At any moment she can reverse her fortune by trading the letters, with their implicit threat of exposure, for Bertha's loyalty. Simon Rosedale governs this alternative plot: he sees Lily at the same time that Mrs. Haffen sees her, and he probably encourages Mrs. Haffen to sell the letters; and he continually urges Lily to sell them back to Bertha. As author of this plot, Rosedale plays the curious role of the demonic realist in opposition to Selden's romantic. Artistic qualities are attributed to Rosedale, who, like the realist, understands the hidden workings of society, the need to cloak and display his wealth with the "right woman to spend it." More important, he is the only one in the novel who knows as much about Lily as do the narrator and reader. Whereas Nettie posits knowledge as the cement of domestic love—"I knew he knew about me"—Rosedale, rather than Selden, is the one who knows about Lily: about her transaction with Trenor and the truth of her relation with Bertha. He knows the story that Selden can read only with difficulty in her checkbook after her death. He knows that the truth value of stories matters less than conspicuousness: "the quickest way to queer yourself with the right people is to be seen with the wrong ones" (257). Nowhere is Rosedale more the realist than in his proposal to Lily: he engages in "plain speaking" by expressing his desire to get into society, which she finds "refreshing to step into the open daylight of an avowed expediency" (259). Yet, to act realistically in "open daylight," according to Rosedale, is to engage in a transaction which both the narrator and Lily find morally repugnant by virtue of reducing everything to "a region of concrete weights and measures" (259).

By burning the letters, Lily treats them as unique content—the intimate knowledge of Selden's past—that cannot be reduced to weights and measures; she refuses to turn them into a medium of exchange and "trade on his name." Yet, by breaking this circuit, she must abandon her self, as well. Wharton thereby divorces her own writing from Rosedale's plot, which treats writing as a medium for exchanging intimacy for power. Wharton saves Lily from Rosedale's plot by extracting her from the circuit of exchange; yet, outside that circuit she can have no self and is left "unsphered in a void of social nonexistence." Wharton thereby refuses to treat writing as the retrieval of knowledge from the wastebasket of intimacy, but in burning those letters she replaces them with Lily, who ends her life "thrown out into the rubbish heap" (308).

Notes

1. Edith Wharton, *The House of Mirth* (1905; repr., New York: Berkley Books, 1981), 3. Subsequent references will be cited parenthetically in the text.

2. See, for example, Judith Fetterley, " 'The Temptation to Be a Beautiful Object': Double Standard and Double Bind in *The House of Mirth*," *Studies in American Fiction* 2 (autumn 1977): 199–211, and Cynthia Griffin Wolff, *A Feast of Words: The Triumph of Edith Wharton* (New York: Oxford University Press, 1977), 109–33. For a psychoanalytic interpretation of Lily's narcissism, see Joan Lidoff, "Another Sleeping Beauty: Narcissism in *The House of Mirth*," in *American Realism: New Essays*, ed. Eric Sundquist (Baltimore: Johns Hopkins University Press, 1982), 238–58.

3. Lewis Erenburg, *Steppin' Out: New York City's Restaurants and Cabarets and the Decline of Victorianism* (Westport, Conn.: Greenwood Press, 1981), 37.

4. This paragraph is based on Erenburg, *Steppin' Out*, chaps. 1 and 2,

and Frederic Cople Jaher, *The Urban Establishment* (Urbana: University of Illinois Press, 1982), 246–79.

5. Erenburg, *Steppin' Out*, 34–40.

6. Erenburg, *Steppin' Out*, 37–40; Frederic Cople Jaher, "Style and Status: High Society in Late Nineteenth-Century New York," in *The Rich, The Well-Born, and the Powerful: Elites and Upper Classes in History*, ed. Jaher (Urbana: University of Illinois Press, 1973), 259–84.

7. Henry James, *The American Scene* (Bloomington: Indiana University Press, 1968), 65; Paul Bourget, *Outre-Mer* (New York: Scribner's, 1895), chap. 4.

8. John Berger et al., *Ways of Seeing* (London: Viking Press, 1973), 83–112.

9. On the relation between the spectacle and the intangible qualities of commodity culture, see Jean-Christophe Agnew, "The Consuming Vision of Henry James," in *The Culture of Consumption: Critical Essays in American History, 1880–1980*, ed. Richard Wightman Fox and T. J. Jackson Lears (New York: Pantheon, 1983), 65–100.

10. Frank Luther Mott, *A History of American Magazines*, Volume 4: 1885–1905 (Cambridge, Mass.: Harvard University Press, 1957), 751–55.

11. Jaher, "Style and Status," 274.

12. James, *The American Scene*, 104.

13. Erenburg, *Steppin' Out*, 51–56.

14. On the centrality of exchange in *The House of Mirth*, see Wai Chee Dimock, "Debasing Exchange: Edith Wharton's *The House of Mirth*," PMLA 100 (October 1985): 783–92. While Dimock demonstrates the pervasiveness of the language of exchange throughout the novel, she does not extend this analysis to writing as an act and medium of exchange.

The House of Mirth
A Novel of Admonition

LINDA WAGNER-MARTIN

◆ ◆ ◆

Historical Context

The New Woman was a harbinger of change—in family life and culture, as well as in women's existences—and it is about the turn-of-the century New Woman that much of Edith Wharton's fiction revolves. Wharton herself was a product of many of the conflicts that the women's movement had set off. She had to face the issues of what an appropriate life for a woman should be and to decide for herself whether or not to marry and bear children, whether she should have a career or profession or become the social butterfly her society preferred. Naturally, Wharton's fiction would show her interest in the possibilities for changes in women's lives in the twentieth century.

In both England and the United States, many women were dissatisfied with their roles during the later part of the nineteenth century. Women of wealth wanted more than to be "protected," but "the long, golden Edwardian garden-party"—with its emphasis on women as beautiful, innocent objects, the desirable icons of an acquisitive patriarchal culture—only reinforced the idea that women needed to be taken care of.[1] The image of women as delicate flowers—too fragile to play sports, study, or earn a living—was a stereotype that had little to do with women's abilities. Their rancor at being suffocated and diminished under the guise of some necessary male shelter had been simmering long before Ibsen's 1879 *A Doll's House* or Kate Chopin's more shocking 1899 *The Awakening*. In those controversial literary works, strong women characters chose to leave the comfort of protective security to find existences of their own. When Chopin's Edna Pontellier chooses to die rather than live that life of "piety, purity, submissiveness and domesticity,"[2] many readers were horrified at her willfulness and boycotted Chopin's writing.

Patriarchal control of women's lives during the nineteenth century was not only economic; it was also religious and sexual. The economic control was clear in men's amassing of immense fortunes and in the gilded-age emphasis on the display of great wealth. According to both the Bible and the nineteenth-century church, women were to marry and be ideal helpmeets for their husbands and True Woman families. The True Woman was sexually naive and pure; virginity was a requirement for any socially approved marriage, and the course of a woman's life was to be self-sacrifice for the good of the family unit. Men, stereotyped by society as less pure and more sexual, could indulge whatever baser sexual appetites they had through appropriate channels (i.e., women of lower class or nonwhite race). In forming what became known as the "double standard of behavior," society recognized that men could do whatever they wanted in relation to women; after all, they controlled all economic power. A common text for sermons during the nineteenth century was the role and duties of the "good" woman. Male physicians became specialists in women's mental health, as well as obstetrics and gynecology.[3] The message was clear: everything that touched a woman's life was in the control of the patriarchy.

Beginning with comments by Harriet Martineau and Sarah Grimke (including the latter's in *Letters on the Equality of the Sexes and the Condition of Women* in 1838), women writers such as Margaret Fuller, Lucretia Mott, and Elizabeth Cady Stanton presented arguments not only for women's right to vote but also for improved educational opportunities, psychological and economic freedom, and the right of women to exercise choice about their lives. The Declaration of Sentiments and Resolutions issued at the Seneca Falls Convention in 1848 was a touchstone document, and momentum from that meeting continued—despite the Civil War—as women drove for social reforms and the vote. Charlotte Perkins Gilman's 1898 text, *Women and Economics*, was so important to the controversy surrounding the role of women in society that Gertrude Stein quoted from it in a speech in Baltimore several years later. Questions about the power of religion to undermine women's physical and psychological freedoms, about ownership of property and wealth, and about women's role in marriage were all threatening to the dominant male culture.

At the International Council of Women in 1888, Elizabeth Cady Stanton noted that, while women did not have the vote, other positive changes had occurred since the early 1800s. If women in 1838 were—as Stanton said—"bond slaves," by 1888 they had access to 563 institutions of higher education, and more than 35,000 female students were enrolled there. Women workers constituted 17 percent of the labor force, amounting to some four million employees by 1890. Most of those women worked at low-paying jobs, but by 1886, 390 women physicians were practicing medicine in twenty-six states. Women were excluded from practicing law in some states, but they could become ministers and professors, architects and scientists.[4]

Such statistical gains, of course, only created more pressure for women choosing to pursue the path of the New Woman instead of following the preference of the culture—and often of their families—and becoming the True Woman. Public opinion was aroused, and the anger of a society that felt insecure as the result of changes in family structure and women's behavior showed itself in satirical cartoons and vindictive essays. When Edith Wharton (née Edith Jones) as an adolescent began to consider becoming a professional writer, her fashionable mother moved up her debut by a year. Expending her energy learning to become a high-society True Woman left Edith little time to explore her possible career as a writer, and that passion was submerged for more than twenty years.[5]

Wharton creates in *The House of Mirth* the impressionable character of Lily Bart, flowerlike in fragility as well as name, who has accepted the social decree that she become a beautiful marriageable object. Wharton's ironic choice in the novel of having Lily be twenty-nine years old at the time of the narrative, instead of nineteen, as a reader might expect, allows her to question the wisdom of Lily Bart's having followed the dictates of her society. As Wharton's protagonist moves from one bad choice to the next, she maintains her virginity and her virtue, but society chooses to blind itself to her purity. Instead, Lily Bart becomes a defamed—and damaged—object of art. As her last chances for marriage falter, the reader is made to question relentlessly the ethics of Lily's seemingly protective society. *The House of Mirth* has nothing about it that is pleasant or comic, and as Wharton draws her condemnatory fiction to its inevitable close, the reader is forced to recognize the dangers of a woman's rebellion against the cultural mandates of True Womanhood.

The Importance of the Work

Wharton's *The House of Mirth*, serialized in *Scribner's* from January to November of 1905, was officially published as a novel on 14 October of that year. The novel had the most rapid sales of any of Scribner's books to that time and rivaled or surpassed the other bestsellers of the year, Upton Sinclair's *The Jungle*, Thomas Dixon's *The Clansman*, and Robert Smythe Hichans's *The Garden of Allah*. It clearly met a demand in American readers that had gone unsatisfied. The poignant but all-too-real narrative of the beautiful Lily Bart, fast aging beyond marriageability, could be read in a number of ways (some conventional, others more subversive). *The House of Mirth* appeared midway in a pattern of writing that explored themes brought to light during the New Woman controversies.

Ibsen's dramas that questioned women's roles in marriage (*A Doll's House*, 1879; *Hedda Gabler*, 1890) and similar world fiction

(Flaubert's *Madame Bovary*, 1857; Tolstoy's *Anna Karenina*, 1877; George Eliot's *The Mill on the Floss*, 1860, and *Middlemarch*, 1872; Hardy's *Tess of the D'Urbervilles*, 1891) supplemented the growing American attention to these themes. Post–Civil War American fiction created the American Girl (Henry James's Daisy Miller in the 1879 novella of that title, and in 1881 his Isabel Archer in *The Portrait of a Lady*), the innocent ingenue whose trust traps her in a morass of European intrigue. More to the point, a number of nineteenth-century American women writers were creating fiction that had female heroes: Elizabeth Stuart Phelps Ward's *The Silent Partner*, 1873, and *The Story of Avis*, 1879; Louisa May Alcott's *Work*, 1873; Mary Wilkins Freeman's *A New England Nun*, 1891; Sarah Orne Jewett's *The Country of the Pointed Firs*, 1889; Charlotte Perkins Gilman's "The Yellow Wallpaper," 1892, and *Women and Economics*, 1898; Kate Chopin's *Bayou Folk*, 1894, and *The Awakening*, 1899.

Readers, though interested in women characters working through what appeared to be real-life dilemmas, could not bear too much reality. The outcry that greeted Chopin's *The Awakening*, with its protagonist's choice of suicide over a life of compromise, was frightening: called "sex fiction," the book effectively marked the end of Chopin's career as novelist.[6] Much the same reception met Theodore Dreiser's comparatively sympathetic treatment of yet another "fallen" (but independent and successful) woman, *Sister Carrie*, published in 1900. The line seemed blurred. Where could the novelist portray women realistically, even in sexual matters, and where would the reader prefer blinders?

Whether conscious of the furor within the literary world or expressing her own place in the continuum of the New Woman, Wharton managed in *The House of Mirth* to choose strategies that appeased the hostile readers. In her choice of a point of view that told the story with seeming objectivity, Wharton was able to show all sides of Lily Bart's personality—her hesitation as well as her ambition, her scruples as well as her understanding of the games society insisted upon playing. Much of the story is given through the eyes of Lawrence Selden, a character who seems to have Lily's best interests at heart. Selden appears to be a high-minded, philosophical young lawyer, himself weary of the social fabric that would catch and doom Lily. In fact, the novel begins and ends with Selden's comments about Lily, making her the social object—the icon—readers would have expected in a novel of manners. Yet, the vitality of the 1905 novel stems largely from the contradictions Wharton was able to incorporate in it. By the end, the reader is not sure that Selden is so admirable—and if he is not, then his authoritative voice should be questioned. When Lily dies, the reader wants some vindication for that death: what has the society paid for its brutal and meaningless vengeance on this woman? By composing a novel that left such important questions unanswered, Wharton foreshadowed the very kind of "open" text the modernists would pride themselves on creating—and the impact of *The House of Mirth*, as well as other of Wharton's fictions, might have been more influential on the younger American modernists than literary history has shown. F. Scott Fitzgerald, for one, was much impressed with Wharton's work.

The House of Mirth, taken with Chopin's *The Awakening* and Gilman's "The Yellow Wallpaper," is a key example of a woman's voice exploring significant women's themes in a covert manner: fiction as disguise. In unraveling the text of Lily Bart's story, through a narrative that appears to be conventional but causes surprising division among its readers, the modern-day reader can recognize the subterfuge women writers needed to employ in order to keep their share of the reading public while expressing potentially unpopular truths.

The House of Mirth provides insight into what Sandra M. Gilbert and Susan Gubar have termed "the anxiety of authorship," the defensiveness and unease women writers experience when they attempt to write stories that focus on human relationships. And it serves as an exciting example of the creation of narrative techniques that allow the expression of an alternate story, as a seeming subtext, under the more apparent plot line of a primary (and perhaps more conventional) text. Learning to read both text and subtext enables today's reader to understand the brilliance, and the subtlety, of women writers' work at the turn of the century.[7]

Critical Reception

As one might expect with a best-selling novel by a woman writer in 1905, critical reaction—though usually approving—had an undercurrent of reservation. The tendency to believe that everything written by a woman was "domestic" or "sentimental" was well established by this point in history, as Nina Baym describes in *Novels, Readers, and Reviewers.*[8] That tendency was less apparent in reviews of *The House of Mirth*, however, because of Wharton's established reputation as an "intellectual" writer. The reviews of her 1905 novel primarily continued the positive tone of the reception of her earlier short story collections (*The Greater Inclination*, 1899; *Crucial Instances*, 1901; and *The Descent of Man and Other Stories*, 1904) and longer fictions (*The Touchstone*, 1900; *The Valley of Decision*, 1902; and *Sanctuary*, 1903). That previous work had been praised for its perfection of style and technique, its attention to characters' motivation, and its seriousness, although some critics found Wharton's treatment of moral issues too intellectualized and her characters sometimes remote. *The House of Mirth* was accordingly seen as an advance for Wharton: it was much more complex, much longer, and much more moving than her earlier work, and the character of Lily Bart was undeniably accessible.

Wharton's protagonist was given high praise. She was described as "complex" and "ill-starred," drawn more fully than any woman character of George Eliot's, and the heroine of a "poignant tragedy." Henry James said of Lily Bart that she was "very big and true—and very difficult to have *kept* big and true."[9] But even as *The House of Mirth* was seen to be Lily's story, that identification led to some disapproval. A few reviewers claimed that unpleasantness was not the province of fiction, that by stressing the "sordid" Wharton did not only her work but her readers a grave disservice ("people rise quicker to a hope" than to unhappiness). The moral purpose of fiction cannot be undermined because of an author's fascination with character. Not all reviewers found Lily Bart poignant or positive. The *Athenaeum* (London) reviewer described her as a woman who needs money; Mary Moss wrote in *Atlantic Monthly* that Lily inspires interest rather than caring; and the London *Saturday Review* described her as "a masterly study of the modern American woman with her coldly corrupt nature and unhealthy charm." Alice Meynell anticipates a somewhat later critical interest in the character of Lawrence Selden, as she finds him—as the spokesman for a "better" world—the important character of the novel.[10]

Throughout the commentary ran the refrain of Wharton's debt to Henry James, though the insistence of that comparison was less obvious in reviews of *The House of Mirth* than it had been in reviews of Wharton's story collections. Her work was also compared with that of Ellen Glasgow, Guy de Maupassant, Booth Tarkington, Howard Sturgis, and George Eliot. Some of this comparison was to privilege Wharton's achievement; some of it worked to limit her accomplishment, as in the blunt *Times Literary Supplement* comment that "Wharton does lack the creative gift at its fullest"—and therefore *The House of Mirth* "is not fiction at its very highest point." Again, an English reviewer has chosen to limit Wharton's success, and it can well be said that American reviewers were, collectively, more enthusiastic about the novel and about Wharton. Perhaps they were better able to understand the fiction and the society it represented; perhaps they were more eager to find American writers who could compete with the English literary figures.[11]

The House of Mirth was recognized both at the time of its original publication and throughout the successive decades of Wharton's writing career as Wharton's breakthrough novel and one of her most important books. In bringing to life the elite New York culture—complete with its villainy and its pride—Wharton found firm ground, much as Sherwood Anderson was to reach in his *Winesburg, Ohio* (1919) and as William Faulkner was to find, at Anderson's urging, in his *Sartoris* (1929). Wharton herself had benefited from the wisdom of Annie Fields and Sarah Orne Jewett, women who cared about the art of fiction and its importance in representing the lives of women characters in authentic, meaningful ways. By placing those women characters in believable contexts, the author could bring value to their daily lives and keep the characterization well above the stereotype of so many fictional characters in turn-of-the-century women's novels. Wharton's aims were complex, and she may not have been entirely conscious of them even as she wrote *The House of Mirth.* Nonetheless, she enjoyed the novel's rapid sale and ubiquitous acclaim, even if she did not realize how important a book it was. In keeping with her usually humble demeanor, she wrote to her publisher, Charles Scribner, that she had had a new photograph taken for use in the postpublication success of *The House of Mirth*, one "with my eyes down, *trying to look modest.*"[12]

Wharton was always much involved in the criticism of each of her works. She wrote to friends with humility, acerbity, and sometimes glee about this reaction or that. The amazingly rapid sales of *The House of Mirth* brought her what she called "a trunkful" of "funny" letters as well as serious ones, and she illustrated the former in this way: "One lady is so carried away that she writes, 'I love, not every word in the book, but every period and comma.' I hope she meant to insert an 'only' after the 'not,' "[13]

She was also very concerned that readers would misread, as some reviewers had, especially those who objected to the novel on the grounds of its moral lapses or its unpleasantness. In a 5 December 1905 letter to Morgan Dix, rector of Trinity Church, in New York, Wharton clarifies her professional commitment, saying that she aims to write fiction "which probes deep enough to get at the relation with the eternal laws." The issue is not "unpleasantness" but whether or not good fiction has as its subject "a criticism of life. . . . *No* novel worth anything can be anything but a novel 'with a purpose.' "[14]

The unprecedented quantity of books and essays published on Wharton's work in the 1970s and 1980s testifies to the surety of the author's aesthetic vision. She was a writer of great talent and versatility, always mindful of her ethical responsibility to write as well as she could, about subjects of value. Current attention to *The House of Mirth* proves the importance of her first major novel and underscores the accuracy of Arthur Hobson Quinn's assessment that, in the 1920s, Wharton was "the foremost living novelist writing in the English language." As Quinn asked then, "which of *us* are as truly alive as Lily Bart, as Ethan Frome, as Ellen Olenska, as May Welland? And which of us will live as long?"[15] There is little question that Edith Wharton is now recognized as a major American writer and *The House of Mirth*, correspondingly, as a major American novel.

The Structure

By dividing *The House of Mirth* into two sections, each written in a different pace, Wharton forces the reader's attention to the pivotal point that centers the novel. Book 1 ends with Lily's despair after she realizes that Selden has, literally, fled from her. [Because Selden is] a man of words, [his] failure to use language either to ascertain or to explain what he thinks is her indiscretion in Trenor's house is heavily ironic. Selden's "love" has no grounding in any reality and, like most sham structures of belief, cannot stand any testing. Again, Wharton plays on the reader's understanding of romance. She draws a narrowly conventional attitude for Selden, who insists that Lily be the pure virginal maiden if she is to win his love. Wharton's irony, which undercuts Selden's disillusion, shows itself in her description of the scene between Lily and Trenor, the scene that sends Selden out of the country so swiftly: "two figures were seen silhouetted against the hall-light. At the same moment a hansom halted at the curbstone, and one of the figures floated down to it in a haze of evening draperies; while the other, black and bulky, remained persistently projected against the light" (160–61). Wharton's vague indefiniteness here leads the reader to question Selden's response. Positive identification of the silhouettes is unlikely; any graceful woman would "float" to the cab. The wry description of the male figure takes on a tinge of Selden's perspective. Trenor, about whom Selden has already felt great repugnance, thinking of his "fat creased hands" (154), deserves no fonder description than "black and bulky"—and persistent.

Selden's running away from knowledge about Lily's behavior

is especially ironic because Selden has praised his own difference from other men in that he is philosophically open-minded. He has insisted that Lily have freedom, that she explore her circumstances rather than simply accept what society mandates. If any man should be willing at least to talk with her about the Trenor house episode, Selden should. Yet Wharton ends book 1 here, adding the emphasis of a major narrative break to the surprise the reader feels at Selden's unexpected behavior.

The first half of *The House of Mirth* has privileged Selden's view of both Lily and the world. Much of the narrative has been seen through Selden's eyes, and recounted through his voice. The reader assumes his credibility and is ready to step into the familiar role of relying on a male narrator, even if that narrator is far removed from the protagonist. As Judith Fetterley has said so well, "recognition and reiteration, not difference and expansion, provide the motivation for reading." Readers want confirmation of expected patterns, and if the male character is not the protagonist, he might well be the narrator, the guide to understanding the story. Fetterley continues, "reading functions primarily to reinforce the identity and perspective which the male teacher/reader brings to the text. Presumably this function is itself a function of the sense of power derived from the experience of perceiving one's self as central, as subject, . . . because [one is] literarily the point of view from which the rest of the world is seen. Thus men, controlling the study of literature, define as great those texts that empower themselves."[17] Wharton has given the reader this expected paradigm, a male narrator and observer, to allow the reader to make sense of the partially hidden motivations of the female protagonist. But with the beginning of book 2, that structure changes. Wharton's narrative method thus supports the complexity of her novel's theme: *The House of Mirth* is not about the typical young woman headed for a good marriage; it is about the maverick young woman who resists the social code that would coerce her into wifehood.

The skill with which Wharton draws Lily has sometimes gone unnoticed. Lily's hesitancy, her almost vacuous acceptance of what Selden tells her, is at the heart of her reality—and Wharton has prepared the reader for that reality in the early description of her, standing "apart from the crowd, letting it drift by her." Lily Bart is *not* complicit in this society's expectations for women; she is herself an observer. Through her choice of narrative method, Wharton forces the reader into asking several key questions. How could Lily Bart—reared by the most self-serving of mothers to think that her only worth was in her beauty, surrounded by a society that plays the marriage game even more ruthlessly than it plays bridge (and for higher stakes), sent into the world with neither formal education nor means of learning other ways to challenge those that prevail—how could this strangely sheltered woman know where to begin to learn about alternate ways of living and choices? Selden's is the only voice that seems to have a wider perspective, that seems to be encouraging her to think differently [from] her friends and relatives.

Whenever Lily follows his lead, however, she ends up with new problems, difficulties that would not have been hers if she had stayed on the expected social track. Selden derides her marrying for money, yet when she loses Percy Gryce, Selden has no alternative. He challenges her to think more philosophically, even if doing so will put her at odds with her society. He approves of her showing her artistic ability—and her beauty—in the very tableau that makes her the target of envy and gossip among her friends. By not marrying, however, Lily is more and more dependent on other people's money, more easily at the mercy of Trenor, Rosedale, and their kind. And when Selden might have spoken his love and given Lily—the reader supposes—some ideal marriage, he runs out with no explanation and, more important, no opportunity for her to discuss the situation. Selden's actions announce that Lily is beneath his notice or support. She is blamed and judged with no defense or appeal and, as book 2 shows, she is rapidly found guilty.

The key to Lily's character lies in the very insubstantiality of personality Wharton draws so carefully in book 1. Despite her age, Lily is a child, and *The House of Mirth* is in some ways a bildungsroman: Lily's story is that of her education. Unfortunately, she has as her school only the society in which she lives, and the mistakes she makes as she tests the system are irreparable. The social group that would protect her were she to behave as she is expected to behave will not aid her when her behavior threatens their social code. Judy Trenor loves the Lily who will play secretary and cosset her cross husband in exchange for hospitality, but she abandons her when she seems to be on too-familiar terms with that husband. A useful Lily is one who serves the system; a defiant, questioning, or uncontrollable Lily is dangerous. Lily's description of Bertha Dorset's relative power (in that Bertha has a house and an opera box, whereas Lily is poor) is as naive as Lily herself at the start of the novel. Bertha has power because Bertha represents the system, and whatever she does, her behavior is sanctioned by that system. To challenge Bertha is to challenge the structure and, consequently, everyone within it.

The early liaison between Selden and the married Bertha is further testimony to Selden's unreliability as narrator. Rather than separate himself from the system, Selden lives off it. Under cover of Bertha's strong social position, their affair has been known but allowed. The affair is over. The letters Lily buys from Mrs. Haffen, in order to "protect" her society and particularly Selden, seem to be entreaties from Bertha, and her behavior when Lily chooses to be with Selden instead of Percy Gryce indicates that she regards Selden as her property still. What Wharton emphasizes in book 2—the flagrant liaison between Bertha and Ned Silverton and its scandalous denouement, which Bertha manipulates to discredit Lily—is a suggestive replaying of what might have been the relationship between Bertha and Selden. Imagined in the role Neddy Silverton plays during book 2, Selden can have little pretense to moral superiority.

The Lily Bart Wharton draws in book 1 is vacillating, thrown off balance by Selden's glowing rhetoric so that she questions the premises that have always guided her. Critical of the society she yet longs to stay a part of, she is hardly the resolute traditional hero. But, given her uncertain position in her social world, given the imperative to play ingenue until she marries, the most promising traits Lily has are her tentativeness and her willingness to question. Frances Restuccia sees the real duality between Selden and Lily as being Selden's need for fixity, a stable understanding of social roles and codes, set against Lily's mutability. Lily will wait and see what she should do, think, become; Selden has to have his proper role established consistently. Describing what she calls "Lily's book-long oscillation," Restuccia notes: "While Lily refuses positions of stability, Selden, faithful to his profession, locates them where they are nonexistent. Selden must transform ambiguity to clarity, as he does in his reading of Lily's story. We might expect, consequently, that, given the instability—the constitutive ambiguity—of language, Selden would shy away from writing."[18] Seeing Lily's wavering uncertainty as positive and strong, this critic only supports the reading that Selden is an untrustworthy narrator and that Wharton's use of his observations is another facet of her deeply entrenched irony.

Between books 1 and 2, Wharton allows Lily Bart to disappear. Much of what the reader would like to know about Lily after Selden's leave-taking—when it is evident that Lily is shaken and confused by Trenor's duplicity—is unstated. Wharton builds to the ending of the first book by showing the reader Lily's long wait for Selden's appearance at tea, her discovery of his departure in the newspaper, and her own invitation to go abroad with Bertha Dorset.

Book 1 stops abruptly, and book 2 begins just as abruptly. The reader is left to imagine the intervening three months. As in the first half of the novel, at the start of the second book Wharton focuses on Lawrence Selden. Several months after his rush away from Lily, Selden has spent the winter working hard at the law and has only recently come abroad again, this time in connection with his work. The irony of Wharton's training the reader's attention on Selden, when Lily is the strong center of interest, establishes the premise for the rest of book 2. Society remains in control, and Selden—as sophisticated intellectual, an integral part of that society—remains an important voice in the narration. The narrative, once again, comes to the reader through his point of view.

The opening of book 2 is reminiscent of the opening of the

novel: Selden is observing society in Monte Carlo. Here Wharton describes his life as a "spectatorship" and his quest as the search for order. Her phrase "his fixed sky" reminds the reader of his frustration early in the novel because he could not "fix" Lily and her movements into the patterns he anticipated. The beauty of the Monte Carlo twilight, in fact, reminds Selden of the last moments of some panoramic "tableau" (183–84). Wharton has deliberately connected the Selden in book 2 with the Selden the reader knew throughout book 1.

After this introduction and stage setting, Wharton focuses Selden's attention (as spectator) on "a consciously conspicuous group of people [obviously Americans]," and soon the reader hears news of Lily Bart. Immediately the action begins, with Lily described as imprudent, or flighty, or something more quixotic. In the words of the astute survivor Carry Fisher: "That's Lily all over, you know: she works like a slave preparing the ground and sowing her seed; but the day she ought to be reaping the harvest she oversleeps herself or goes off on a picnic. . . . Sometimes I think it's because, at heart, she despises the things she's trying for" (189).

Book 2 is a series of climactic and defeating episodes for Lily. In almost every instance, Selden observes; he often helps her make an escape, but the fact is that Lily is on the run, pursued by the machinations of Bertha Dorset—and the reader cannot forget that Bertha's initial anger with Lily occurred over Selden. The irony of his adopting the role of Lily's "rescuer" in light of his also being part of the cause of Bertha's pursuit is inescapable.

Lily's problems are exacerbated by her poverty. Wharton structures *The House of Mirth* so that immediately after Bertha has ordered Lily off the *Sabrina*, the novel moves with cinematic quickness to the reading of Mrs. Peniston's will. Changed after news of Lily's supposed liaison with George Dorset has reached Mrs. Peniston, the will leaves Lily only ten thousand dollars, in effect disinheriting her.

The visible decline in Lily's fortunes, both financial and emotional, is drawn in Wharton's clipped, fast-paced narrative: the pace of the story distances the reader from Lily's futile attempts to recover. There is to be no recovery, however, even when Rosedale urges Lily to go to Bertha with the letters and demand apology and restitution in society.

Wharton's reliance on the packet of Bertha's letters—and her mention of it throughout the book—reminds the reader of the duplicitous social system and of Lily's innocence in contrast to that system. Just as Mrs. Haffen mistakes Lily for the author of the letters, so society judges her falsely. Yet Lily's goodness—which prompts her to purchase the letters in the first place—prevents her using them, either with Bertha or with Selden. When she throws the shadowy packet into Selden's fire after yet another inconsequential and indirect interchange, the reader feels that the letters symbolize Lily's last hope. Selden's utter inability either to see or to hear what Lily has come to is one of the more poignant scenes in the novel. Lily goes on talking, insistently, and the narrative voice describes the urgency the reader feels: "Whether he wished it or not, he must see her wholly for once before they parted" (307).

After their conversation, Lily tells Selden good-bye in several ways, throwing the letters into the fire. Whatever good the letters might have been in some previous life, they have no efficacy in Lily's present bleak world. They seem, to her, completely unreal.

Wharton concludes the scene with the letters burned, with no use ever to be made of their words, their presence. Just as Selden did not care about those words—for Mrs. Haffen had found the letters in his wastebasket—so he does not know how to care for Lily's words. He literally cannot understand them, nor can he reply to them. Wharton ends the scene with the image of Selden, "tranced . . . still groping for the word to break the spell" (310). Reminiscent of the language of fairy tales, Selden's "spell" is a selfish luxury. Lily, still cold and wet from being caught in the rain, kisses him goodbye and walks back to her solitary room. Her kiss has not awakened him, any more than has her language.

Following Wharton's clues, the reader knows now that there will be no rescue by Selden, for Selden himself has been cast in the role of love object, in need of both awakening and rescue.

Lily's kiss may have had a long-term effect, for the ironic opening of Wharton's last chapter shows an ebullient Selden hurrying toward Lily's flat at only nine in the morning. Clearly now awakened from his trancelike state, Selden is both ready to act and armed with the word which has previously eluded him. Wharton has called the reader's attention to the metaphor of exchanging words when she has, just a page earlier, shown Lily's inability to find a word for which she groped, "some word she had found that should make life clear between them" (323), going into the drugged sleep that would mean her death. In this "mild and bright" morning scene, part of Selden's "youthful sense of adventure" shows itself in his confidence—in both language and self. He is, clearly and ironically, completely in charge: "Nine o'clock was an early hour for a visit, but Selden had passed beyond all such conventional observances. He only knew that he must see Lily Bart at once—he had found the word he meant to say to her, and it could not wait another moment to be said. It was strange that it had not come to his lips sooner—that he had let her pass from him the evening before without being able to speak it. But what did that matter, now that a new day had come?" (324). Wharton's rhetorical question, "But what did that matter," punctures the mood of both Selden and reader. For time has mattered, and Selden's complete insensitivity to Lily's physical and mental state has kept him from responding as he might have, and when he might have.

Wharton continues her reversal of expected imagery by stressing the brilliance of Lily's death bed: "The irresistible sunlight poured a tempered golden flood into the room, and in its light Selden saw a narrow bed along the wall, and on the bed, with motionless hands and calm unrecognizing face, the semblance of Lily Bart" (325). The narrow, and chaste, bed symbolizes Lily's life—pure, inviolate, crowded next to a wall in a modest room, never to escape from sterile loneliness into the warmth of care and wealth.

When Wharton describes Lily's figure as a "semblance," the reader is alerted to the fictionality of Selden's observations. As at the beginning of the novel, the reader is in the power of Selden as narrator: the account of Lily's denouement will come from his eyes, and Lily dead is even more the object that Selden had described her as being in chapter 1.

It is significant that Wharton never lets Selden touch Lily. He thinks of laying his face along hers, he considers some passion in a leave-taking, but his legalistic mind interrupts and warns that time is short. So Selden—hardly destroyed by his passion—begins his scrutiny of Lily's effects and nearly judges wrong when he comes to the financial matters. His shallow comprehension, his inaccurate guesses, are nowhere more obviously exposed than in Lily's room, and Wharton's care to make the reader see Selden's bumbling only intensifies Lily's separateness. If the man who could have married her, the man she would have loved, is only this inept interpreter, then Lily's life of loneliness might not have changed so much in marriage as she would have wished.

Wharton's last four paragraphs serve as an ironic coda, an authorial statement about Selden's vapidity so cleverly phrased, in what might have been his own words, that the reader wonders at the range of possible interpretations. Read literally, the section adds to Selden's self-congratulation: he has loved Lily, he claims, and he is somehow helping her at that moment. He would be comforted in his nostalgia; he would have the memory of their love, even if he had never spoken of it to her. "But at least he *had* loved her—had been willing to stake his future on his faith in her—and if the moment had been fated to pass from them before they could seize it, he saw now that, for both, it had been saved whole out of the ruin of their lives" (329).

More than ironic, Selden's statement is also vapid and meaningless. How could the moment be saved for *both* when Lily is already dead? Selden's obeisance to "fate," the rationalization that what had happened to Lily was bound to happen, is even further mockery of her belief in him. Wharton's setting Selden in the position of Lily's rescuer now appears to have been a device of biting censure, as the reader sees that the central trait of Selden's personality is his unwillingness to take any stand that calls for action. And his meaningless phrase, "the ruin of their lives," is another empty nod to the sentimental novel. While Lily is unquestionably dead, Selden's life is hardly a "ruin." It might be said to be flourishing, in fact. Selden has escaped not only marriage to Lily but also any involvement in her unfairly maligned life—and with her burning of Bertha's letters, Selden has also escaped any later ramifications of that affair.

Selden's definition of "love" in this passage is also self-serving. Staking his future on his faith in her does not represent Selden's behavior as Wharton has described it throughout the book. Where was Selden's faith when Lily left the Trenor house at midnight? Where was his support during the long two years when she fell so thoroughly out of place, and out of sight, of the society to which he also belongs? What Selden's words in this concluding chapter show, forcefully, is that he will use all events to aggrandize himself. Even though he could rightly be contrite, could blame himself for being the last person to see Lily alive and the last who had some chance of saving her, he never admits to any complicity. He instead ennobles his part in the travesty of Lily's decline by creating a fiction about what he and Lily have shared. In Selden's rhetoric, they shared this great love; they shared this moment; and, finally, they shared "the word which made all clear" (329).

In this chapter, Wharton uses Selden's words against him. First, he claims to know the word, and then he claims to share that word with Lily—as if any understanding about a subject as complex as love could be captured in a single word, even if the dead woman were able to hear it. If the legalistic Selden doesn't realize the quixotic evanescence of words, Wharton does. And so do Wharton's readers, who have just read a novel of thousands of words and now find that they have no idea what word Selden refers to. The riddlelike effect of the ending—Selden's calling attention to a word that he does not name and the reader cannot guess—adds to the reader's dismay. Here, at the end of Lily's story, Selden not only is shown as seriously limited in his use of language; he also appears as a self-serving egoist. As Dale M. Bauer points out: "Lily is the text that remains incomprehensible for Selden; he is no critic, no identificatory reader, able to transform the text or himself from confronting alien thoughts and allowing the division to occur between the subject formed by his culture and his experience of the effects of that ideology in Lily's death . . . because the finalizing word is left unsaid, the novel remains open-ended. Lily does not deliver a final word about herself; her suicide serves, instead, as a means to stave off others' essentializing discourse about her."[19]

Perhaps Wharton's fullest irony is that even Lily's death does not leave Selden at any loss for words. Selden not only "explains" and justifies throughout the scene in Lily's death room; he also convinces himself by the end of his time there that he and Lily have had a monumental love affair and that her death has kept their love pure, safe from the tawdry dailiness of actual living relationships. It is Selden's self-praise that makes the concluding chapter so revelatory and turns him from a character who bores and frustrates the reader into one who disturbs. For if the narrative of women's lives falls into hands such as these, to be told through a voice such as this and in such inaccurate language as this, readers have no chance of ever learning the significance of women's stories.

Wharton's choosing to write this concluding section so as to bring the reader into an intimate relation with Selden—in all his vacuous and offensive hypocrisy—does several important things. First, it conveys an indisputable argument for Lily's naiveté. The very man she thought was so superior to her, the man to whom she looked for guidance and encouragement, was incapable of recognizing her very substantial strengths. Selden never saw Lily at all *as she was*. He saw her first as the manacled victim of the society that had made her, and he saw her, dead, as the woman he had loved tragically, whose love he had been fated to lose.

Second, the novel's ending acknowledges the complicity of Lily's society—*all* her society—in her death. If Selden is presented as somehow superior to the herd, then his superiority is itself egregiously flawed. As Wharton said to Sara Norton, Selden is a "negative hero," and her publisher's urging that her next novel have stronger men because he was tired of critical comments about Selden reinforced the sense that many readers of *The House of Mirth* found that character irritating.[20]

Perhaps most important, at least to readers contemporary with the novel's publication in 1905, the conclusion allows *The House of Mirth* a traditional "marriage novel" structure. If the expected ending was the marriage of the protagonists, then the scene of the lamenting Selden, kneeling near Lily's dead body, is a satisfactory denouement—the marriage novel frustrated. A lover's sorrow is as acceptable as a lover's happiness, especially when the bereaved can make such poetic and heartfelt use of his loss. With Lily's death, many readers critical of her sometimes unpredictable behavior are satisfied; because she has disappeared from the story, the reader need make no judgment about her behavior or her life. And, because her death has been "accidental," the reader has nowhere to place any blame. The reader can join with Selden in the self-congratulation of their sensitive response to Lily's tragic—and unnecessary—death.

As Wharton knew well, however, a great many of her readers would not accept that final chapter as a traditional ending and would see it as the subtle unmasking of the still inaccurate narrator, Lawrence Selden.

Notes

1. Kate Caffrey, *The 1900s Lady* (London: Gordon Cremonesi, 1976), 165.

2. Barbara Welter, *Dimity Convictions: The American Woman in the Nineteenth Century* (Athens: Ohio University Press, 1976). See also Carroll Smith-Rosenberg, "The Female World of Love and Ritual: Relations between Women in Nineteenth-Century America," *A Heritage of Her Own: Toward a New Social History of American Women*, ed. Nancy F. Cott and Elizabeth H. Pleck (New York: Simon & Schuster, 1979).

3. Barbara Ehrenreich and Deirdre English, *For Her Own Good: 150 Years of the Experts' Advice to Women* (Garden City, N.Y.: Doubleday, 1979); Elaine Showalter, *The Female Malady: Women, Madness, and English Culture, 1830–1980* (New York: Pantheon Books, 1985).

4. Ann R. Shapiro, *Unlikely Heroines: Nineteenth-Century America Women Writers and the Woman Question* (Westport, Conn.: Greenwood Press, 1987).

5. R. W. B. Lewis, *Edith Wharton: A Biography* (New York: Harper & Row, 1975), 154.

6. Cecilia Tichi, "Women Writers and the New Woman," in *Columbia Literary History of the United States*, ed. Emory Elliott (New York: Columbia University Press, 1988), 595. Tichi also points out that, under the guise of being "local color" writers, many of these women were presenting truthful, if not happy, accounts of real women's lives.

7. Sandra M. Gilbert and Susan Gubar, *The Madwoman in the Attic: The Woman Writer and the Nineteenth-Century Literary Imagination* (New Haven, Conn.: Yale University Press, 1979); Rachel Blau DuPlessis, *Writing beyond the Ending: Narrative Strategies of Twentieth-Century Women Writers* (Bloomington: Indiana University Press, 1985).

8. Nina Baym, *Novels, Readers, and Reviewers* (Ithaca, N.Y.: Cornell University Press, 1984). An anonymous reviewer had written of Wharton's 1903 novel, *Sanctuary*, that it demonstrated "a beautiful, tender sentimentality peculiar to women, whether they are writers, mothers, or missionaries" ("Edith Wharton's New Novel," *Independent* 55 [10 December 1903]: 2933–35).

9. See representative reviews in *Spectator* 95 (28 October 1905): 657; *Literary Digest* 31 (9 December 1905): 886; and *Bookman* 22 (December 1905): 364–66. The Henry James remark, as well as other information about the book's reception, appears in Lewis, *Edith Wharton*, 150–56. See also Marlene Springer, *Edith Wharton and Kate Chopin: A Reference Guide* (Boston: G. K. Hall, 1976), and Katherine Joslin, "Edith Wharton at 125," *College Literature* 14, no. 3 (1987): 193–206.

10. Reviews in *Independent* 59 (16 November 1905): 1151, 1155; *Athenaeum* (London) 4074 (25 November 1905): 718; *Atlantic Monthly* 97 (January 1906): 52–53; *Saturday Review* (London) 101 (17 February 1906): 209–10; *Bookman* (London) 29 (December 1905): 130–31.

11. *"The House of Mirth," Times Literary Supplement*, 1 December 1905, 421. Important considerations of Wharton's novel as expressing a particularly American theme are H. D. Sedgwick, "The Novels of Mrs. Wharton," *Atlantic Monthly* 98 (August 1906): 217–28; Erskine Steele, "Fiction and Social Ethics," *South Atlantic Quarterly* 5 (July 1906): 254–63; and Charles Waldstein, "Social Ideals," *North American Review* 182 (June 1906): 840–52 and 183 (July 1906): 125–36.

12. Wharton to Scribner, 11 November 1905, *The Letters of Edith Wharton*, ed. R. W. B. Lewis and Nancy Lewis (New York: Scribner's, 1988), 85.

13. Wharton to Edward L. Burlingame, 23 November 1905, *Letters*, 98.

14. Wharton to Dix, 5 December 1905, *Letters*, 99.

15. Arthur Hobson Quinn, "Edith Wharton," pamphlet, n.d., as quoted by Joslin, "Edith Wharton at 125," 205.

16. *The House of Mirth* (New York: Penguin, 1985), 3. Page numbers from this edition appear in the text subsequently.

17. Judith Fetterley, "Reading about Reading," in *Gender and Reading*, ed. Elizabeth A. Flynn and Patrocinio P. Schweickart (Baltimore: Johns Hopkins University Press, 1986), 150.

18. Frances L. Restuccia, "The Name of the Lily: Edith Wharton's Feminism(s)," *Contemporary Literature* 28 (1987): 223–38.

19. Dale M. Bauer, *Female Dialogics: A Theory of Failed Community* (Albany: State University of New York Press, 1988), 126. See also Susan Gubar, " 'The Blank Page' and the Issues of Female Creativity," *New Feminist Criticism*, ed. Elaine Showalter (New York: Pantheon, 1985), 292–313.

20. Lewis, *Edith Wharton*, 155, 159.

"The Word Which Made All Clear"

The Silent Close of The House of Mirth

SHARI BENSTOCK

◆ ◆ ◆

> It almost seems to me that bad & good fiction (using the words in their ethical sense) might be defined as the kind which treats of life trivially & superficially, & that which probes deep enough to get at the relation with the eternal laws; & the novelist who has this feeling is so often discouraged by the comments of readers & critics who think a book "unpleasant" because it deals with unpleasant conditions. . . . *No* novel worth anything can be anything but a novel "with a purpose," & if anyone who cared for the moral issue did not see in my work that *I* care for it, I should have no one to blame but myself—or at least my inadequate means of rendering my effects.
>
> —Edith Wharton to Dr. Morgan Dix, Rector, Trinity Church, 5 December 1905

From Magazine to Book

The House of Mirth was not the first of Edith Wharton's nineteen novels and novellas to be serialized. It was, however, the work that first brought her to the attention of a large reading public and established her reputation as a critic and satirist of American society. She was to have a long career in the pages of literary and popular magazines, earning vast sums (in the millions of dollars at today's rates) from the serial rights to her works. She later said that writing *The House of Mirth* under pressure of editors' deadlines and printers' schedules had taught her "the discipline of the daily task" and transformed her "from a drifting amateur into a professional."[1] Made at thirty years' remove from the period in which *The House of Mirth* appeared in the pages of *Scribner's Magazine* (January to November 1905), this statement seems disingenuous. Wharton had produced nine books in the eight years preceding 1905, including a two-volume historical novel set in eighteenth-century Italy (*The Valley of Decision*, 1902). But there was a difference: during the two decades of her literary apprenticeship she had followed, more or less, her own thematic interests in fiction and had set her own timetable for writing and publication.

From the moment the first installment of *The House of Mirth* appeared on newsstands, Wharton faced an impatient readership desirous to know more of Lily Bart and Lawrence Selden. Serial publication was, then, the crucible of her artistic maturation, forcing her to a strict production schedule.[2] Even though she considered the general reading public "fickle and featherheaded," she learned to speed the pace of her writing to keep up with the rhythms of serial publication.[3] This pattern of work eventually took its toll on her physical health and, some would say, on the quality of her writing. By the time she was in her sixties, in the 1920s, the decade of her greatest productivity, she had become so dependent on the income generated by serial publication that she could not afford to slow her writing pace.

What were the artistic and personal costs of this pressure to perform for her reading public? On the surface, the narrative of Edith Wharton's life differs radically from that of her heroine, Lily Bart. Wharton lived a long and successful life, making her name as a writer, and earning a substantial fortune in literary royalties, through her criticism of the very society that "killed" Lily. She could not leave high society behind, not only because it provided her subject matter but because she could not (and did not desire to) escape her own social class. Royalties from *The House of Mirth* allowed her to leave New York and reinvent her American style of life *à la française*, but the money that supported a Paris lifestyle always came from the American middle class (especially its women), who first read her novels in serial publications.

The House of Mirth was officially published in book form on 14 October 1905, a few days ahead of the November *Scribner's Magazine* supplement, which contained the shocking final chapter that turned the arch comedy into tragedy and gave the novel its somber twist of fate. The news of Lily Bart's death flashed across the country. One woman reported that when she read the final installment, she was so overcome with emotion that she telegraphed a friend: "Lily Bart is dead."[4] The shock of the novel's ending electrified the reading public, and the first and second book editions sold out during the advance publication period. By 28 October, two weeks after the official publication, the third edition was, in the parlance of the publishing trade, "almost exhausted." The book climbed quickly to the top of the best-seller list (surpassing Upton Sinclair's *The Jungle*) and received excellent reviews both in America and England.[5] The ending of the novel spurred sales. Readers asked themselves and each other: Why did Lily Bart have to die?

By late November 1905 a debate about the meaning of the novel had opened in the pages of the *New York Times Saturday Review of Books* between two readers who identified themselves as "Lenox" and "Newport." The argument focused on the accuracy of Wharton's picture of high society as deceitful, pleasure-seeking, and immoral. Was Lily's a "sordid career"? Was Selden strong or weak? "Newport" thought the book unjustly characterized New York society. "Lenox" responded that "Newport" refused to recognize the truthful, if unflattering, portrait of society and failed to see the book's "entire scheme and purpose." Others entered the discussion and refocused debate on the dramatic last chapter. One reader confessed: "The tragic death of the unfortunate Lily Bart gave me, for one, a very bad quarter of an hour, and any one coming suddenly upon me at that moment would surely have thought that I had met with some great personal affliction. But when all was over, I realized the perfection of the author's art, and I would not have desired a different ending to the book. Had

I been writing it (again forgive my impertinence) I could not have resisted the temptation of making, Selden, during that last meeting with Lily, send surreptitiously for a clergyman to marry them forthwith. Only thus could she have escaped that fatal dose of chloral."[6]

In general, those who saw Lily as society's victim objected that the ending was too brutal and tragic. Those who thought that Wharton had misrepresented society found Lily deserving of death. And a third group felt that the society Wharton drew with such precision was too superficial and self-serving to inspire passion. Mary Moss, writing for the *Atlantic Monthly*, spoke for this third segment of Wharton's readership: "For all its brilliancy, *The House of Mirth* has a certain shallowness; it is thin. At best, Lily can only inspire interest and curiosity. You see, you understand, and you ratify, but unfortunately, you do not greatly care." Nearly everyone agreed that the novel offered no admirable characters (Burlingame had expressed "disappointment" a year earlier at "a certain monotony of motives in the [character] types"), and many readers objected to Selden's passivity. Remarking on public reaction to Selden's emotional and moral detachment, Charles Scribner wrote to Wharton: "In the next book you must give us a strong man, for I am getting tired of the comments on Selden."[7]

Words That Somehow Must Be Said

That neither Lily nor Selden had spoken a last "word which made all clear" opened a textual space quickly filled by readers and reviewers who provided revised endings, offered moral encomiums, and cheered heartily the author's "genius" or loudly lamented the novel's fatalism. The dramatic last chapter of *The House of Mirth*, so inevitably plotted yet so surprising and shocking, was made all the more powerful by the profound silence that surrounded its final dumb show.

Editing the closing chapters of the novel for *Scribner's Magazine* in June 1905, Burlingame commented to Wharton that he thought they represented the best work she had ever done.[8] They had been written at lightning speed, as though Wharton herself were driven by the powers of darkness that closed in on her heroine. Holograph and typescript versions of these chapters reveal remarkably few alterations to the text, but the few that were made in manuscript accentuate the fatalism of the novel's close.[9] The reader observes Selden's effort to "unravel . . . the story" as he stands looking at Lily's inert body on the bed: "But at least he *had* loved her—had been willing to stake his whole future on his faith in her—& if the moment had been fated to pass from them before they could seize it, he saw now that, for both, it had been saved [whole] out of the *seemed seeming failure* [ruin] of their lives. It was this moment of love, this fleeting victory over themselves, which *alone lived in the* had kept *them both from gradual the gradual atrophy* kept their lives sweet in spite of them [both] from *gradual* atrophy & extinction."[10] Rather than softening the blow ("seemed seeming failure"), Wharton revised her prose to give the full impact of the tragedy—"the ruin of their lives"—even as she underscored Selden's belief that he had loved Lily and "had been willing to stake his whole future in his faith in her." The irony, of course, is that Selden had taken no risks on Lily's behalf, even the risk of telling her how he loved her. There is no "gradual atrophy and extinction" in the final version: atrophy and extinction fall at once, a deathblow.

But was Lily's death suicide or an accident? Did she at last take her life in her own hands, if only to end it? We desire to know her intentions, but the author withholds the crucial piece of information, thus clouding the death in mystery. Gerty Farish reports to Selden on his arrival: "The doctor found a bottle of chloral—she had been sleeping badly for a long time, and she must have taken an over-dose by mistake. . . . There is no doubt of that—no doubt—there will be no question—he has been very kind" (325). The doubt that Gerty and the doctor hope to dispel—that Lily took her own life—is raised by the language of this statement. The repetition of the word *doubt*, the ellipses, and the phrase *must have taken*, stress the "facts" while also casting doubt on them. Motivations are not disclosed, appearances deceive. Any hint of suicide must be silenced. The doctor gives the cause of death as "accidental": "he has promised that there shall be no trouble," Gerty tells Selden (326). Society thereby enforces its codes even beyond the end of life: the truth of Lily's existence—her poverty, desperation, and death—are hidden from public view by conventional phrases and elliptical explanations.

The manuscript and published versions of these crucial sentences are identical, yet Wharton's notes on the novel make clear that Lily does take her own life.[11] Her tragedy is forecast in the opening moments of the novel, dramatized in a series of casual incidents and minor indiscretions that, in Hamilton W. Mabie's words, eventually "forge an iron chain of fate" that draws her inexorably to social exclusion and death. Increasing the dose of chloral was just another of the "careless compromises" that characterized Lily's behavior throughout the novel.[12] Any doubt that she took her own life was, for Wharton's contemporaries, rhetorical rather than "real."

Is it possible to distinguish the reality of Lily's death apart from the rhetorical and fictional modes that represent it? Can one interpret the meaning of her death separate from the social contexts of her life, "her little world" (135), as Selden calls it? How does the shift in narrative perspective in the last chapter shift the focus of the novel's social critique? These questions concern the storytelling methods and themes of *The House of Mirth*, but they also open onto a broader set of issues: Wharton's contributions to the novel of manners and her place in the historical transition between what might be called the nineteenth-century "novel of ethics," with its emphasis on moral issues, and the twentieth-century "novel of aesthetics," with its display of literary artifice. To pose the question otherwise, where does Edith Wharton, a woman writer who insisted on the ethical referentiality of art, stand in relation to Victorian and modern aesthetic modes?[13]

Before moving on to these larger issues, let us look at two moments of heightened aesthetic (but also ethical) awareness in *The House of Mirth*. Lily represents the tension between society's moral claims to honesty and forthrightness and the deceptions and devices of its social forms. A false morality, whose ethics are drawn from the masculine world of business, is veiled by a practiced gentility of manners that her society (and ours) ascribes to the feminine. In this context, Lily's fragile beauty elaborates an aesthetics of the feminine; her everyday survival depends on her ability to sustain graceful illusions and "tread a devious way" (127) as she negotiates society's twisting paths.

In the tableaux vivants scene, where Lily appears as Sir Joshua Reynolds's "Mrs. Lloyd," she so successfully masters illusory arts that she becomes, at one and the same time, both her subject and herself. Her creation is so "real" that the audience sees not the artist's brushwork but "the flesh and blood loveliness of Lily Bart" (134). The narrative voice, positioned within the novel's authorial perspective, assures us that such reinventions of reality are not easy to effect: "*tableaux vivants* depend for their effect not only on the happy disposal of lights and the delusive interposition of layers of gauze, but on a corresponding adjustment of the mental vision. To unfurnished minds they remain, in spite of every enhancement of art, only a superior kind of wax-works; but to the responsive fancy they give magic glimpses of the boundary world between fact and imagination" (133). Distinctions blur in this boundary world, and one cannot merely draw aside the veil of artifice to reveal the reality it hides: artifice and actuality intermesh.

The afternoon entertainment of the tableaux vivants in the Wellington Brys' drawing room foreshadows the tableau mort of Lily's death scene. Driven out of the society she had so desperately courted, she has returned alone to her boardinghouse room and is now face-to-face with her destiny. She performs her last acts in solitary silence, paying the bills with the unexpected bequest from her aunt, undressing in the lamp light, measuring out the sleeping potion. In contrast to the tableaux vivants scene, where the reader was one of the spectators, this later scene draws the reader into Lily's thoughts by a narrative that shifts back and forth between omniscient narration (the "Victorian" mode) and free indirect style (the "modern" mode):[14]

> She could bear it—yes, she could bear it; but what strength would be left her the next day? *Perspective had disappeared*—the

> next day pressed close upon her, and on its heels came the days that were to follow—they swarmed about her like a shrieking mob. She must shut them out for a few hours; she must take a brief bath of oblivion. She put out her hand, and measured the soothing drops into a glass; but as she did so, she knew they would be powerless against the supernatural lucidity of her brain. She had long since raised the dose to its highest limit, but tonight she felt she must increase it. She knew she took a slight risk in doing so—she remembered the chemist's warning. If sleep came at all, it might be a sleep without waking. But after all that was but one chance in a hundred: the action of the drug was incalculable, and the addition of a few drops to the regular dose would probably do no more than procure for her the rest she so desperately needed. (322, emphasis added)

The reader, like Lily, loses perspective in these final moments; in a dizzying collapse of distance from the subject, the narrative mimes her actions and self-justifications. She wants sleep ("a brief bath of oblivion"), she wants to halt the nervous wakefulness and anguish of exhaustion, and she wants the "supernatural lucidity of her brain" to cease: "darkness, darkness was what she must have at any cost" (322).

But does Lily want death? At this crucial moment the reader is both an observer of the scene and inside her thoughts as she struggles to remember the word she must tell Selden, "some word she had found that should make life clear between them." The word that would clarify things lingers "at the far edge of thought," then "fade[s]" and sleep enfolds her. We see her struggle against sleep, then relax into it, then start up again "cold and trembling from the shock" (323), then sink again.

We never learn the word she seeks, nor do we know until the following morning—when Selden arrives to tell her his own word ("he had found the word he meant to say to her, and it could not wait another moment to be said")—that hers is now the sleep of death (324). Selden enters the room alone, standing at the side of her narrow bed, the place where the reader had stood only a few pages earlier. We enter his private thoughts, as we had entered hers, and at the same time we follow his activities. Like a detective searching for clues, he looks at the letters she has addressed, lifts the lid of her desk, opens her checkbook. Seeing that she has written a check to Gus Trenor, he arrives at partial understanding of events: "It was true, then, that she had taken money from Trenor, but true also, as the contents of the little desk declared, that the obligation had been intolerable to her, and that at the first opportunity she had freed herself from it, though the act left her face to face with bare unmitigated poverty" (329).

Selden can carry the story no farther because Lily can tell him nothing: "The mute lips on the pillow refused him more than this—unless indeed they had told him the rest in the kiss they had left upon his forehead" (329). He then interprets her kiss of the evening before, translating it as her pardon of his "detachment" and "spiritual fastidiousness." That is, Selden reads—as a literary critic would—Lily's mute sign. He takes it into his own (unspoken) language: "Yes, he could now read into that farewell all that his heart craved to find there; he could even draw from it courage not to accuse himself for having failed to reach the height of his opportunity" (329). Selden has the last "word," but an attentive reader of the novel, a reader who has listened carefully to Lily's unspoken thoughts, recognizes Selden's self-serving egotism as he detaches himself once again from her.

Selden adopts an attitude of penitence and reconciliation: "He knelt by the bed and bent over her, draining their last moment to its lees; and in the silence there passed between them the word which made all clear" (329). But this time the reader is not given entry to the character's thoughts. In front of this tableau mort, one asks: What was the secret word? Was it the same word that "lingered vague and luminous at the far edge" of Lily's thoughts a few hours earlier? Was it "love"? "faith"?

Wharton decided, by her choice of narrative method, to deny readers access to Lily's last thought and to keep secret the word that Selden arrived too late to tell her.[15] Manipulating the narrational method in these final pages, she chose to emphasize psychological verisimilitude (Lily falls into unconsciousness) rather than to underscore omniscient authority. In this way, the author kept open the question of Lily's and Selden's (mis)understanding of each other while at the same time clouding the issue of Lily's intentions to commit suicide. The choice of shifting narrative modes was no doubt made for aesthetic reasons, but it opens ethical questions: To what degree was Lily responsible for her death? What responsibility does society bear for these events? These were precisely the issues that "Lenox" and "Newport," and many others like them, tried to interpret, and they were questions Edith Wharton tried to answer in her own life. As a daughter of Old New York, she had learned the value of taking responsibility for her actions, and she believed (as did her parents) that social privilege entails social responsibility.

The strength of the novel for its early readers was that it held a mirror up to reality. They saw Wharton's characters as living human beings who congregated daily in the damask-lined drawing rooms of Fifth Avenue. To my knowledge, only one reader spoke to her of the tension between the novel's social realism and its rhetorical structures. Howard Sturgis, a London-born Bostonian who lived most of his life in England, a close friend of both Wharton and Henry James, took issue with the narrative perspective of the last two chapters. She had tricked the reader, he said, into believing in the "reality" of her characters and their situation and then intruded on this "fiction" by entering Lily's mind in the last moments of her life.

A novelist himself, Sturgis focused on the final scene in Lily's room, when the narrative enters the mind of a dying woman. His letter continued a discussion already under way with Wharton.

> Yes, of course one xrays the character one is most interested in, and by the rules of the game you are perfectly justified in doing it when she's dying as well as when she's alive, if you are willing to profit by this convention; but somehow to me, there *is* a difference, because as long as Lily lives she might have told what she felt to Gerty Farish, or Edith Wharton ("or

> whatever" as Henry [James] says) *or* she might herself be writing the book in the 3rd person. It is unlikely you would know just what she thought & felt on any particular occasion, *but not impossible*, whereas what she thought & felt just before she died alone, *she could not tell any one*, nor could she write it (being dead) and whenever I come across it in a book it falsifies the whole thing to me, somehow—I *know* it is *done*, & done by the higher authorities; but it always gives the show away—I say: "Halloa, hold on; Mrs. Wharton *can't* know this; she's inventing; perhaps she has invented the whole thing; perhaps it isn't true after all, perhaps there never was a Lily Bart." Of course with the ordinary novel one doesn't say: "*Perhaps* there never was"—one says for certain: "There never was"—but I felt right up to that last chapter that all *your* people were alive & walking about in New York; I could have sworn to it, and it came like a douche of cold water. . . . The illusion is so terribly hard to give, so fatally easily destroyed. It is for the same reason that I deprecate the constant *shifting* of the point of view in most novels, the going first behind one character, then behind another. As long as one tells the story entirely from the point of view of one character, it is open to the reader, as I say.[16]

One can imagine Wharton's amusement at Sturgis's rather naive and literal-minded complaint that she had broken the frame of social realism she had so perfectly put in place. Nor would she have agreed that verisimilitude in fiction required that the author maintain a single point of view.[17]

Twenty years after the publication of *The House of Mirth*, having read James Joyce and Virginia Woolf, Wharton stated her objections to the abrupt shifts from external to internal perspectives that characterized the modern novel. Like Sturgis, she situated her complaint on the grounds of verisimilitude: "Verisimilitude is the truth of art, and any convention which hinders the illusion is obviously in the wrong place. Few hinder it more than the slovenly habit of some novelists of tumbling in and out of their characters' minds, and then suddenly drawing back to scrutinize them from the outside as the avowed Showman holding his puppets' strings."[18] Wharton had captured psychological realism in Lily's last moments—the failure of human memory to recover a word at the edge of consciousness. But what about her decision to keep back Selden's last word, the word of the survivor? His word, "the word which made all clear," haunts the last moments of the novel. It refuses the ending it invites.

Tethered in Native Pastures

We know less about the writing process of *The House of Mirth* than we do of Wharton's later works. Only a small number of letters to her editors at Scribner's about its composition still exist, and references to the novel's progress in letters to her two closest women friends, Sara Norton and Mary Cadwalader Jones, reveal little. We do know, however, that in 1903 and 1904 Wharton was profoundly depressed by reviews of her recent work. She was particularly disheartened by the continuing references to Henry James as the model for her narrative methods. In Wharton's view, James's great work was *The Portrait of a Lady*, but she repeatedly remarked that she found his late fiction unreadable. Although she cherished him as a dear friend, she took less and less enjoyment in his writing. James never served as her literary Master (the term applied to him by several disciples, including Howard Sturgis), and she treated his commentaries on her own work as the opinions of a respected colleague. She parodied James's style in private writings, and in 1926, ten years after his death, she published "The Velvet Ear-Pads," a comic send-up of the themes of his 1909 story, "The Velvet Glove."

In June 1904, she expressed to William Crary Brownell, one of her editors at Scribner's, her discouragement with the reviews of her recently published short-story collection, *The Descent of Man.* "I have never before been discouraged by criticism," she wrote, "because when the critics have found fault with me I have usually abounded in their sense, & seen, as I thought, a way of doing better the next time; but the continued cry that I am an echo of Mr. James (whose books of the last ten years I can't read, much as I delight in the man), & the assumption that the people I write about are not 'real' because they are not navvies & char-women, makes me feel rather hopeless. I write what I see, what I happen to be nearest to, which is surely better than doing cowboys de chic."[19]

Brownell sympathized with her feelings: "Do you remember the paper that called you 'a masculine H.J.?' Unpleasant not to have one's uniquity recognized but [you] sometimes seem to come out better than he does." Brownell admitted that he did not fully understand her feeling of discouragement. She would be indifferent to "*private* opinions of critics," he wrote, and then added in a postscript: "It's a relief to know you can't read H.J. [In] the efforts I made to read *The Ambassadors* I broke one tooth after another."[20] His letter was perhaps intended to tease Wharton out of her depression. She had great respect for Brownell, who was himself a literary critic, but she must have felt that, sympathetic as he was to her, he was also blinded to her real concerns—the *public* opinions of critics who, unable to place her work in any other literary context, made her a clone of Henry James (inverting her gender as they did so). Brownell's behavior might be explained by his intellectual attitudes: a puritan of sorts, he was closed to experimentation in either the form or subject matter of the novel as a genre. Thus, he would have had no natural affinity for James's work; nor would he have thought James an appropriate "master" for Wharton's developing literary skills. And yet Brownell refused to address directly Wharton's analysis of her place in American letters.[21]

In literary history, Wharton stands under James's protective wing; she *descends* from his paternalism. In life, we know, James was awed by his Angel of Devastation, his *oiseau de feu*. Her restless energy and high spirits, her wide-ranging intellectual pursuits and cultural interests, her fashionableness—all this fascinated and frustrated him. He wanted her to settle down, to draw her chair close to the fireside and *stay there*.

In 1902, although they did not yet know each other well, Wharton sent James a copy of her two-volume historical novel, *The Valley of Decision*, set in eighteenth-century Italy. On 17 August, he wrote in appreciation of the novel, adding that he longed to talk with her about it: "Even, however, were I prepared to chatter to you about *The Valley*, I think I should sacrifice that exuberance to the timely thought that the first duty to a serious & achieved work of art is the duty of recognition *telle quelle*; & that the rest can always wait." He then goes on to "admonish" her toward "the *American Subject*": "Don't pass it by—the immediate, the real, the ours, the yours, the novelist's that it waits for. Take hold of it & keep hold, & let it pull you where it will."[22] Three days later, he expounded on this theme to Edith's beloved sister-in-law, Mary ("Minnie") Cadwalader Jones.

> Mrs. Wharton is another affair, and I take to her very kindly as regards her diabolical little cleverness, the quantity of intention and intelligence in her style, and her sharp eye for an interesting *kind* of subject. I had read neither of these two volumes [*Crucial Instances* and *The Touchstone*, which Minnie had sent him] and though the "Valley" is, for significance of ability, several pegs above either, I have extracted food for criticism from both. As criticism, in the nobler sense of the word, is with me enjoyment, I've in other words much liked them. Only they've made me, again, as I hinted to you other things had, want to get hold of the little lady and pump the pure essence of my wisdom and experience into her. She *must* be tethered in native pastures, even if it reduce her to a backyard in New York. If a work of imagination, of fiction, interests me at all (and very few, alas, do!) I always want to write it over in my own way, handle the subject from my own sense of it.[23]

James's language betrays an element of sexual aggression ("pump the pure essence of my wisdom and experience into her") and latent desires to dominate, even intimidate, "the little lady." She threatened and worried him, and in this letter he tries to reduce her genius to a "diabolical little cleverness" and to contain her creative spirit: "she *must* be tethered in native pastures, even if it reduce her to a backyard in New York." He wants to "write" her work "over in my own way." That is, he wants to appropriate her subject and style to his own ends.

Wharton may never have been fully aware of James's designs on her work, but she knew that they viewed fiction-writing rather differently. She felt that the elaborate style of his late period blurred his subject and clouded the narrative point of view. By contrast, she was working toward greater clarity of language and moral perspective in her fictions. As she wrote to Dr. Morgan Dix after the publication of *The House of Mirth*, "if anyone who cared for the moral issue did not see in my work that *I* care for it, I should have no one to blame but myself—or at least my inadequate means of rendering my effects."[24] In Wharton's view, James failed to "render his effects." By this time, she had deep-seated doubts about his writing, and it is hardly likely that she would have abandoned her long search for her own voice, subject, and style to follow his advice. Still, literary historians and biographers continue to claim that it was James's wisdom by which Wharton found her way to her real subject, "Old New York."

By mid-spring 1902, some four months before James offered the advice quoted above, Edith Wharton was already at work on a novel set in modern-day New York and Long Island. By autumn, she had drafted seventy pages of a book entitled "Disintegration" but then abandoned it, even though Burlingame was enthusiastic about her subject and her methods. Her decision not to continue the novel coincided with the onset of the first serious episode of her husband's mental illness, a suicidal depression.[25] One year later, she began to write *The House of Mirth* (September to December 1903), but again Teddy's illness stalled progress on it. In August 1904, she took up the novel again, after a period of "black despair" and struggle. By early October, she announced to Burlingame: "I am fatuously pleased with 'The House of Mirth.' "[26] The following week, Henry James arrived for his first extended visit to The Mount. In the mornings, while he worked on his prefaces for the New York edition of his works, she was propped up in bed, looking out toward Laurel Lake, writing her novel.

Another year later, in November 1905, having read the serial installments of the novel, James wrote to her: "Let me tell you at once that I very much admire that fiction, and especially the last three numbers of it: finding it altogether a superior thing. . . . The book remains one that does you great honour—though it is better written than composed; it is indeed throughout *extremely* well written, and in places quite 'consummately.' " James had much to say about *The House of Mirth*, more than could be contained in the letter; he even proposed to return "to the U.S. to deliver a lecture on 'The question of the *roman de moeurs* in America—it's deadly difficult.' "[27] It was not the close of the novel itself that posed a problem for him but rather, he implied, the very genre of the novel of manners *in America*. Unfortunately, he never wrote the lecture he proposed on the subject, and we do not know whether he might have shared the opinion of many American critics who not only praised Wharton's treatment of her subject but commended the strong moral stance that she took. The reviewer for the *New York Times* commented that the novel "will be acclaimed largely because of its moral side—its vivid, pitiless portrayal of the folly which pervades a newly builded, imperfectly founded, social structure."[28] A question remains, however, one that even Henry James appears to have overlooked: how does the novel's *ending*—its complex narrative structure, its shifting point of view—affect the "moral side" of human behavior that the novel portrays?

Writing beyond the Ending

In *The Writing of Fiction* (1925), Wharton plotted a double genealogy for the modern novel: "the novel of psychology was born in France, the novel of manners in England . . . out of their union in the glorious brain of Balzac sprang that strange chameleon-creature the modern novel, which changes its shape and colour with every subject on which it rests."[29] She called this new form the novel of character or manners (using the terms interchangeably) and distinguished it from the novel of situation, which was, in her view, an outmoded genre dominated by machinations of plot. She described herself as a novelist of character: characters came to her first, and their development, or situation, emerged from their personalities and psychologies. Form (understood as order and incident) followed character, and the novel of manners, "with its more crowded stage, and its continual interweaving of individual and social analysis," presented the most difficult questions of appropriate form.[30]

In *A Backward Glance*, Wharton discussed the problem of interweaving individual and social analysis in *The House of Mirth*. "The problem was how to extract from such a subject the typical human significance which is the story-teller's reason for telling one story rather than another. In what aspect could a society of irresponsible pleasure-seekers be said to have, on the 'old woe of the world,' any deeper bearing than the people composing such a society could guess? The answer was that a frivolous society can acquire dramatic significance only through what its frivolity destroys. Its tragic implication lies in its power of debasing people and ideals. The answer, in short, was my heroine, Lily Bart."[31] Wharton's commentary reopens familiar questions about *The House of Mirth*: If Lily took her own life, then how is society implicated? If her death was accidental, is society exonerated? Behind these questions lurks another, one that Wharton does not address: If frivolous New York society was complicit in the killing of Lily Bart, what role did it play in the creation of Edith Wharton, writer and social critic?

The closing moments of *The House of Mirth* do not figure either or choices; instead, the meaning of Lily's death flickers within the terms the novel sets for her life and lifestyle. She cannot be extricated, even in death, from her social—and therefore moral—context; the novel poses the question of human subjectivity in terms of the "social." Rachel Blau DuPlessis comments that "Lily's ambiguous suicide, occurring as a gambled side effect ('one in a hundred') of delivering herself from the temporary insanity of insomnia, is not willed; thus it is like all of Lily's decisions when she does not see that one option may genuinely foreclose another. In its coming, death is sensual, a seduction into the drug climaxing in her illusion of maternal bliss. Lily has been compromised by money, time, sexuality: all the high-risk components of female life. And yet she has arranged herself as a beautiful object so that her bier resonates with both narcissism and the failed *community* of the earlier tableaux scene." DuPlessis sees gambling as a "root metaphor" of *The House of Mirth*, and she argues that Lily "is open to speculation."[32] That is, Lily is a subject who refuses to act (action closes out options), and is therefore a subject of compromise.

Wharton took a double gamble in *The House of Mirth*. She held the mirror of art up to her own social set, the society in which she moved. Although her values were those of an earlier, less affluent, and less worldly community, she understood the double standard of "modern" society's mores, the tensions between personal desires and public codes of behavior.[33] She rewrote the denouement of the novel of manners to reflect these tensions. The classic ending of comedy (in which marriage renews society and extends its power) and tragedy (where death is a cleansing and renewing social force) draw together in a single closing image in *The House of Mirth* that combines both meanings: death-in-marriage and marriage-in-death. There is no place outside marriage or the conventions that lead to marriage, no moment for the word that Selden and Lily might whisper to each other: "love," separate from the social customs that enclose it, dares not speak its name.

In the thirty years of active publishing that followed *The House of Mirth*, Wharton took many risks, addressing subjects considered to be unfeminine, immoral, or outside her range of experience. But only one other time did she risk sacrificing a woman's life in the cause of social criticism. In *The Fruit of the Tree* (1907), a novel of social conscience, Wharton examined the abuses of power and the profit motive in New England mills. Her heroine, Justine Brent, a surgical nurse with strong ethical convictions, commits a mercy killing. She takes the life of her childhood friend Bessy Westmore, a woman, like Lily Bart, made to society's measure, who had inherited the mill after the death of her first husband.

Wounded in a riding accident, with little hope that she can resume a normal life, Bessy is being kept alive by medical science until her second husband, John Amherst, can return from South

America. Suspended between life and death, suffering intensely, she is "wrapped in a thickening cloud of opiates—morphia by day, bromides, sulphonal, chloral hydrate at night."[34] Bessy finds a way to tell Justine of her suffering: "I—I—can't bear it . . . The pain . . . Shan't I die . . . before [he comes home]?" (410). Several days later, when Bessy's pain has become so terrible that she can produce only "vague animal wailing" (432) in place of words, her eyes beg for Justine's help to relieve the pain. Justine, acting on the moral principle that medical science must not prolong useless suffering, administers a lethal dose of morphine.

Justine later marries John Amherst, who uses the fortune Bessy left him to improve working conditions at the mill. But, instead of the joy of a lifetime of work together in the common cause of bettering workers' lives, their happiness is shadowed by Bessy's death, the true circumstances of which eventually come to light. As with the ending of *The House of Mirth*, the moral directive of the novel remains an open question. Is Justine a hero? A murderer? To what degree was Bessy a victim of society's false self-serving morality, and in what degree did she contribute to it?

Contrasting New York society with the lives of mill workers, *The Fruit of the Tree* broadened Wharton's critique of social values. But this wider canvas presented narrative difficulties that she was unable to resolve. The novel's social subject, based on her personal observations of mill towns near Lenox, Massachusetts, where she summered, is not successfully integrated with the book's psychological drama. But these were not the only reasons that *The Fruit of the Tree* was not the popular success that *The House of Mirth* had been. Serialized in *Scribner's Magazine* (January–November 1907), its publication in book form coincided with a financial crisis on Wall Street that depressed sales. Scribner's had paid Wharton an $8,000 advance against royalties (about $120,000 today) in the expectation that sales would match, if not exceed, those of *The House of Mirth*. The publishing firm never recovered its initial investment.

Wharton did not publish another novel for six years (*The Custom of the Country*, 1913), and, instead of killing off her society heroines—the beautiful, decorative, self-absorbed Lily Barts and Bessy

Westmores—she watched them suffer slowly as they wrestled with their unfulfilled desires and lived through the dry seasons of unhappy marriages. This kind of suffering, a slow spiritual death, mirrored the pain she experienced in her own marriage. Marriage became the instrument of death in Wharton's later fictions, and even modern, quick-fix divorces did little to alter the psychological pain in which her heroines faced their destinies.[35] There are several reasons for the shift in her perspective. Her love affair with William Morton Fullerton between 1907 and 1911 opened to her an unknown world of women's experiences that included the pleasures (and power) of sexual desire, and she saw the danger of confusing sex with love or love with marriage. In 1913, after twenty-eight years of marriage, she divorced Edward Wharton, who was by this time severely mentally ill. The decision was without doubt the most difficult of her life and followed several years of intense self-scrutiny and moral anguish. Ironically, the divorce convinced her that marriage offered the only possibility for true intimacy.[36]

The family was the core unit of civilized society for Wharton, and the effect of shifting social mores on familial relations was always a major theme of her fiction. Although she realized that marriage fostered women's economic and emotional dependence on men and that parents often behaved irresponsibly with regard to their children, she could envision no other form of social organization so well suited to the nurturance and preservation of civilization.[37] World War I, a war that she felt threatened the very foundations of civilization, only intensified her commitment to the family. All her war work was directed toward preserving the family and protecting its most vulnerable members—women and children. Her charities provided an integrated form of life for the refugees and gave them far more than food, clothing, shelter, and medical care. She refused to separate family members, except in cases of extreme illness. While women worked at lace making, sewing, or weaving, their children attended school, where they studied the full range of academic subjects and also learned a trade. Daily activities were balanced between work and leisure;

the schools and workrooms fostered independence and encouraged cultural and artistic interests.

Edith Wharton took a personal interest in the refugees her charities served, and she maintained lifelong relationships with many of them. In her early fifties when the war began, she was an older Justine Brent, a woman of courage and commitment; indeed, Justine portrays the future role of Edith Wharton as social activist. The war gave Wharton the opportunity to act on the moral principles that underwrote her art: She used her social and economic privileges for the greater good of others. Again, Wharton differs from Lily Bart, who appears to have no social conscience.

When she looked back at Old New York after the war, Wharton saw it as though through the reverse end of a telescope (*The Age of Innocence*, 1920; *Old New York*, 1924). The hidebound community into which she had been born no longer existed. Transmuted over time, it had been taken over first by the robber barons of the mid-nineteenth-century, then by greedy midwestern tycoons, and now it was dominated by postwar commercialism that fostered irresponsible self-indulgence. The "Jazz Age" disgusted her no less than a renewed American puritanism (prohibition and the return to religious fundamentalism) that drove some Americans to "Gay Paree."

Still America's most respected woman writer, and now a war hero who proudly wore the rosette of the French Legion of Honor, Wharton restated her authority as social critic. She portrayed the self-destructiveness of high society and the middle class that aped its bankrupt values in a series of popular novels: *Glimpses of the Moon* (1922), *Twilight Sleep* (1927), and *The Children* (1928). Nor was she afraid to expose the false virtues of social forms that denied spirituality and constrained creativity, driving people to excess or bizarre forms of self-sacrifice (*The Mother's Recompense, 1925*). Her two-volume study of the novelist in modern society (*Hudson River Bracketed*, 1929; *The Gods Arrive*, 1932) understood her belief in the novel as an instrument of social change.

Wharton insisted—more outspokenly than ever—on the ethical referentiality of art. Yet, in her personal life, she was caught up in the very money-seeking conventions that her art decried. The war had left her ill and exhausted (she suffered a major heart attack in 1917); her literary income was diminished because the war work had allowed little time for writing. After the armistice, she needed money both to support her public charities (the convalescent homes for tubercular patients) and to provide assistance to several ill, aged, and infirm dependents, including family members and household staff. In 1919, she retreated to the country, where she wanted to spend her time gardening and writing fiction. She renovated an eighteenth-century *pavillon* north of Paris and a fortified château (formerly a nunnery) on the south coast. Banking on her literary earnings to support her new life, she divided her time between the two residences until her death in 1937.

She had changed publishing firms before the war, believing that Scribner's had not adequately advertised and marketed her writing. She was now served primarily by Appleton's in New York, and her editor, Rutger B. Jewett, a man of her own social class, was eager to increase her literary reputation. He knew that the way to make money in a competitive postwar literary marketplace was through serialization rights. Popular magazines (the pictorials) paid large sums, and he was able to negotiate profitable contracts for Wharton's new novels.[38] These monies were enormous, even by today's standards. Delighted in her new earning power, she also discovered two drawbacks to the arrangements: she had to write far more quickly than was comfortable for her, and some magazine editors, fearing that the "modern" subject matter of her fiction (adultery, divorce, illegitimacy, incest) would offend the middle-class Christian readership of their magazines, wanted her to tame her social criticism and provide happy endings to her novels. It fell to Jewett to negotiate such impasses, and he was a strong advocate for Wharton's literary methods. He reminded editors that her name would increase the prestige of their magazine and draw a wider, and more sophisticated, readership to it.

Wharton's literary reputation skyrocketed in the 1920s; she

won the Pulitzer Prize in 1921, received an honorary doctorate from Yale in 1923, was nominated for the Nobel Prize in 1926, and was inducted into the American Academy of Arts and Letters in 1930. When magazine editors asked her to write *à mésure de la publique*, however, she told Jewett that someone of her stature should have free rein in artistic matters. She was understandably perplexed by the attitudes of magazine editors, their puritanism seeming to contradict the facts of Jazz generation excesses. Hers was the view from Paris, of course, and magazines served readerships in the American Midwest and the Bible Belt.

In a letter regarding publication of *Glimpses of the Moon*, Jewett explained that the editor of the *Pictorial Review*, which had published serially *The Age of Innocence*, found it "somewhat above the heads of his subscribers, who are more at home with Kathleen Norris and Booth Tarkington." For this reason, he had asked Jewett to instruct her about *Glimpses:*

> Please explain to Mrs. Wharton that this story is planned to be run serially in a popular magazine, for the privilege of running it serially we are paying her a great sum of money [$18,000], and that we would most certainly appreciate it if she could divide her story in four parts, so that each part leads up to a climax or interesting situation that will leave the reader in suspense and eager to get the next issue of the magazine. Now please do not misunderstand me. I do not expect Mrs. Wharton to do a dime novel or family-story-paper break, but it can be done in a dignified artistic way. . . . The outline as you told it to me has possibilities of a good serial, if she will tell the story for all it is worth.[39]

From Wharton's point of view, these requests struck at the core of the author's artistic freedom.

The following spring, as she continued work on the novel, Jewett wrote to say that the magazine editors "are praying for a happy ending to the story, hoping that your young hero scores heavily with a novel or some book so that he wins not only golden ducats but also his wife and his soul's desire."[40] Wharton refused to provide a happy ending, and her judgment proved correct: the novel was a runaway best-seller.

She adamantly refused to temper her social criticism, to turn away from the depressing, often grim, subjects of her fiction, or to alter the narrative structure of her stories to accommodate the magazine trade. In holding firm to the line of artistic integrity, she knew she risked turning away the very readership she wanted to educate as well as losing the monies on which she had become increasingly dependent. In 1926, perhaps the most economically secure year of her life, Wharton wrote to Jewett: "I appreciate very much all the trouble you take in my behalf, but you must not think that it will be a surprise to me if I find that the editors of these popular magazines do not consider my novels adapted to their purpose. As you say, it would be impossible for me (even if I could remember to do so) to write a novel with a climax at the end of each instalment. This being so, it would seem to me natural that other novelists should be preferred, and I am all the more grateful to you for the trouble you take to place my fiction to such good advantages."[41] This letter strikes an ominous note, as though she foresaw the moment when magazines would reject her work. Yet popular magazines continued to buy her writing, often paying very substantial prices for it.[42]

In 1933, however, her story "Duration" was rejected both by the *Woman's Home Companion*, a popular women's magazine, and by the *Atlantic Monthly*, the most respected literary periodical in America and one that had been publishing her work since she was seventeen years old. Although the *Companion* had purchased the story after Wharton had rewritten its ending at the request of its editor, Gertrude Lane, the magazine then refused to print it. Angered and frustrated, Wharton wrote to Jewett.

> When I think of my position as a writer I am really staggered at the insolence of her letter, and if it were possible to make any one of that kind understand what she had done, I should not be sorry to do so. . . . The fact is I am afraid that I cannot write down to the present standard of the American picture magazines. I am in as much need of money as everybody else

> at this moment and if I could turn out a series of pot-boilers for magazine consumption I should be only too glad to do so; but I really have difficulty imagining what they want. I never supposed that their readers took much interest in my work, but I thought the magazine editors required a few well-known names. If what they want is that I should write stories like those I see in their pages, I am afraid it is beyond my capacity.[43]

When asked why they refused to publish the story, the editors of the *Woman's Home Companion* explained that the opening pages promised a more dramatic ending, and Jewett speculated that the popular magazines wanted something with more action.[44]

"Duration" is a satire of changing family mores among upper-class old Boston families, and its dramatic *point de départ* is a highly publicized hundredth-birthday party of a spinster who for all the long years of her life had been a most unremarkable (and thus easily forgettable) family member. Ellery Sedgwick, editor of the *Atlantic Monthly*, was a member of an old Boston family himself, and a longtime friend of Wharton. In rejecting the story, he agreed, in effect, with Gertrude Lane and told Jewett that the story, a grotesque satire, "is cutting, but not cutting enough. Mrs. Wharton's reputation is a real American possession, and in my judgment it would be a mistake for her to have the story printed in anything like its present form. A story of this kind, to be effective, ought to draw blood, and I think it fair to say that this does not break the skin."[45]

Was it possible that Wharton had slowly, even unconsciously, shaped her writing to public taste, softening the edge of her social satire? Or had she lost her acute powers of perception in her final years? The closing chapters of Wharton's life and writing career are as dramatic and as open to interpretation as the final scenes in any of her novels. She devoted these years wholly to her writing, the career that in her own life narrative had replaced the marriage plot that was so often the subject of her fictions. But, unlike society women who had married well (the "successful" Lily Barts), Edith Wharton could not retire in her later life and live on her husband's investments. She found herself instead working harder, faster, and under greater pressures to support herself and those who depended on her. The postwar economic expansionism of the 1920s led her to believe that the rewards of writing (and the royalties from theater productions and Hollywood films that were its by-product) would continue to increase.

The year 1929 marked the reversal of her fortunes, as it did for many Americans in Europe. In the spring, she had suffered a severe stroke (the first of several); six months later, the New York stockmarket crash reduced the value of the dollar and the French franc and led to a crisis in American publishing that forced her to work even faster for less economic gain. Jewett, himself growing older and working under great stress, could no longer secure for her the enormous advance monies on which she relied, and by 1932 her literary income had been reduced by three-quarters. The New York real-estate market had collapsed, and two commercial rental properties of which Wharton was part owner underwent foreclosure; next, her Paris bank, Munroe's, whose founder had been a family friend, collapsed; finally, property taxes in France quadrupled, and American income tax was increased. At her death, Wharton owed back taxes in both France and the United States, and her château at Hyères was sold to help pay these debts.

She regained her physical and mental strength several times after the 1929 illness and experienced long periods when she wrote well and quickly. She produced some excellent short fiction, wrote a skilled and popular autobiography (*A Backward Glance*, 1934), and, at her death, left an incomplete manuscript of *The Buccaneers*, one of her finest narratives. It is not an exaggeration to say, however, that her financial dependence on the American publishing market and the effort to meet its demanding schedules created a vicious cycle of overwork and illness that eventually killed her.

In her last years, Edith Wharton shared something else with her tragic heroine, Lily Bart: she could not admit to anyone the extent of her financial worry, although its effects were apparent in her rapidly declining health. The huge success of *The House of Mirth* some thirty years earlier had forged a link in her mind between the creative powers of authorship and the economic power her writing gave her. To lose the financial power of her pen, a fear that had long haunted her, was to lose the chance of fulfilling the desires that fed her creativity (travel, gardens, beautiful homes) and of sharing her bounty with friends, family members, staff, and dependents whom she supported. Like Lily, her last desire was to be freed from all responsibility, to be taken care of. In late July 1937, when she knew she could not live much longer, she unburdened herself to Elisina Tyler, the woman who had served as coadministrator of her war charities. Edith then made her friend residuary legatee of her estate and signed over power of attorney to her. Elisina promised Edith that no one would learn of her financial problems and that her public reputation would be preserved. Edith was then at peace: "not since I was eighteen have I felt so free," she told Elisina.[46] Two weeks later, in the late afternoon of 11 August, Edith Wharton died peacefully at her home north of Paris.

She did not die in silence like Lily Bart; she did not die in great pain like Bessy Westmore, her eyes pleading for release. At the end, she spoke "the word which made all clear" to a woman friend, who then acted on her wishes. Edith's actions differed from Lily's in two ways. She acknowledged the costs (and rewards) of taking responsibility for all the dimensions of her life, from worldly desires to artistic creativity, from moral imperatives to the dictates of social conscience. The "word which made all clear" was not passed between lovers, accomplices like Lily and Selden to the social necessity of marriage, but between women whose friendship and mutual trust developed during the dark days of World War I, when they were comrades together in the cause of social justice. Finally, Edith Wharton had lived a thoughtful and self-conscious life, and her death, at age seventy-five, was not, as Lily Bart's may have been, either a tragedy of lost opportunities or merely the last in a series of "careless compromises."

Notes

1. Edith Wharton, *A Backward Glance* (New York: Scribner's, 1934), 208–9.

2. Wharton detested writing under these kinds of pressures, but she came to understand that "many an editor begins the publication of a serial novel long before the last chapters are even written," she wrote her sister-in-law Mary Cadwalader Jones on 1 May 1919. Edith Wharton Collection, Yale Collection of American Literature, Beinecke Library, Yale University (YCAL). Archival material will be cited in full in the first note, and by the acronym of the respective collection in subsequent notes.

3. Quoted in William Crary Brownell's answer to Edith Wharton, 6, July 1904, Scribner's Archive, Firestone Library, Princeton University (FL).

4. R. W. B. Lewis, *Edith Wharton: A Biography* (New York: Harper & Row, 1975), 152.

5. *Publishers Weekly*, 28 October 1905, p. 1094. Wharton recorded in her diary on that day: "H. of M. bestselling book in New York." Wharton Archive, Lilly Library, Indiana University, uncataloged.

6. Letter from M. L. A., Oxford, N.J., 27 November 1905, *New York Times Saturday Review of Books*, 2 December 1905. "Lenox" wrote from New York on 24 November 1905, "attribut[ing] the feminine gender without hesitation" to "Newport": "women are not apt to spare each other." In a later letter, 15 December 1905, "Lenox" restored "Newport" to his—we assume—proper manhood. By contrast, the writer who would have sent for a clergyman assumed that "Newport" was a man and "Lenox" "a woman who knows the heartlessness of the world" (27 November 1905). The letter regarding Lily's "sordid career" was signed by "Bettine of Cranmere" (28 November 1905).

7. Mary Moss, review of *The House of Mirth*, *Atlantic Monthly* 97 (1905): 52–53; E. L. Burlingame to Edith Wharton, 21 September 1904, FL; Charles Scribner to Edith Wharton, 20 November 1905, FL. She tried to provide a strong hero in *The Fruit of the Tree*, her next novel (1907), but failed. Indeed, she was never able to portray strong men. Biographers and critics have speculated that she failed because her father, whom she loved deeply and who died when she was only twenty years old, was weak. See Lewis, *Edith Wharton*, and Cynthia Griffin Wolff, *A Feast of Words: The Triumph of Edith Wharton* (New York: Oxford University Press, 1977).

8. Edward L. Burlingame to Edith Wharton, 5 June 1905, FL.

9. The authoritative text of *The House of Mirth* is the 1905 Charles Scribner's Sons edition (New York), printed from the plates of the *Scribner's Magazine* serialization, with Wharton's corrections of printers' errors. My references are to the 1969 Scribner's reprint of this first edition; subsequent quotations will hereafter be cited parenthetically by page

number. Wharton's method of rewriting was to "cut and paste" manuscript versions, so that it is often impossible to discover major changes (reordering of scenes, etc.). She wrote in minor word changes above the manuscript lines.

10. Holograph manuscript, YCAL. Words in italics were crossed out in Wharton's text; words in brackets are her additions.

11. On 26 May 1909, Wharton wrote to Richard Watson Gilder, then editor of the *Century Magazine*, proposing a short story for publication. In the letter she admitted that she was a "bad hand" at writing resumes of her work: "I produce a very bald & often erroneous effect, & I can only ask you to believe that the part I leave out is *always* what constitutes, for me, the psychological value of the story" (YCAL). Her comment applies very well, I believe, to the synopsis of the death scene in *The House of Mirth* that she sent to her publishers: "Then she comes home and takes chloral" (FL, box 1, folder 5).

12. Hamilton W. Mabie, *Outlook*, 21 October 1905, 406.

13. I am grateful for Alison Booth's guidance in framing the ethical and aesthetic terms of Wharton's fiction. The phrase *ethical referentiality of art* is hers.

14. These two narrational forms, which are at times difficult to separate clearly from each other, allow access to a character's consciousness. Free indirect style, which was in use before the Victorian period, is a mediate position between externalized third-person narration and internalized stream of consciousness. The free style relies more heavily than does omniscient narration on the character's vocabulary and manners of speech. It creates the fiction of the narrator's absence from the narrational scene.

15. For a discussion of a similar moment in Joyce's *Ulysses*, see my *Textualizing the Feminine: On the Limits of Genre* (Norman: University of Oklahoma Press, 1991), 187–89.

16. Howard Sturgis to Edith Wharton, 5 December 1905, YCAL, emphasis in original. Wharton's response to Sturgis no longer exists.

17. See her discussion of shifting viewpoint in *The Writing of Fiction* (New York: Scribner's, 1925), 88–98.

18. Ibid., 89.

19. Edith Wharton to William Crary Brownell, 25 June 1904, FL.

20. W. C. Brownell's notes on a letter to Edith Wharton, 6 July 1904, FL.

21. Brownell resisted Wharton's effort to get Scribners to publish Howard Sturgis's novel *Belchamber*, perhaps because he was offended by

its unpleasant subjects—adultery, illegitimacy among the British upper classes (see Lewis, *Edith Wharton*, 142).

22. Henry James to Edith Wharton, 17 August 1902, in *Henry James and Edith Wharton Letters: 1900–1915*, ed. Lyall H. Powers (New York: Scribners, 1990), 34.

23. Henry James to Mary Cadwalader Jones, 20 August 1902, in *Henry James Letters*, ed. Leon Edel, 4 vols. (Cambridge, Mass.: Harvard University Press, 1984), 4: 237–38.

24. Dr. Dix, who had performed the marriage service in 1885 of Edith Newbold Jones to Edward Robbins Wharton, wrote to her on 1 December 1905 to praise *The House of Mirth*: "This book places you at the head of the living novelists of our country or of the English-writing authors of our day. It is a terrible but just arraignment of the social misconduct which begins in folly and ends in moral and spiritual death. . . . To me the reading of your book has been like walking the wards of some infirmary set apart for the treatment of pestilential disease: the same ghastly wrecks of humanity, the same mephitic odours, the same miasma of afflorescent corruption" (YCAL).

25. "Disintegration" was revised and incorporated twenty years later into *The Mother's Recompense*. Wharton had plotted "Disintegration" before she began writing *The Valley of Decision* in 1901.

26. On Wharton's "black despair," see her 1905 diary, LL; Edith Wharton to E. L. Burlingame, 7 October 1904, FL.

27. Henry James to Edith Wharton, 8 November 1905. See Edel, *James Letters*, 4:373–74, and Powers, *James and Wharton Letters*, 52–53. What James meant when he said the novel was better written than composed or why he thought the question of the novel of manners in America was "deadly difficult" remains open to speculation.

28. *New York Times*, Sunday, 15 October 1905.

29. Wharton, *Writing of Fiction*, p. 61. Balzac is the writer whose work is generally considered to have had the greatest influence on Wharton's fictional methods.

30. Ibid., 81. See the chapters entitled "Constructing a Novel" and "Character and Situation."

31. Wharton, *Backward Glance*, 207.

32. Rachel Blau DuPlessis, *Writing beyond the Ending: Narrative Strategies of Twentieth-Century Women Writers* (Bloomington: Indiana University Press, 1985), 17, emphasis mine. Because Lily must become an object of beauty and desire, she opens herself to the speculation of the male gaze; the

marriage game is played according to the rules of scopophilic desire so powerfully dramatized in the tableaux vivants scenes. This game is Lily's "work," as serious a business for her as Wall Street is for men in this society. For a helpful discussion of the marriage quest as career in Wharton's fiction, see Wendy M. DuBow, "The Businesswoman in Edith Wharton," *Edith Wharton Review* 8, no. 2 (fall 1991): 11–18.

33. Wharton distanced herself from the American society scene by moving to France, first renting an apartment from the George Vanderbilts (1907 and 1908) and then in 1909 taking a long lease on an apartment of her own. Her charitable activities during the war brought her back into contact with New York and Newport "high society" when she solicited money from rich Americans to support her convalescent houses and sanatoria for tuberculous patients.

34. Edith Wharton, *The Fruit of the Tree* (New York: Scribner's, 1907), p. 423. Subsequent quotations from this edition will hereafter be cited parenthetically by page number.

35. Divorce was one of Wharton's major subjects, beginning with *Madame de Treymes* (1908), and was a staple of all her postwar fiction.

36. Contrary to some popularly held views, Wharton never considered marrying Morton Fullerton (nor did he ask her), and her decision to divorce Teddy was not directly linked to her friendship with Fullerton.

37. Edith Wharton was particularly sensitive to children's places in the family structure. She was a lonely (and perhaps even unwanted) child, born when her mother was almost thirty-eight years old. Her two brothers were twelve and sixteen years older than she. Contrary to the myth that she disliked, or was afraid of, children, she seems to have been immensely interested in them.

38. Jewett did not receive an agent's commission. He was salaried at Appleton's and served only informally as Wharton's fiction agent, as did Minnie Jones, who was her proofreader and drama representative in New York. Edith for many years provided financial assistance to Minnie and her daughter Beatrix.

Serial sales functioned in Wharton's lifetime rather like the paperback market does today—they were the source of "big monies." Unlike Scribner's, Appleton's did not have an in-house magazine. Jewett sold Wharton's novels twice: once to a magazine, once to Appleton's for book publication. Thus, he doubled her advance income on every novel. In the early years of her career, when she was not yet well known, Wharton had had the advantage of double publications with Scribner's (magazine and book), which drew wider interest in her work.

39. Mr. Vance of the *Pictorial Review*, quoted in Rutger B. Jewett to Edith Wharton, 14 October 1920, YCAL.

40. Rutger B. Jewett to Edith Wharton, 9 June 1921, YCAL.

41. Edith Wharton to Rutger B. Jewett, 21 December 1926, YCAL.

42. During the 1920s, Wharton received between $1,500 and $1,800 per short story, which would translate into fifteen times that amount now—$22,500 and $27,000. In the early 1930s, during the worst years of the Great Depression, she had difficulty placing her more serious work, but the *Saturday Evening Post* paid $2,000 for "A Glimpse" (1932) and *Hearst's International-Cosmopolitan* paid a record $5,000 for "Charm Incorporated" (1934), printed under a new title, "Bread upon the Waters," in its February 1934 issue. After the First World War, Wharton refused to publish with Hearst's magazines because she thought William Randolph Hearst had taken a pro-German stance during the war. Needing money during the depression years, however, she backed away from her political conviction and claimed that his magazines were the only ones that published worthwhile fiction.

43. Edith Wharton to Rutger B. Jewett, 26 October 1933, YCAL. See *The Letters of Edith Wharton*, ed. R. W. B. Lewis and Nancy Lewis (New York: Scribner's, 1988), 571–72.

44. Rutger B. Jewett to Edith Wharton, 29 December 1933, YCAL.

45. Quoted in Rutger B. Jewett to Edith Wharton, 11 January 1934. "Duration" appeared in the short-story collection, *The World Over* (New York: Appleton-Century, 1936). Although not one of her strongest stories, "Duration" is yet a powerful, if understated, comment on living "beyond the ending" of the old values and on the competition for recognition under the terms of modern society.

46. See Elisina Tyler's commentary on Edith Wharton's last days, LL.

The "*Perfect* Jew" and *The House of Mirth*

A Study in Point of View

IRENE C. GOLDMAN-PRICE

◆ ◆ ◆

WHEN EDITH WHARTON received a copy of F. Scott Fitzgerald's *The Great Gatsby*, she thanked the author, saying: "it's enough to make this reader happy to have met your *perfect* Jew" (emphasis Wharton's), and went on to praise the luncheon scene and the characterization of Meyer Wolfsheim as the parts of the novel that "make me augur still greater things!" (6/8/1925 in Lewis & Lewis 481). Wolfsheim, of course, was the man looking for a "gonnection," the man who fixed the 1919 World Series. Nick describes him as: "A small, flat-nosed Jew . . . with two fine growths of hair which luxuriated in either nostril," who eats "with ferocious delicacy" and talks about witnessing the gangland murder of his old friend, Rosy Rosenthal (69–71). In short, Wolfsheim is physically repugnant, socially unacceptable, morally reprehensible, and stinking rich. This, in 1925 at least, is Edith Wharton's *"perfect"* Jew.

The House of Mirth, conceived around 1900 and largely written during 1903–early 1905, presents another socially unacceptable rich Jew: Simon Rosedale. He is one of the suitors for the hand of the heroine, Lily Bart, and his social success offers chiastic contrast to Lily's decline. He is described as having "that mixture of artistic sensibility and business astuteness which characterizes his race," and "his race's accuracy in the appraisal of values," and when we first meet him he is unmistakably vulgar and distasteful: ". . . a small, glossy looking man with a gardenia in his coat," ". . . a plump, rosy man of the blond Jewish type, with smart London clothes fitting him like upholstery, and small sidelong eyes which gave him the air of appraising people as if they were bric-a-brac" (16).

Critics generally consider Rosedale, if they consider him at all, either as an outsider (Ammons, Lidoff, Showalter) or as the embodiment of the American business climate (Westbrook) or of a lower-class society that will inevitably be successful in entering the upper class (Trilling).[1] Often they mention him only in passing, but, interestingly, every critic, with the notable exceptions of Joan Lidoff and Wai Chee Dimock, in mentioning Rosedale labels him "a Jew" or "Jewish," despite the fact that they never mention any religious practices or habits. Evidently his Jewishness, for the critics as well as the author, has some important key to his identity and to his role in the novel unrelated to his actual religious behavior.

So what does it mean to Wharton to make Rosedale a Jew? Unlike George Eliot, who studied Jews and Judaism carefully for her *Daniel Deronda*, Wharton is not interested in depicting Jewishness from the inside. Rather, she views him very much from the outside, and she expects her reader to have the same associations with the term that she does. Therefore, for us to understand the characterization of Rosedale, and hence his role in the novel, we will require a shared understanding with Wharton of the categorization "Jew."

This understanding seems to me both quite crucial and long overdue, for Rosedale is a significant character in the novel. His position in society is a key indicator of what Wharton is trying to say about society, and society is the stated subject of her novel. In August of 1902, Henry James adjured Wharton in the strongest terms to "DO NEW YORK!" (*Letters* 33), something one assumes she was already thinking, as her first notes for the novel are in a notebook dated 1900. Wharton claimed in her memoirs that *The House of Mirth* was a study of "fashionable New York," "in all its flatness and futility," "a society of irresponsible pleasure-seekers" whose deeper bearing was its power of destruction. "Its tragic implication lies in its power of debasing people and ideas" (*Backward* 206–7).

If society is the focus of Wharton's novel, her message about it is not a simple one. Lily Bart, with her fine discriminations in taste and ethics, represents what it has bred at its best, and also what it destroys. But what does Simon Rosedale represent? Surely he is a foil for Lily, and his successes and increasing acceptance into society mirror her failures and rejection. But there is more. I will argue that Wharton uses Rosedale's Jewishness to illuminate economic issues and social hypocrisies in the society that would otherwise remain underground; by being a member of a race reputed to be vulgar and economically savvy, Rosedale can speak about subjects that are taboo to the others. He is, further, something more than a flat stereotype; Wharton's complex feelings of distaste yet sympathy, anti-Semitism yet admiration, create a complicated irony surrounding his characterization. I shall undertake an analysis of this characterization by looking beyond the text at Wharton's and her friends' experience of and attitudes toward Jews and at prevailing attitudes toward race in general around the late nineteenth century. With this information in mind, I shall suggest a fuller reading of the novel and a darker interpretation of Rosedale's presence in it.

By the time Wharton was writing *The House of Mirth*, there were three different Jewish communities inhabiting New York City: the Sephardic Jews, the German Jews, and the Eastern European Jews. The last group, most newly arrived, were then inhabiting the Lower East Side tenements, some of which were owned by Wharton's contemporaries. They were the least Americanized, of course, and the most alien to the old guard. But the Sephardic Jews, those of Spanish and Portuguese descent, came to this country at the same time as Wharton's own Dutch ancestors, shared similar occupations, and were largely assimilated, even to some degree into the "Old New York" society. Well into the 1890s, Hendrickses, Lazaruses, and Nathans (all Jews) belonged to the Union Club, the most exclusive club in the city, to which Joneses, Stevenses, and Schermerhorns (all Wharton's relatives) also belonged.

The second population of Jews to arrive in America, and the one from which Rosedale must have been drawn, were the German Jews, most of whom emigrated between 1837 and the 1880s. One of the earliest, and certainly the most prominent to Wharton's eyes, was August Belmont, who came to New York in early manhood on business for the house of Rothschild (Black). He married a society girl, and, as one New York socialite put it, "gained entrance to New York Society through the social position of his wife, coupled with his own participation in national affairs" (Van Rensselaer 172).

The issue of Belmont's name change illustrates how Anglo-Dutch prejudices colored society's vision of a man's life. It was long believed that Belmont's original name was Schoenberg and that he changed it himself in order to infiltrate society. Neither is true; such rumors seem to have arisen from society's self-important view that of course a socially ambitious man would want to change his name to fit in with them. Rather, his family name, Simon (much less Jewish-sounding), had been officially changed to Belmont in Alzey in 1808 under Napoleon's orders that all Jews take French surnames (Black, Katz). Yet this victimization was seen by society as his desire to become assimilated.

It has been argued that Belmont was the model for Simon Rosedale, but I don't share this opinion. Belmont was already long married into and accepted by good society by the time Wharton was born. Though he never converted from Judaism, he was married by a minister, and his children were baptized in the Episcopalian church. Further, he came to America already well schooled in European standards of fine foods, music, art, and aristocratic living and was in fact a force in forming taste rather than having it formed for him, as happens to Rosedale. Wharton herself mentions the Belmonts several times in *A Backward Glance*, and evidently they were among the families she visited both in

New York and in Newport; a good friend of hers married one of Belmont's sons.

Rosedale is much more of an outsider than Belmont. He seems to be drawn from the wealthy German Jewish businessmen making fortunes in retailing and investment banking at the end of the century (such now-familiar names as Seligman, Bamberger, Altman, Bloomingdale, Lehman, Goldman, Sachs, Bache, Schiff, Kuhn, Loeb). Those who were Wall Street investment bankers—bankers who loaned money in return for stock rather than for a note, like the Yankee commercial bankers—were indeed, like Rosedale, in the position to give "tips." Wharton and her set would not have seen much of them up close, as they maintained their own social lives apart from the "old New York" society. Nevertheless, their paths did cross on occasion, mostly in the political arena, but in others as well. Addie Wolff, for instance, daughter of a Kuhn, Loeb partner, had her debut in 1894 at Sherry's, the very place frequented by Lily Bart and her friends (Birmingham). Wharton's friend Theodore Roosevelt was one of the guests of an 1883 Purim party that took place in several houses in New York City (Glanz, 21–22). Otto Kahn became the first Jew on the board of directors of the Metropolitan Opera in 1903, until then an all-society board, and gradually other such boards accepted Jewish members.

Roosevelt, with whom Wharton dined at least once while writing *The House of Mirth*, and other of Wharton's politically active friends were of necessity involved with the Jews because of the bankers' strong patriotism and financial support of government activities. But rarely would they have met at private parties. A visiting Polish prince, for instance, when he mentioned a weekend he had spent at the Seligman home on the New Jersey shore, was taken aside in the Knickerbocker Club and instructed that, in America, one didn't socialize with Jews after business hours (Birmingham 263–66). As president, Roosevelt denounced overt public anti-Semitism and appointed a Jew, Oscar Straus, to be secretary of commerce. But when he went to a luncheon given by the Seligmans where at least half the guests were Jewish, he wrote to his sister that "I felt as if I was personally realizing all of Brooks

Adams' gloomiest anticipations of our gold-ridden, capitalist-bestridden, usurer-mastered future" (Dyer 125). Brooks's brother, Henry Adams, a good friend of Wharton's, was notoriously anti-Semitic and complained consistently from the 1860s until his death, from such diverse places as Vienna, Paris, Washington, D.C., and South Carolina, of being surrounded by Jews.[2]

While Wharton was coming of age, anti-Semitism became more and more visible and public among the upper class of the country. A watershed event was the 1877 incident at Saratoga, New York, where Joseph Seligman and his family were turned away from the Hilton-owned Grand Union Hotel. Though reparations were made and apologies issued, it became more acceptable publicly to deny access to jobs, housing, and privileges to "Hebrews." It was a time of social and financial insecurity on the part of the old guard. They were having to work harder to make their money and to keep their exclusive aristocratic status, and a variety of gestures toward consolidating and enhancing their privileged position were made. In 1887, when Wharton was twenty-five, the New York Social Register was first copyrighted, and the only German-Jewish name among the 2000 was Belmont's, though it also contained a number of the Sephardic Jews. Ward McAllister began talking about "the Four Hundred" most important New Yorkers (just enough to fit into the Astors' ballroom) in the late 1880s, and the Daughters of the American Revolution was founded in 1890. Between 1893 and 1897, America experienced a financial depression that exacerbated both the anti-immigration and the anti-Jewish feelings of the nation. Wharton's friend Senator Henry Cabot Lodge introduced legislation designed deliberately to keep Jews and southern Europeans, "who are most alien to the great body of the people of the United States" (qtd. in Weiss 133), from entering the country.

Racial ideologies were growing in importance as a way of understanding history, designing political policy, and perhaps reinforcing the wavering sense of superiority of the Anglo-Dutch upper class. Lodge, Adams, and Roosevelt were firm believers in and purveyors of this ideology. According to one historian:

> The force of race in history occupied a singularly important place in Roosevelt's broad intellectual outlook. In fact, race provided him with a window on the past through which he could examine the grand principles of historical development. None of human history really meant much, Roosevelt believed, if racial history were not thoroughly understood first. (Dyer 47)

Such men as Lodge, Adams, and Roosevelt—all friends of Wharton whom she was actively visiting during the time she was writing *The House of Mirth*—believed that American democracy derived from the Anglo-Saxon, Teutonic peoples and that the Aryan race was superior to others. Though originally a linguistic differentiation, in the nineteenth century the terms "Aryan" and "Semitic" took on a physical, anthropological meaning, and, despite research to the contrary (Fishberg), the Jews began to be considered a separate race. And to be a separate race meant more than just to have certain physical characteristics. Race meant, as Lodge put it:

> the moral and intellectual characters, which in their association make the soul of a race, and which represent the product of all its past, the inheritance of all its ancestors, and the motives of its conduct. The men of each race possess an indestructible stock of ideas, traditions, sentiments, modes of thought, an unconscious inheritance from their ancestors, upon which argument has no effect. What makes a race are their mental, and above all, their moral characteristics. . . . (Weiss 134)

Thus, the traits of avarice, business astuteness, and social vulgarity were seen as inherent to Jews.

Wharton's own ideas on race probably came from her early readings of Hippolyte Taine and William Lecky, whom she called, along with Darwin and Spencer, "the formative influences of my life" (to Sara Norton 3/16/08 in *Letters* 136).[3] Taine, in his famous Introduction to *History of English Literature*, noted that three sources contributed to a man's [*sic*] moral state: race, surrounding, and epoch ("race, milieu, et temps").

> What we call the race are the innate and hereditary dispositions which, as a rule, are united with the marked differences in the temperaments and structure of the body. They vary with various peoples. There is a natural variety of men, as of oxen and horses, some brave and intelligent, some timid and dependent, some capable of superior conceptions and creations, some reduced to rudimentary ideas and inventions, some more specially fitted to special works, and gifted more richly with particular instincts. . . . We have here a distinct force,—so distinct, that amidst the vast deviations which the other two motive forces produce in him, one can recognize it still. . . . (17)

William Lecky, Wharton's other influence, wrote a great deal specifically about the Jews. Patiently and with evident sorrow, he chronicled the various persecutions of the Jews all over the world and throughout time. But in "Israel among Nations," an 1893 review of Anatole Leroy-Beaulieu's book of that title, while still showing great sympathy and outrage at the persecution of the Jews, he nevertheless embraces certain attitudes about race and stereotypes about Jews that we would today refute. While marking their achievements in many fields, he characterizes the Jews as "shrewd, thrifty, and sober," with a "rare power of judging, influencing, and managing men," and asserts that "great Jewish capitalists largely control the money markets of Europe" (108). He then goes on at great length about the "physiological force and tenacity of the Jewish race-type" (109). Among his other observations, Lecky tells us that, although "great is the power of assimilation the Jewish race possesses, the charm and grace of manner seem to have been among the qualities they most slowly and most imperfectly acquire" (114). He discusses their *parvenu* status among the good society of Europe: their "love of the loud, the gaudy, the ostentatious, and the meretricious," and their inability to "master the happy mean between arrogance and obsequiousness" (115).

As the nineteenth century drew to a close, many books and pamphlets with anti-Semitic propaganda were published, far more than in earlier years (Singerman 6–14). These came particularly, though by no means solely, in conjunction with the debate on bimetallism and charged that the Jews ran the banks of England, France, and the United States, a charge that was never accurate, though certainly there were powerful Jewish financiers.

In popular literature, Jews were represented in stereotyped ways as aggressive and corrupt, frequently usurers and arsonists with names like Burnupsky and Blazenheimer. Wharton's literary friends and acquaintances, while somewhat less crude in their depictions, also included Jews in their writing, some in more, some less flattering ways. Henry James, in "Glasses" (1896), has a resort peopled gratuitously by "thousands of chairs and almost as many little Jews . . . wagg[ing] their big noses" (317). An heiress in his earlier "Impressions of a Cousin" (1883) is defrauded of her inheritance by a mysterious and sinister financier named Caliph, believed by the narrator (although we never know for sure) to be a Jew. Owen Wister, whose family was on close terms with the Whartons, published in 1903 *Philosophy 4*, a novel of undergraduate life at Harvard which contains a Jewish boy subject to ridicule both by his friends and by the narrator. And Henry Adams, in *Democracy*, gives us the Schneidekoupons (coupon-clippers), a surprisingly mild portrayal of a Jewish financier and his wife. Wharton, too, has a Jew in her story "The Last Asset," about which more later.

Further, Wharton most likely discussed with Henry James his fear of the Eastern European Jews who inhabited New York's Lower East Side. James was making his famous return trip to America while Wharton was writing the novel, and he saw her both at The Mount and in New York City. This was the trip he would write up in *The American Scene* with its famous chapter on the "swarming" of Israel, likening the Jews to fish, squirrels, monkeys, and ants, fearful of their masses, their poverty, their future blight upon the nation, and their stain upon the linguistic purity of his sacred English.

Such was the atmosphere in which Wharton was writing *The*

House of Mirth. To summarize: Wharton and her set believed that all people belong to a particular race and that this racial inheritance accounted for not just physical attributes but intellectual, linguistic, moral, and spiritual characteristics, as well. (Hence Wharton gives us her own long and detailed pedigree in *A Backward Glance* as a way of explaining how she became what she was.) She and her friends found Jews at best distasteful, although, when cleaned up, on an individual basis they could be quite presentable (she was shortly to count among her close friends two nonpracticing Jews: the Comtesse Robert de Fitz-James and Bernard Berenson). But, in the main, with their foreign ways, their natural bad taste, and their incorrect usage, their suspicious ability to make money quickly and to spend it quickly, Jews were to be at best avoided, at worst abhorred.

Wharton drew on her racial beliefs in writing *The House of Mirth.* She made racial references, not just to Rosedale but to a number of other characters in the novel, including Gus Trenor, Jack Stepney, Hudson Bart, and Percy Gryce. Lily herself is the product of "inherited tendencies" (311), and, most sad, finds her deepest impoverishment to come from a rootlessness born precisely of her having failed to connect to any family place, tradition, or loyalty. In a passage toward the end, we have a sense of Wharton's understanding of inheritance:

> as [Lily] looked back she saw that there had never been a time when she had had any real relation to life. Her parents too had been rootless, blown hither and thither on every wind of fashion, without any personal existence to shelter them from its shifting gusts. . . . *In whatever form a slowly accumulated past lives in the blood—whether in the concrete image of the old house stored with visual memories or in the conception of the house not built with hands but made up of inherited passions and loyalties—it has the same power of broadening and deepening the individual existence, of attaching it by mysterious links of kinship to all the mighty sum of human striving.* (331) (emphasis mine)

All of Lily's friends suffer more or less from this loss of their inheritance because of the "disintegrating influences" (332) of

ily from being raped
s, the hand of inher-
ith Gus in Rosedale's
or had the safeguard
erstep them because
mine). To Wharton,
heritance.
lale? Being a wealthy
ne necessary skills to
way into high society
the necessary polish
of society, or one of
ares Lily's "intuitive
ilgar and dangerous.
ild be an act of mis-
alter the purity of
ties, Rosedale is im-

e English language.
ge and a consequent
ard Glance she spends
-speaking about "the
in my childhood,"
in speaking English
goes on to speak of
ing:

il of the accepted
of the well-bred.
or the niceties of
ted their language
as their friends. It
bad" English, and
)

foundedly gone on
(186), offends both

nce of many of the

ı more serious is his
l need. "Never talk
ıs possible" was, ac-
f conversation," and
ackward 57). And yet
ıkness. The fact that
s not just to a judg-
his purposes in the

›ws the ideas of the
racial beliefs, all Jews
at appraising values"
ıbility to trade value
dmits his willingness
rovide him. Lily and
cs, and so, perhaps,
nt; Wharton is using
ticed covertly by all
nce of private life by
of course, as several
ted, in the market to
Dorset, too, offers Lily
ily ignores Selden to
erial resources. Rose-
when other society
›nomics, nevertheless
ıving to do with it.
ıch a pretense of ig-
ı the novel, she tells
ey one must have a
at one "might as well
ir is to have enough
tement. Nevertheless,
money, a truth Lily's
Jew, who "naturally"

speaks openly of such things, to force the old society to reexamine the hypocrisy of its feigned indifference to money? In this sense she uses the stereotype of the Jew in order to comment not on Rosedale's character but on his surroundings.

Here, as in "The Last Asset" (1904), the Jew takes blame for the avaricious and cruel behavior of the society member. In that story, although the marriage of a young innocent is accomplished by "a superlative stroke of business" (59) on the part of the girl's society mother, the man through whose eyes we see the action sees the situation as the result of her taking up with the Jewish baron, who marks for him "the first stage of his friend's decline" and who contributes to the "mephitic air" surrounding the young girl (69–70). Rosedale, who seems to Lily dangerous, socially ambitious, overly familiar, and too interested in money, is actually less of all of these things than are Lily's so-called friends. Bertha Dorset, for instance, is far more dangerous than Rosedale in the way she almost singlehandedly destroys Lily's reputation and hence her ability to earn a living. And why does Bertha do this? To retain her own money and power: precisely the motives ascribed to Rosedale in particular and Jews in general. And, as for familiarity, it is Gus Trenor, one of her own set, who imposes on her physically and socially, not Rosedale. It is Trenor, not Rosedale, who exhibits a distinctly ill-bred, sexually charged manner toward Lily in Rosedale's opera box and later comes close to raping her. And Selden, while purporting to love Lily, is always ready to believe the worst of her, while Rosedale knows that the behavior they accuse her of "ain't [her] style" (301). Rosedale acts at once as the scapegoat for and the emblem of the secret identities of society insiders.

Yet, while he might not be as bad as some, Rosedale, too, with his stock-taking eyes, is ill bred according to society standards. Though he turns out to have a number of good qualities—he is honest, he likes children, and he genuinely cares for Lily—he never loses his essential vulgarity. The irony of his increasing social acceptance as Lily becomes less and less acceptable cuts several ways.

One irony that Wharton does not seem to intend is that of

society's hold on Rosedale; how awful to be "mad to know the people who don't want to know" you (86). In this light, society has debased Rosedale as much as it claims itself debased by his presence. One could feel a poignancy at his financial and social success, which might be as empty for him as is David Levinsky's in Abraham Cahan's 1917 novel, particularly since he never gets the woman he loves. But the narrator does not exhibit this kind of sympathy for Rosedale; it seems that Rosedale's inner life was not of interest, or at least of use, to Wharton.

It is more likely that she intended a different kind of irony. If we embrace her view of Jews as impossibly vulgar and morally reprehensible (as Lily does, for instance, when she considers marrying him, thinking: "he would be kind . . . kind in his gross, unscrupulous, rapacious way, the way of the predatory creature with his mate" [259]), then his successful entry into society is a devastating indictment, particularly in light of Lily's expulsion. His very acceptance deep into the folds of society becomes proof that society is in an irretrievable decline.

Still, as we have seen, this outsider, this representative of a rapacious, predatory, vulgar outside world, is no worse, and may be better, because kindlier and more honest, than anyone inside the sacred society. Wharton knew this. It is no accident that even Selden, the supposed savior of Lily and her counterpart in retaining the refined sensibilities of an earlier age, is known to have had an affair with a married woman, Bertha Dorset, the most reprehensible character in the book. So the ultimate message to be read from Wharton's making her interloper a Jew might be that this society is *so* frivolous, *so* irresponsible, *so* wasteful, cruel, and self-serving, that even a vulgar Jew is better than they are.

This is a very dark reading of Wharton's feelings about Jews. It may or may not be the ultimate one of Rosedale's presence in the novel. One of the indicators of Wharton's accomplishments as a writer is that her portrait of Rosedale goes well beyond stereotype. Instead of simply making Rosedale rich and vulgar, she makes him a real person to us, and she has him change over time. His sins are primarily against taste rather than morality; we never actually see him perform an immoral act. Though he does suggest that Lily commit blackmail, he doesn't carry it out without her. Thus, we cannot easily judge or dismiss him. His racial characteristics may be used to comment on society, but his humanity, his love for Lily, his growth in social and moral perception, make him a central character in the book, a character in his own right, one whom we wonder about and perhaps care about more than we do the flatter characters, like the Dorsets and the Trenors, who populate society. The ambiguity and subtlety of his characterization make it impossible to come to a firm conclusion about him or about Wharton's use of him.

This investigation into the characterization of Simon Rosedale demonstrates the complexity of the use of racial stereotypes, particularly in the period from the 1870s to the 1930s. Critics have frequently unconsciously shared in the stereotyping by calling Rosedale a Jew despite any reference to his religious behavior. The challenge to literary critics, then, is to stop either unconsciously sharing literary stereotypes or glossing over them with labels such as "anti-Semitic" and to open the doors to full conversation on the depiction of Jews and other ethnic minorities in literary works.

Notes

The author wishes to acknowledge the Ball State University Office of Research for its assistance in funding some of the research and the members of the Edith Wharton Society, particularly Annette Zilversmit, for encouraging and assisting with this work.

1. Several Wharton scholars are now working on the issue of Rosedale's Jewishness, including Clare Colquitt and Annette Zilversmit.

2. Derogatory references to Jews abound in the correspondence of Henry Adams. To cite only a few, all available in W. C. Ford's 1938 collection: to Elizabeth Cameron, 8/10/1901, 8/14/1901; to C. M. Gaskell, 1/23/1894, 7/13/1896: "We are in the hands of the Jews. They can do what they please with our values," 2/19/1914; to Sir Robert Cunliffe, 2/17/1896.

3. I am indebted to Elsa Nettels for my first thoughts about Taine's influence on Wharton.

Works Cited

Ammons, Elizabeth. *Edith Wharton's Argument with America*. Athens: University of Georgia Press, 1980.

Auchincloss, Louis. *Edith Wharton: A Woman in Her Time*. New York: Viking, 1971.

Birmingham, Stephen. *Our Crowd: The Great Jewish Families of New York*. New York: Harper, 1967.

Black, David. *The King of Fifth Avenue: The Fortunes of August Belmont*. New York: Dial, 1981.

Cohen, Naomi W. *Encounter with Emancipation: The German Jews in the United States 1830–1914*. Philadelphia: Jewish Publication Society, 1984.

Dimock, Wai Chee. "Debasing Exchange: Edith Wharton's *The House of Mirth*." *PMLA* 100 (1985): 783–92.

Dyer, Thomas G. *Theodore Roosevelt and the Idea of Race*. Baton Rouge: Louisiana State University Press, 1980.

Fishberg, Maurice. "Materials for the Physical Anthropology of the Eastern European Jews." *Memoirs of the American Anthropological Association* 1905–7. New York: Kraus, 1964.

Fishman, Priscilla. *The Jew in the United States*. New York: Quadrangle, 1973.

Ford, Worthington Chauncey, ed. *The Letters of Henry Adams, 1892–1912*. Boston: Houghton, 1938.

Glanz, Rudolph. "German Jews in New York City in the Nineteenth Century." *YIVO Annual* 11 (1956): 9–38.

Hertzberg, Arthur. *The Jews in America*. New York: Simon and Schuster, 1989.

James, Henry. *The American Scene*. 1907. Bloomington: Indiana University Press, 1968.

———. "Glasses." *The Complete Tales of Henry James*, ed. Leon Edel. Vol. 9. Philadelphia: Lippincott, 1964. 317–70.

———. "The Impressions of a Cousin." *The Complete Tales of Henry James*, ed. Leon Edel. Vol. 5. Philadelphia: Lippincott, 1963. 111–93.

———. "To Edith Wharton 8/17/1902." In *Henry James and Edith Wharton: Letters: 1900–1915*, ed. Lyall H. Powers. New York: Scribner's, 1999. 33–35.

Katz, Irving. *August Belmont: A Political Biography*. New York: Columbia University Press, 1968.

Lecky, William E. H. "Israel among the Nations" (1893). In *Historical and Political Essays*. London: Longmans, Green, 1910.

Lidoff, Joan. "Another Sleeping Beauty: Narcissism in *The House of Mirth.*" *American Quarterly* 32 (1980): 519–39.

Madison, Charles A. *Eminent American Jews, 1776 to the Present.* New York: Ungar, 1970.

Nettels, Elsa. "Henry James and the Idea of Race." *English Studies* 59 (1978): 35–47.

Showalter, Elaine. "The Death of the Lady (Novelist): Wharton's *The House of Mirth.*" *Representations* 9 (1985): 133–49.

Singerman, Robert. *Anti-Semitic Propaganda: An Annotated Bibliography and Resource Guide.* New York: Garland, 1982.

Taine, Hippolyte. *History of English Letters,* Vol I: *1883.* Trans. H. Van Laun. Repr., New York: Ungar, 1965.

Trilling, Diana. "*The House of Mirth* Revisited." In *Edith Wharton: A Collection of Critical Essays,* ed. Irving Howe. Englewood Cliffs, N.J.: Prentice Hall, 1962. 103–18.

Van Rensselaer, Mrs. John King. *The Social Ladder.* New York: Henry Holt, 1924.

Weiss, Richard. "Racism in the Era of Industrialization." In *The Great Fear: Race in the Mind of America,* ed. Gary B. Nash and Richard Weiss. New York: Holt, Rinehart and Winston, 1970.

Westbrook, Wayne. "Lily-bartering on the New York Social Exchange in *The House of Mirth.*" *Ball State University Forum* 20 (1979): 59–64.

Wharton, Edith. *A Backward Glance.* New York: D. Appleton-Century, 1934.

———. *The House of Mirth.* 1905. New York: NAL, 1964.

———. "The Last Asset." 1904. In *The Hermit and the Wild Woman.* New York: Scribner's, 1914. 43–93.

———. *The Letters of Edith Wharton,* ed. R. W. B. and Nancy Lewis. New York: Scribner's, 1988.

Another Sleeping Beauty

Narcissism in The House of Mirth

JOAN LIDOFF

◆ ◆ ◆

DESPITE THE PRESENT renewal of interest in *The House of Mirth*, reminiscent of the enthusiasm that greeted its publication in 1905, criticism has not yet explained the single most powerful aspect of the novel: the extraordinary appeal of its heroine, Lily Bart. Lily somehow exceeds the bounds of critical definition as she does the intentions of Edith Wharton's narrative structure. She is one of the most compelling of the female spirits—Emma Bovary, Anna Karenina, Maggie Tulliver, Edna Pontellier—struggling to forge their own destinies, whom, as Diana Trilling points out, literary convention customarily destroys.[1] Critics have recognized the super-added energy of *The House of Mirth*[2] and acknowledged Lily's "mysterious appeal."[3] "Lily Bart is by far the most vivid of Mrs. Wharton's heroines," writes Louis Auchincloss.[4] "Simply as an example of imaginative portraiture," Irving Howe proclaims, she is "one of the triumphs of American writing."[5]

To Edith Wharton, Lily is an inevitable victim of destruction by social institutions' collective necessities. Wharton's declared intent was to illuminate the tragic possibilities of the idle society of the wealthy by showing what that society destroys.[6] Lily is "a captured dryad subdued to the conventions of the drawing-room" (11), conquered by the constant tension between social discipline and the spontaneous feeling of individual impulse. Yet, she rises out of the sea foam of this deterministic world with a power that far exceeds her role as a pawn of hostile social forces. Writes Irving Howe, "before the pathos of her failure, judgment fades into love,"[7] and readers do regularly fall in love with Lily. Lily charms the reader as she does the other characters in the novel (and as she has her creator). We are bewitched by the beauty of her grace and vitality of spirit, as well as her appearance. Irrationally, we wish with her for a prince to transport her from her troubled poverty to the paradise of wealth and security she craves; we concur in her yearning to live happily ever after.

These fairy-tale expectations are generated by the emotional structure of the plot; they are thwarted by that same structure. Lily dies at the novel's end, destroyed by the tyranny of social manners, but she is first the victim of the limitations of Wharton's fictive world. Richard Chase has declared that, "whenever it turns out to be a brilliant and memorable book, the American novel of manners will also be a romance."[8] *The House of Mirth*, I wish to argue, is primarily a romance of identity. Though it purports to be a novel of social realism (which Gary Lindberg convincingly places in the tradition of the novel of manners), it is controlled by a deeper underlying dynamic. Before the society the novel portrays makes life impossible for Lily, the novel's structure itself forbids the realization the character and plot seek. At the same time, Lily derives her extraordinary appeal from the nexus of primordial feelings the romance taps.

Traditionally, the romance form makes its external world out of its hero's inner world.[9] It populates a hero's journey of self-discovery with token figures representing aspects of himself which he must learn to confront and accept. Reading *The House of Mirth* as a romance, we see the conflicts. Lily encounters as internal: the other characters appear as aspects of her own needs and feelings. Her fate measures the success with which she resolves, or fails to resolve, these developmental conflicts.

The romance form generally permits resolution: an ending in which the hero reclaims the divided aspects of himself in a new personal and societal integration. Women's heroic journeys often end in failure because society offers women no adequate forms of active adulthood. When reality thwarts the forward progress of maturation by perpetuating childlike passivity in adult roles, dissonances are felt subtly within the female psyche. Lily is unable to move toward integration; she remains locked in the regressive emotional state of primary narcissism, which in turn mirrors her fictive world. This early developmental stage is characterized by a fusion of one's feelings and desires with the outside world. Difficult aspects of the self are projected onto others so that, rather than becoming coherent and realistic, the self-concept remains idealized. In this initial mechanism of projection, romance and narcissism are alike; however, while romance allows for recognition and thus reintegration, narcissism prohibits this self-knowledge.

In narcissism, the distinction between fantasy and reality is not clear. Similarly, Wharton's fiction confounds realism with romance. Failing to clarify the difference between the social world and the psychological, her novel does not stay consistently within either framework but tries to resolve issues from one dimension in terms of the other. What purports in her plot to be a mimetic description of the social world is often unconvincing as realism: a persistent inability to acknowledge aggressive drives (consistent with cultural images of femininity) results in a confusion within Wharton's narrative framework of the dynamics of moral causality with the psychological determinism of fantasy. Wharton provides many cues which encourage reading her novel of social realism as a romance. Lily's allegorical progress from house to house down the social scale invites us to read in romance's allegorizing, abstracting mode, as do the symbolically suggestive names: Lily and Rosedale, Bellomont, Stepney. Like the typical romance hero(ine), Lily is an orphan, powerless and alone in her quest for identity. None of the secondary figures are real Others with whom it would be possible for her to have a significant relationship. Silent spaces between characters remain unbridgeable because the characters themselves are the simplistic projections of unintegrated fragments of personality. Paradoxically, Wharton's fiction operates from a narcissistic fantasy of ecstatic oneness, while it creates a world in which communion is impossible and isolation inevitable.

In his introduction to the Gotham Library edition of *The House of Mirth,* R. W. B. Lewis notes that the drama in the human encounters in this novel is unrealized—artfully, he says, suppressed. But it is the drama of the novel as a whole that is inadequately realized. Emotional connections are not made, feelings and events are stopped short of completion. Lily is another Sleeping Beauty, slumbering in a dormant presexual state from which she never awakens.[10] Wharton's narrative not only portrays this state but itself suffers the same frustrations. A dynamic of repression animates, and de-animates, this fiction. The first book of *The House of Mirth* is consistently powerful; the scenes in Book II set up to mirror scenes of emotional force in Book I are, however, frequently inadequate. Lily's charged walk with Selden at Bellomont is reflected structurally by another walk with Rosedale which lacks all of the color and appeal of the first. Her visit to the working girl Nettie Struther and her infant and the death scene that concludes the novel are both stock sentimental pieces substituted for scenes of emotional climax or resolution. Even before the limitations of Lily's character doom her, she is damned to destruction by the constrictive walls of the inhibited psychic world from which Wharton has constructed her novel. This is the real locus of the determinism of Wharton's fiction, in which the consequences of social inhibitions are felt.

Simultaneously, however, Lily derives her potency as a character from the very emotional configuration which dooms her. In her later, more perfectly structured novel, *The Age of Innocence,* Wharton controls in a more balanced way the feelings she releases with Lily Bart, but no single character in that novel has quite Lily's appeal. Wharton's language most clearly reveals the potent emotional sources from which Lily is drawn. Lily is described by a consistent pattern of metaphors of unrestrained gratification and sensual delight that belong to the universal fantasy of Eden and appeal with the force of lost paradise.

Wharton surrounds Lily with the libidinal imagery of wish fulfillment. She is presented to us cushioned in pleasure: "Her whole being dilated in an atmosphere of luxury; it was the background she required, the only climate she could breathe in" (23). Having a totally sustaining environment, where "everything in her surroundings ministered to feelings of ease and amenity" (37), is not a luxury for Lily but a necessity. Her life is nourished, like an infant's, by an amniotic bath of sensual satisfactions. Her images are fluid: "She was like a water-plant in the flux of the tides, and today the whole current of her mood was carrying her toward Lawrence Selden" (51). With Selden, "the horizon expanded, the air grew stronger, the free spirit quivered for flight . . ." and a "sense of buoyancy . . . seemed to lift and swing her above the sun-suffused world at her feet" (62). Lily's characteristic motion is the graceful swing of free flight; she lives not in an earthbound world of gravity but in an unbounded fantasy world, free from the weight of cause and effect. The verbs which regularly describe her are: "glow," "throb," "dilate," "dazzle," "kindle," "shine," "delight," "quiver," "swing," "soar," "flow," "thrill"—expressions of quick sensual response, of energy that admits of no channeling. Lily is "buoyant," "charming," "radiant," "vivid," "intoxicating," "delicious," "elegant," "clear," "exhilarating"; this is the aura of her presence. Being wealthy is another metaphor for this safe and harmonious life of perfect and effortless pleasure. Marrying money, Lily assumes, would let her "soar into that empyrean of security [where] she would be free forever from the shifts, the expedients, the humiliations of the relatively poor" (47). In this world of wealth, sunlight "caresses" the furniture, rooms afford a view of "free undulations of a park" (37). In this Eden, one's beauty is sufficient magic to make all one's desires automatically materialize. And Lily is beautiful.

Wharton repeatedly uses chiaroscuro lighting to illuminate Lily's beauty dramatically against the background of drabness (moral and physical) of the other women around her. Lily feels that "the dinginess of her present life threw into enchanting relief the existence to which she felt herself entitled" (32). The first view we have of Lily is through Selden's eyes; he sees her among the throngs at the train station and wonders, "Was it possible that she belonged to the same race? The dinginess, the crudity of this average section of womanhood made him feel how highly specialized she was" (3). (Selden too has features that "[give] him the air of belonging to a more specialized race.") Lily explicitly articulates the perception that she is "a creature of a different race . . . with all sorts of intuitions, sensations and perceptions that [others] don't even guess the existence of" (46).

Lily is persistently characterized by this metaphor of specialness: she sits, stands, and walks apart from others. The special race to which Wharton makes Lily and Selden belong is that of the fairy-tale royalty of Freud's family romance, a fantasy generally outgrown, or suppressed, with childhood. Freud describes the typical childhood notion that one is a changeling, the offspring of royal parents mistakenly placed among commoners but in truth exalted above them. This fantasy is an attempt to preserve the narcissistic image of perfection in the face of inevitable disappointments.[11] The dark underside of this glorification is the instability formed of the child's fears and feelings of powerlessness.

Similarly, beneath the metaphors of beauty and specialness runs another strain of Lily language. Holistic and absolute, Lily's moods swing between the intoxicating rush of triumphant excitement and dull despair. The brilliance and intensity of her highs is predicated on the bleak emptiness of her lows. Beneath the free air where her spirit quivers, expands, and swings buoyantly (62) is a "prison-house of fears" (61). When things go wrong, she feels not moderate disappointment or frustration but a deep self-disgust. Never seen as a competent, adult woman, Lily is regarded as a commodity, a beautiful object of art,[12] but she is also often imaged as a troubled, helpless child, "longing for shelter, for escape from . . . humiliating contingencies" (94). Lurking under the imagery of sensual gratification is a second language of intense, ungratifiable neediness and fear, of a tenacious hunger for comfort and security.

Lily's encounters with Selden elicit from her both extremes of feelings. In the splendid scene at Bellomont, the luxurious country house where they are guests, Lily walks through the gardens and woods to sink into a rustic seat in a set romantic scene. She knows the charm of the spot is enhanced by the charm of her presence, "but she was not accustomed to taste the joys of solitude except in company" (58). She wilts: "She felt a stealing sense of fatigue as she walked; the sparkle had died out of her, and the taste of life was stale on her lips. She hardly knew what she had been seeking, or why the failure to find it had so blotted the light from her sky: she was only aware of a vague sense of failure, of an inner isolation deeper than the loneliness about her" (58). When Selden appears, she instantly bubbles back into the luxury of enjoyment and gaiety that comes with their meetings. The fluid joy of unspoken communication between them brings a feeling of oceanic oneness, but it is in fact extremely fragile. With any disagreement, "the flow of comprehension between them was abruptly stayed." "It was as if the eager current of her being had been checked by a sudden obstacle which drove it back upon itself. She looked at him helplessly, like a hurt or frightened child: this real self of hers, which he had the faculty of drawing out of the depths, was so little accustomed to go alone" (92).

The fragility of Lily's self-image becomes increasingly apparent. Like a "sea anemone torn from [its] rock" (295), she is unable to exist alone. The first book ends with a statement that quakes with unintended irony: "It would take the glow of passion to weld together the shattered fragments of her self-esteem" (171). Lily's glow feeds on the absence rather than the abundance of internally animating energies; the intensity of her intoxication manifests her dependence on others for all of her self-esteem. Isolation is terrifying to her: her whole sense of being requires another's presence. Yet, she is prohibited by her own emotional structure, and that of the novel she inhabits, from any possibility of receiving from or giving to others. She appears lovely, a fantasy of perfection. But coexisting with this idealized self is another, characterized by a deep void of deficient confidence and stability. As the glowing Edenic imagery of the first book fades, the novel's second book is progressively dominated by language of deprivation, anxiety, resentment, and fear. The persecution and disintegration that Lily experiences in the plot are not unrelated to her loveliness; they are intrinsic to it. As her charm plays out the graces of narcissistic pleasures, so her fall from social grace, her progressive isolation, and her victimization by vengeful characters who have the power she does not to initiate action enact the underside of the narcissistic fantasy.

THE TERM "NARCISSISM" is now in vogue in the currency of social criticism. As a psychoanalytic concept, it is undergoing reformulation at the hands of Heinz Kohut and Otto Kernberg.[13] I mean it here neither in the diluted common usage as "self-love" nor in the clinical sense as a specific pathological personality structure. While narcissism is dysfunctional as an overall personality defense, Kohut elaborates Freud's formulation to argue that the infant's universally shared primary narcissism can be perpetuated in adults as one in a repertory of responses, a residue we retain from the infant's initial feeling of oneness with the mother. Lily partakes of both its appeals and its dysfunctions. Derived from the intense, instinctual level of experience, the narcissistic state is wedded to libidinal energy and sensual pleasure. A striving to return to the elation of this oceanic fusion informs mythologies of Paradise and symbols of Eden's garden. Its sensuality and illusion of oneness exercise continuing appeal in sexuality and in mythologies of romantic love.

The libidinal imagery that defines Lily and her sense of specialness are those of the infant's Eden; the fantasy she speaks to of eternal power, wealth, youth, and beauty derives from this paradise free from both work and mortality. Originally, the infant experiences all his needs as being gratified instantaneously and completely by the nurturing mother, whom he perceives as an extension of his own being. Believing his needs and desires to be congruent with [those of] the external world, the infant does not feel the necessity of producing effects by generating causes, of earning his own satisfactions. Wishes, not actions, motivate his world. The expectation of automatic fulfillment and delight translates into a sense of specialness, of exemption from the laws of causality that govern others' fates.

The habit of perception characteristic of infant narcissism is called "primary process thinking." For sequential, linear causality, it substitutes symbolism and holistic magic. Monolithic, this world view does not allow the possibility of change or development; everything seems absolute, permanent. All perceptions are rigidly polarized—black or white, on or off, with no tolerance for ambiguity or doubt. The emotional affects of narcissism are either elation or despair, without modulation.

This polarization is absolute because the narcissistic state precedes the development of initiative or assertion; narcissistic thinking cannot acknowledge drives—the wish to act autonomously to attain one's desires, or the capacity to do so. While narcissism presumes magical security and gratification, it in fact entails vulnerable and passive dependence on the generalized environment to provide satisfaction. Its idealized self-image of omnipotence and perfection is preserved only by projecting aggressive feelings onto others, whose helpless, innocent victim the narcissist then becomes. Otto Kernberg explains the need to cling to the narcissistic self-concept: "To accept the breakdown of the illusion of grandiosity means to accept the dangerous lingering awareness of the depreciated self—the hungry, empty, lonely, primitive self surrounded by a world of dangerous, sadistically frustrating and revengeful objects."[14] Kernberg's description of narcissistic dynamics summarizes the latter half of *The House of Mirth.*

In Wharton's fiction, as in narcissistic thought, characters and alternative actions frequently are presented as black or white, good or bad. There are no possibilities of compromise or moderate resolution. This fictive world suggests the romance realm of fairy tales, wherein, as Bruno Bettleheim explains, such polarization and externalization of fantasy can be used to work developmental conflicts through to resolution.[15] *The House of Mirth* is sprinkled with fairy-tale allusions. Wharton often uses the language of fairy-tale magic for Lily and gives her magical powers. She has a Prince Charming in Selden, a frog prince in Gus Trenor, a wicked stepmother in Bertha Dorset, and an evil stepsister in Grace Stepney. Lily herself plays Sleeping Beauty, though one who fails at her initiation rites of awakening (as she is failed by those who should help her in those tasks). Wharton appears to be writing an adult version of the stories which, in her childhood, were too frightening for her to face. She writes, in *A Backward Glance*, "I never cared much in my little-childhood for fairy tales, or any appeals to my fancy through the fabulous . . . my imagination lay there, coiled and sleeping, a mute hibernating creature." "Fairy tales bored me," she declares.[16] Cynthia Griffin Wolff's biography of Wharton suggests that this boredom was in fact a defense, that as a child, Wharton was "made acutely uncomfortable by their primitive emotional directness." When writing gave Wharton the tools to begin to reexamine feelings that were overwhelming to her when she was young, she was able to return to those emotional depths and began to write her own fairy tales—in the form of romance.

Lily's appeal testifies to the success with which Wharton was able to free the rich resonances of early narcissistic longing and the elation of wish fulfillment. At the same time, Wharton maintained some of her earlier ambivalence about acknowledging these emotions, manifested in the novel's unsettled combination of realism and romance. The novel is uneasily cast in a satiric mode, a rigid protective style of distancing emotion by rational and verbal artifice. But Wharton's various strategies of narrative control are only partially successful, their fragility belied by the way feeling repeatedly breaks through. When Lily is pressed by Judy Trenor to participate in the nightly gambling at Bellomont, she is afraid to get involved. Like Pope's "The Rape of the Lock," this card game proceeds on a level of sexual double entendre. Lily fears "the gambling passion" that overtakes her. She "knew she could not afford it" (24). Once caught up in its exhilaration, her spending and repentance are both profligate. Lily has realized that "the luxury of others was not what she wanted." Beginning "to feel herself a mere pensioner on the splendor which had once seemed to belong to her," she is becoming "conscious of having to pay her way" (23). But the ambivalent activity of gambling is the only form of adult responsibility available to Lily. For both Lily and the novel itself, when feeling is released, it does run out of control, because there are no realistic channels to shape it.

Wharton casts this story, dominated by emotional issues, into social and financial terms. Both characters and narrator persistently confound the language of love and money: love is spoken of in terms of cost, expense, value, while the stock market is discussed in the language of dependence and independence, betrayal, suffering, and sympathetic affection (cf. 117). Wharton's intent in this metaphorical interchange of love and money is sometimes patently satiric, but it is not always clear that she is controlling, rather than controlled by, the substitution. "The underflow of a perpetual need" that tugs at Lily's family is as much a need of emotional security as it is "the need of more money" as Wharton declares. This metaphoric confusion reflects the narrative's inconsistent intermingling of romance with realism.

Wharton's attitude toward her heroine is similarly inconsistent. Although, like Selden, she tries to make Lily a satiric object, Lily's charm exceeds the confinement of that characterization; Wharton's deepest sympathies are aroused by her heroine. At the same time, her punitive assessment of Lily is harsh in the extreme, taking its ultimate form in Lily's death. The judgmental dichotomizing in Wharton's thinking prevents her beautiful child from becoming a heroine as much as do the real constrictions in Lily's social world that prohibit her from overcoming her childishness.

Polarizing characters and action with the absolutism of primary process fantasy, Wharton establishes impossible alternatives for her heroine; Gerty Farish, especially, is used blatantly "to throw [Lily's] exceptionalness into becoming relief" (86). "Fatally poor and dingy" (86), Gerty provides a dim background against which Lily glows. They are set up as diametrical opposites. Gerty's "eyes were of a workaday grey and her lips without haunting curves" (86). Her gown is of a "useful" color, her hat has "subdued lines" (86). Lily finds "something irritating in her assumption that existence yielded no higher pleasures" (86); and, indeed, Gerty is as excessive in her expectation of too little pleasure from life as Lily is in hers of too much. When Lily considers whether she should marry Percy Gryce, she sees only two choices for herself: "It was a hateful fate—but how to escape from it? What choices had she? To be herself, or a Gerty Farish." To be Gerty means to live in an environment "cramped," "cheap," "hideous," "mean," "shabby," "squalid," while Lily enjoys one of total luxury, beauty, and charm, of softly shaded lights, lace, silk, embroidery, perfume (23).

In her conception of Gerty and Lily, Wharton makes a complete and exclusive dichotomy of pleasure and usefulness: Lily's mode is all pleasure, Gerty's all use. There is no connection, for character or narrator, between cause and effect, activity and gratification, work and pleasure. Wharton describes Lily's family life as alternating between "grey interludes of economy and brilliant reactions of expense" (26). The passive expectation of swinging between extremes is all that is available to Lily, who is inhibited from action by thinking she has only two rigidly conceived and equally unsatisfactory choices. This all-or-nothing thinking is immature, but within the terms of the novel it is realistic. Wharton gives Lily only the two radical alternatives (or nonalternatives) she perceives for herself.

The one instrument with which Wharton allows Lily to initiate action works only by holistic magic. The source of Lily's power to move others is felt to be her beauty, which is conceived as a Platonic ideal, not an expression of adult sexuality. To look on Lily's "loveliness was to see in it a natural force, to recognize that love and power belong to such as Lily" (162). Selden considers Lily's beauty a part of "that eternal harmony" (131), and Lily herself believes it part of "her power, and her general fitness to attract a brilliant destiny" (85). (Her mother has trained her to feel that she can give her beauty "a kind of permanence" and use it to win her fortune.) Wharton shares this fantasy of beauty's permanence and power; at the end, she will preserve Lily for us by her death, forever beautiful, forever young.

In one of the novel's key scenes, the tableau vivant in which Lily displays herself, literally, as an art object, Wharton shows that Lily does have some of the transforming powers she believes she

has. The tableau scene is set to give us "magic glimpses" into "the boundary world between fact and imagination" (130). With Selden we "yield to vision-making influences as completely as a child to the spell of a fairytale" (130) and give ourselves to "the desire to luxuriate a moment in the sense of complete surrender" (132). Lily's audience reacts to her beautiful self-presentation with a "unanimous 'Oh' " (131), in an undifferentiated collective spirit whose warm bath makes her joyful. She is pleased to find herself the center of a "general stream of admiring looks" (133). "The individual comments on her success were a delightful prolongation of the collective applause. . . . Differences of personality were merged in a warm atmosphere of praise, in which her beauty expanded like a flower in sunlight" (133).

Lily evokes from others the response of preautonomous oceanic pleasure in which she thrives. "The completeness of her triumph gave her an intoxicating sense of recovered power" (133). While Lily's elation, the excitement of a successful performer after charming an audience, is credible, it is also illusory; she mistakes the confection of general admiration for substantial emotional sustenance. Her pleasure stands in ironic and inverse proportion to her real isolation. Loved by everyone in general, she is loved by and loves no one in particular. The autointoxication of this scene is the drunkenness of displaced sexual attraction but, significantly, its pleasures remain nonspecific and nonsexual. Both her audience's responses and her own are global and diffuse, not active but passive, not other-oriented but incorporative, oral without being genital.

Lily's, and Wharton's, choice of Lawrence Selden as a love object is a primary manifestation of the confusion of passive with active modalities. Wharton suggests that Lily and Selden are possible lovers, but, like Selden's "Republic of the Spirit," their love has no material base. That both they and Wharton believe it might leads to Lily's destruction. Selden is the one character who elicits Lily's romantic longings. Yet, in Lily's relationship with Selden, Wharton dramatizes most concretely Lily's inevitable isolation. When Lily charms Percy Gryce on a train, miraculously making materialize for him a little table of delicacies and bewitching him into eloquence, Wharton satirizes the fairy-tale scene she sets up and the magical powers with which she endows her heroine.[17] But in Lily's scenes with Selden, Wharton herself concedes to the romanticism. They meet in paradisal atmospheres, imbued with the sensual color and protected security of the Edenic fantasy, but also with its comcomitant passivity. On a hill looking down on Bellomont, "the soft isolation of the falling day enveloped them: they seemed lifted into a finer air. All the exquisite influences of the hour trembled in their veins, and drew them to each other as the loosened leaves were drawn to earth" (70). Characteristically, they "stay silent while something throbbed between them in the wide quiet of the air"; "neither seemed to speak deliberately . . . an indwelling voice in each called to the other across unsounded depths of feeling" (64). For Lily and Selden, silences remain unbreakable; there is never any possibility of completed intercourse—verbal or physical—between them. Invariably, their encounters culminate in frustration, not climax; the novel itself concludes with a silence made permanent by Lily's death. Scenes between Lily and Selden operate with the intensity of suppression; they remain frozen in magical expectations without pragmatic means of realization.

The limitations of this characteristic imagery of hazy softness, miracle and magic are immediately apparent in their inappropriateness to practical financial dealings. While the need for money to sustain life is a social reality of utmost immediacy, Lily's attitudes toward money manifest her expectation that the material world should operate as fantasy does. She thinks about money in the language of magic: she is upset when she cannot "conjure back" a "vanished three hundred dollars" (25). Needing cash, she goes to Gus Trenor "with the trustfulness of a child." "Through the general blur her hopes dilated like lamps in a fog. She understood only that her modest investments were to be mysteriously multiplied without risk to herself; and the assurance that this miracle would take place in a short time, that there would be no tedious interval for suspense and reaction, relieved her . . ."(82).

When Gus Trenor lures Lily to his deserted townhouse, his

attempt to use his financial and physical power to coerce her sexually makes explicit the real connections among money, power, and sex that Lily has purposefully kept from her awareness. But the language and imagery Wharton uses in this scene show her own confusions, deeper than the social drama, though undeniably arising from it. Unlike any of the romantic and always frustrated scenes with Selden, the handsome prince, the scene of the attempted rape is the only one in the novel written in the rising and completed rhythms of sexual climax.

Contrasted with Lily's "freshness and slenderness" (77), Gus Trenor, sweaty, "red and massive" (77), with a "puffing face" cast in deep crimson by a match's glow, is her frog prince. (When a fairy-tale princess matures beyond her youthful fears of sexuality, she kisses the frog, who is then revealed as a handsome prince; Lily, however, is unable to transcend her early repugnance to unite the two figures.) Lily's scenes with Selden are filled with throbbing and blushing. With Gus, these reactions are intensified, but in fear and anger. His resentful verbal attack makes her feel her "frightened heart throbs." "The words—the words were worse than the touch: Her heart was beating all over her body in her throat, her limbs, her helpless, useless hands" (142). "Trenor's face darkened to rage: her recoil of abhorrence had called out the primitive man." He comes closer "with a hand that grew formidable" (141–42). "She felt suddenly weak and defenseless: there was a throb of self-pity in her throat" (142). When he threatens her verbally "the brutality of the thrust gave her the sense of dizziness that follows on a physical blow" (141). "She flamed with anger and abasement." "Over and over her the sea of humiliation broke—wave crashing on wave . . ." (143). When, at the last minute, Gus withdraws, "the sharp release from her fears restored Lily to immediate lucidity. The collapse of Trenor's will left her in control" (144).

Although this is a scene of verbal confrontation whose explicit emotions are fear and anger, its imagery builds in a pattern of sexual tension and release. Its aftermath for Lily is severe shock. "All the while she shook with inward loathing. On the doorstep, . . . she felt a mad throb of liberation." But, once outside and safe, "reaction came, and shuddering darkness closed on her" (144). Lily reacts with terrified dissociation: "She seemed a stranger to herself, or rather there were two selves in her, the one she had always known, and a new abhorrent being to which it found itself chained" (144). "There was a great gulf fixed between today and yesterday. Everything in the past seemed simple, natural, full of daylight—and she was alone in a place of darkness and pollution" (145).

Although Lily is a creature of beauty and sensual charm, sexuality is not an acceptable part of her self-image. Responsibility is transferred to a male character; sexuality becomes Gus Trenor's domain, as hostility will be projected onto Bertha Dorset. The passionate imagery of fulfillment is therefore released from its pressurized control only in the context of brute force and coercion (in short, rape).

The brutality of Lily's encounter with Gus Trenor is complementary to the recurring frustration of her emotionally and physically unconsummated relation with Selden. Inhibited by the same fears that constrain Lily. Wharton has divided her characters in such a way that sexuality is isolated from both loving concern and romantic longing. The only male character who is realistic in his daily behavior and genuinely concerned about Lily is Simon Rosedale, whom she finds wholly unattractive. Structurally, Wharton suggests that Rosedale would be a proper mate for Lily and has named him accordingly. But she is ambivalent toward him.[18] From the start, each encounter between Lily and Rosedale attempts a negotiation of intimacy, but since Lily is incapable of the closeness he offers, it remains unattractive to her. The first chapter of *The House of Mirth* begins with Lily's tête-à-tête with Selden and ends with her shunning Rosedale's proffered escort; this is the destructive movement of the novel as a whole.

While Selden, like the narrator, sees Lily through an aesthetic haze and simultaneously passes harsh moral judgments upon her, Rosedale understands her plainly and accepts her simply. He is the only man who is genuinely kind to Lily and the only one to tell her he loves her. Unlike any of the other voices in the novel, including the narrator's, Rosedale does not confuse the language of love and money but talks of money when he means money and love when he means love. Lily and Rosedale engage in honest dialogue and confrontation as Lily and Selden never do, but neither Lily nor the novel can accept familiarity because any intimacy is perceived as threatening. Rosedale's advances seem to Lily excessive, "intrusive," "odious"; they freeze her into repugnance (111).[19]

Selden and Rosedale are repeatedly juxtaposed in consecutive or reflecting scenes which should make Rosedale's virtues apparent but instead highlight Selden's appeal. Book I ends as Lily awaits Selden in her drawing room; Rosedale comes instead. Selden has deserted her; Rosedale offers marriage, but Lily feels such extreme disappointment over Selden's absence that Rosedale's presence is nothing but an irritation. When in Book II Lily walks with Rosedale, Wharton explicitly recalls her earlier golden September walk with Selden, which evoked the soaring freedom of flight. In contrast, this November day "outlined the facts with a cold precision unmodified by shade or color, and refracted, as it were, from the blank walls of the surrounding limitations" (247). As she did with Gerty Farish, Wharton makes a life of practical action within accepted limitations seem intolerably harsh.

Considering that she might one day have to marry Rosedale, Lily feels that he stands for "one of the many hated possibilities hovering on the edge of life." Unlike Lily, or Selden, Rosedale operates from a real material base; he "set about with patient industry to form a background for his growing glory." "I generally *have* got what I wanted in life" (172), he tells Lily. It is just the possibilities which make life possible that violate Lily's world of oceanic narcissism. As Gus Trenor was her frog prince, so Rosedale is her Rumplestiltskin, representing qualities she is unable to integrate within her own personality. An adult figure of autonomous in dustry, Rosedale shows the initiative and assertion that Lily fears and shuns—as she does him.

In the novel's only congenial scene of domestic "repose and stability" Wharton shows Rosedale with Carry Fisher's daughter, in a pose of "simple and kindly" "homely goodness" (243). But Lily is unable to decide whether this sight "mitigated her repugnance, or gave it, rather, a more concrete and intimate form" (244). When she considers Rosedale's offer of marriage, she cannot imagine further than her betrothal: "after that everything faded into a haze of material well-being . . . there were . . . certain midnight images, that must at any cost be exorcised—and one of these was the image of herself as Rosedale's wife" (242–43).

No image of Lily as wife is possible in the imaginative world of this novel. Dividing essential qualities among disparate male characters, Wharton has not created a hero whom Lily might marry. But marriage is more than a literal solution for Lily and for the plot; it is a symbolic affirmation of maturity. Lily cannot marry because she is incapable of love. Both ability to love and the capacity for moral responsibility are predicated on the integration of sexual and active impulses. Wharton, however, rejects all assertive drives in symbolically coherent metaphors of pollution. In her Aunt Peniston's house, Lily resents the smell of wax and soap; she "behaved as though she thought a house ought to keep clean of itself, without extraneous assistance." Lily's encounters with the cleaning woman she here resents thread through the novel from beginning to end as moments of moral crisis. When Mrs. Haffen comes to Lily offering her letters with which to blackmail Bertha Dorset and restore her own good name, Lily shuns her offer with disdain, as she has earlier evaded her flood of soap suds. Wharton suggests that Lily's disgust and sense of contamination are noble, that her refraining is an act of moral courage (102). It is also, however, a refusal to get her hands dirty in taking practical action on her own behalf. Lily obscures the necessity of acting to promote her own needs or of acknowledging her potent desires for revenge; she maintains the idealized purity of her self-image at the ultimate cost of preserving her life.

The specific metaphor of dirt and cleanliness in which Lily's avoidance of adult responsibility is expressed recalls an oft-quoted reminiscence of Wharton herself, one which suggests a specific connection to childhood mothering. In her autobiographical *A Backward Glance*, Wharton tells of her first "novel," which began:

> ' "Oh, how do you do, Mrs. Brown?" said Mrs. Tompkins. "If only I had known you were going to call I should have tidied up the drawing-room." ' Timorously I submitted this to my mother, and never shall I forget the sudden drop of creative frenzy when she returned it with the icy comment: "Drawing-rooms are always tidy."[20]

C. G. Wolff's biography demonstrates that this anecdote is not anomalous but typical of Wharton's impaired relation with her cold and demanding mother.

The array of mother figures in *The House of Mirth* also suggests a pervasive psychic configuration of inadequate maternal nurturance and support. Lily's troubles with sexual love and adult responsibility are symptomatic of a deeper problem. The key to Lily's relation with the male figures of the novel is in her relation to the female figures. The primary motivations that determine the plot of *The House of Mirth* are not actions with or among the men but feelings of resentment and revenge among the women. Lily encounters a host of inadequate mother figures as she sinks from one to another down the social scale. Maternal intimacy suffers the same fate in this novel as sexual intimacy and is in fact the model for it. The women who are concerned about Lily are made unattractive and powerless. Gerty Farish, truly generous and reliable, is persistently undercut by being made working-class, poor and drab, and a martyr who lacks sufficient sense of emotional preservation. When Carry Fisher is seen with her daughter in a maternal light, Lily finds her affection rather distasteful (as she does Rosedale's paternal pose in the same scene). Judy Trenor, an affectionate and giving friend at the start, is seen ultimately to be only a shallow, socially contingent creature who "could not sustain life except in a crowd" (38).[21]

While Lily's good-mother figures are only ambivalently good and tend toward satiric caricature, the bad mothers are selfishly neglectful or powerfully destructive. Lily's Aunt Peniston, her official guardian whose home Lily finds ugly and impersonal, is caricatured with some of the vicious grotesquerie with which

Flannery O'Connor images her potent and oppressive mother figures (cf. p. 32). In the money-for-love metaphor of this novel, Mrs. Peniston, the essence of female passivity and repression, gives her niece erratic gifts of money that encourage dependence, rather than the trust necessary for autonomy and self-regard (cf. p. 36). Influenced by Lily's poor cousin, Grace Stepney, the wronged and vengeful fairy-tale stepsister, Mrs. Peniston disinherits Lily. In the end, both love and money fail.

The woman whose actions are most immediately responsible for Lily's fate and for the mechanical workings of the novel's plot is Bertha Dorset. Just as Gus Trenor was made the villain of disowned sexuality, so Bertha becomes a malevolent presence, allowing Lily to be seen as the innocent victim of her manipulations and desires. The only fully enfranchised adult woman in the novel, Bertha is active, sexual, rich, powerful—and ruthlessly evil. She is made as vicious as the wicked stepmother of fairy tales, the cruel being created from the projected hostility of a child's resentment at wrongs done and love not given, from fears of retaliation for forbidden wishes. Like the feminine figure of projected evil in romances of male development, as long as she cannot be owned and reintegrated, her existence conceptually impedes the heroine's maturation.

While Wharton describes "an unavowed hostility" and a "thirst for retaliation" (116–17) between the two women, she attributes them not to Lily but to Bertha. Bertha first sabotages Lily's designs on Gryce, out of envy of Lily's relation with Selden (who has been Bertha's lover); finally, Bertha camouflages a real love affair of her own by implying that Lily is having an affair with her husband. In a brilliant scene in a restaurant, Bertha ruthlessly destroys Lily's reputation by exposing her to public humiliation. The metaphors of Lily's encounters with Bertha are of battles in which words are weapons, weapons that "could flay [their] victims without the shedding of blood," and Bertha is "unscrupulous in fighting for herself" (207).

This triangle with the Dorsets is a variant of the earlier scenario with the Trenors. In both, by a series of thin coincidences of bad luck and bad timing, Lily is observed in what seem to be sexually compromising situations. Her reputation is polluted; the resulting social ostracism indirectly causes her death. Unconvincing as literal plot, these scenes are rather unexamined Oedipal fantasies which both project responsibility onto the powerful figures of Gus or Bertha and punish Lily for specious guilt. The unresolved Oedipal triangle, however, is a more specific symbol of the pervasive psychic configuration of this novel's world: where inadequate nurturance and support lead to undeveloped self-esteem and a consequent inability to love or to work, the heroine remains fixed in passive dependency and the hungers of the unnurtured childhood state. The mode of primary narcissism remains her dominant emotional style.

The erratic giving and withholding of maternal affection or support is reflected by Lily's male lovers. Selden, especially, is critical and judgmental; he lets her down whenever she needs him most. Yet, Lily is compelled to seek in the global fantasies of romantic love, of which he is the focus, a regressive mother-love of total acceptance and nurturance. The language of dark and hollow craving that surfaces repeatedly in the latter parts of the book reveals the extent to which Lily is controlled by the pervasive childlike neediness that is the underside of her narcissistic ecstasy. With no home, "no heart to lean on" (145) in moments of crisis, craving "the darkness made by enfolding arms" (145), Lily runs to Gerty Farish in "the open misery of a child" (162), and Gerty holds her "as a mother makes a nest for a tossing child" (164).

The scenes in which Wharton attempts to restore Lily to a nurturing relationship do not work. When Lily visits the working girl Nettie Struther and her infant, Wharton tries to use Nettie's good marriage and the baby, who reappears in Lily's fantasies as she drifts into the dream of her ambiguous suicide, to suggest the transcendence of the need for mothering in becoming a mother and experiencing nurturing feelings for a new infant. But the scene is drawn from fiction's stock, not from the novel's deeper sensibilities. The retreat to conventional devices is only a fragile aesthetic response which cannot match or resolve the resilience, richness, and provocativeness of her earlier evocations of positive narcissistic feelings. (By contrast, in a similar scene in *Jane Eyre*, Brontë recognizes both the anger at deprivation and the need for self-nurture and so is able to conclude her novel in a more realistic, if violent, emotional rhythm.) Wharton's narrative strategy, however, never integrates needs or angers in personality or in plot. Her heroine's hidden anger turns inward in self-destruction, but even this dynamic is unclear for Wharton, whose handling of it is more sentimental than cathartic. Deprivation and anger remain undercurrents pulling beneath the plot; unacknowledged, they undermine the structure in which Wharton tries to confine them.

In *The House of Mirth*, Wharton transforms a personal psychic despair into a pessimistic social determinism, locating in society the forces of inevitable destruction of spirit that proceed from within. Ultimately, of course, there is a reciprocal relation between psyche and society. The narrative sensibility that creates the social world of this novel is itself shaped by development in society. Wharton shows Lily's destruction by the contradictions and limitations of needing to be independent and adult in a social context that neither equips nor permits her to be. In this, Lily, like many other heroines, acts out a cultural dilemma: when society provides no adult female role of active responsibility and initiative, women are confined to passive and childlike states and cannot mature.

Within the psychic structure of Wharton's fiction, Lily's destruction *is* determined. Her undoing is implicit in the very illumination of her initial descriptions; what attracts us most to her is what dooms her. Reading the novel in this psychological mode is not to deny the destructive effect of social arrangements on women's development but rather more fully to demonstrate it. The ultimate locus of damage by inadequate social structures is within the individual. The internal arena of the author's sensibility becomes the demonstration ground of the social harms she criticizes; the flawed structure of her novel, as much as her heroine's death, shows the debilitating effects of the constrictions on realistic self-assertion. Wharton's statement about the destructiveness of her limited social world is ultimately strikingly successful, only more indirect than she may have intended.

Wolff's biography suggests that the unresolved narcissism of the world of *The House of Mirth* parallels Wharton's own delayed emotional maturation. Wharton had not resolved the dilemma of integrating sexuality and assertiveness when she wrote this novel. "Every one of the early fictions," writes Wolff, "had been devoid of genuine adult passion. . . . The terms in which Wharton experienced sexual passion were indelibly colored by the fearful shades of an earlier, more primitive, and more inclusive hunger . . . a threatening resurgence of that infantile sense of unsatisfied, insatiable oral longing" connected with earlier problems with maternal love.[22] In this context we can understand differently Wharton's determinism. Tied by excessive fears about the destructive powers of assertive passions, Wharton was unable to free herself from believing in the necessary control of the strict code of manners of the society whose rigid constraints on the human spirit she so pointedly criticized.

Lily has to die because she cannot live. A grown and beautiful woman, she can no longer exist as a child, but neither can she become an adult. We feel the pull of human character in Lily, a growing sympathy and self-knowledge, but society cannot support her development. All her romance "helpers" fail her. Her evil mother figures have more power to hurt than the good ones do to help. She has only a defective Prince Charming who has the magical power to change her complacent vision of the world but is unable to transport her to a kingdom beyond. *The House of Mirth* is both a failed romance of identity and a romance of failed identity. It ends not with wisdom, integrity, and social reintegration but with regression to infancy and death (like many female *bildungsromane*). Not only does Lily fail in her attempts at growth and self-sufficiency, but Wharton too fails to create a sustained aesthetic structure to legitimate the integrity of her struggle. She is able to make her heroine noble only as a suffering victim; she cannot create a responsible adult of moral dimensions—a tragic heroine. In her inability to image woman's responsibility for herself, Wharton shares a larger cultural tradition. Lily's stock death acts out the social prohibitions that deny women active maturity (as well as the punitive judgment that blames victims for their victimization). Wharton writes within a central tradition of American thought that manifests itself in literature in the favored use of the polarizing, simplistic form of romance.

Still, something of considerable power is going on in this fiction. In *The House of Mirth*, Wharton is able to tap the well of childhood narcissism and use those resonant feelings to create a brilliantly memorable character. While others of Wharton's novels have a more perfectly balanced structure, Lily's fire appeals directly to those sustained remnants of narcissism in adults. Like a child or a lover, she speaks to our capacity for narcissistic projection; the strength of our response to her derives from the potency of those feelings in us. The historical mythology of romantic love testifies to the intensity of suppressed and withheld passions; thwarted feeling paradoxically heightens aesthetic effects. As we are charmed by doomed lovers and by dreams of Eden—with all their permanent remoteness in time and place, their nostalgia of impossibility and loss—so we are charmed by Lily Bart. She is able to find in her readers' hearts the place she could never find in her world. In fiction's own magical transformation of constriction to transcendence, the repression of sexual and active energy becomes the potent pressurizing force that forges the lasting power of Lily's appeal.

Notes

1. Diana Trilling, "The Liberated Heroine," *Times Literary Supplement* 13 (Oct. 1978): 1163–67.

2. Patricia Spacks, *The Female Imagination* (New York: Knopf, 1975). She writes, "*The House of Mirth* has the energy of a parable" (241). Gary Lindberg detects in Lily "psychic energies that are unmalleable to social forms." See Lindberg, *Edith Wharton and the Novel of Manners* (Charlottesville: University Press of Virginia, 1975), 122.

3. R. W. B. Lewis, ed., *The House of Mirth* (New York: New York University Press, 1977), vi. This is the text of Wharton's novel used here.

All page numbers, indicated in parentheses after quotations from *The House of Mirth*, are to this edition.

4. Edith Wharton, *The House of Mirth* (New York: New American Library, 1964), Afterword, 343.

5. Irving Howe, ed., *Edith Wharton: A Collection of Critical Essays* (Englewood Cliffs, N.J.: Prentice Hall, 1962), 125.

6. In *A Backward Glance* Wharton writes of *The House of Mirth*: "The problem . . . how to extract from such a subject . . . a society of irresponsible pleasure seekers . . . any deeper bearing than the people composing such a society could guess? The answer was that a frivolous society can acquire dramatic significance only through what its frivolity destroys. Its tragic implication lies in its power of debasing people and ideals. The answer, in short, was my heroine, Lily Bart" (207). Wharton here establishes a confusion between tragedy and determinism that plagues criticism of the novel in an unresolved debate about Lily's stature as a tragic heroine. All of Wharton's characters live in an essentially deterministic universe. Without a modicum of free will and interior spirit, the moral responsibility necessary for tragedy is hardly possible. Yet, the feeling that Lily is a tragic character keeps reemerging. In both Irving Howe's and Edmund Wilson's criticism, the dimensions of tragedy and determinism seem paradoxically to coexist. Cf. Howe, ed., *Edith Wharton*, and Wilson, "Justice to Edith Wharton" (1941) in *The Wound and the Bow* (New York: Oxford University Press, 1947). But R. W. B. Lewis states blankly that Lily "is not a tragic heroine" (xx), and Wharton's most reliable early critic, Blake Nevius, writes, "we are deceiving ourselves if we try to account for the compelling interest of *The House of Mirth* by the nature or intensity of the moral conflict." See Nevius, *Edith Wharton: A Study of Her Fiction* (Berkeley: University of California Press, 1953).

7. Howe, ed., *Edith Wharton*, 127.

8. Richard Chase, *The American Novel and Its Tradition* (New York: Doubleday, 1957), 160.

9. See Joseph Campbell, *The Hero with a Thousand Faces* (1949; repr., Princeton, N.J.: Princeton University Press, Bollingen Series 17, 1968); and Northrup Frye, *Anatomy of Criticism* (Princeton: Princeton University Press, 1957).

10. Elizabeth Ammons, in " 'Fairy-Tale Love' and *The Reef*," *American Literature* 47 (1975): 615–28, observes a similar use of fairy-tale motifs to expose female fantasies about love and marriage generated by cultural limitations encouraging economic dependence and sexual repression.

11. See Sigmund Freud, "Family Romances," *The Standard Edition of the*

Complete Psychological Works of Sigmund Freud, ed, and trans. James Strachey (London: Hogarth Press, 1955), 9: 1906–8.

12. Cynthia Griffin Wolff's reading of *The House of Mirth* in "Lily Bart and the Beautiful Death," *American Literature* 46 (1974): 16–40, elaborates this perception of Lily as an object of art. "The death of a beautiful woman as seen through the eyes of her lover" was a set piece of American literature. Wharton, however, shows us "what it would be like to be the woman thus exalted and objectified," revealing "the self-alienation that a woman suffers when she accepts the status of idealized object" (39).

13. See Heinz Kohut, *The Analysis of Self* (New York: International Universities Press, 1971); Heinz Kohut "Forms and Transformations of Narcissism," *Journal of the American Psychoandytic Association* 14 (1966): 243–72; Otto Kernberg, "Contrasting Viewpoints Regarding the Nature and Psychoanalytic Treatment of Narcissistic Personalities: A Preliminary Communication," *Journal of the American Psychoanalytic Association* 22 (1974). This issue is entirely devoted to discussions of narcissism. Also see Marion Michel Oliner, "*Le Narcissisme:* Theoretical Formulations of Bela Brumberger," *Psychoanalytic Review* 65 (summer 1978): 239–52.

14. Kernberg, "Contrasting Viewpoints," 265–66.

15. Bruno Bettleheim, *The Uses of Enchantment: The Meaning and Importance of Fairy Tales* (New York: Random House, 1977).

16. Edith Wharton, *A Backward Glance* (New York: D. Appleton-Century, 1934), 4. Quoted in Cynthia Griffin Wolff, *A Feast of Words: The Triumph of Edith Wharton* (New York: Oxford University Press, 1977).

17. Wharton's language in this scene is explicitly that of fairy tales and narcissistic fantasies: "With the ease that seemed to attend the fulfilment of all her wishes," Lily makes the tea table materialize. Gryce sees this feat as "miraculous"; the tea becomes "nectar," though Lily is reluctant to taste it, still savoring the "flavor" of another prince's kiss. Lily's effect on Gryce is magical: he "grew eloquent," feeling "the confused titillation with which the lower organisms welcome the gratification of their needs, and all his senses floundered in a vague well-being" (18–19).

18. Karl Miller, in "Edith Wharton's Secret," *New York Review of Books* 23 (Feb. 1978), 10–15, makes this observation in a different context. As a dark, Jewish foreigner, he explains, Rosedale had the ambivalent attraction/repulsion of an outsider. Since his otherness made him socially unacceptable in Wharton's world as a love object, he could become the locus of disowned feelings of sexual attraction.

19. Wharton's language makes Lily's revulsion quite physical and concrete: Lily shrinks "in every nerve from the way in which his look and tone made free of her" (252). She draws "away instinctively from his touch." When Rosedale's "smile grew increasingly intimate" (111), she withdraws with a "repugnance which kept her in frozen erectness."

20. Quoted by Wolff, *A Feast of Words*, 10, and Wilson, "Justice to Edith Wharton" (19–20).

21. Wharton accuses one of her characters of "woman like" accusing of the woman (158), and that is her own habit. Blame for the inadequacies of the whole socializing process is placed on the women who teach and enforce social paradigms.

22. Wolff, *A Feast of Words*, 191, 206.

Lily Bart and the Drama of Femininity

CYNTHIA GRIFFIN WOLFF

◆ ◆ ◆

I WROTE an essay [in 1974] entitled "Lily Bart and the Beautiful Death," an argument I still think true, though it did not answer certain questions adequately (Why must Lily die at the novel's conclusion? What are we to make of Selden—of his passivity and his self-important moral pronouncements? What is the meaning of Nettie Struther and her belated appearance?). If, as I argued, Edith Wharton's knowledge of the visual arts provided insights into the *The House of Mirth*, perhaps the answers to these persistent questions about her first New York novel can be found by exploring another of her artistic interests—the busy, varied world of Edwardian drama.

Between 1890 and 1905 (when *House of Mirth* was published), New York theater life was lively and colorful. There was a relatively flexible sense of international theater: major productions in London and Paris were regularly reviewed in the New York papers; touring companies traveled back and forth across the Atlantic. Moreover, turn-of-the-century stage was an art form for average Americans, not just for a wealthy elite. There were old-fashioned melodramas (like *Uncle Tom's Cabin*, which was still playing to enthusiastic audiences); historical dramas (both costume pageants and extravagantly staged tragedies); musical reviews (like the first New York production of *Little Johnny Jones* in 1904); burlesque presentations (with women in scandalously revealing tights); adaptations of Shakespeare that were remarkably various; an unending assortment of drawing-room dramas; and—the most avant-garde group of offerings—the problem plays of dramatists like Ibsen and Shaw.

Despite this apparent diversity, virtually all stage productions with an even rudimentary plot shared several assumptions about narrative, especially the conventions of the *pièce bien faite* (or well-made play, as it was known in England and America) and the *pièce à thèse* (a well-made play intended to convey a moral lesson). Invented in about 1850 by the French playwrights Augustin-Eugène Scribe and Victorien Sardou, the regulations that shaped the plot of a well-made play persisted for more than a century.

These plots are based on some secret, usually known to the spectators but withheld from certain characters; there is a pattern of increasingly suspenseful events, often connected with radical changes in the hero's fortunes; this pattern parallels a series of misunderstandings, obvious to the onlookers but not to the characters; and the crescendo of these vicissitudes builds to a sharp contrast between the hero's lowest point (peripeteia) and highest moment—the *scène à faire*—when secrets are disclosed, virtue triumphs, and the hero gains a rightful reward. Unless exclusively comedic or farcical, the well-made play was devised consciously to inculcate a moral lesson. In the most ambitious, skillfully managed *pièces à thèse*, the *scène à faire* became a coup de theatre—the disclosure of a withheld truth that, once revealed, conveyed a climactic and cathartic moral judgment.[1]

Much of Edwardian theater, including costume drama, labored strenuously to convey a true-to-life effect. Yet, as even some critics at the time observed, this realism was specious, achieved by neat and plausible explanations of [the play's] ingenious and unlikely principal situations. The illusion of reality was identified with an entirely visible and unbroken chain of circumstantial causality" (Meisel 79). Thus, stage events did not represent the complicated, sometimes contradictory, reactions of character, did not devolve from the intrinsic nature of the hero or other principal players. Instead, the plots tended to be action driven events were constructed to move the play ineluctably forward to its necessary, tidy conclusion. The plot pulled the principal characters in tow.

Because these dramas were elaborately produced and a great deal of money was spent to make the onstage activity *seem* real, it was easy for the audience to suppose that the stage artifice was transparent, no more than a pleasing rendition of the way things usually happen—or, even more subtly treacherous, a vivid lesson in the way things *ought* to happen. Several novelists, intrigued by the problem presented by this discrepancy, undertook to write for the theater, including Henry James, W. D. Howells, and Wharton herself. Thus, throughout the several years when she was intermittently at work on *House of Mirth*, Wharton was also writing extensively for the stage. In fact, the earliest sketch of the character who eventually became Lily Bart was almost certainly concocted in 1900 for a drawing-room drama entitled *The Tightrope*, the full text of which has disappeared (Lewis 109). Altogether, between 1900 and 1902, Wharton worked on four plays, concluding with a translation of Hermann Sudermann's *Es Lebe das Leben*, which was performed on Broadway.

Wharton shared the reasons that had moved James and Howells to experiment with writing plays, but she also felt a powerful additional motive. The theater was one of the few arenas in which women exercised some real (if limited) power. At the turn of the century, Sarah Bernhardt and Eleonora Duse were in the waning years of their careers, but their performances in London and Paris still commanded full-length reviews in the *New York Times*; and the next generation of actresses was extraordinarily successful in perpetuating the notion that the theater was a medium uniquely suited to a woman's graceful talents. Often a particular play became the vehicle for a particular actress, and not infrequently the actress herself arranged the deal. Such was the case with Wharton's fourth dramatic venture.

In 1902, the celebrated English actress Mrs. Pat Campbell produced a number of plays for the recently opened Theatre Republic in New York City. Her first presentation was a translation of Sudermann's *Magda* with herself in the title role, and it was a tremendous success. A few months later, hoping to achieve a second such personal triumph, Campbell approached Wharton to translate Sudermann's *Es Lebe das Leben* (which the actress-producer insisted upon calling *The Joy of Living*). Wharton completed the work, which received such enthusiastic reviews that Campbell urged her to translate another Sudermann play, *Es War*. This time, however, Wharton refused. She could not conveniently find the time. For she also seems to have concluded that her talents lay elsewhere.

This brief but busy excursion into the theater added yet another dimension to Wharton's understanding of women's roles. Although Edwardian drama proclaimed an interest in women's lives (and the most coveted roles were those commanded by actresses, not actors), the plays themselves were almost invariably written by men. Moreover, critics and theoreticians of the stage were overwhelmingly male. The standard plots were meant to defend a male-dominated society—especially when the plot dealt with the relationship between the sexes. In these dramas, then, the action was driven by one imperative—to buttress male power. Consequently, no matter how much a play might appear to stress its female characters, their natures were rendered only superficially, and their principal job—perhaps their only job—was to please and placate the male audience. In this unique respect the stage accurately, if grimly, reflected social reality.

The tradition begun in France with Sardou and Scribe was elaborated in Edwardian England most successfully by Arthur Wing Pinero and Henry Arthur Jones, who developed a version of the *pièce à thèse* that came to be known as the "society play." These plays were even more didactic about women's roles than their French predecessors and were often praised in the press as a repository of wisdom concerning woman's essential nature. Pinero's heroines were especially praised as sensitive portrayals of the decorative, dependent attitudes that made *true* femininity so beguiling. Thus, when Pinero's *Letty* opened in September 1904, the *Times* review rhapsodized, "The English master playwright has laid bare another woman's soul."[2]

Having rejected the feminine ideal that her own upbringing had prescribed, Wharton understood the real-life price that society exacted from women who did try to satisfy this requirement for an appearance of effortless, "natural" femininity. Moreover, this mutilation of women's nature was not an isolated example of social corruption. In Wharton's estimation the deformities of a debased society will always be shown most clearly in the plight of those who are disempowered. The hypocrisy of this demand for a real-life drama of femininity indicated the more general viciousness that pervaded wealthy New York. The confusion, pain, and destruction that attend the heroine of *House of Mirth* in her efforts to present that necessary *performance* "Lily Bart" are but the visible signs of society's comprehensive corruption, an emblematizing of its vaster cruelties. Throughout the novel, a steady pattern of references both to playacting in general and the contemporary theater in particular mark the method of Wharton's satire.

In 1905, readers of *House of Mirth* would catch its many allusions to contemporary drama. When Gus Trenor stands next to Selden, his affinities with the broadly limned low villain of traditional melodrama are unmistakable: "the unpleasant moisture of his intensely white forehead, the way his jewelled rings were wedged in the creases of his fat red fingers" (248). Rosedale has his origins in the stage Jew. Selden's diffident intellectualism, so frustrating to Wharton's readers today, captured the habits of the *raissoneur* when he appeared in turn-of-the-century society drama as the apologist for conventional wisdom and the onstage affirmation of dominant male authority.

As if doubly to confirm their power, certain actor-managers regularly preempted the role of the *raisonneur*, bridging the boundary between the stage and the world whose myths it reified. Thus, the courtship of the *raissoneur* reflected his wisdom and authority, rather than his ardor: "His wooing is mature, rational, immune from effusive outbursts. In comparison to this role model of appropriate masculine behavior, the emotional declarations of younger men . . . appear callow and ultimately silly. The implication of the plays is that the younger men will eventually realize this and emerge as potential *raissoneur* figures themselves" (Clarke 48). Yet, the most unambiguous theft from the theater in Wharton's novel is not a stereotyped role but a stage prop passed from character to character—the MacGuffin that holds the crucial secrets of the story—the bundle of love letters that Lily ultimately burns.

Comedy, tragedy, farce, historical pageant, even burlesque, in 1905, were all most likely to share this one element—a plot that turned upon the concealment, interception, destruction, or revelation of a letter. " 'The letter!' " exclaimed the director of the French Academy upon welcoming Sardou into membership, " 'It plays a major part in most of your plots, and every detail of it is vital, container and contents. The envelope, the seal, the wax, the stamp, the postmark, the shade of the paper, and the perfume that clings to it . . . ' " (qtd. in Stanton xxiii). If Sardou can be credited with perfecting the legerdemain of the letter on stage, his technique was copied by so many dramatists in Europe and America that few of Wharton's readers could have misunderstood the dramatic potential of Bertha Dorset's letters to Selden—"the words, scrawled in heavy ink on pale-tinted note-paper" (166–67).[3]

Although all of the major characters in *House of Mirth* have their counterparts in Edwardian drama, they all also transcend their stage stereotypes, and Wharton often emphasizes the tension between the platitudes of simplistic stage reality and the intractable complexity of real life in their choice of language. Thus, Trenor (the low villain) recoils at having been misused when Lily rebukes his clumsy sexual overtures: "Don't talk *stage-rot*," he expostulates, "I don't want to insult you. But a man's got his feelings—and you've played with mine too long" (234, emphasis added). Only Rosedale discerns her deep moral probity and the poetic injustice of the poverty in which she ultimately finds herself: "It's a *farce*—a crazy *farce*, he repeated, his eyes fixed on the long vista of the room reflected in the blotched glass between the windows" (482, emphasis added). Unlike the usually authoritative *raisonneur*, Selden is not a reliable guide to the moral structure of

Tableaux Vivantes is
when she's most feminine
except its a performance

the fiction. However, perhaps the most difficult character to identify with a single stage stereotype is Lily Bart herself—Wharton's elegant, protean heroine. Her similarity to the heroines of Pinero's society dramas, which played to adulatory New York audiences in the years just before 1905, is inescapable, and it is with these plays that we must begin if we are to comprehend her complexities.

Wharton would have been compelled to note the triumphal progress of Pinero's *Iris*: Campbell had begun her performance of Wharton's translation of Sudermann only weeks after *Iris* opened, and the heroines of the two works were often compared in newspaper reviews and commentaries.[4] Indeed, the correspondences between *House of Mirth* and *Iris* are so comprehensive that the Pinero play, along with all the narrative conventions upon which it depends, constitutes what Roland Barthes has called a "*dejà-lu*" for Wharton's novel: a set of "words, structures, functions, sequences, plot"—of "intertextual interlockings"—that establish audience expectations for a narrative pattern (Brooks 98–99; see Barthes 19–20). The story of Iris had become this culture's quintessential portrait of "the good woman who falls through mere weakness. In happy circumstances no one could be more sincerely charming or more truly virtuous, but she has neither the courage of pride nor the courage of affection. It only needs the necessary test to make her doom . . . inevitable" (*Iris* 10). The spectacle of sumptuary life that was a necessary production value of the society drama had become a requirement of everyday life for Pinero's Iris. She "is extravagant, but not reckless . . . and to [her], poverty is martyrdom as much because it takes away the ability to do kind things as because it forces her to personal discomfort" (10). So it is with Lily Bart, who "was not made for mean and shabby surroundings, for the squalid compromises of poverty. Her whole being dilated in an atmosphere of luxury; it was the background she required, the only climate she could breathe in" (39–40). For Pinero, the fall of a woman like this was always the result of personal weakness (the action of his plays drove irresistibly to this conclusion). For Wharton, tyrannical social conventions were largely responsible for the fate of such women.

Despite this patent similarity to Pinero's Iris, Lily's repertoire of histrionic attitudes is by no means exhausted by the conventions of society drama. Sometimes "she liked to think of her beauty as a power for good . . . liked to picture herself as standing aloof from the vulgar press of the Quirinal and sacrificing her pleasure to the claims of an immemorial tradition" (54–55), a construction based on Bernhardt's legendary performances in *La Tosca.* At other times, when confronted with reversals, Lily personates a kind of moral imperiousness well enough, drawing "herself up to the full height of her slender majesty, towering like some dark angel of defiance" (362). Sometimes she seems like one of Lydia Thompson's "British Blondes," as in the tableaux vivants when she portrays the *undress* of Sir Joshua Reynolds's *Mrs. Lloyd*; for here she dispenses "with the advantages of a more sumptuous setting" (219) in order to display her form as boldly as a girl in tights. And when Lily discusses the difficulties of her situation with Selden, she may even sound like one of the women from the new problem plays of Ibsen and Shaw—Nora musing about the role of woman and wife in *A Doll's House*, for example. Yet Lily does not have Nora's moral fortitude: she cannot leave her "House" of "Mirth" to face the world alone.

Perhaps Lily Bart might best be characterized as a heroine in search of an appropriate scenario. Too virtuous to enact the society drama, she is not virtuous enough to reject the role, nor is she original or brilliant enough to invent a role for herself. Without some available narrative that is both socially viable and personally acceptable, she cannot *be.* Lily's frantic quest for a role gives force to Wharton's statement about the origins of the character. This frivolous society has destroyed Lily Bart because it can give her no story adequate for the construction of her adult identity, a tragedy not just for Lily Bart but also for all the other women who could find no such narrative.

Too much of Lily's life has been contaminated by the pursuit of admiration—an occupation that has produced no coherent plot, no starring role, and no happy ending. Still, no action is more characteristic of Lily's moments alone than the ritual of examining her life as a narrative, rehearsing past acts and estimating present options in order to formulate some story that will affirm an acceptable self.[5] Indeed, she is drawn to Selden largely because of his willingness to participate in these narrative musings. Yet, the myths that inform the order of this society, the same myths that were purveyed on stage, have invaded the terms of their mutual storytelling: Lily and Selden have learned the didactic lesson of this influence too well.

One of the explicit values of society drama was the clarity of its formulas for life—the lack of ambiguity in its rules for judging good and bad, the deceptively unambiguous strokes with which character was drawn, and the promising simplicity with which happiness was defined. Pinero even claimed that the task of creating homilies was the primary mandate of his profession: "I believe . . . that the playwright's finest task is that of giving back to the multitude their own thoughts and conceptions illuminated, enlarged, and, if needful, purged, perfected, transfigured" (qtd. in Clarke 28).

Not everyone agreed with this notion. Problem plays were concocted to prove that melodramatic homilies could not be transformed into strategies for existence. Yet, their audiences were ambivalent about such a corrective view. For example, in 1905, performances of *Mrs. Warren's Profession* created major scandals in New Haven and New York. In the same year, the young Ethel Barrymore's performance in *A Doll's House* was reviewed with pious reserve because the play did not represent those feelings that were deemed appropriate to a young woman.[6] Audiences and critics were more comfortable with familiar moralisms about women than with shocking innovations intended to proffer reform.

Jones, whose plays shared preeminence on the Edwardian stage with Pinero's, defended the political underpinning of his plays—especially of their reductive treatment of women—and ventured some theoretical statements on the subject, using "scientific" data:

> It is a physiological fact that throughout life a woman's brain and general anatomy is much nearer and more allied to a child's than a man's brain and anatomy. . . . My incessant pro-

test is not against knocking down faulty human institutions, but against the folly . . . of treating such primary instincts as sex, religion, and patriotism as if they were opinions; instead of being, as they are, impulses and emotions which we cannot root out, but must guide and control as best we may. (qtd. in Clarke 44)

This notion of innate femininity suffused late-nineteenth-century drama; because these plays rested upon the conviction that women were naturally submissive, the women in them were never permitted to enact independent social roles. Their only role, their only reality, was in relation to a man. In treating sexual issues, such drama took a double standard more or less for granted, and when a woman's action rose to heroic proportions, it most often took the form not of assertion but of renunciation. Not surprisingly, then, marriage was judged to be the central fact of a woman's life: it enabled her to express her "natural" femininity, since it stabilized her necessarily dependent relationship to men; not trivially, it also afforded her security and a clear, unimpeachable public identity—her only reliable means of achieving social stability.

Female characters who failed to adapt to these stereotypes could not be awarded a permanent role in the narrative, and their only appropriate action was to drop out of the play. Shaw commented acidly that the society play was "a tailor's advertisement making sentimental remarks to a milliner's advertisement in the middle of an upholsterer's and decorator's advertisement" (*Major Critical Essays* 14). And when he published the introduction to *Mrs. Warren's Profession* in 1902 (the very year that Pinero took New York by storm with *The Notorious Mrs. Ebbsmith, The Second Mrs. Tanqueray*, and *Iris*), Shaw referred to the "unwritten but perfectly well understood theater convention that members of Mrs. Warren's profession shall be tolerated on the stage only when they are beautiful, exquisitely dressed, and sumptuously lodged and fed." He also noted the mandate that they shall, "at the end of the play, die." Shaw cited Pinero in general and Pinero's great success *Iris*, in particular, as odious examples of these truths (*Plays*

34). Mrs. Ebbsmith, having grappled with the ideal of free love, flings her Bible into the fire in a fit of antisocial rage but then remorsefully picks it out again and is saved. The title heroine of *Iris* is granted no such magical happy ending; near the close of the play, the poor but honest suitor whom she should have married returns from a two-year adventure to seek his fortune, and his immense success comes to represent the automatic happiness that would have accompanied the virtuous choice she failed to make.

If the New Woman of Shaw and Ibsen was meant to correct these stereotypes, Edith Wharton's personal experiences had taught her that a New Woman is considerably easier to create on stage than in life. Wharton knew that most women in her culture had constructed a self by internalizing didactic patterns like the ones guiding the society dramas—that everyday life was laced together with the various narratives of the world to which women had, of necessity, accommodated themselves. Most daunting of all, any woman who wanted to invent some new way to be—some new *story* of self—had to struggle not only against the strictures of an outside world but also against the habits of identity she had already (adaptively) constructed. She needed great strength of will to change these accumulated narratives. Moreover, such stories are seldom told in solitude: the drama of a life is enacted with others, and understanding is completed only by response. So she also needed the positive assistance of at least one other person. For Lily, Selden seems to be that other person.

Although Lily and Selden have both been shaped by the narratives of wealthy, fashionable New York, both are also to some extent outsiders, having declined to accept all its myths and rituals. Indeed, the abstract configuration of their characters is remarkably similar: both respond powerfully to aesthetic forces; both crave luxury as a given of life; both cultivate a moral fastidiousness (more often manifested in astute criticism of others than in ethical activity); and both fancy that they are above the common lot of pleasure seekers who populate their world. They are fatally different, however, in their views of the possibilities of courtship. Unable to abide the standard plot of gender and marriage, Lily has never been willing to play her role to its compulsory conclusion; by contrast, marriage for Selden is an option, not a necessity, and he can linger at the peripheries of commitment—taking pleasure in the perquisites of empowered masculinity and titillated by the aesthetic spectacle of dependent femininity seemingly displayed for his benefit. The only circumstances under which communication between them can take place, then, are those moments—like the evening of the tableaux vivants—when Lily reverts to corrupt but familiar representations of femininity. The complexity that typifies the dialogue between these major characters is reiterated in the novel's fundamental configuration. The structure of *House of Mirth* mirrors that of a five-act play (or a four-act play with an epilogue, both common forms during this period). Each act contains a scene in which Selden and Lily attempt discourse and fail, and often the scene's significance is signaled by an allusion to some form of stagecraft.

The first act (centered on the tea ceremony in Selden's flat) establishes both Lily's place in the scheme of things and her self-consciousness about the implications of that place. Their conversation is really more a business talk than an intimate exchange. His dialogue falls patly into the *raisonneur's* line: "Isn't marriage your vocation? Isn't it what you're all brought up for?" (13)—both a description and a defense of society's gendered power structure. By contrast, Lily's behavior is organized as an attempt to escape from the prescribed narrative, and what she most seeks from Selden is cooperation: "Don't you see . . . that what I want is a friend? . . . Sometimes I have fancied you might be that friend—I don't know why, except that you are neither a prig nor a bounder" (12). "Prig" and "bounder" are opposite extremes of the suitor on stage. *Male friend is not in the play*. By stipulating it, Lily announces her desire to create a new social narrative. Lily has no alternative plot to offer, but she is trying to make one with Selden's collaboration.

The quest continues at their next encounter (act 2) when Selden postulates his "republic of the spirit" (108). Appealing as this ideal is to Lily, she challenges its purely theoretical nature, arguing that citizenship necessitates having enough money. Selden answers by recurring to the norms of theatricality that reveal his own commitment to all the half-truths and illusions that lend plausibility to the standard plot: "[T]he queer thing about society is that the people who regard it as an end are those who are in it, and not the critics on the fence. It's just the other way with most shows—the audience may be under the illusion, but the actors know that real life is on the other side of the footlights" (111). What he fails to realize (and what Lily fully understands) is that even as they speak, she is enacting agreeable femininity for his credulous appreciation. She knows not merely how much money has gone into producing this charade but how much calculation must attend even the most apparently spontaneous gesture if she is to succeed in achieving that unvarying aesthetic performance that is "Lily Bart."[7]

When she is most frightened and uncertain of her hold over his allegiance, she resorts to the self-dramatizing talent that she only half-scorns. There is no higher moment of make-believe in the novel than its centerpiece (act 3) the tableaux vivants, an explicit piece of stagecraft—"Lily Bart" produced from behind the curtain. Lily's artistic skill has been entirely focused on creating this theatrical effect—a gorgeous, static, utterly silent rendition of self. Paradoxically, it is here Selden finally supposes that he has glimpsed the real Lily Bart and that he might love her. Yet, it is also here that Lily despairs of realizing true comradeship. The very terms of her success have revealed the impossibility of concocting a new narrative with Selden. She no longer even asks for friendship but instead sadly inquires, "Why can't we be friends? You promised once to help me" (222).

Before their last tea ceremony (act 4), Lily seems tempted to deploy the one weapon she has against Selden by using the incriminating letters to expose him. However, if she cannot enact an acceptable love scene, she is at least determined to demand another kind of standard theatrical moment, the recognition scene. So, instead of presenting herself as an aesthetic display, she tells Selden of her ethically motivated decision to leave Mrs. Hatch's employment. By this point Lily has made her most strenuous effort to escape the standard scenario, having internalized his injunctions and integrated them into her behavior. However, Selden still cannot acknowledge Lily's *real*, albeit imperfect, efforts at moral self-reclamation—cannot respond to this actualizing of his abstract moral pronouncements—a failure Wharton stresses by creating a coup de theatre that fails to take place, the novel's least understood remnant of turn-of-the-century drama, that is, the moment when Lily burns the letters between Selden and Bertha Dorset.

In a standard well-made play, this moment would be a *scène à faire* that might take place this way: Lily drops the love letters into the fire. Selden turns and catches sight of the missives and seizes the bundle (as Mrs. Ebbsmith had seized her Bible), realizes that Lily knew of his frailty and nonetheless protected him at her own expense. He says something like "Ah, my beloved, my redeemed Lily"; they embrace, and the curtain falls. Yet, this sequence never happens (frustrated readers know that *something* is missing but cannot easily identify the absence). Instead, Selden is so preoccupied with his inspection of Lily's now much-diminished person that he literally does not see what has happened, does not notice that she is burning the incriminating letters. Lily's long moral journey toward self-esteem culminates in this act, while for Selden it is a nonevent. A once-beautiful woman struggling to achieve some morally admirable way of life can be little more than "an embarrassment to him" (496). At last Lily comprehends the harsh truth that, where women are concerned, the only reality that the world of pleasure seekers will acknowledge is masquerade.

The notions of femininity that inform Selden's thinking—that informed virtually all dramas of the Edwardian age—are not of course eternal verities but gendered propaganda upholding a specific social arrangement. One form of satirical insight into this propaganda inheres in the relationship between *House of Mirth* and plays like Pinero's *Iris*. A second is offered by the novel's female-gendered, "omniscient" narrator, who repeatedly exposes the behind-the-scenes machinery of fashionable make-believe (by revealing the secrets that women must know and must keep hidden from men—the petty deceptions, rigorous disciplines, and minor humiliations that produce "natural" femininity). This presents an audacious challenge to a reader. Will you become so captivated by Lily's decorative elegance (it asks) that you fail to appreciate the narrator's account of its cost? Will you see the principal characters as tragic (or pathetic) hero and heroine or understand them as ordinary people maimed by the society that has shaped them? Will you react by rote to the familiarity of the underlying theatrical form (with its didactic implications) or be disgusted by this society's casual destructiveness?

The novel's penultimate scene with Nettie Struther—so often a puzzle to modern readers—is Wharton's final marker for her message. Although a reader today may have difficulty making the appropriate connection, a playgoer of 1905 would have recognized Nettie Struther's literary ancestry in Pinero's successful drama *Letty*, the tale of a working-class girl who is sorely tempted to become the pampered kept woman of a rich man. Pinero's play follows her temptations and indecisions. It concludes with a scene in which Letty delivers a monologue holding a baby in her arms. Her words extol the simplicity of married life far from the luxury of high society.

Letty's speech sounds like a moral that might be read unchanged into *House of Mirth*, but there is a crucial difference between Pinero's scene and Wharton's adaption. Always loyal to aristocratic values, Pinero is concerned only with sorting out class differences and with maintaining the status quo. Letty's speech acknowledges that she belongs in the lower class and that it was a mistake to suppose she might join the life of her social superiors. By contrast, Wharton's is a class-neutral conviction that everyone should denounce the false values of society and that all have an overriding need for emotional honesty.[8]

However, there is another difference. Nettie Struther has found a mate who can help her formulate a new narrative of self; together they have begun a life that renounces pretense and affirms frank disclosure and compassion. It is the narrative of this new life—and, above all, of her new self—that Nettie recounts; and although it presents a "central truth of existence" (517) and suggests a remedy for the misery that has overtaken Lily, it is a remedy of which the faded, but still elegant, Miss Bart cannot avail herself.

Perhaps Lily's deepest need is to enact the closure of some recognizable theatrical scenario. Thus, as the novel concludes, just before she dies, she falls into the activity that has most characterized her life. Obsessively her imagination recollects and recombines the events of her existence—searching for a narrative that will confirm "Lily Bart" with finality. "She had not imagined that such a multiplication of wakefulness was possible: her whole past was reënacting itself at a hundred different points of consciousness" (520). It is not simply that Lily chooses to die. In nineteenth-century theater, heroines *did* die. If they had been virtuous, they died tragically; if they were no more than fallen women, they died trivially. In either case death was a suitable ending, and Wharton's theatrical heroine had nowhere else to go.

Notes

Substantial portions of this essay have appeared in Cynthia Griffin Wolff, "Lily Bart and Masquerade Inscribed in the Female Mode" in *Wretched Exotic: Essays on Edith Wharton in Europe*, ed. Katherine Joslin and Alan Price (New York: Peter Lang, 1993), 259–93.

1. The reader will recognize some of these conventions as essentially melodramatic. The well-made play was, in many ways, an outgrowth of melodrama—an ambitious formulation that could, for example, aspire to convert mere melodrama into high tragedy.

2. Edith Wharton was certainly not the only woman to notice the male monopoly of stage mores. The outspoken actress-activist Mary Shaw was outraged. In 1903, she gave an interview voicing protest in language that is an interesting commentary on the language of today's discussions of gender:

> Most of our plays and books and laws are masks. They lull us to sleep, give us moral peace. Ibsen had the courage to lift one corner of the mask and look at the dreadful thing, and there was a chorus of shrieks. Then, when he tore the mask away, pande-

> monium. The grinning mask which Ibsen tears away in *Ghosts* is the duty of wifely sacrifice in woman. (Chinoy and Jenkins 99)

In another interview she observed:

> Although 75 per cent of the theatre-going public is composed of women and consequently the managers are lying awake nights trying to secure productions which will make a hit with them, they obstinately refuse to accept woman's judgment. No matter what an author says, the play is remodelled and whipped into shape by those men in charge, who cause the heroines to talk and act not as real women would but as men think that women ought to talk and act. (106)

Chinoy and Jenkins provide an immensely instructive guide to the male domination of early-twentieth-century theater. By 1900, even the great Bernhardt was looking for ways to evade the limiting prescriptions for actresses. No longer young (and thus no longer able to play those ingenue roles that were both so decorative and so popular), Bernhardt dared to cross-dress and play Shakespeare's tragic hero Hamlet. The production was a striking event (in Paris [1899] and New York [1900]). The *New York Times* rhapsodized over this Hamlet in terms that were confusingly gendered (one does not know to what extent the gender confusion was justified by the performance): "So low of stature, so wonderfully graceful . . . , so agile, and so restless most of the time, but so incomparably effective in repose; . . . the daintily molded limbs . . . this odd, pathetic, eloquent, courtly, gracious, lithe, explosive, grotesque, hysterical Hamlet of splendid contradictions." The *New York Times* waxed eloquent on Pinero's sensitivity to the "woman's issue":

> Mr. Pinero has offered his hospitable arm to the actresses of his generation. . . . It is a quite justifiable . . . phrase to say that Mr. Pinero has walked into fame arm in arm with the young women of his creation. Who are these young women, and what are they? The inquiry is not without point, for as Pinero is the best of the English playwrights of our generation, so these young women are the most notable of the products of the modern English drama. (*Iris* 10)

3. Waid seems unaware of these stage traditions and especially of the stage implications of the letter (this despite the fact that she quotes

Selden's musings about "costume-plays" [23]). Waid's discussion of the possibility that Lily might rival Bertha Dorset as an author of letters (24–26) brings late twentieth-century notions of the power of inscription to bear somewhat anachronistically upon this text. The discussion also seems to retain the notion that *of course* every woman wants to best her female rival and win her man.

4. By contrast with Pinero's work, the Sudermann play was designed to show that the existing social conventions sometimes cramp the spirit and deaden the soul (see *Joy*). It is important to understand that insofar as Wharton involved herself with the theater, she did so in ways that were distinct (to a contemporary audience) from the society dramas and their heroines. Paula, the heroine of *The Joy of Living*, was an unconventional woman who could not find happiness within the confines of a perfectly benign marriage because she was in love with another man. The play more or less accepts her right to some alternative—though it forbears stipulating it. The *New York Times* gives a long plot summary of Pinero's *Iris*:

> Instead of being a woman of immoral life, or yet a Trafalgar Square advocate of the sanctity of love as against the sanctity of marriage, Iris is a woman of the fashionable world, who is not only irreproachable in her life but who exerts a positive charm and a force of beneficence among her friends. Her fall is the result of a nature that loves luxury, and that, when the necessity comes for facing poverty and discomfort, brings her lower and lower in the scale of life.
>
> She is in love with a young and impoverished gentleman but is prevented from marrying him by a clause in her late husband's will providing that if she marries, the property shall cease to be hers. Instead of deciding for or against the young man and poverty, she drifts into relations with him that are clearly more than platonic.
>
> The catastrophe of the story is the result of the loss of her estate. A trustee absconds, leaving her only a matter of $700 or so a year to live on. Even now, however, she is not past redemption. She has only to marry the young man and go with him to face life anew in America. She decides instead to wait, living on the remnant of her husband's fortune.
>
> She has a fabulously wealthy admirer, Maldonado, a Spanish-

> American Jew, who seizes upon the opportunity to win her love. The means by which Iris is led step by step to accept money from him, and finally to become his mistress, are too intricate and subtle to be described here. But her fall is complete.
>
> When the young man returns from America he finds her living with Maldonado. After a painful scene, in which her emotions rise to extreme heights, he leaves her crushed. His only words are, "I am sorry. I am sorry." Maldonado, when he in turn discovers that Iris has never loved him, casts her angrily forth in to the streets. (25–26)

5. Telling the story of a life is the necessary precursor to enacting the life of that story: one plots "its meaning by going back over it to record its perpetual flight forward, its slippage from the fixity of definition" (Brooks 33). Lily is frozen into inaction because she can neither discover nor invent an appropriate plot, though she tries to do so by obsessively rehearsing the memories of her actions.

6. "Times change in the theatre as well as out of it. Not so many years ago the youthful actress seeking recognition as an artist of the higher order would probably have selected 'Juliet' as the medium of her ambition. Today the study of the rich warm glow of youthful impulse and passion gives way to the cold, gray, and barren shadows of life as it is understood in the bleak Northland."

7. Leonard's recent argument that *House of Mirth* is an instantiation of the Lacanian notion of "masquerade" is perhaps shortsighted. As a description of some of the masquelike elements, Leonard's essay is useful. However, far from seeing masquerade as pandemic, Wharton quite explicitly identifies it as an indication of social corruption; perhaps the most useful way to read *House of Mirth* is as a denunciation of *all* pronouncements that would define such "femininity" as either necessary or normal.

8. *Lefty* may also provide a clue to the meaning of the final line in *House of Mirth*; "and in the silence there passed between them the word which made all clear." What is the "word"? Possibly Selden, too, is recollecting the ending of *Letty* (which concluded with the hero's echoing of Letty's own monosyllabic response to the termination of their relationship—" 'Thanks' ") Selden may most resemble Lily in having no deeper desire than the wish to enact some appropriately theatrical love scene.

Works Cited

Barthes, Roland. *S/Z*. Trans. Richard Miller. London: Cape, 1975.

Brooks, Peter. *Reading for the Plot: Design and Intention in Narrative*. New York: Vintage, 1984.

Chinoy, Helen Krich, and Linda Walsh Jenkins, eds. *Women in American Theatre*. Rev. ed. New York: Theatre Communications, 1987.

Clarke, Ian. *Edwardian Drama: A Critical Study*. London: Faber, 1989.

Review of *A Doll's House*, by Henrik Ibsen, with Ethel Barrymore. *New York Times*, 2 May 1905, p. 9.

Review of *Hamlet*, by William Shakespeare, with Sarah Bernhardt. *New York Times*, 26 Dec. 1900, p. 6.

Review of *Iris*, by Arthur Wing Pinero. *New York Times*, 28 Sept. 1902, p. 10+.

Review of *The Joy of Living*, trans. Edith Wharton. *New York Times*, 26 Oct. 1902, p. 9.

Leonard, Garry. "The Paradox of Desire: Jacques Lacan and Edith Wharton." *Edith Wharton Review* 7.3 (1990): 13–16.

Review of *Letty*, by Arthur Wing Pinero. *New York Times*, 13 Sept. 1904, p. 6.

Lewis, R. W. B. *Edith Wharton: A Biography*. New York: Harper, 1975.

Meisel, Martin. *Shaw and the Nineteenth-Century Theater*. 1963. New York: Limelight, 1984.

Pinero, Arthur W[ing]. *Iris: A Drama in Five Acts*. 1902. Boston: Baker, 1905.

———. *Letty: An Original Drama in Four Acts and an Epilogue*. 1904. Boston: Baker, 1905.

Shaw, George Bernard. *Major Critical Essays: The Quintessence of Ibsenism. The Perfect Wagnerite. The Sanity of Art*. London: Constable, 1932.

———. *Plays:* Mrs. Warren's Profession. . . . New York: NAL, 1960.

Stanton, Stephen S. Introduction. Camille *and Other Plays*. Ed. Stanton. New York: Hill, 1957. vii–xxxix.

Waid, Candace. *Edith Wharton's Letters from the Underworld: Fictions of Women and Writing*. Chapel Hill: University of North Carolina Press, 1991.

Wharton, Edith. *The House of Mirth*. New York: Scribner's, 1905.

Wolff, Cynthia Griffin. "Lily Bart and the Beautiful Death." *American Literature* 46 (1974): 16–40.

Engendering Naturalism

Narrative Form and Commodity Spectacle in U.S. Naturalist Fiction

LORI MERISH

◆ ◆ ◆

I. Billboard Love

In a well-known passage from Theodore Dreiser's *Sister Carrie*, the eponymous heroine, Carrie Meeber, "an apt student in fortune's ways," learns a lesson from her lover in the art of feminine public appearance. Carrie, a young woman from the countryside recently arrived in Chicago, walks with her lover, Drouet, and "pick[s] . . . up" from him the trick of attentively watching women who pass along the street:

> Drouet had a habit . . . of looking after stylishly dressed or pretty women on the street and remarking upon them. He had just enough of the feminine love of dress to be a good judge—not of intellect but of clothes. He saw how they set their little feet, how they carried their chins, with what grace and sinuosity they swayed their bodies. A dainty, self-conscious swaying of the hips by a woman was to him as alluring as the glint of rare wine to a toper. He would turn and follow the disappearing vision with his eyes . . .

"Did you see that woman who went by just now?" he said to Carrie, on the very first day they took a walk together.

It was a very average type of woman they had encountered, young, pretty, very satisfactorily dressed so far as appearances went, though not in style. Drouet had never seen the perfectly groomed ladies of the New York social set, or he would have been conscious of her defects. Carrie had spied her first, though with scarce so single an eye.

"Fine stepper, wasn't she?"

Carrie looked again and observed the grace commended.

"Yes, she is," she returned cheerfully, a little suggestion of possible defect in herself awakening in her mind. If that was so fine she must look at it more closely. Instinctively she felt a desire to imitate it. Surely she could do that too. (99)

This passage reads like an allegory of feminine consumer education in the turn-of-the-century capitalist public sphere. Occurring on the "very first day" Carrie and Drouet walk together, the incident is framed as an urban initiation, one which begins to map out the coordinates of Carrie's physical and psychological relocation from rural "periphery" to urban "center." Although Dreiser lapses here (as, at times, elsewhere) into a Darwinian rhetoric of "instinct," the scene in fact foregrounds Carrie's desire—specifically, her *taste*—as a *cultural construction*, one thoroughly enmeshed in a politics of class, gender, and sexuality—as well as nationality.[1] And perhaps because Dreiser's was the era when the consumer public sphere, with its conventionally heterosexist erotic economy, was an emerging social form, the passage details that construction (and its politics) in a refreshingly straightforward way. Notably, if this is a scene in which Carrie is made into a desirable (because appropriately desirous and tasteful) "woman," it is also a scene in which she is reconstructed as an "American" and incorporated within an emerging national commodity market. Born in rural Wisconsin to the children of German immigrants, Carrie here officially begins her transformation from country girl to "American woman." In this scene, Carrie's protofeminist desire for "freedom" and escape from the patriarchal family is scripted into a national consumerist form. What we are witnessing here is the making of the modern American consumer whose "civilized" desires constituted a salient marker of national identity and increasingly appeared—in political discourse as well as advertisements—as both motive and justification for U.S. imperial expansion. In *Sister Carrie*, Dreiser constructs taste as an expressly "feminine" cultural practice, and underscores the new, *public* orientation of women's consumer identities in mass culture.

Carrie's transformation is fundamentally, I have suggested; a transformation in her subjectivity and desire—a desire reshaped here through the visual parameters of modern urban experience. For Carrie's desire is decidedly visual: if in this passage she is learning to *desire*, she is also learning to *look*. She is, to be sure, an avid student: the "spectacle of warm-blooded humanity" on the street had struck her as powerfully absorbing from her first moments in the city, so that her favorite occupation while at her sister Minnie's flat, where she stays when she first comes to Chicago, is "standing at the street door looking out" (76, 53). Drouet, who has "just enough of the feminine love of dress" to appreciate the cultivated graces of feminine appearance, guides and coaxes Carrie's desire, directing her attention toward the "young, pretty, very satisfactorily dressed" woman who passes by. Carrie had "spied her first," but Carrie's look, though precocious, is coded as a naive gaze, "scarce so single" as Drouet's, a look which is, as yet, uncultured and uncultivated. Carrie's look, Dreiser suggests, must be trained: specifically, it must be filtered through Drouet's own ("Carrie looked again and observed the grace commended"). (Partially) identifying with Drouet's look, Carrie sees the (other) young woman as well as herself: she is developing the art of "comparison shopping." Watching the "fine stepper" that Drouet eyes appreciatively, Carrie finds a "little suggestion of possible defect in herself awakening in her mind." What is awakening here is the practice of compulsory self-scrutiny that feminists have seen to be endemic to consumer culture. While Carrie is "learning to look"—becoming an active consumer subject—she is also learning to see herself as an object according to increasingly exacting commodity standards of taste and social distinction. Crucially, the gaze which determines value in this scene is male, as well as culturally (i.e., racially, class, nationally) specific; that gaze is authorized by a masculine aesthetics underwritten by male economic power.

Carrie must learn to see as Drouet sees, but with a difference. What for Drouet is the studied appreciation of the would-be connoisseur is for Carrie an identificatory longing that is primarily a desire to *be* the other woman: to remake her own body in the image of the "young, pretty, very satisfactorily dressed" woman; to build a new body, through the imitation of gesture and aesthetic surface, that closely resembles the (feminine) object of her desire. Carrie's longing to "creat[e] a good impression" (43)—a longing here *produced* in public—converts an apprehension of value into gestures of bodily reconstruction and emulation. Notably, the exchange of bodies which Carrie imagines takes place wholly in the visual register: the woman who catches Drouet's and Carrie's eye is flattened out into a material image and is of interest only as a visual representation of desirability and allure. Such visual exchanges were being institutionalized in the consumer public sphere, largely through the burgeoning advertising industry. During the 1890s, with the arrival of the screen halftone, which enabled the mass reproduction of illustrations and photographs, advertisements became more pictorial in emphasis and advertising images became increasingly realistic. Ads from the period frequently featured images of women, such as the "Sozodont Girl" (used to advertise Sozodont Dentrifrice) and the "Gibson Girl," images which became, in the words of one historian, a "popular means of attracting attention" to an advertisement (Presbrey 382). Indeed, the "pretty girl picture" was a pervasive presence in American advertising by the turn of the century; as Bella Landauer notes, around 1900 the "bathing beauty" gained ascendancy as an icon in advertising, replacing the verbal and textual orientation of earlier ads, which had typically featured literary allusions and references to well-known authors from Mother Goose to Shakespeare (149). What Dreiser depicts as Carrie's desire to inhabit the bodies of anonymous (female) others was the *effect* of an historically specific technology of gender, one which produced new forms of (class, racial, sexual, and national) consumer subjectivities. In order to demonstrate what part naturalism played in this moment, I will turn from *Sister Carrie* to Edith Wharton's *The House of Mirth*, a novel whose representations of consumerism are even more explicitly regendered in terms of the opposition between observing subject and object of the gaze.[2] Indeed, this novel might well be considered an allegory of naturalism's rewriting of the subject-object opposition to address late-nineteenth-century economic conditions and popular anxieties about them.

II. Consumption and Visibility

Recently, feminist theorists have reevaluated the politics of women's consumption and have begun viewing women's bodily reconstruction through consumption as an empowering political act. In important work on late-nineteenth-century consumer culture, Miriam Hansen has argued that mass consumerism challenged the bourgeois gender hierarchy of public and private and opened up a space for the public representation and social recognition of women's desires. Drawing upon Oscar Negt and Alexander Haug's theory of the "proletarian public sphere," Hansen suggests that by acknowledging human needs more concretely than the bourgeois public sphere, albeit for the purpose of appropriation, the branches of consumer culture "brought into view a different concept of the public sphere: that of a 'social horizon of experience' " (55). Others have contended that consumer reembodiment has accorded women the power to reproduce, in the sphere of consumption, the political reembodiment of constitutional self-making—historically, the prerogative of elite white men (Norton, Berlant). Late-nineteenth-century consumer culture engendered new possibilities of identification and desire, challenging normative scripts of heterosexuality and maternity (Fuss; Radner 35–65). In Dreiser's novel, Carrie's desire for reembodiment, enacted through consumption and commodity display and epitomized in her acting career, registers what Hansen terms the "utopian" political dimensions of mass consumption. However, the text simultaneously registers the limits of consumerism as a site of female power. These limits, Dreiser suggests, inhere in women's unstable construction as both subjects and objects of exchange.[3] This instability is especially apparent in the fashion system, a symbolic structure that historically has entangled signs of liberation and oppression—of feminine pleasure and autonomy, and masculine power and domination—within the image of the fashionable female body.[4] In the passage with which this essay begins, Dreiser shows how the positions of "subject" and "object" collapse into one another in the consumer public sphere. Feminine taste appears as a *regulatory* medium, one which proscribes a certain relation of female "subject" to her own body—in some sense, the object of all (commodity) objects, incorporating cultural codes that regulate them all (Armstrong, "Occidental").

With the rise of a national market and national advertising in the late nineteenth century, feminine consumption emerged as a primary cultural problematic (Lears; Dijkstra; Bowlby). Numerous cultural texts from the period—from literature and paintings to political cartoons and advertisements—featured the "woman consumer," whose public, extradomestic practices constituted new possibilities for fantasy and erotic investment. The often reproduced statistic that women controlled "90 percent of her family's expenditures" bespoke the new authority ascribed to feminine consumption while reframing that authority within the heterosexual presumption of the nuclear family as the basic economic unit. The genre of naturalist fiction, in particular—perhaps following the lead of Zola's *Au Bonheur des Dames*—featured the female consumer as a new cultural type whose commodity desires often outstripped, and certainly redefined, her sexuality.[5] If earlier novels tend to depict feminine eroticism as the primary narrative problematic—characteristically "resolved" through narrative endings of marriage or death—late-nineteenth-century texts activate a different erotic economy, in which female consumption complicates—and restructures—sexual desire.

Late-nineteenth-century scientific discourses attempted to contain the power of consuming—its potential for reconfiguring feminine desire and identification—by casting consumer practices in the categories of sexual deviance: consumption disorders such as "kleptomania" and "oniomania" ("the inability to stop shopping") were newly codified in medical and sexological literature and were typically tied to the dis-ease of women's reproduction. Like the contemporary sexological taxonomies of sexuality, classifications of consumer deviance operated to police consumer desire, deploying a binary logic which constituted certain practices (and subjectivities) as normative (Abelson 148–72). At the same time, naturalist literary practice—defined by its oft-noted "scientific" objectivity—emerged as a cultural movement in explicit response to the "feminizing" influence of women's literary consumption and the cultural authority of "feminine" taste. Naturalist authors themselves often cast their project in gendered terms, as a revolt against a feminized and genteel Victorianism: David Graham Phillips, for instance, applauded the forceful vigor of the period's journalistic realism as a welcome eruption of the "eternal Masculine"; others called for a "roast beef" of narrative style and an unremitting clarity of vision as against the "drama of the broken teacup" and the proprieties of popular sentimental fare (Wilson 152, 58). In a real sense, naturalist fiction might be generically defined as an effort to contain feminine consumption as a cultural force. Simultaneously fascinated and repelled by women's new role as consumers, scientists and naturalist novelists both explored and aimed to control the disruptive power of feminine consumer desire. That control was exercised both discursively and visually, through the scientific gaze of medical literature and the masculine social gaze of naturalist narrative.[6]

I will argue below that naturalist texts enact gendered fantasies of surveillance that work to contain the radical potential of feminine consumer desire and to redefine the female consumer subject as commodity *object*.[7] Naturalism has a gender, I contend, because it deals with the problem of the feminine consumer at precisely the moment when American culture was beginning to see itself as more dependent on consumption than on a form of production that could be understood as masculine in character.

Naturalism dealt with this problem by collapsing the difference between consumer and commodity. Thus, as we saw in the passage from *Sister Carrie*, naturalism circumscribes consumer agency by turning the female consumer quite literally into the things she desires. By so transforming the desiring subject into the objects of her desire, naturalism subordinates such objects to the masculine observer. Once visibility becomes the basis for differentiating subject from object, in other words, it is a rather simple matter to resubordinate the female, as someone who cannot control objects, to the male who is able—by virtue of a gender that differentiates him from objects—to do so. Where the male has the power to choose what kind of consumer to be, the female no longer does, at least not in *The House of Mirth*, a novel that plays out this cultural logic to its all-or-nothing conclusion.[8] The only alternative to life as a hapless commodity destined by the laws of the market to lose value that Wharton allows her heroine even to imagine is a life of Christian renunciation, an alternative inscribed in the text's sentimental vision of (re)absorption into domestic invisibility.[9]

In *The House of Mirth*, the affective possibilities engendered by mass consumption, as well as their regulation through naturalist narrativization, are equally apparent. The novel's two main characters, Lily Bart and Lawrence Selden, are potential lovers, and their unfulfilled "romance" constitutes the text's dominant narrative thematic. But Lily Bart's "femininity" and Selden's "masculinity" are tenuous constructions, while their heterosexual "passion" is ambiguously presented in the text. As with Undine Spragg (*The Custom of the Country*), Lily Bart's passion for men is much less convincingly rendered than her passion for things. Obviously disturbed by Lily's (hetero)sexual "coldness," which he contrasts with her intense desire for commodities, R. W. B. Lewis once pathologized Wharton's heroine as a "nymphomaniac of material comfort" ("Edith Wharton" 144).

For his part, Selden's general skittishness in love and his emotional vacillations regarding Lily—criticized as moral spinelessness by Wharton's feminist readers, as by Wharton herself—bespeak a certain sexual ambiguity, as does his characterization as a bachelor-professional—a type whose historical relationship to the emergence of gay identities Eve Sedgwick has examined at length. But, under the disciplinary gaze of the naturalist text, these erotic ambiguities give way to the gender binary of heterosexual romance—thus narrativizing gender as sexual difference and reinforcing "the epistemic regime of presumptive heterosexuality" (Butler x). That regime is policed by a specular logic that is economically determined in Wharton's novel.

Foregrounding this specular logic, *The House of Mirth* explores in detail the complex relationships among vision, gender, and desire in the emergent consumer culture. Visual relations are determined in *The House of Mirth* by what Wharton terms the "invisible laws" of commodity exchange. Indeed, the market figures in that text as an "impersonal power," constituting the invisible referent of social relations (Poirier 131–32).[10] According to the narrator, diverse social and political phenomena—from the "allotment of executive power" to the forms of social entertainment—betray a "sympathetic" relation to the market, to the distribution of "railway stocks and bales of cotton" (120). Most of the novel's action takes place in semipublic spaces of consumption and commercial amusement: in the lavish homes of the rich, typically designed for the "display of festal assemblage[s]," rather than as "frame[s] for domesticity" (131); at the horse show; or in the opera hall, spaces of public transportation (e.g., the train), casinos, expensive hotels, and fashionable restaurants. The market in *The House of Mirth* is an inescapable, controlling environment, a subterranean network which organizes the text's relations of visibility and which is largely controlled by *men*. The Wall Street world of "tips" and "deals" manipulated and managed by men such as Simon Rosedale and Gus Trenor is beyond Lily's range of vision. Like many nineteenth-century women's novels, *The House of Mirth* represents the marketplace as a space of male predation and female danger—especially sexual danger. Lily's sentimental approach to the market and cultivated inattention to "money matters"—a posture deemed genteel in a wealthy matron but deadly in a "horribly poor" single woman (10)—leaves her vulnerable to the lascivious designs of men such as Trenor and ultimately leads to her downfall.

The ubiquitous presence of the market is signaled in the novel's opening pages. As Lily Bart tells Selden in the novel's first scene, she is without economic means but "very expensive" (10): raised in an atmosphere of "studied luxury," she has grown accustomed to the "external finish" of life (40, 25), although she can no longer afford to gratify her expensive tastes. Plotting her capture of Percy Gryce, the last in a series of prospective husbands, Lily takes great pleasure in the prospect of finally "doing over" her own drawing room, and the novel begins with Lily several hundreds in debt to her dressmaker and jeweler. What Wharton calls the "amusement of spending" is further indicated by Lily's susceptibility to the "gambling passion" (27). But if Lily is represented as an avid and enthusiastic consumer, she is also marked quite plainly as a commodity. "The beautiful Miss Bart" (196) occupies the increasingly specularized and "feminized" space of the commodity in late-nineteenth-century culture—a space organized, Wharton indicates, by male economic power and male desire. In a legal and socioeconomic context in which women were collectively defined as men's sexual property and in which men controlled much of the wealth women spent, women's self-presentation as public subjects, Wharton suggests, inevitably competed with their objectification by men and their status as men's (sexual) objects. In *The House of Mirth*, Lily's desire to buy is framed by men's desire to buy *her*.

Lily's status as a commodity is made absolutely explicit in *The House of Mirth* Lily's body is considered a marketable "possession" by most of the novel's characters. Lily's mother, for instance, sees her daughter's physical beauty as her main "weapon" and economic asset (37), and Rosedale, evincing what Wharton calls his "collector's passion" (113), admires the "rarity" of Lily's beauty and manner because she projects the air of "cost[ing] more" than any woman he has ever seen (176). Lily herself is acutely self-conscious of the economic value of her cultivated body as an article of "superfine human merchandise" (256) and views her beauty as a "possession" to be preserved and improved. In order to enhance the desirability of her property, Lily wears luxurious and low-cut dresses, cares for her skin and hair, and displays herself to advantage. As a single woman on the market for a husband, Lily [finds that her] status as commodity is publicly marked, and the requirement to remain "brilliant and predominant" (122)—to keep herself, in Lily's words, "fresh and exquisite and amusing" (266)—is an economic necessity. Remaining "vivid" and desirable in a consumer society, Lily pointedly notes, costs a lot of money, and her efforts to do so lead her to accept economic "backing" from Trenor which, in turn, intensifies her need to find a prospective buyer. In Lily's case, the positions of "consumer" and "commodity" are inextricably interwoven: the "amusement of spending" is inseparable from the exigencies of self-marketing. In *The House of Mirth*, Lily's public "conspicuousness" is represented as dependent—economically and formally—on the invisible presence of men, on male capital and male desire.

The omnipresence of the proprietary male "look" is principally figured by the novel's "negative hero," Lawrence Selden. Selden, a genteel lawyer with fastidious tastes who relishes his "spectatorship" as a form of "indolent amusement" (8), is particularly charmed by the "wonderful spectacle" of Lily Bart (66). Selden, in fact, is represented as Lily's most interested spectator: the novel opens with his perspective, and his voyeuristic interest in Lily is indulged throughout the novel. As I have already suggested, Selden at first glance would seem to be an unlikely incarnation of male power and authority. Selden, as Wharton repeatedly notes, *can't afford* Lily: with only a modest income, he has, as he tells Lily, "nothing to give" her (72). But Selden, who learned from his mother to appreciate the "luxury of charm" (152), is a connoisseur and collector who invests in aesthetic objects "as much as a man who has no money to spend" (10). In fact, it is precisely because he *can't* afford (but *appreciates*) Lily that Selden best enacts  the dynamics of visual desire in consumer culture. In her characterization of Selden, Wharton dramatizes the compelling, apparently irresistible nature of the commodity spectacle and the new pleasures of "just looking" in a specularized social milieu. It is Lily's exorbitant "price" that, for Selden, marks her as desirable *precisely because out of reach*. And it is because Selden remains *just* a spectator—in a suspended state of visual desire—that he best evinces the fantasies of proprietorship engendered by modern consumerism.

III. Gender, Publicity, and the Commodified Body

Selden's pleasure in looking at Lily, and the politics of looking which structure their relationship and generate his pleasure, are foregrounded in *The House of Mirth*. One might say, in fact, that Selden's visual pleasure initiates the narrative: the novel opens with his surprised but pleasurable "sighting" of Lily Bart in the crowded train station, a vision which "refreshed" his eyes (3). Selden takes "a luxurious pleasure" (5) in Lily's appearance and eyes her with "a purely impersonal enjoyment" (10); the narrator tells us, "as a spectator, [Selden] had always enjoyed Miss Bart" (4). Selden's favorite stance is that of detached viewer: aloof and remote, he is consistently depicted as a spectator scanning the stage of life, surveying the spectacle and requiring only that the production be "aesthetically pleasing" (212). And the most aesthetically pleasing production in the novel is of course Wharton's heroine, "the beautiful Miss Bart" (196).

The complexities of Lily's position, and of Selden's visual investment in Lily, are legible in the opening scene. The novel begins *in medias res*: "Selden paused in surprise. In the afternoon rush of the Grand Central Station his eyes had been refreshed by the sight of Miss Lily Bart" (3). The narrative opening, which frames the novel with Selden's arrested gaze and Miss Bart's arresting appearance identifies as the motive for spectatorial "pause" and narrative interest the appearance of a beautiful, mysterious woman. "One or two" other passersby "lingered to look" for, according to the narrator, "Miss Bart was a figure to arrest even the suburban traveller rushing to his last train" (4). But Selden's look in particular is riveted by Lily's presence, and he immediately engages in "speculation" about her motives and intentions, his interest provoked by her simultaneous embodiment of "publicity" and "privacy," transparency and reserve:

> It was a Monday in early September, and he was returning to his work from a hurried dip into the country; but what was Miss Bart doing in town at that season? If she had appeared to be catching a train, he might have inferred that he had come on her in the act of transition between one and another of the country-houses which disputed her presence after the close of the Newport season; but her desultory air perplexed him. She stood apart from the crowd, letting it drift by her to the platform or the street, and wearing an air of irresolution which might, as he surmised, be the mask of a very definite purpose. It struck him at once that she was waiting for some one, but he hardly knew why the idea arrested him. There was nothing new about Lily Bart, yet he could never see her without a faint movement of interest: it was characteristic of her that she always roused speculation, that her simplest acts seemed the result of far-reaching intentions. (3)

Selden's visual desire is stirred at once by the aesthetic pleasure of Lily's image and by his belief that that image conceals an unexpressed interiority and occludes a hidden reservoir of meaning. The two poles of Selden's visual interest—aesthetic valorization and a desire for possession of intimate knowledge, or what feminist psychoanalytic and film critics term "fetishism" and "voyeurism"—structure his desire throughout the novel (Mulvey). Like other men in the novel, such as Rosedale, Trenor, and Ned Van Alstyne, Selden is charmed by Lily's attractive physical surface, her beauty and elusive, refined manner: in particular, he appreciates Lily's grace and the "high finish" of her beauty (3). But Selden's proprietary desire is especially moved by breaks in that surface, what Wharton later calls the "hint of weakness" in Lily, penetrable gaps in her manner through which the "fluctuations of the spirit were sometimes tragically visible" (68, 191). Selden's proprietary desire extends to Lily's *subjectivity* and entails a desire for privileged and exclusive knowledge of an interiority—what he repeatedly calls the "real Lily"—invisible to all but himself. Selden flatters himself that he enjoys privileged access into what makes Lily tick. He ascribes to himself a god-like omniscience enabling him to survey Lily's most "private" self—a fantasy which culminates in his exhilarated "revelation" when he catches sight of Lily at Bellomont later in the novel: "That is how she looks when she is alone!" (69).

In her discussion of this scene, Amy Kaplan contends that "by introducing the main character through Selden's confusion," the novel "introduces itself as a more accurate 'speculation' " on Lily Bart's character and implicitly promises to "clarify the mystery" of Wharton's heroine. According to Kaplan, the "mystery" which produces both Selden's and the reader's interest is generated by the visible distinction between the "dull tints" of the "crowd" of working-class women, described later in the scene as the "shallow-faced girls in preposterous hats, and flat-chested women with paper bundles and palm leaf fans" (5), and Lily's radiant image. Kaplan argues that the narrative capitalizes on this discrepancy and is motivated by an effort to (re)construct buried connections between the social classes, gradually "unfolding the relation between the veiled figure of the lady and the crowd that surrounds her" (88). Kaplan deftly analyzes the importance of class relationships in the novel and the significance of public display in the representation of class power (88–103). But Selden's "confusion" and visual interest in Lily in the novel's opening pages derives from other, equally significant sources. Lily exhibits for Selden what Freud would later describe as the "enigma" of femininity: "woman's" concurrent embodiment of accessibility and inaccessibility, assent and withholding, "publicity" and "privacy."[11] Selden feels himself simultaneously in possession and not in possession of Lily Bart. Selden configures this doubleness in terms of a series of related dichotomies: surface and depth, appearance and reality—and, finally, art and nature.

Seized by an "impulse of curiosity" in the train station, Selden approaches Lily hoping to penetrate her mystery but finds himself endlessly elaborating new possibilities of concealment, so that even Lily's apparently spontaneous responses—her "imprudences" as well as her "discretions"—are imputed to "the same carefully-elaborated plan" (5). As the narrator notes, Selden "could never be long with [Lily] without trying to find a reason for what she was doing" (11): while he finds it "pleasant" to look at her, this pleasure in her appearance and performed actions is generated and sustained by his fascination with her interior motives and by a suspicion of even her most insignificant expressions and gestures. The gap Selden compulsively investigates between revealed appearance and concealed secret is reconstituted later in the scene as a distinction between art and nature. When the two converse in Selden's apartment where he has invited Lily for tea; Lily appears to him "a captured dryad subdued to the conventions of the drawing-room," and the narrator notes that, for Selden, "it was the . . . streak of sylvan freedom in her nature that lent such savour to her artificiality" (13). Selden's visual interest in her is in fact produced by the seeming artfulness of her physical self-presentation. Selden's unspoken preoccupations while he walks beside Lily on their way to the Benedick might be summed up by the now-familiar question "Does she or doesn't she?"

> As [Lily] moved beside him, with her long light step, Selden was conscious of taking a luxurious pleasure in her nearness: in the modelling of her little ear, the crisp upward wave of her hair—was it ever so slightly heightened by art?—and the thick planting of her straight black lashes. Everything about her was at once vigorous and exquisite, at once strong and fine. He had a confused sense that she must have cost a great deal to make, that a great many dull and ugly people must, in some mysterious way, have been sacrificed to produce her. He was aware that the qualities distinguishing her from the herd of her sex were chiefly external: as though a fine glaze of beauty and fastidiousness had been applied to vulgar clay. (5)

The narrator encodes the contradictions which Selden finds embodied in Lily's presence in a chain of dual significations—she is both vigorous and exquisite, strong and fine, mortal flesh (unadorned "vulgar clay") and polished artifact. Lily's embodied synthesis of art and nature similarly connotes both the aristocratic ideal of nonchalance—the art that conceals all art—and the prosaic platitudes of bourgeois consumerism.

The visually titillating ambiguities encoded in Lily's synthesis of art and nature—the commingling of the natural and the commodified body—are intensified in this scene by the material presence of Lily's veil. The veil foregrounds and in effect stages the mysterious process by which raw materiality is converted into the visually fascinating commodity.[12] According to the narrator, Lily's "radiant" and "vivid" physical presence is heightened by the veil which covers her face, restoring to her "the girlish smoothness, the purity of tint" which the twenty-nine-year-old heroine is starting to lose (4). The veil, by simultaneously revealing and delicately concealing Lily's image, externalizes the dynamic of "semiconcealment"—the concomitance of public and private, external sign and interior, invisible motive—which piques Selden's interest. This tension between consent and refusal, giving and withholding, emblematized by the veiled body was identified by Wharton's contemporary, the sociologist Georg Simmel, as the defining characteristic of femininity. Simmel observed that veiling the body with clothes and "the girdles and petticoats that fulfill the function of a fig leaf" render concealment itself ornamental, marking the body as "eminently worthy of attention" while concealing what is adorned. "From the perspective of the man," Simmel notes, the woman thus attired appears as a "Not-Yet, an unredeemed promise, an unborn profusion of obscure possibilities that have not yet developed far enough beyond their psychic location to become visible and apprehensible" (147–48)[13] In *The House of Mirth*, Lily's veiled body displays the "Not-Yet" of femininity—the "semiconcealment" and flirtatious foregrounding of the private, "unattainable" self—that magnetizes the masculine social gaze and produces male erotic interest.[14]

For her part, Lily Bart recognizes that the codes of fashionable display and the ornamental concealment of the body form a specifically feminine language, one in which women must be well versed. Drinking tea in Selden's apartment, she directs Selden's attention to the social imperatives surrounding feminine dress: "Your coat's a little shabby—but who cares? It doesn't keep people from asking you to dine. If I were shabby no one would have me: a woman is asked out as much for her clothes as for herself. The clothes are the background, the frame, if you like: they don't make success, but they are a part of it. Who wants a dingy woman? We are expected to be pretty and well-dressed till we drop—and if we can't keep it up alone, we have to go into partnership" (12). The imperative of specifically *feminine* sartorial conspicuousness was, in fact, a fairly recent phenomenon: fashion historians point out that during the late eighteenth and early nineteenth centuries, ornate dress—made up of vivid colors, luxurious fabrics, and elaborate decoration and defined by the rapidly changing codes of fashion—which had during the fifteenth, sixteenth, and seventeenth centuries been a prerogative of the aristocratic elite and a sign of social class was increasingly associated with women, while most men adopted some version of the plain, dark, uniform three-piece suit. With gender replacing social class as the principal category of sartorial distinction, fashionable appearance and sumptuary display became material markers of femininity (Silverman). The gender division of "conspicuousness" to which Lily Bart alludes in this scene was famously theorized by Thorstein Veblen. "The function of woman," Veblen wrote, is "to exhibit the pecuniary strength of her social unit by means of a conspicuously unproductive consumption of valuable goods" (200). Like the narrator's numerous references to Lily's "adaptability" and her capacity to "harmonize herself with her [material] surroundings" (192), the enforced identification of femininity with sartorial ornamentation that Lily analyzes in Selden's apartment similarly foregrounds the equivalence the novel constructs between (female) body and (commodified) "thing."

Notably, Wharton's own childhood ambition was to be "the best-dressed woman in New York"—an ambition partly owing to her mother's scrupulous fashion sense and "inexhaustible" interest in the "details of dress" (*Backward* 20, 17).[15] Constructing a fashionable appearance is, Lily knows, the key to social success, a central part of an attractive woman's physical allure: as she asks rhetorically, "Who wants a dingy woman?" Dressing well, as she tells Selden, is "part of the business" (12). But fashionable clothes are also, quite plainly, a form of advertising : what Wharton calls the "enhancements of dress" (116) attract attention to a woman and court the gaze of her audience—a crucial business for, as Lily's mother had warned her, "People can't marry you if they don't see you" (35). Feminine fashions call attention to the female body and intensify a woman's "conspicuousness," vividly embodying the conflicting values of self-display and self-concealment and staging the giving and withholding of self.

For his part, Selden responds to Lily's social analysis with silent "amusement," finding it "impossible, even with her lovely eyes imploring him, to take a sentimental view of her case" and dismissing her concerns with the clever rejoinder, "There must be plenty of capital on the lookout for such an investment" (12). Still, as I have suggested, it is precisely the erotic promise emblematized by feminine sartorial display—that of knowledge withheld, of private experience unshared by others—which fascinates him. In this scene, Wharton defines the stance that Selden will maintain throughout the novel vis-à-vis Lily Bart: Selden oscillates between spontaneous interest in Lily and a restrained detachment. The detachment of Wharton's "negative hero" has often been noted by critics (e.g., Michelson, Wolff). Wharton identifies this detachment as a product of Selden's natural circumspection and "fastidiousness," depicted in the novel as a genteel—and inherited—unwillingness to take "risks." But this detachment is also due to Selden's inability to afford Lily. Selden, because he has no "capital" to "invest," can only look on. Selden's posture of "admiring spectatorship" thus suits him perfectly: it "costs" him nothing, involves few "risks," and allows him to take his "pleasure in [Lily's] nearness" for free.

Selden's ambivalence—alternating between fascination and reserve—structures his relationship to Lily throughout the novel and establishes that relationship as a lengthy flirtation. Throughout the text, Selden eyes Lily with detachment and self-restraint, characteristically approaching her with the "aesthetic amusement which a reflective man is apt to seek in desultory intercourse with pretty women" (66, 68). This "personal detachment" (187) occasionally lapses into cruelty, as during the pastoral interlude at Bellomont where Selden and Lily enjoy a few hours of intimate conversation and the "finer air" of an elevated vista, and at the Van Osburgh wedding. At Bellomont, Selden, who had long before, Wharton informs us, renounced "sentimental experiments," proves himself up to the task: hesitant and cautious in his conversation with Lily, he alternates between abrupt declarations of feeling and self-protective, sarcastic retorts, as if he fears the "chance of his having to pay up" (151). Similarly, at the Van Osburgh wedding, Selden meets the appeal of Lily's "helplessness" and sincerity with a mixture of aesthetic amusement and voyeuristic suspicion. Selden leans against the window jamb, "a detached observer of the scene," and attentively studies Lily, letting his "eyes rest on her in frank enjoyment of her grace" and following with apparent irony her social maneuvers with Rosedale and Trenor (94).

But it is during the tableaux vivant scene at the Wellington Brys that Selden's visual operations are most clearly delineated. It is there—where Lily's veiled body is on public display—that Selden imagines himself in possession of the "real Lily" and resolves to profess his love and propose marriage. Tableaux vivants, the narrator tells us, "depend for their effect not only on the happy disposal of light and the delusive interposition of layers of gauze, but on a corresponding adjustment of the mental vision. To unfurnished minds they remain, in spite of every enhancement of art, only a superior kind of wax-works; but to the responsive fancy they may give magic glimpses of the boundary world between fact and imagination" (133). Selden, apparently, has just such a "responsive fancy": "He could yield to vision-making influences as completely as a child to the spell of a fairy tale" (133). As Reynolds's *Mrs. Lloyd*, Lily exemplifies the magic of spectacular illusion: according to the narrator, she has selected "a type so like her own that she could embody the person represented without ceasing to be herself. It was as though she had stepped not out of, but into, Reynolds's canvas, banishing the phantom of his dead beauty by the beams of her living grace" (134). Captivated by the vision of Lily's alluring, veiled body, and by her synthesis and simultaneous embodiment of a series of oppositions—illusion and truth, art and nature, "Mrs. Lloyd" and "Lily Bart"—Selden is overcome and fancies himself in intimate possession of the "real Lily Bart" (135). After her performance, he lingers before approaching her to "prolong" the "exquisite" moment and to "luxuriate . . . in the sense of complete surrender" (136). When he finally reaches her, he finds "the expected look in her eye," confirming his belief in her performance's intimate address and that it was, in the narrator's words, "for him only that she cared to be beautiful" (137). That belief—and Selden's sense of Lily's "value"—is compromised the following evening by the scene he witnesses on Trenor's doorstep, which seems to indicate Lily's "promiscuity" and the possibility that she "belongs" to other men as well (160–61).

Selden's (mis)perception that Lily is "cheap" convinces him—at least until the novel's last scene—that investing in her is simply not worth the risk. Indeed, the predominant feeling Selden "nourishe[s]" after his near-proposal to Lily is "one of thankfulness for his escape," and he imagines himself as a traveler who has been rescued from a "dangerous accident" (187). But, although Selden attempts to mitigate what Wharton describes as the "sharp shock of . . . disillusionment" (187) by fleeing to Havana and then by burying himself in his work, he cannot long resist the riveting spectacle of Lily Bart. Experiencing a "renewed zest of spectatorship" after a season's reprieve, Selden visits Monte Carlo—where he unexpectedly happens upon Lily and her New York traveling companions (183–84). Selden's seemingly inevitable return as Lily's audience in the novel suggests the irresistible power of Lily's charms, a power to fix Selden's gaze which apparently displaces the boundaries between proprietor and property, subject and object. But Wharton's depiction of Selden's almost compulsive return principally works to reinscribe the male look and male desire as the novel's structuring presence. Feminine "conspicuousness" in Wharton's novel is but one half of a vital exchange and depends on male spectatorship to realize and ratify its significance. If, as

Kaplan argues, Lily's set needs the visual interest of the "gaping mob" to demarcate the "little patch of purple" and invest it with value, Lily Bart would seem to require the presence of the erotically engaged male spectator to constitute her identity as a ("desirable") woman.

IV. Selling Gender: Commodity Self-Fashioning

In his position as detached spectator, one marginal to much of the novel's action, Selden enjoys what Mark Seltzer calls the "privilege of relative disembodiment" (*Bodies* 9) vis-à-vis the "brilliant and predominant" Lily Bart. It is a privilege to which Lily refers when she contrasts her own need to construct an attractive appearance with Selden's less taxing social invisibility. This privilege—the privilege of disembodied abstraction—reflects a broader gender division of embodiment in late-nineteenth-century consumer culture.[16] This gender division of embodiment is suggested in *The House of Mirth* by the fact that male economic providers in the text—most notably Lily's father Mr. Bart—are spectral individuals, mere "supernumerar[ies] in the costly show for which [their] money paid" (85), who hover in the background of the narrative and are "seen" only when their economic funds are needed. Men's material *invisibility* relative to women in *fin-de-siècle* America was noted by numerous cultural critics and observers, including Thorstein Veblen and Wharton's close friend Henry James.[17] However, unlike James, Wharton suggests that men's social invisibility in modern culture is not a sign of their marginality but rather an index of their economic and political power. *The House of Mirth* both probes and questions the cultural logic according to which women's bodies are used to display men's wealth and men's wares and in which the social rituals over which women conspicuously preside theatrically exhibit male power.

This gender division of embodiment is legible, as I have shown, in the novel's opening scene and structures the representation of

Selden and Lily's relationship throughout the novel. In Wharton's text, the privileges of spectatorship and the novel's relays of looks encode this gendered division: Selden, occupying the position of spectator, is imaged (and imagines himself) as partially relieved of material constraints of the body; Lily, projecting feminine display and appearance, bears the weight of more complete embodiment. Selden's spectatorship expresses a desire that is erotic and proprietary and extends sexual and economic relations of control. Lily's emphatic embodiment signifies, in part, her subjection to male power and her status as marketable commodity.

In *The House of Mirth*, Selden's comparatively less intense embodiment vis-à-vis Lily is manifested spatially and is registered in terms of his physical mobility. Selden approximates in many of his characteristics a late-nineteenth-century masculine "type": the *flâneur*. The *flâneur*, the impassive urban stroller or "man of the crowd" who goes, in Walter Benjamin's memorable phrase, "botanizing on the asphalt," embodied new forms of modern experience, especially the privilege to move about the spaces of the city observing but not interacting, consuming the sights through a controlled and controlling gaze—a gaze both covetous and erotic which was directed as much as other people as at goods on display (Pollock 66–70). In *The House of Mirth*, Selden enjoys the easy mobility and urbane detachment of the *flâneur*. He shows up everywhere in the novel, often unexpectedly: he arrives without notice at Bellomont, where he comes to see Lily, and exits the scene as abruptly, and he surfaces as a spectator at the Van Osburgh marriage, the Wellington Brys, and again on the French Riviera. Selden describes himself as "amphibious" (70) and believes himself able to enter into Lily's fashionable social set and to depart essentially untouched. Lily questions the viability of this self-characterization, wryly observing that he "seems to . . . spend a good deal of [his] time in the element [he] disapprove[s] of," but the novel itself reinforces Selden's view of his unproblematic mobility. Selden exemplifies what Wharton depicts as the *male* capacity to traverse all the spaces of the city—both public and private—and remain unscathed and untouched. Exemplifying the "accepted social axiom that a man may go where he pleases"

(131), Selden passes easily from the public spaces of his profession to the social spaces of Lily's milieu, and he can visit Lily in the hotel apartment of the "disreputable" Norma Hatch without concern for his social standing or reputation.[18] Being a member of the male audience, Wharton suggests, entails a mobility that seems, when compared with Lily's more rigid strictures of appearance and performance, a kind of freedom.[19] Selden's marginality is, Wharton indicates, a form of power: he can weave in and out of the novel's social world, and can disappear and reappear without his "social credit" (261) diminishing.

But if Selden can thus flaunt his independence from the sphere of commercial "publicity" by voluntarily "disappearing and reappearing" in public, Lily Bart has no such option. Unlike Selden, Lily enjoys little freedom of movement: her position requires that she remain consistently before the public eye. In fact, the moment of her disappearance from high society marks, for Lily, the beginning of the end, leading directly to her suicide. Even Lily's moments alone are structured by the imperative to "be seen" by someone. Lily's compliance with the vicissitudes of male surveillance and her awareness of her status as beautiful object are documented throughout Wharton's novel. They are most clearly legible in the passage describing Lily's solitary walk at Bellomont:

> [Lily's] thoughts so engaged her that she fell into a gait hardly likely to carry her to church before the sermon, and at length, having passed from the gardens to the wood-path beyond, so far forgot her intention as to sink into a rustic seat at a bend of the walk. The spot was charming, and Lily was not insensible to the charm, or to the fact that her presence enhanced it; but she was not accustomed to taste the joys of solitude except in company, and the combination of a handsome girl and a romantic scene struck her as too good to be wasted. No one, however, appeared to profit by the opportunity; and after a half hour of fruitless waiting she rose and wandered on. She felt a stealing sense of fatigue as she walked; the sparkle had died out of her, and the taste of life was stale on her lips. She hardly knew what she had been seeking, or why the failure to

> find it had so blotted the light from her sky: she was only aware of a vague sense of failure, of an inner isolation deeper than the loneliness about her. (61)

Viewing herself as an "opportunity" for a potential male observer, Lily experiences a vague sense of failure when no passerby arrives to "profit" from her ritual of self-display. Importantly, it is *Selden* whom Lily anticipates: as the narrator notes, Selden had a way of "re-adjusting [Lily's] vision" so that she consistently "found herself scanning her little world through his retina" (55). In Lily, Wharton registers the constitutive nature of feminine commodity subjectivity.[20]

Lily's decline in the novel, as numerous critics have noted, is materially marked by her "shrinking existence" (263) and residence in increasingly constricted social spaces, proceeding from the lavish spaces of Bellomont to her final "resting place," a "narrow room" in a "shabby" boardinghouse (287). But this descent is more pointedly charted out as a decline from "conspicuousness" to "obscurity" and social invisibility. Here, again, Wharton underscores the specular, commodity coordinates of modern feminine "subjectivity." The plot is in fact significantly shaped by struggles among women for the social space of conspicuous desirability: Lily's "drab," poor cousin Grace Stepney resents Lily and relays rumors about her to Lily's Aunt Peniston because the young woman had slighted her, treating her as "insignificant" by excluding her from a fashionable dinner party, and Lily's power to charm Selden at Bellomont and her success on the Riviera prompt Bertha Dorset's malicious insinuations. Lily herself had entered the "sacred precincts" of high society with the "confidence of assured possessorship" of that territory, but she gradually finds herself struggling for a "foothold" (280, 38). Her triumph at the tableaux vivants, where she is "lifted to a height apart by that incommunicable grace which is the bodily counterpart of genius," demonstrates that Lily is "still conspicuous" in her world and temporarily recuperates her social value (116, 113). But, while Lily's position as "a star" in the "sky" of high society (286) is threatened at the novel's opening by the fact that the twenty-nine-year-old heroine has been "too long before the public" in her unmarried state (87), it is seriously compromised by the scandal on the Riviera. After Mrs. Peniston disinherits Lily in favor of Grace Stepney, the family snubs her. During the reading of the will, the narrator observes, "Lily stood apart from the general movement [to Grace], feeling herself for the first time utterly alone. No one looked at her, not one seemed aware of her presence; she was probing the very depths of insignificance" (223). Although Lily vows to keep herself "visibly identified" with her old social circle "as long as the illusion could be maintained" (268), her "eclipse" (275) is virtually certain from the moment of her disinheritance. Lily's "social credit" further diminishes when she associates herself with the uncultured parvenu Mattie Gormer, and especially when she takes a position as private secretary for Mrs. Hatch, a wealthy divorcée of uncertain background who is the most substantial figure in the "pallid" and "dimly lit" world of the Emporium Hotel (274). Here, Lily has "the odd sense of being behind the social tapestry" rather than prominently displayed within it, "on the side where the threads were knotted and the loose ends hung" (276). Lily's move from center stage to "obscurity" (267) is sealed by her work as a milliner and her residence in a boardinghouse, a "utilitarian" structure devoid of decorative attractions. By the novels end, the narrator notes that "something of her mother's fierce shrinking from observation and sympathy was beginning to develop in [Lily]" (287). Thus, while social disappearance marks in Selden's case the affirmation of his private self and social independence, public invisibility thrusts Lily beyond the reaches of collective interest and transform her into an internal exile or excommunicant. "Inconspicuousness" ensures Lily's social, and then her literal, death.

The visual dimensions of "desirability" are clearly marked in the text, and the social extremes that Lily must avoid are embodied by characters who figure as negative exemplars. Lawrence Selden's cousin, Gerty Farish, is characterized by Lily as "good" but "dingy," and she is decidedly unversed in what Wharton calls the "complex art of civilized living." As Lily confides to Selden, Gerty "[h]as a horrid little place, and no maid, and such queer things to eat. Her cook does the washing and the food tastes of soap" (7). Gerty is also conspicuously *single*—she is, as Lily observes, decidedly not "*marriageable*" (7) [and therefore] is positioned outside the novel's nexus of visibility and desire. In fact, Gerty's singleness is not only represented but *performed* in the novel, in Selden's unwitting rejection of Gerty (and his blindness to her love) in favor of Lily Bart. Lily's imagined choice—"to be herself, or a Gerty Farish" (25)—are thus depicted by the novel as no choice at all: Gerty's situation is dismissed out of hand by Lily as undesirable because Gerty quite simply refuses to embody what the novel establishes as the conditions of *being* desired. At the other extreme is Mrs. Norma Hatch. The garish ostentation of Mrs. Hatch inversely connotes an "easy promiscuity" (234) and the excessive conspicuousness of the prostitute. Lily's task is to successfully negotiate these different cultural codes and social requirements. In order to maintain her high "price" and embody desirability, Lily must remain both "conspicuous" and elusive, distinctly *visible* and yet fastidiously aloof.

Lily's tenuous position is that of a single woman who must exhibit an air of lofty exclusiveness and elusiveness while simultaneously projecting availability; in other words, she must "show herself to advantage" without appearing, in the novel's Jack Stepney's phrase, "up at auction" (136, 157). Lily must court the approval of many; she must appease and appeal to all—especially potential or existing economic "backers" such as Rosedale and Trenor—while promising herself to none until a satisfactory buyer comes along. Lily, in other words, must *flirt*: she must simultaneously embody proximity and distance, consent and refusal. Lily's flirtatious, seductive manner is evident in an exchange with her father, recalled early in the text, in which she appeals to him for money to have a centerpiece of fresh flowers sent each day for the family luncheon (30). In Wharton's description of this exchange, Lily "lean[s] confidently toward her father" while she asks his permission to instruct the florist to send lilies-of-the-valley every day: according to the narrator, Mr. Bart "seldom refused her anything," and Mrs. Bart has taught Lily to use her fresh charms to plead with him when Mrs. Bart's own entreaties

failed (30). Lily similarly couples the "trustfulness of a child" and the seductive "appeal of her exquisite nearness" in her efforts to secure Gus Trenor's monetary "backing," thus flattering him with the intimacy of her address (she "ma[de] him feel that he understood her better than her dearest friends") and her professed faith in his economic prowess (84). After accepting the money Trenor earns for her, Lily attempts to appease him with an alluring manner and by occasionally "letting her eyes rest on his" (118) in seductive communion, but Trenor soon wearies of this: he resents the fact that he, whose money has paid for Lily's "good clothes" and fine public image, should reap "no return [on his investment] beyond that of gazing at her in company with several hundred other pairs of eyes" (138, 116). Lily had inwardly dismissed the twinge of discomfort produced by the sexual "claim at which [Trenor's] manner hinted," confident that she can handle such a "coarse dull man" as he (85), but that claim becomes increasingly more insistent in the text until it is expressed as attempted rape (85). Similarly, Lily appeals to Rosedale—who seeks the "privilege" of familiarity and knows the value of "being seen" with Lily—by projecting an air of elusive superiority, an "exquisite inaccessibleness" and "sense of distance" conveyed through gestures, look, and manner (254), while teasing him with confiding glances and gestures of intimacy. The requirements of Lily's position are perhaps most clearly legible in the tableaux scene. Here, after the "triumph" of "showing her beauty in public," Lily basks in the "general stream of admiring looks" and serially meets the succession of men who approach her with an intimate, "answering gaze," conferring on each the look that he "dreamed of capturing for himself" alone (116, 137, 136).

In trading on the "promise" of sensual gratification for money, Lily enacts the dynamics of commodity attraction in *fin-de-siècle* consumer culture. Lily embodies what Wolfgang Haug has termed the commodity's "insatiable desire to please": like commodities, she must "cast wooing glances" at potential buyers while holding herself aloof until the transaction is complete. The trick of the commodity, according to Haug, is to create the illusion of direct, personalized, and exclusive address to a potential consumer while "smil[ing] invitingly on everyone" and indiscriminately appealing to "the wide world of anyone with money" (151, 86).[21] Like that of the commodity, Lily's position is one of managed conspicuousness: she must appear with frequency before the "public" ("they can't marry you if they don't see you") while avoiding being "too long before" it and risking marketplace saturation.[22] Lily's self-marketing entails balancing the imperatives of display and withholding, of publicity and privacy, in order to remain both "conspicuous" and desirable. Indeed, Lily's managed gestures and gazes constitute what advertisers were calling "come-ons," visual and/or verbal "hooks" designed to stimulate proprietary desire. By underscoring throughout the novel Lily's status as "superfine human merchandise," Wharton makes absolutely explicit the identification between commodity and feminine display in the newly specularized public sphere.

V. Domestic Nostalgia; or, The House of Mourning

In response to the feminine commodification depicted as endemic to modernity, the novel gestures toward a radical invisibility, a perfect "shelter" from the realm of specularized value which can only be recuperated nostalgically. In the final pages of *The House of Mirth*, Wharton mobilizes the twinned, nineteenth-century discourses of domesticity and Christianity to define an "alternative" to the specular logic of the consumer public sphere. Ironically, Wharton's "solution" to the commodification of women within the consumer public sphere is to (re)confine them within the heterosexual economy of nineteenth-century domesticity.

According to the binary specular logic of Wharton's novel, "conspicuousness" is inseparable from the exhibition and commercialization of self, entailing incorporation within the realm of commodity exchange, while invisibility signifies escape from this pervasive commodification. It is in these terms that Lily's most significant action, in terms of plot—her decision to burn Bertha's love letters to Selden, rather than use them to blackmail Bertha and profit by them—must be viewed. These letters—which, crucially, Lily herself does not read—contain inscriptions of personal sentiment and represent the availability of private subjectivity to the arena of exchange. The poor charwoman Mrs. Haffen sells Lily the letters to support her unemployed husband and family, and both George Dorset and Simon Rosedale tempt Lily with the opportunity to trade the contents of the letters in exchange for economic security and social prominence. Lily purchases the letters out of the "feeling that Selden would wish the letters rescued" (105), and her refusal to profit by selling them is ascribed by Wharton to an outdated genteel morality, to "all the instinctive resistance of taste, of training, of blind inherited scruples" (104). But, while the narrator questions the wisdom of Lily's actions from a practical standpoint, the novel very much invests in Lily's efforts to extricate the letters—and thus, in some sense, herself—from the network of commodity exchange.

The novel's final vision of invisible, uncommodified virtue is an essentially Christian one. Christian goodness, as Hannah Arendt has written, harbors a tendency "to hide from being seen or heard": when goodness appears openly, it loses the specific character of goodness, of being done for goodness's sake alone, and can easily become—or seem to become—hypocrisy (74–75). Lily's act of burning the letters, an act unperceived even by Selden (though in some sense he dictates it), is performed inconspicuously, outside the arena of social recognition and economic profit. The novel's search for an alternative to the commodified realm of publicity results in a (re)inscription of the Christian ideal of self-sacrifice. It is in that reinscription that he emotional force of the novel's final scenes lies.

The novel's Christian vision of invisible virtue and uncommodified action structures its concluding depiction of sentimental domesticity. Beginning with James, many critics have argued that the novel falters in the second book and especially in the final scenes, slipping from astute social criticism to banal sentimentality. That sentimentality is especially evident in Wharton's depiction of Nettie Struther's sentimental maternity and family life and in the scenes preceding and immediately following Lily's death.

Wharton's ambivalent relationship to nineteenth-century domestic fiction has often been noted by critics (Showalter). But in Nettie Struther's warm kitchen, Wharton delineates an alternative to the realm of publicity in *home life*—not the home life of the rich, whose houses are "well-designed for the display of . . . festal assemblage[s]" but are deficient as "frame[s] for domesticity" (131), but an essentially middle-class model of domestic intimacy. Indeed, *The House of Mirth* appeals nostalgically to the vision of uncommodified value presented in domestic fiction. As Jeanne Boydston has observed, Lily Bart's story reprises the central theme of nineteenth-century domestic fiction: Lily is "above all an orphan in search of a home" (34). And, in nineteenth-century domestic fiction, the home was depicted as the primary sphere of private and uncommodified value. In "woman's fiction," domesticity was figured as a realm of perfect sincerity in which virtue could be safely performed because inconspicuous—materially sheltered from publicity and commercial exchange—and because actions thus performed would be a transparent reflection of interior sentiments. In *The House of Mirth*, the "shelter" of domesticity, localized in Nettie's kitchen, spatializes and embodies the novel's vision of escape from "publicity" and commodity exchange.

VI. The Pleasures of the Text

Given the gendered relations of visual desire and commodification which structure *The House of Mirth*, where does Wharton's novel place the reader? How do these relations inform Wharton's representation—and the reader's apprehension—of "feminine" character? How, exactly, is the reader implicated in the novel's gendered relations of visibility, spectatorship, and embodiment?

The problems and pleasures of readerly spectatorship are thematized and directly addressed in many realist and naturalist texts, as several critics have noted (e.g., Howard; Miller). Because of their generic commitment to "hold steadily visible" *all* reality, these novels are particularly engaged with questions of compulsory and compulsive visibility.[23] Naturalist novels appeal to readerly fantasies of omniscience—generalized surveillance and perspectiveless disembodiment—to which Selden aspires ("*that* is how she looks when she is alone!"). In other words, they engender the pleasures of unseen seeing, extending to the reader the "privilege of relative disembodiment" and readerly invisibility vis-à-vis the textually represented objects of narrative. This fantasy of readerly disembodiment vis-à-vis textually delineated, objectified characters frequently, in naturalist novels, encodes specific class positions. Wharton's novel suggests that the pleasures of naturalist surveillance are informed by gender, as well.

In *The House of Mirth*, the technology of gender which emerged in the turn-of-the-century consumer public sphere is enacted both thematically and formally. In fact, Wharton implicates the reader quite explicitly in the novel's gendered nexus of visibility and objectification. In the novel's initial pages, Wharton constructs point of view so as to explicitly force our collusion with Selden. Selden stands as a kind of surrogate for the reader we first see Lily through his eyes, and our initial encounter with the heroine is mediated by his thoughts and perceptions. Selden's look is, at least initially, a structural analogue for the reader's gaze, and Selden's construction of Lily as an enigmatic, mysterious woman frames readerly interest in Wharton's heroine: as the novel initially positions us, we, like Selden, are fascinated by the beautiful woman in the train station, and, like Selden, we are curious about what motivates her. Selden's position as male spectator is, as I have demonstrated, intermittently reinscribed in Wharton's novel, and his look is reasserted in the final scene. By framing the narrative with Selden's perspective Wharton identifies the structural underpinnings and motivating force of the narrative—both the initiating and closing gestures—with a *masculine* viewpoint, with male voyeuristic fascination with the feminine and with a gendered bifurcation of subject and object ratified in Lily's death. Wharton thus establishes a structure of looking/reading which encodes certain dominant conceptions of "man" and "woman," "subject" and "object" while exposing the disciplinary violence of these visual/textual practices.

The fantasies of surveillance inscribed within naturalist texts are also fantasies of ownership and are embedded within the gendered logic of commodity desire. Notably, it is Selden's original "speculations" about Lily's character that draw the reader into the story and frame the reader's interest in Lily. And it is Selden's desire for the possession of privileged knowledge about the "real Lily" that is both ironically gratified and travestied in the death scene. There, where the "little impalpable barrier" which has separated them falls away (326), Lily's objectification is perfected and Selden's subjectivity fully redeemed. Selden enjoys an intimate communion with the dead Lily Bart: over her silent body Selden "construct[s] an explanation of the mystery" of Lily's character, and he "read[s] into" the scene "all that his heart craved to find there" (329). Selden's self-satisfied account of Lily's life and his own role in it supplies him with the "courage not to accuse himself for having failed to reach the height of his opportunity" and enables him to find solace for their "moment of love," which, he believes, "had been saved whole out of the ruin of their lives" (329). Wharton's depiction of Selden's "reconciliation" with Lily thus both foregrounds and ironizes his will-to-possession.

Naturalism's structure of masculine voyeurism is thus itself placed under scrutiny in Wharton's novel, through a productive disjuncture between the narrative inscription of male visual desire and its anthropomorphized embodiment in the character of Selden. However, naturalism's gendered relations of visibility have often been reinscribed rather than analyzed in contemporary criticism. The idea that an oedipalized proprietary desire—a desire for the completion of meaning, for closure—structures the reading of *all* realist and naturalist narrative has, in fact, become an axiom of narrative theory. In Roland Barthes's formulation, what animates us as readers of these texts is *la passion du sens*, the passion for meaning that occurs when the narrative "sentence" reaches full predication in closure. As Barthes puts it in his erotics of reading, *The Pleasure of the Text*, what produces textual desire is "intermittence," the unexpected "flash" of significance ("the staging of appearance-as-disappearance") that incites readerly longings for the truth's perfect unveiling (10, 14). Foregrounding this dynamic of visual desire both thematically and formally, *The House of Mirth* insists that the textual desire for possession of/in naturalist narrative is, at heart, a gendered affair.

Notes

For their helpful comments on the many incarnations of this essay, I especially wish to thank Carolyn Porter, Susan Schweik, Karen Jacobs, Eric Peterson, and Nancy Armstrong and the editorial board of *Novel*.

1. For an analysis of the role of "taste" in the construction of the domestic woman and the cultural identity of the middle class, see Armstrong, *Desire*. In Dreiser's text, "taste" is reconstituted from the property of the *private* domestic woman to a commodity acquired and displayed in *public*.

2. Wharton's preoccupation with what she termed "visibility in fiction" has often been noted. Vision—as metaphorical perception and as social action—is thematically foregrounded in much of her work (Wharton, "Visibility"; Baril).

3. That instability is emphasized throughout Dreiser's text. For example, Dreiser emphasizes the consumer orientation of Carrie's desire by designating the department store (Chicago's The Fair), a "show place of dazzling interest and attraction," as a principal setting for Carrie's urban education (22). However, he also underscores the *instability* of Carrie's identity as consumer subject, her slippage from subject to object of exchange, focusing on the construction of her charismatic allure as a celebrity: repositioning Carrie from public consumer to publicly consumed commodity, Dreiser parallels the desiring gaze of the female shopper with the desiring gaze of the male spectator/owner. Strikingly, it is during her public performance as Laura that both Hurstwood and Drouet feel closest to Carrie and experience a passionate desire to possess their "idol" (192): Hurstwood feels a "deep sympathy" for her and fancies that "she was talking to him" alone (189); while Drouet is driven to a "most harrowed state of affection" for Carrie and impetuously resolves to ask her to marry him (192). Like the trinkets on display at The Fair, Carrie on stage embodies the simultaneity of availability and distance, invitation and aloofness which, according to sociologist Georg Simmel, is the essence of "price." In the theater, as in the department store, late-nineteenth-century spectatorial desire is produced by a dialectic of pub-

licity and privacy, the interplay between the object's *public* appeal and its (imagined) identity as a "private" possession.

4. The critical literature on the fashion system, and its ambiguous relationship to feminism, is vast (Gaines and Herzog; Benstock and Ferriss). Below, I suggest that this ambiguity derives, in part, from the history of women's fashion practices.

5. Examples include Dreiser's *Sister Carrie*, Frank Norris's *McTeague* and *Vandover and the Brute*, and much of Wharton's work, especially *The House of Mirth* and *The Custom of the Country*.

6. Since its initial formulation by feminist film theorists in the mid-1970s, feminist theorists have debated the concept of the "male gaze"—not the gaze of an individual man but an effect of the male/subject-female/object structuring of the symbolic order which constitutes woman as paradigmatic object. (For a foundational presentation of the feminist formulation of the "male gaze" and the gendered bifurcation of positions ["active/looking" and "passive/looked at"] in film spectatorship, see Mulvey. Critics of Mulvey's essay have taken particular issue with her masculinization of the spectator position, which would seem to render the position of "female spectator" a logical impossibility.) Wharton's novel suggests that the historical and discursive construction of the new feminine consumer subject was articulated with a "male gaze" that operates to contain the emerging forms of feminine publicity and desire.

7. On the visual, disciplinary forms of naturalist narration and the spectatorial relations that organize realist and naturalist texts, see Seltzer, *Henry James*; Howard. While Seltzer's analysis is Foucauldian and Howard's is Lukácslan, both critics suggest that spectatorial/readerly pleasure and "freedom" are underwritten by the construction of narrative subjects as textual objects. As I hope to show, naturalism's poetics of vision emerged as a specifically *gendered* response to the new economic and political visibility of women in the late nineteenth century.

8. Wharton has often been viewed by critics as marginal to the naturalist canon—an assessment owing, at least in part, to her class as well as her gender position. For important critical examinations of Wharton's naturalism, see Poirier and Michaels. As will become clear, I am less interested here in definitively classifying Wharton as a naturalist, or in entering into the "realism vs. naturalism" debate to decide under which rubric she best fits. As I suggest below, Wharton's writings contain a variety of literary languages, from sentimentalist discourse to social satire

to the deterministic rhetoric usually identified as the characteristic feature of naturalist narrative. I argue below that Wharton engages the languages of naturalism, especially its deterministic idiom and tropes of gendered visibility, and—by foregrounding their gendered investments—places them under critical scrutiny.

9. The reverberations generated by the emergence of the "woman consumer" were not merely "domestic" in scope. Political writers and policymakers envisioned U.S. external imperial expansion during the 1890s (culminating in the Spanish American War) as a response to what was widely termed "overcivilization" through excessive (feminine) consumption, an attempt to restore male authority at home by remasclinizing American manhood and by securing new markets for the "surplus commodities" that were seducing the American consumer public. In *The House of Mirth*, the dynamic of imperial expansion as a response to feminine "domestic" authority informs the consistency with which Lily Bart's male suitors—notably, Dillworth and Selden—are whisked off to the imperial outposts of India and Havana when she exerts threatening (sexual/economic) power over them. Revealing the imperial coordinates of the American consumer's construction, this narrative pattern maps a relay of looks through which the disciplinary male gaze instantiated in naturalism is reinforced by (and inseparable from) "scientific," disciplinary structures of imperial control.

10. As Diana Trilling observed in 1962, "*The House of Mirth* is always and passionately a money story" (122). See also Dimock. Michaels has argued that *The House of Mirth* "exemplifies" the inescapable power of the market, which thoroughly determines the narrative's terms so that "the novel refuses the role of critique" (227). In particular, he contends that the novel's discourse of "personal freedom" and agency reinscribes the imperatives of market capitalism, so that Lily's spontaneous impulses—which apparently register her resistance to New York's calculating commercial society—in fact signify her "complete commitment to the practices of speculation" and risk-taking (228). Michaels's reading, which proceeds by rhetorically invoking and then deconstructing an opposition between subjects and markets and by abstracting from the narrative a disembodied, ungendered subject-position as "representative," rehearses and, in effect, formalizes the logic of the market itself.

11. In this doubleness, Lily projects what Wharton's contemporary, Georg Simmel, calls the "essence of 'price' ": the concurrence of having and not-having, accommodation and denial which inheres in "the prox-

imity and interpenetration of the ability and inability to acquire something" (134).

12. The power of the veil to transform "vulgar clay" into desirable artifact was the central theme of "The Veiled Beauty," a film produced two years after Wharton published her novel. In the film, a veiled young woman is pursued by several men who attempt to force their attentions on her, one suitor, after beating up his rivals, follows the woman into Dreamland amusement park, where she explores its commercial attractions while ignoring the young man's attentions. He finally succeeds in inviting her to dinner, where she lifts her veil, revealing an ugly, misshapen face. Peiss discusses this movie and its reception in nickelodeons (139).

13. My analysis of the seductive allure of the fashionable female in Simmel's text is indebted to Apter (87–89). For a feminist critique of the veil as a philosophical metaphor of femininity, see Spivak. Fashion historians have characterized the years between 1890 and 1914 as those in which filmy, semitransparent undergarments became popular (Steele 192–210). Contemporary observers were often quite explicit about the erotic appeal of the intimately veiled body. The British writer Mrs. Pritchard, in her book *The Cult of Chiffon* (1902), insisted that "lovely lingerie" did not belong "only to the last" and went so far as to blame failed marriages on wives' unwillingness to wear "dainty undergarments" and dress seductively for their husbands (as seen in Steele 195). According to Mrs. Pritchard, even married women must continue to embody feminine allure and inaccessibility—to maintain their *price*—in order to sustain their husbands' interest and, presumably, their willingness to "pay." Pritchard's book was contemporary with the widespread circulation in the West of photographs of veiled Muslim women (Alloula; Fanon). The turn-of-the-century "cult of chiffon" in the West suggests the complex articulation of colonialism with the regulation of female consumer desire: it "domesticates" the colonialist venture by reinscribing the colonial logic of the veil at "home." For an analysis of this interarticulation in the English national context, see Armstrong, "Occidental."

14. The metaphorical power of veiling to mobilize proprietary desire is suggested by the original advertisements for Wharton's novel. Scribner's first promoted *The House of Mirth* with the following jacket advertisement: "For the first time the veil has been lifted from New York society." Wharton responded with an angry letter to her publisher: "I thought that, in the House of Scribner, the House of Mirth was safe

from all such Harperesque methods of réclame" (as seen in Lewis, *Edith Wharton* 151). The advertisement and Wharton's letter suggest the erotically charged tension between publicity and privacy that structured the commodity marketplace in which her novel—and her heroine—were enmeshed, as well as Wharton's ambivalence toward this social frame.

15. Many scholars have noted the autobiographical significance of *The House of Mirth.* Wharton herself expressed exasperation at readers' attempts to draw easy parallels between her life and art, insisting that the novel originated in the "mysterious other-world of invention" and expressing impatience with readers of the novel who are "curious only to discover which of the heroes and heroines of the 'society column' are to be found in it" (*Backward* 210–11, 212). But the resemblances between Edith Jones and her heroine, Lily Bart, are, in fact, quite striking. Edith had been nicknamed "Lily" by her Newport friends, the Rutherfords. And, indeed, her own account of her intellectual and social development as a professional author in *A Backward Glance* reprises the themes and even the language of Lily Bart's personal history, notably giving that earlier story a happier ending. With the publication of her first book, Wharton writes, "I felt like some homeless waif who, after trying for years to take out naturalization papers, and being rejected by every country, has finally acquired a nationality. The Land of Letters was henceforth to be my country, and I gloried in my new citizenship" (119). Wharton apparently found possibilities for personal "freedom" and "liberty" in the "publicity of print" not available in fashionable society: publishing, Wharton writes, "broke the chains which had held me so long in a kind of torpor": "seeing one's self in print" brought with it novel possibilities of selfhood (212, 122, 112). Evidently, for Wharton, the "publicity of print" restructured the imperatives of feminine "conspicuousness" and public appearance, creating a mediated relation to the social gaze by redirecting that gaze from the author's material body to the created body of the literary text.

16. Scarry, who argues that a (relatively) "more intense embodiment" is a condition of "those without power," comments on the gender division of embodiment in contemporary consumer culture: "The newsstand in almost any city tends to present to all who pass on the street a proliferation of images of women unclothed or effectively unclothed, which is distressful to at least half of the population who pass by each day. (It subverts women's autonomy over their own bodies; their power to determine the degree to which they will or will not

reveal their own bodies is pre-empted by the prior existence of such images in the most public, most communal, of spaces.) Opposition to pornography is sometimes deflected into discussion of the particular content of the photographs or drawings. . . . But . . . much more crucial is the framing fact that, comparatively speaking, men have no bodies and women have emphatic bodies. That the very serious political problem here is independent of the tone and content of the images can be illustrated with section I of the Sunday *New York Times*: the steady presentation of the disembodied male voice of the news column side by side with the drawings and photographs of women announces, iconographically, a relation between the two halves of the population that makes any discussion of the isolated content of the images irrelevant" (359–60).

17. In *The American Scene*, James writes memorably of the "woman-made society" to which women have claimed "peerless possession." According to James, it is in the political capital of Washington, D.C., "alone in the American world" that one can witness the "return of the male": there, James observes, "Man is solidly, vividly present, and the presence of Woman has consequently for the proposed intensity, to reckon with it" (244–52, 349).

18. Lily, on the other hand, is more constrained in her movements—a constraint that bears the traces of the sexual double standard. She can't "be seen" in certain places or situations without suffering severe consequences—consequences apparent in the novel from the very start. After impulsively visiting Selden in the Benedick for tea, Lily must suffer the consequences of her imprudence by incurring Rosedale's suspicion and being thus in his "debt"; later, when Lily is seen by Selden and Van Alstyne on the Trenors' doorstep, the mere appearance of misconduct brings the same consequences as the actual performance of any crime: both "cheapen" her, because they entail censurable lapses in vigilance and discretion.

19. In *The House of Mirth*, gossip operates as a regulatory medium and an extension of the novel's structure of surveillance. As Showalter observes, "To become the object of male discourse [in Lily's world] is almost as bad as to become the victim of male lust" (136). See also Bauer. In Wharton's novel, gossip polices female sexuality and affirms male privilege, although the locus of gossip is women's sphere.

20. Hochman has interpreted Lily's "wish for an audience" as evincing phenomenological imperatives of "recognition" and the vitalizing

dynamic of reciprocal interchange. Hochman sees Lily as a figure for the author, and claims that Lily's characterization registers Wharton's own ambivalent relationship to her readership. According to Hochman, "For Lily, as for the novelist herself, the process of generating images and meanings is reciprocal: it cannot proceed without an audience." But Hochman's phenomenological account of Lily's need to "be seen" ignores what Hochman herself refers to as the "gender specific aspect" of this imperative (147–61).

21. Haug emphasizes the "feedback loop," whereby "commodities borrow their aesthetic language from human courtship" while, conversely, "people borrow their aesthetic expression from the world of the commodity" (19). The "femininity" of the commodity form has been inscribed by numerous male writers, from Marx to Benjamin to Haug. The gendered language these writers use to describe commodities simultaneously acknowledges the sexual commodification of women in capitalism *and* reduces that commodification to a rhetorical metaphor. In *The House of Mirth*, Wharton takes as her explicit narrative subject the sexual politics of commodification.

22. Lily's friend, Carry Fisher, for instance, after the fiasco on the Riviera, proposes that Lily keep herself "out of sight" until her friends "realize how much they miss" her (236).

23. Seltzer identifies the "frequent association" of late-nineteenth-century realism with "a sort of dissection, vivisection, or surgical opening of the body" as exemplifying this imperative of compulsory visibility (*Bodies* 95–97).

Works Cited

Abelson, Elaine S. *When Ladies Go A-Thieving: Middle-Class Shoplifters in the Victorian Department Store.* New York: Oxford University Press, 1989.

Alloula, Malek. *The Colonial Harem.* Trans. Myrna Godzich and Wlad Godzich. Minneapolis: University of Minnesota Press, 1989.

Apter, Emily. *Feminizing the Fetish: Psychoanalysis and Narrative Obsession in Turn-of-the-Century France.* Ithaca: Cornell University Press, 1991.

Arendt, Hannah. *The Human Condition.* Chicago: University of Chicago Press, 1958.

Armstrong, Nancy. *Desire and Domestic Fiction: A Political History of the Novel.* New York: Oxford University Press, 1987.

———. "Occidental Alice." *differences* 2.2 (1990): 3–40.

Barthes, Roland. *The Pleasure of the Text*. Trans. Richard Miller. New York: Hill, 1975.

Baril, James Ronald. *Vision as Metaphorical Perception in the Fiction of Edith Wharton*. Boulder: University of Colorado Press, 1969.

Bauer, Dale. *Feminist Dialogics: A Theory of Failed Community*. Albany: State University of New York Press, 1988.

Benstock, Shari, and Suzanne Ferriss, eds. *On Fashion*. New Brunswick: Rutgers University Press, 1994.

Berlant, Lauren. "National Brands/National Bodies." *Comparative American Identities: Race, Sex, and Nationality in the Modern Text*. Ed. Hortense J. Spillers. New York: Routledge, 1991. 103–31.

Boydston, Jeanne. " 'Grave Endearing Traditions': Edith Wharton and the Domestic Novel." *Faith of a (Woman) Writer*. Ed. Alice Kessler-Harris and William McBrien. Westport Conn.: Greenwood, 1988. 31–40.

Bowlby, Rachel. *Just Looking: Consumer Culture in Dreiser, Gissing, and Zola*. New York: Methuen, 1985.

Butler, Judith. *Gender Trouble: Feminism and the Subversion of Identity*. New York: Routledge, 1990.

Dijkstra, Bram. *Idols of Perversity: Fantasies of Feminine Evil in Fin-de-Siècle Culture*. New York: Oxford University Press, 1986.

Dimock, Wai Chee. "Debasing Exchange: Edith Wharton's *House of Mirth*." *PMLA* 100.5 (1985): 783–92.

Dreiser, Theodore. *Sister Carrie: The Unexpurgated Edition*. New York: Penguin, 1981.

Fanon, Frantz. "Algeria Unveiled." *A Dying Colonialism*. Trans. Haakon Chevalier. New York: Grove, 1967. 35–67.

Fuss, Diana. "Fashion and the Homospectatorial Look." *Critical Inquiry* 18 (1992): 713–37.

Gaines, Jane, and Charlotte Herzog, eds. *Fabrications: Costume and the Female Body*. New York: Routledge, 1990.

Hansen, Miriam. "Adventures of Goldilocks: Spectatorship, Consumerism, and Public Life." *Camera Obscura* 22 (1990): 51–71.

Haug, Wolfgang. *Critique of Commodity Aesthetics: Appearance, Sexuality and Advertising in Capitalist Society*. Trans. Robert Bock. Minneapolis: University of Minnesota Press, 1986.

Hochman, Barbara. "The Rewards of Representation: Edith Wharton, Lily Bart, and the Writer/Reader Interchange." *Novel* 24.2 (1991): 147–61.

Howard, June. *Form and History in American Literary Naturalism*. Chapel Hill: University of North Carolina Press, 1985.

James, Henry. *The American Scene*. Ed. Leon Edel. Bloomington: Indiana University Press, 1969.

Kaplan, Amy. "Crowded Spaces in *The House of Mirth*." *The Social Construction of American Realism*. Chicago: University of Chicago Press, 1988. 88–103.

Landauer, Bella C. "Literary Allusions in American Advertising as Sources of Social History." *New York Historical Society Quarterly* 31.3 (July 1947): 144–52.

Lears, T. J. Jackson. *No Place of Grace: Antimodernism and the Transformation of American Culture, 1880–1920*. New York: Pantheon, 1981.

Lewis, R. W. B. *Edith Wharton: A Biography*. New York: Harper, 1975.

———. "Edith Wharton and *The House of Mirth*." *Trials of the Word: Essays in American Literature and the Humanistic Tradition*. New Haven: Yale University Press, 1965. 129–47.

Michaels, Walter Benn. "Action and Accident: Photography and Writing." *The Gold Standard and the Logic of Naturalism*. Berkeley: University of California Press, 1987. 217–44.

Michelson, Bruce. "Edith Wharton's House Divided." *Studies in American Fiction* 12 (1984): 199–215.

Miller, D.A. *The Novel and the Police*. Berkeley: University of California Press, 1988.

Mulvey, Laura. "Visual Pleasure and Narrative Cinema." *Screen* 16.3 (1975). 6–18. Rpt. in *Visual and Other Pleasures*. Bloomington: Indiana University Press, 1990.

Norton, Anne. *Republic of Signs: Liberal Theory and American Popular Culture*. Chicago: University of Chicago Press, 1993.

Peiss, Kathy. *Cheap Amusements: Working Women and Leisure in Turn-of-the-Century New York*. Philadelphia: Temple University Press, 1986.

Poirier, Richard. "Edith Wharton: *The House of Mirth*." *The American Novel: From James Fenimore Cooper to William Faulkner*. Ed. Wallace Stegner. New York: Basic, 1965. 117–82.

Pollock, Griselda. "Modernity and the Spaces of Femininity." *Vision and Difference: Femininity, Feminism and Histories of Art*. London: Routledge, 1988. 52–70.

Presbrey, Frank. *The History and Development of Advertising*. 1929. New York: Greenwood, 1968.

Radner, Hilary. *Shopping Around: Feminine Culture and the Pursuit of Pleasure*. New York: Routledge, 1995.

Scarry, Elaine. *The Body in Pain: The Making and Unmaking of the World.* New York: Oxford University Press, 1985.

Sedgwick, Eve Kosofsky. *Epistemology of the Closet.* Berkeley: University of California Press, 1990.

Seltzer, Mark. *Bodies and Machines.* New York: Routledge, 1992.

———. *Henry James and the Art of Power.* Ithaca: Cornell University Press, 1984.

Showalter, Elaine. "The Death of the Lady (Novelist): Wharton's *The House of Mirth.*" *Representations* 9 (1985): 133–49.

Silverman, Kaja. "Fragments of a Fashionable Discourse." *Studies in Entertainment: Critical Approaches to Mass Culture.* Ed. Tania Modleski. Bloomington: Indiana University Press, 1986. 139–52.

Simmel, Georg. "Flirtation." *Georg Simmel: On Women, Sexuality, and Love.* Ed. and trans. Guy Oakes. New Haven: Yale University Press, 1984. 133–52.

Spivak, Gayatri Chakravorty. "Disruption and the Discourse of Woman." *Displacement: Derrida and After.* Ed. Mark Krupnick. Bloomington: Indiana University Press, 1983. 169–95.

Steele, Valerie. *Fashion and Eroticism: The Ideals of Feminine Beauty from the Victorian Era to the Jazz Age.* New York: Oxford University Press, 1989.

Trilling, Diana. "*The House of Mirth* Revisited." *American Scholar* 32.4 (1962–63): 113–28.

Wharton, Edith. *A Backward Glance.* New York: Scribner's, 1934.

———. *The House of Mirth* 1905. New York: Scribner's, 1969.

———. "Visibility in Fiction." *Yale Review* 18 (1929): 480–88.

Wilson, Christopher P. *The Labor of Words: Literary Professionalism in the Progressive Era.* Athens: University of Georgia Press, 1985.

Wolff, Cynthia Griffin. *A Feast of Words: The Triumph of Edith Wharton.* New York: Oxford University Press, 1977.

Veblen, Thorstein. "The Economic Theory of Women's Dress." *Popular Science Monthly* 46 (1894): 198–210.

The Crumbling Structure of "Appearances"

Representation and Authenticity in The House of Mirth *and* The Custom of the Country

CHRISTOPHER GAIR

◆ ◆ ◆

"Did you ever hear of Christopher Columbus?"

"Bien sûr! He invented America, a very great man. And is he your patron?"

—Henry James, *The American*

The highest level of intensity lies behind us. The lowest level of passion and intellectual illumination lies ahead of us.

—Jean Baudrillard, *Cool Memories*

At one point in *The House of Mirth* (1905), Carry Fisher, Lily Bart's social facilitator and general fixer for the seemingly endless supply of monied Americans seeking the contagious prestige gained through association with faded British aristocracy, complains that " 'the London market is so glutted with new Americans that, to succeed there now, they must be very clever or awfully queer' " (188). The utterance appears to invite readings of selfhood as something tentative or provisional, with the metaphor of society as a stock exchange confirming the impression that identity is speculative and depends on a combination of inventiveness and chance. At the moment of Carry's pronouncement, it would seem that the value of American selfhood is down in the old world, the victim of a saturated market, and that only the production of an even newer, improved model will be enough to generate fresh interest among the discerning names of London society.

With her next remark, however, Mrs. Fisher undermines such speculative uncertainty by asserting that if the "new American" in question, Mrs. Bry, could " 'be natural herself—fat and vulgar and bouncing—it would be alright' " (188). While this might appear to be an improbable road to success in a society where every gesture is scrutinized and where, as Lily learns to her cost, intention and interpretation engage in constant battles to control meaning, Mrs. Fisher's observation does alert us to the novel's frequent erasure of comfortable oppositions between "natural" and "cultural," spectacle and spectator, authentic and imitation, or "new" and "old." These pairings, evident here in the emphasis on "*new* Americans" and throughout the novel in characters' attempts to define "self" and "culture" as stable constructs in the face of overwhelming evidence to the contrary, point to the issue I wish to examine in this essay, that is, representations of the relationship among self, ethnic, and national identities in and immediately preceding the Progressive Era and in particular in the New York sections of Wharton's novels *The House of Mirth* and *The Custom of the Country*, published eight years later, in 1913.

Such searches for fixed and meaningful identities were taking place in a rapidly changing world—in her autobiography, *A Backward Glance* (1934), Wharton recounts the cultural upheavals transforming what, until the 1880s, had seemed (at least to her privileged and long-domiciled social group) to be "unalterable rules of conduct" into "observances as quaintly arbitrary as the domestic rites of the Pharaohs" (6)—and were responses to at least three interrelated factors. The closing decades of the nineteenth century witnessed a rapid technological transformation, a massive increase in immigration from Eastern and Southern Europe (New York being "glutted" with a very different kind of "new American"), and the perception, famously articulated by Frederick Jackson Turner, that the frontier was closed and that there was no more free land. As a result of the combination of these factors, the already antiquated Jeffersonian image of the American family as unit both of domestic harmony and of work was finally banished by a combination of rapid urbanization and what Alan Trachtenberg has called the "Incorporation of America."

One of the principal effects of this transformation was the erasure of a separate domestic sphere. The development of a culture of consumption moved women increasingly into the public domain, where female leisure-class identity required constant updating if it was to conform to the latest fashions. Instead of inhabiting the private space of "the kitchen and the linen room," immersed in what Wharton calls the "household arts" (*Backward* 41), the new woman became a public spectacle, subject to the scrutiny of press, acquaintances, and fellow citizens and compelled to demonstrate her nonproductive role via her clothing and behavior. As Thorstein Veblen observed in 1899:

> It needs no argument to enforce the generalization that the more elegant styles of feminine bonnets go even further towards making work impossible than does the man's high hat. The woman's shoe adds the so-called French heel to the evidence of enforced leisure afforded by its polish; because this high heel obviously makes any, even the simplest and most necessary manual work extremely difficult. The like is true even in a higher degree of the skirt and the rest of the drapery which characterizes woman's dress. The substantial reason for our tenacious attachment to the skirt is just this: it is expensive and it hampers the wearer at every turn and incapacitates her for all useful exertion. The like is true of the feminine custom of wearing the hair excessively long. (121)

For Veblen, the leisure-class woman represents a combination of nonproductivity—in addition to external symbols of leisure, the use of the corset "[lowers] the subjects vitality" (121)—and wastefulness. Thus, she epitomizes the transformation from utility to the "flux and change" of fashion as the economy shifts from producer to consumer capitalism, with the latter's success depending upon the generation of a limitless desire for newness (122). Indeed, in *The House of Mirth* Lily Bart's demise commences with her need for money to purchase the symbols of leisure-class nonactivity (such as clothes and the ability to gamble) and concludes with her patent unsuitability for the manual labor of the millinery establishment where, "tired and confused" (286), she has neither the skill nor the stamina to survive.

The erasure of the private, domestic sphere not only transformed the role of the leisure-class woman in New York. In addition, it paralleled a reconfiguration of the architecture of the city. One effect of this alteration was the construction of palatial mansions by the newly rich—what Henry James called, echoing Veblen's description of leisure-class women, "the outward show of the fortunate life" (*American Scene* 11)—a feature to which I will return when I examine Lily Bart's tableau vivant. But, if the role of affluent women in New York represented the shift from utility to conspicuous wastefulness, then the geography of much of the city signified the opposite, with every space being exploited to its maximum potential. As a result of economic and demographic transformation, the "old" New York of Wharton's childhood had, in James's words, been "violently overpainted," replaced by the "multitudinous sky-scrapers standing up to the view . . . like extravagant pins in a cushion already overplanted, and stuck in as in the dark, anywhere and anyhow" (*American Scene* 7, 60).[1]

Plainly, for the James of *The American Scene*, returning to New York after more than twenty years, this transformation elicits a sense of crisis, with the city's modernity posing a threat to the values he sees in continuity and history. He represents New York as a "colossal set of clockworks, some steel-souled machine-room of brandished arms and hammering fists and opening and closing jaws" (59) and feels that the skyscrapers are "Crowned not only with no history, but with no credible possibility of time for history, and consecrated by no uses save the commercial at any cost" (60–61). In a world governed by economics and machine culture, permanence is impossible—"sky-scrapers are the last word in economic ingenuity only till another word be written" (61)—and "beauty" is marginalized. Even when James does manage to pick out the spire of Trinity Church, commenting on its "charming elements" in a desperate attempt to recollect the past, he focuses on its "caged and dishonoured condition" (61) and the manner in which its presence is dwarfed by what surrounds it. As we shall see, it is precisely this marginalization of the past and its "culture" that necessitates Lily Bart's own increasingly desperate speculative entry into the twentieth century and provides the rationale for Wharton's attempts to reconstruct an American history in the novel.

It is clear that for a James there is a link between spatial and social transformation. In *The American Scene*, New York's sheer size—and, in particular, the ways in which this mitigates against privacy—makes it a "huge, continuous fifty-floored conspiracy against the very idea of the ancient graces" (71); here and elsewhere, he repeatedly comments on the absence of "manners" in the city. "The Jolly Corner" (1908), for example, a tale apparently committed to the elevation of old New York above the "new" amoral concern with profit, finally admits that the old values are anachronistic and are, in any case, contaminated. It even features a protagonist, Spencer Brydon, who, on his belated return to America, discovers "a capacity for business and a sense for construction" as he supervises the conversion of his house into "a tall mass of flats" (354–55).[2] The moral appears to be twofold: the city has the power to transform even the most settled identities, and, in any case, identities unable constantly to refashion themselves within ever-changing conditions will perish.

A similar pattern is present in *The House of Mirth* and *The Custom of the Country*, though with the focus very much on female identity. What is probably apparent to anyone with even a passing familiarity with either or both of these novels is that, for Wharton, the problem of "American" identity is more directly concerned with the effects of publicity and the culture of consumption than with mass immigration from Central and Southern Europe or with Melting Pot ideologies.[3] Though the latter clearly inform the reading public who, like Lily's sometime acquaintance the working-class Nettie Struther, follow the progress of their own fantasies "in a world where conspicuousness passed for distinction, and the society column had become the roll of fame" (*House* 216), it is the acquisition and *display* of new wealth that undermine deep-rooted definitions of national and personal identity. Of course, hostility to the assimilative desires of the newly rich *is* demonstrated repeatedly in the narrator's and Lily's own (albeit increasingly qualified) aversion to Simon Rosedale, the "little Jew who had been served up and rejected at the social board a dozen times" (15). Yet, it is not only the Jew—a figure carrying the burden of centuries of distrust—who is the target of such hostility and suspicion. Lily's combination of disdain for and financial dependency on a whole series of new arrivals in the society column, and her need to constantly reinvent herself within the relational matrix of the *fashionable* leisure class world, prompt a reassessment of how we should read her sense of Americanness.[4]

That this identity is in crisis is clear from the opening chapter of the novel, when Lily visits a fellow "old" New Yorker, Lawrence Selden. Emerging from Selden's apartment and from their reassuring discussion of Americana—a discussion blending the security offered by the knowledge of a unique cultural heritage, to which Lily has a claim by birth, with her belief that this combination of knowledge and birthright will secure her own future centrality within this culture—Lily encounters Rosedale outside the building. That Rosedale "happens" to own the Benedick (as he immediately informs Lily) neatly encapsulates the near-obsessive concern with a perceived lack of space in America at the turn of the century, here, typically, linked with the arrival of other races and classes.[5] Whether in James's *American Scene*; in Turner's frontier thesis; in the dystopian fictions of, among others, Ignatius Donnelly and Jack London, predicting massive escalations in urban violence; in adventure stories representing the search for new lands; or in novels, paintings, and museum displays seeking to recreate a "vanished" (imaginary) America, "old" Americans repeatedly display their anxieties about the *new* New World. Indeed, in *The Custom of the Country*, Wharton explicitly links the disappearance of the "old" families with the earlier passing of other American cultures, squeezed into smaller and smaller spaces. Ralph Marvell, representative of long-established New York "Society," "sometimes called his mother and grandfather the Aborigines, and likened them to those vanished denizens of the

American continent doomed to rapid extinction with the advance of the invading race. He was fond of describing Washington Square as the 'Reservation and of prophesying that before long its inhabitants would be exhibited at ethnological shows, pathetically engaged in the exercise of their primitive industries" (47).[6] In a passage extending the emphasis on constraint and supervision implied by Selden's occupation of a few rooms within Rosedale's building, Wharton makes a number of significant observations about the shifting status of a once-hegemonic social group.

First, there is a sense of the inevitability of extinction, coupled with a vision of history in which "progress" is marked by the repeated arrival of new invading races. Thus, where the Indian's demise had been guaranteed by the advance of the pioneer, the latter are now condemned to the same fate by the ascendancy of the next generation of pioneers, that is, the new capitalist hegemony of speculators. In Wharton's fiction, the result is a situation in which identification with the Indian becomes a way to sustain American identity in the face of cultural transformation, but only at the expense of death.[7]

Association with the Indian is not unique to the early twentieth century: Michael Rogin has suggested that Andrew Jackson and his fellow Indian hunters identified with Indians through the act of hunting them, since, as Walter Benn Michaels has summarized, "the violence of the Indian required the violence of the Indian hunter who, in killing the Indian, became a version of him" ("Armies" 130). In canonical American literature, identification with aspects of Native American culture, albeit within Euro-American romantic configurations, is evident in the work of Cooper and Hawthorne, though, as Hester Prynne's "native courage" makes clear, the "estranged point of view" she shares with the "wild Indian," represents individual, rather than collective, marginalization (Hawthorne 199).

By the end of the nineteenth century, ambivalence about machine culture and incorporation increasingly led to the Indian being associated with unconquerable and inflexible individualism—the function already anticipated in Hester's case—in a more widespread, systematic fashion. Because the Indian was seen as unresponsive to change and therefore not only unsuited to, but also subversive of, the Taylorization processes of machine culture, he or she must be destroyed. It is this logic which informs the conclusion to Twain's *A Connecticut Yankee*, in which Hank Morgan's recognition that his "white Indians" do not correspond with his dictum that "Training is everything. . . . Training is all there is to a person" results in his decision to exterminate them (qtd. in "Armies" 129). As Michaels has argued: "Morgan's recognition that *his* Indians can be neither trained nor conquered is thus a recognition of their rocklike character and his commitment to exterminating them is not an attack on their savagery but a tribute to their individuality" ("Armies" 130).[8] It is for this reason that Ralph Marvell can make what might initially seem the extreme gesture of correspondence between his family and the Indian. Both are imagined as resisting the changes inherent to American life, in particular after the Civil War, and as such are doomed to perish because inflexible "character" is no match for an impersonal speculative economy. When he makes the analogy, Ralph imagines himself at a critical distance from his ancestors, but his own fate, at the hands of a woman defined by her "pioneer blood" (37) and her midwestern upbringing, suggests that such a distancing is not possible.[9] As a result of his "inherited prejudices" (294), Ralph does not contest, or even consider, the divorce settlement through which the courts award sole custody of his son to his (ex-)wife, since he believes that the idea of *her* having or even wanting the boy is "preposterous" (273). Ralph's misunderstanding stems from a failure to comprehend fully the speculative, fluid nature of the "new" American like his wife, wherein—in a direct parallel with James's description of New York's architectural impermanence—ontological "character" is replaced by identification constructed via consumption and repeated reinvention of the self in a variety of roles. Although his marriage to Undine Spragg implies a recognition of her adaptability, since he plans to save her "from the ranks of the cheaply fashionable" by taking advantage of "her freshness, her malleability" to mold her into his type (53), Ralph does not appreciate the gulf between his embodiment of tradition and what he misperceives as her desire to imitate it. He loses custody of his son and commits suicide as a result of what *he* sees as his own and his family's "innate" weakness, "some hidden hereditary failing" (274).

I have already noted that Wharton's fiction manifests widely shared anxieties about a perceived lack of space in America at the turn of the century. The squeezing of Selden into a small apartment in Rosedale's building, within which both Selden and Lily are subject to the scrutinizing and speculative gaze of both the masses and a new financial elite, equates with Marvell's representation of Washington Square as the "Reservation." If this description is contrasted with Henry James's own earlier assertion that the "ideal of quiet and genteel retirement, in 1835, was found in Washington Square" (*Washington* 39), it is possible to start to understand the historical transformation within which Wharton's novels operate.

In James's novel, Dr. Sloper moves to Washington Square because he has only an "indirect" interest in the "commercial development" of New York (39). The Square offers privacy and an alternative to the "mighty uproar" (39) of trade to be found elsewhere in New York. It is markedly juxtaposed with the residence of Arthur Townsend, the "stout young stockbroker" (50), who seeks to live within the developing market economy. In contrast to the permanence sought by Sloper, Townsend claims:

> "At the end of three or four years we'll move. That's the way to live in New York—to move every three or four years. Then you always get the last thing. It's because the city's growing so quick—you've got to keep up with it . . . ; it's a great advantage to have a new house; you get all the latest improvements. They invent everything all over again about every five years, and it's a great thing to keep up with the new things. I always try to keep up with the new things of every kind." (50)

In *Washington Square*, Arthur Townsend makes only a brief appearance and, as Ian Bell has argued, is "the voice of the *distanced* power structure of a market economy that provides an accurate picture of living within the city's transformations" (Bell 45; emphasis added). His type poses little threat to Dr. Sloper in his abode, since, in 1835, this is also new: "a handsome, modern, wide-fronted house," embodying "the last results of architectural science" (39). While Townsend's acquisitive fascination with "things" may well anticipate Undine Spragg's desire for new husbands at similar intervals, it remains marginal and excluded from the still-central, fashionable solitude of Washington Square. In sharp contrast, in *The Custom of the Country*, it is Undine's insatiable urge for new "things" (remember James's observations on the "commercial at any cost" and the destruction of the past) that forces Ralph out of the already threatened realm of the Square and into the hostile world of commerce for which he is entirely unsuited.

Nevertheless, two points about James's novel are significant in terms of my present interest in Wharton's fictions of New York. First, even his representation of the city of the 1830s and '40s provides a sense of impending doom for the denizens of old Manhattan, with the "embryonic" streets further uptown (40) threatening to crush the old world values of Washington Square by sheer weight of numbers. Second, James is writing his novel retrospectively, with what Bell terms, recalling the title of Wharton's own autobiography, "the warm glow of a *backward glance*" (Bell 45; emphasis added). For James,

> It was here, as you might have been informed on good authority, that you had come into a world which appeared to offer a variety of sources of interest; it was here that your grandmother lived, in venerable solitude, and dispensed a hospitality which commended itself alike to the infant imagination and the infant palate; . . . it was here, finally, that your first school . . . enlarged the circle both of your observations and your sensations. (James, *Washington* 39–40)

Bell is surely correct to suggest that "James's dispersal of time belongs in part to his tactic of removal from what he finds distasteful in the early manifestations of the Gilded Age" and also to argue that "such vocabulary . . . emphasizes itself as a warning against the elisions whereby nostalgia and memory discolor the experience of history" (45–46)—a criticism fully illustrated by the fate of Ralph Marvell in *The Custom of the Country*. But I believe that Bell is mistaken to suggest that James's memories "deliberately fudge the conditions of history" (45–46), since these conditions are already inscribed in James's need for a retrospective narrative, in his fusion of the romance and the novel at a time of accelerated economic transformation in the United States of the 1870s, and in the *implicit* filling-in of the spaces described by Arthur Townsend, a filling-in whose textuality is clearly equated with James's own act of writing American history.

That Dr. Sloper's mid-nineteenth-century sense of detachment is no longer either relevant or appropriate to the early twentieth century is evident when we return to Ralph Marvell's musings on familial identity.[10] Instead of privacy, Washington Square is now under surveillance, with its inhabitants soon to be "exhibited at ethnological shows, pathetically engaged in the exercise of their primitive industries" (47). The choice of image is significant on two interconnected counts, both of which will ultimately also return us to Lily Bart's sense of selfhood. Ralph both imagines the "old" Americans in terms of ethnicity and, by extension, implicitly associates the need for such ethnic identification with the historically specific emergence of particular forms of representation such as ethnographic display and the American Museum of Natural History, to whose trustees Henry Fairfield Osborn reported in 1908: "Nature teaches law and order and respect for property. If these people cannot go to the country, then the Museum must bring nature to the city" (qtd. in Haraway 237). I will return to this cross-reference below, since the link between Edith Wharton's refined New Yorker gentility and the city's famous Natural History Museum may seem rather curious.[11] First, however, I want to develop my observation that Ralph imagines himself as belonging to an ethnic group.

It should be obvious that Marvell's ethnic self-definition is an invention, given both the limited time within which the American aristocracy constructed itself—that is, usually within one or two generations of a financially successful founding father—and the fact that, with a few notable exceptions, there is no *racial* difference between *new* and *old* Americans in Wharton's novels. She makes the point explicit in *A Backward Glance*, observing that "Colonial New York was mostly composed of merchants and bankers" and noting that her mother had a "hearty contempt for the tardy discovery of aristocratic genealogies" in an "old New York . . . composed of Dutch and British middle-class families" (9). This sense that American aristocracy is an invention of the modern world is also amply illustrated by other novels of the late nineteenth and early twentieth centuries, most notably, perhaps, in *The Rise of Silas Lapham* (1885), where Howells's Bromfield Corey, the son of a prosperous merchant, disguises superficial cultural differences as inherent biological determinants. Although it is hard to decipher precisely what Corey "means" (given his slippery irony), his reminder to his son that " 'we are Essex County people . . . just a little beyond the salt of the earth' " (66–67) and his hostility to the poor syntax and etiquette of Silas Lapham mask the cultural construction of his own aloofness, stemming from his own youth when, "with his father's leave he *fixed himself* at Rome, where he remained studying art and rounding the being inherited from his Yankee progenitors, till there was very little left of the ancestral angularities" (70, emphasis added).

But the fact that such an identity is an invention should not, in itself, lead us to dismiss it as irrelevant or unimportant, given the by now critical commonplace that all of the modern world is made up of cultural constructs. Indeed, Corey's association of selfhood with aesthetic sensibility equates with the anthropologist James Clifford's assertion that "ethnography is an 'art,' " in the sense that "the making of ethnography is artisanal, tied to the worldly work of writing" (Clifford 6). Despite all of the narrator's and his own attempts to make himself appear *un*worldly, Corey's inscription of a self concurs with Clifford's definition of ethnographic writing in several ways: Corey's construction of a meaningful identity through rhetorical resistance to hegemonic capitalism and its expressive conventions; his (ideological) recognition that, to quote Clifford, "the authority to represent cultural realities is unequally shared and at times contested" (6); and, most memorably, his generically different use of paint, all contribute to the creation of a "coherent" ethnographic identity, which is a fiction "based on systematic, and contestable, exclusions" (Clifford 6).

This insight can be extended through a consideration of Ernest Gellner's argument: "Nationalism is not the awakening of nations to self-consciousness; it *invents* nations where they do not exist" (qtd. in Sollors xi). As Werner Sollors has pointed out, "this understanding of nationalism . . . could be helpful toward an interpretation of ethnicity, too" (xi), since the latter peaked during the industrial revolutions of the late eighteenth to early twentieth centuries, when technological innovations and economic transformation resulted in the dislocation of older senses of order.[12] Although, as with Bromfield Corey's or Ralph Marvell's sense of difference, ethnic groups are often represented as being natural and inflexible (what Sollors calls "always already in existence" [xiv]) and are thus seen as threatened from without, in particular by the danger of assimilation, it should already be plain that such a perception is an illusion. As Sollors continues, "It is always the specificity of power relations at a given historical moment and in a particular place that triggers off a strategy of pseudo-historical explanations that camouflage the inventive act itself" (xvi).[13]

Sollors poses a series of challenges to the idea of ethnic "authenticity," to many of which our reading of Wharton, James, and Howells can already provide an affirmative response. He asks, among other questions:

> Are not ethnic groups part of the historical process, tied to the history of modern nationalism? Though they may pretend to be eternal and essential, are they not of rather recent origin and eminently pliable and unstable? Is not modernism an important *source* of ethnicity? . . . Even where they exist over long time spans, do not ethnic groups constantly change and redefine themselves? . . . Are not the formulas of "originality" and "authenticity" in ethnic discourse a palpable legacy of European romanticism? . . . Does not any "ethnic" system rely on an opposition to something "non-ethnic," and is not this very

> antithesis more important than the interchangeable content (of flags, anthems, and the applicable vernacular)? (xiv)

I cite Sollors at such length because, although his collection of contributors markedly avoids any discussion of "old" Americans in the sense implied by Wharton and Howells, his questions are as relevant to the study of their sense of ethnic identity as they are to the essays on Mexican, German, African, or Jewish Americans. Clearly, Corey's and Marvell's sense of ethnic selfhood is both recent and unstable, whatever *they* may believe to the contrary. It is a product of a modernity in which a romantic desire for "origins" and "authenticity" appears to be the only alternative to an increasingly standardized national identity, locatable in Wharton's time in the combination of Progressive Melting Pot ideologies and the Man-Management ethos of machine culture. Finally, it can be defined only through contrast with what it is not—that is, the amorphous modern self, able to colonize any space in its quest for economic and cultural domination. Before the transformation of New York, Wharton that her class was unaware that its "unalterable rules of conduct" were ethnic at all. They become significant only once the invasion by a plethora of *other* social codes renders her group's manners "as quaintly arbitrary as the domestic rites of the Pharaohs," a subject which must be studied and displayed before it vanishes forever.

Crucially, however, the sense of difference is held not only by the ethnic group themselves. Howells exploits the Laphams' sense of inadequacy when invited to the Coreys' dinner party to great comic effect, as when Silas's "large fists . . . looked, in the saffron tint which the shop-girl said his gloves should be of, like canvassed hams" (188), and, although Howells's attitude to both the Laphams and the Coreys is complex and ambivalent, the families share a sense of each other's *Otherness*, which even the marriage between Tom and Penelope cannot overcome. Likewise, in *The Custom of the Country*, Undine Spragg, despite being informed largely by "the glowing pages of fiction" and despite mistakenly erasing the gap between wealth and "class" in "fashionable society" in her early pursuit of Ralph Marvell, imagines herself to be an "intruder" (40) and finds any kind of contentment only at the end of the novel, when she remarries Elmer Moffatt, as much of a social "pioneer" as herself and by now defined through his association with economic and industrial success as the "billionaire Railroad King" (366). At this moment, Wharton makes clear her own sense of impassable cultural difference since, although Moffatt has become "the greatest collector in America" (365), she recounts—again reminding us of the public face of the domestic space—that the books in his library remain unread, "too valuable to be taken down," and that "the wigged and corseleted heroes on the walls" are *not* Moffatt's ancestors (363), and she repeatedly represents his acquisitions in terms of their inflationary impact on art and precious stone prices, rather than in tribute to a conversion to Marvellian (or *Marvellous*) understanding (365–66). Significantly, this sequence of representations is focalized through Paul Marvell, the son of Undine's marriage to Ralph, and the clash of cultural constructs between Undine and her various husbands makes it impossible for him to arrive at a meaningful interpretation of what he sees. His desire to impose a narrative of "origin" or "authenticity" is destroyed by the reader's knowledge of the imitative quality of the rooms, in which authentic works of art now construct a false history, superficially granting the Moffatts access to an ethnographic heritage to which they cannot lay claim through even a single generation. In order to assure themselves and their descendants of a present and a future—that is, acceptance within the inner sanctum of American social life—they need to construct a past.[14]

We are now, finally, ready to return to Lily Bart's situation in *The House of Mirth*, since her value is a product of a combination of the factors we have examined. Although the Moffatts' textual genealogy is false, in the sense that it is purchased, it could well be argued that this falsehood is only a recreation of a similar act by Corey, or the earlier Marvells, especially given that they, too, are implicitly contrasted with the aristocratic family of Undine's third husband, a French nobleman whose cultural treasures *do* represent centuries of familial history but which, ironically, he is forced to sell as a result of Undine's extravagance. But, for the inhabitants of Lily's New York, the difference between old and new Americans *appears* to be real and provides the source of her value, as well as the inevitability of her death. Thus, while the Moffatts' acquisition of the trappings of an aristocratic the history remains merely superficial, exposed by the gaze of Paul Marvell, who is instinctively attracted to the one genuine picture in the house, a photograph of the young Elmer looking "infinitely *noble* and charming" (362; emphasis added), Lily's own membership in an old family offers Rosedale, or any other wealthy new American who wishes to marry her, the chance of access to a club impregnable via purely financial means. For, although Lily's own pressing need to marry stems from her father's "ruin," Lily's ancestors, like her guardian, Mrs. Peniston, "belonged to the class of old New Yorkers who have always lived well, dressed expensively, and done little else" (37). It is this genealogy, combined with her famous "beauty," that gives Lily value, even when she is financially destitute.[15]

The point is first made through the discussion of Americana I mentioned in my introduction. Lily requires information on the subject because she is contemplating marrying Percy Gryce, inheritor of the celebrated "Gryce Americana" (21). She reckons, correctly as it transpires, that a knowledge of this cultural heritage, alongside Gryce's knowledge of her own value as old American, will draw him to her.[16] Although she has an unpleasant vision of what the marriage will mean to her, since it will reify her as a piece of Americana, this pales beside the alternative, that "she would have to be civil to such men as Rosedale" (57), and Lily insists that she will marry Gryce. But Lily Bart is unable to take such a cold-headed economic step; like Marvell's, her actions are governed by a romantic vision of the world in which "the landscape outspread below her seemed an enlargement of her present mood" and within which, to Selden, "her quick-breathing silence seemed a part of the general hush and harmony of things" (64).[17] As a result of a walk with Selden and the contrast this evokes between him and Gryce, who looks like a "baffled beetle" as he is seen departing "mournfully, in a dust-hood and goggles" in a motor car (67), Lily loses the chance to marry Gryce. Her romanticism, the possible source of her financial salvation, precludes the possibility of singleminded devotion to the task of making Percy think he is pursuing her.

Of course, this is not the only occasion on which Lily's inherited value is illustrated. Most notable, in terms of our present interest, is the famous tableau vivant scene, in which she poses as Reynolds's "Mrs. Lloyd." In order to consider the effects this generates, we need first to consider its context, that is, the "general entertainment" offered by the ("fat and vulgar and bouncing") Mrs. Bry, as a means of "attack[ing] society" (130). The tableaux, along with expensive music, "were the two baits most likely to attract the desired prey," and the guests respond by dressing "rather with an eye to Mrs. Bry's background than to herse!" (131–32). Indeed, as with the description of the Moffatts' new collection at the end of *The Custom of the Country*, Wharton goes to great lengths to illustrate the illusory nature of real "things":

> [The "Welly Brys' "] recently built house, whatever it might lack as a frame for domesticity, was almost as well designed for the display of a festal assemblage as one of those airy pleasure-halls which the Italian architects improvised to set off the hospitality of princes. The air of improvisation was in fact strikingly present: so recent, so rapidly evoked was the *mise-en-scène* that one had to touch the marble columns to learn they were not of cardboard, to seat one's self in one of the damask-and-gold arm-chairs to be sure it was not painted against the wall. (132)

Instead of generating an impression of authenticity, the real marble and real gold only contribute to the theatricality of a domestic space now constructed for the purpose of *public* spectacle.[18] The guests respond with a recognition of their dual status as both onlookers and objects of others' gazes, dressing to "present a surface of rich tissues and jewelled shoulders in harmony with the festooned and gilded walls, and the flushed splendours of the Venetian ceiling" (132). As with the contents of the Moffatts' library, history is replaced by a succession of depthless and recycled images of the past.

At the center of this spectacle and, as we have seen, deliberately selected to entice Mrs. Bry's "prey," is Lily Bart, who is perceived as being different from her hostess and the guests in a number of ways. We are made aware that the tableaux may be *correctly* interpreted only by, a select few. The facts that "to the responsive fancy they may give magic glimpses of the boundary world between fact and imagination" and that "Selden's mind was of this order: he could yield to vision-making influences as completely as a child to the spell of a fairy-tale" (133) immediately alert us to the romantic elements of such an interpretation: Wharton's close paraphrase of Hawthorne's definition of the environment of the romance-writer as "a neutral territory, somewhere between the real world and fairy-land, where the Actual and the Imaginary may meet" (Hawthorne 36) and the knowledge that Selden shares Lily's ethnic heritage are clear signs of the kind of world constructed by Lily's tableau, within which her presence offers a nostalgic vision of a wholeness "lost" in the modern world.

Such impressions are enhanced when we move to Wharton's description of Lily's effect. I will quote the passage at some length, since it brings together a number of issues I have outlined earlier:

> Here there could be no mistaking the predominance of personality—the unanimous "Oh!" of the spectators was a tribute not to the brush-work of Reynolds's "Mrs. Lloyd" but to the flesh and blood loveliness of Lily Bart. She had shown her artistic intelligence in a type so like her own that she could embody the person represented without ceasing to be herself. It was as though she had stepped, not out of, but into, Reynolds's canvas, banishing the phantom of his dead beauty by the beams of her living grace. (134)

The power of Lily's performance is her ability to erase the distinction between her own "living flesh" and the subject of the original painting, that is, to create the impression of authenticity and depth when surrounded by surface and imitation. That she is able to achieve such an erasure is a result of her "artistic intelligence"—in other words, her *inherited* romantic sensibility—and the acceptance by the spectators of her genetic right to such an inheritance. It is here that Selden "seemed to see before him the real Lily Bart . . . catching for a moment a note of that eternal harmony of which her beauty was a part," and, as the ironically labeled "experienced connoisseur" Ned Van Alstyne puts it: " 'there isn't a break *in the lines* anywhere, and I suppose she wanted us to know it!' " (135, emphasis added). Lily's seamless ability to place herself within a painting exhibited, significantly, in 1776 is a result of her already ethnically inscribed, or reproduced, ability to go beyond mere impersonation. In its place, she possesses what the Moffatts or the Welly Brys lack: the paradoxical ability to what passes for an *authentic* representation of an original image.[19]

Of course, we must remember that this persuasive illusion of authenticity has been selected because of its ability to attract guests to the party. It belongs, too, to the world of fashion, and, even if it may appear to be one of Walter Benjamin's "tiger's leap[s] into the past," Lily's action "takes place in an arena where the ruling class gives the commands" (Benjamin 253).[20] As with Marvell's fears about Washington Square becoming a "Reservation," subject to the scrutiny of the new "pioneers," or Gryce's earlier attempt to put Lily on display, the effect here is to turn Lily into a museum piece. Her pose thus immediately starts to self-deconstruct through its participation in a system mediated by economics and fashion, rather than aesthetics, in which, in 1905, Reynolds's "Mrs. Lloyd" was in a private collection owned by the Rothschilds. Selden's perceptions of the effect Lily creates quickly remind us of the historical conditions within which she is being displayed and "the standards by which she was fated to be measured!" (135), and he is repeatedly disillusioned with her as a result of her willingness to participate in the speculative contemporary world. Indeed, for Selden, Lily appears to share the "caged and dishonoured condition" associated with the spire of Trinity Church by James in *The American Scene*.

This does not entirely dissipate Lily's own understanding of her situation, however, in which, alongside her pressing need to find a husband, "she liked to think of her beauty as a power for good, as giving her the opportunity to attain a position where she should make her influence felt in the vague diffusion of refinement and good taste" (35). Like Henry Fairfield Osborn's contemporaneous desire to teach "law and order" by bringing "nature to the city" via the American Museum of Natural History, Lily perceives her own role as educational, implying that her own *natural* beauty can be used to elicit a cultural imitation. Her place in the tableau vivant claims to restore an original and promises that the association will result in the contagious transformation of the spectator.

The parallel between Lily's representation and those to be found in the Museum can be illuminated through a brief consideration of Donna Haraway's description of the animals in the tableaux of the Akeley African Hall. Although Haraway's account insists on the "death and literal representation" of the animals, it bears many parallels to Wharton's account of Lily's tableau:

> the Hall threatens to dissolve into the chaos of the Age of Man. But it does not. The gaze holds, and the wary animal heals those who will look. There is no impediment to this vision. There is no mediation, nothing between the viewer and the animal. . . . [T]he gaze invites his visual penetration. The animal is frozen in a moment of supreme life, and man is transfixed. . . . Taxidermy fulfills the fatal desire to represent, to be whole; it is a politics of reproduction. (243)[21]

Of course, Lily's pose is temporary, rather than permanent, although it does anticipate her death, when Selden feels the "real Lily was still there" and that "time had ceased in this room" (326). Nevertheless, for its duration, Lily both transfixes her audience and invites the penetrative gaze of prospective husbands or admirers. It is only when the curtain falls that the "note of eternal harmony" (135) collapses into the general "circulation" defined by Lily's place within an economy of "success" (136).

But, alongside the ability to heal and the invitation to penetrate both sexually and socially—the dual promise that is the condition of Rosedale's interest—there is an equally "fatal" side to Lily's own "politics of reproduction." For, despite the effect she has upon her male viewers, and despite her own recognition that she must make her act of reproduction a commercial one, there is also the implicit inability to act beyond the "unalterable rules of conduct" (again remembering *A Backward Glance*) of her kind. Like Marvell, and like Twain's "white Indians," Lily is finally inflexible, unable to adapt herself to the fluid speculative economy that surrounds her in a turn-of-the-century America identifiable to commentators as diverse as James and Veblen by its constant "newness." By constructing a biological self ("living flesh") definable only within a logic of ethnic reproduction, Lily precludes the possibility of what would have to be cultural transgression.[22] Thus, it is a mistake to distinguish, as has Cynthia Griffin Wolff, between the artificiality of Lily's usual behavior, virtually always "a deliberate piece of acting," and the "spontaneity" of "those few impulses for which she pays so dearly" (*Feast* 128).[23] Instead, we must recognize that the latter are defined by their lack of spontaneity or by what we have seen to be the elision of the gap between self and ethnic group or between reproduction and "original." For Lily Bart, like the "Aborigines" both identified and represented by Ralph Marvell, is doomed to perish, the victim of what she must *act out* as inflexible *nature*. To belong to her ethnic group—that is, to resist the entreaties of the "nonethnic" market and, paradoxically, to thus inflate her market value—Lily must perform "ethnically." But to act in this way—to reproduce a history of "good taste"—is finally to price herself out of the market, and Lily dies because she cannot be bought, because her self is not "fat and vulgar and bouncing," because, as Ralph Marvell recognized in *The Custom of the Country* the only way to remain pure is to perish. As Selden tells us, there is "nothing new" about Lily Bart, but her reproduction of authenticity can never move beyond the merely theatrical performance of *history* within an economy of imitation and representation.

Notes

1. James's reading of the skyscrapers is analogous to Veblen's account of female fashion. The buildings are "simply the most piercing notes in that concert of the expensively provisional into which your supreme sense of New York revolves itself" (*American Scene* 61).

2. The erosion of private space in American life had been a concern of James's as long ago as *The Bostonians* (1886). In that novel, Selah Tarrant's craving for publicity and Matthias Pardon's desire to report on domestic conversations threaten to turn Olive Chancellor's house—hitherto a sanctuary from the outside world—into a target for public scrutiny.

3. Of course, Cynthia Griffin Wolff is correct to identify the "menacing spectral presences" of poor immigrants in *The House of Mirth*, since "they represent for Lily Bart a physical emblem of the poverty she so fears" (Introduction x). Nevertheless, as this essay will make clear, Lily can never *be* a "new American" of any kind.

4. Wharton thus makes explicit what is implicit in William Dean Howells's *The Rise of Silas Lapham*, published two decades earlier, in 1885. For Bromfield Corey, Howells's ironic representation of the "old" American "aristocracy" (like Lily Bart a figure increasingly reliant on "taste" and "origins" as alternatives to wealth), "[Money] is the romance, the poetry of our age. . . . The Englishmen who come here are more curious about the great new millionaires than about anyone else, and they respect them more" (64). Wharton's substitution of "new Americans" for "new millionaires" confirms the sense that wealth functions within a complex network of competing constructions of what "American" should mean. It clearly renders Carry Fisher's call for Mrs. Bry to " 'be natural herself' " meaningless, since the "new American" is definable only through imitation and constant change.

5. The encroachment is further illustrated by the "persistent gaze" of the charwoman with "a broad sallow face, slightly pitted with smallpox, and thin straw-colored hair through which her scalp shone unpleasantly," whom Lily passes on the stairs as she leaves Selden's flat. The danger of Lily's situation is thus evoked though a combination of

racial and class anxieties, with Lily "flushing" under their dual "interrogative" stares (13–14).

6. Note the similarity between this and James's description of Washington Square in *The American Scene*. For James, the "good easy Square . . . [is] a cool backwater for time as well as for space," full of the signs of "a pleasantly primitive order" (7).

7. See Michaels, "Race into Culture," for an important discussion of the significance of association with the "Indian" as a strategy for asserting nationality in American literature. He identifies this as a product of the 1920s and provides examples from Cather's *A Lost Lady* and Fitzgerald's *The Great Gatsby*, explicitly arguing that "the major writers of the Progressive period—Drelser, Wharton, London—were comparatively indifferent to the question of American national identity" (670). That his periodization is inaccurate is implied by this paper and is illustrated in greater depth in my " 'The Way Our People Came.' "

8. My discussion of this aspect of *A Connecticut Yankee* is largely informed by Michaels's argument.

9. In *A Backward Glance*, Wharton traces the transformation of New York back to the 1880s and "the earliest detachment of the big money-makers from the West" (6). The figures behind the economic imperative to remove the Native American population are thus also seen as being responsible for the destruction of the "aboriginal" population of old New York.

10. Mary E. Papke has attributed Ralph Marvell's fate to his "love of romantic illusions" (139) and to the fact that he "never fully surrenders his romantic view of Undine" (140). Her reading of the novel highlights the disparity between Ralph's misreading of the marriage and Undine's pragmatic decision to cut her losses and look elsewhere for a man providing access to genuine wealth and status. While Papke's account is persuasive in its recognition of this juxtaposition, her principal concern is with the heroine, and she fails to explore further the reasons for Ralph's form of self-definition. This absence, though understandable to the extent that Ralph is a relatively minor character in the novel, seems curious if we link his representation of Indians and pioneers with his insistence on defining his family ethnically, as I do below. Joan Lidoff describes the novel as "primarily a romance of identity" "sprinkled with fairy-tale allusions" (239, 244) and reads Lily's relationship with Selden as "Edenic fantasy" (248). Lidoff's forceful psychoanalytic reading of the novel breaks down with her failure to historicize *universal* "truths." By

attributing Lily's identity to her status as "orphan, powerless and alone" (240), Lidoff denies the importance of cultural heritage in the construction of social identity. The significance of the absence generated by such an omission will become clear as I develop my argument.

11. Nancy Bentley has recently addressed the relational matrix of fiction and ethnography. She examines the ways in which novels and ethnographies generated a master discourse of "culture" in the mid to late nineteenth and early twentieth centuries.

12. Such transformations reached their peak in the United States in the late nineteenth century, eliciting the sense of crisis felt by writers such as Wharton, Howells, Twain, and James.

13. Think, too, in this context, of Twain's mocking treatment of the subject in his representation of the First Families of Virginia in *Pudd'nhead Wilson* (1893).

14. In a sense, what we witness here is an early anticipation of the more typically postmodern investigation of the simulacrum as a cultural problem. In particular, the scene can be compared with those in Ridley Scott's movie *Blade Runner* (1983) which focus on photography and memory. Scott's film is obsessively concerned with photographs as not merely substitutes for but as conditions of memory and "history." For the Replicants, and especially for Rachel (Sean Young), who is such a perfect simulation of the human that she believes she *is* what she simulates, photographs of childhood or of ancestors *prove* the right to a present existence. A witty intertextual example of the process occurs in Martin Scorsese's adaptation of Wharton's *Age of Innocence* (1993), with a background painting depicting the star (Daniel Day-Lewis) in his earlier role as Natty Bumppo in *Last of the Mohicans.*

15. A similar point could be made about the "purchase" of the Prince by Adam Verver in James's *The Golden Bowl* (1904).

16. Gryce has inherited his fortune from his father, who made it "out of a patent device for excluding fresh air from hotels" (22). That Percy himself is decidedly *not* an old American is confirmed by his repeated association with motor cars and by the description of him as being a "lower organism . . . [whose] interest in Americana had not originated with himself" (21). As with Elmer Moffatt in *The Custom of the Country*, Gryce is seeking to purchase a past (and present) different from the "reality" of his ancestors' experiences.

17. The opening pages of chapter 6 (63–65) are suffused with such romantic imagery.

18. See Amy Kaplan for an excellent analysis of the theatrical function of the architecture in this passage (94–95). Also compare James's description in *The American Scene* of New York "in *villeggiatura*": "The ample villas, in their full dress, planted each on its little square of brightly-green carpet, and as with their stiff skirts pulled well down, eyed each other, at short range, from head to foot; while the open road, the chariots, the buggies, the motors, the pedestrians . . . regarded at their ease both this reciprocity and the parties to it" (11).

19. It is thus only partly true to claim, as does Peter Messent, that it is "Lily's physical beauty that makes her valuable in this social world" (190). As a result of this simplification, Messent overstates his claim that "money is collapsing traditional class boundaries. The stress on the elaborate codes of the leisured world . . . is based on the very finest of distinctions. . . . The stress on such distinctions . . . cannot hide the fact that this 'aristocratic' world has no real prop on which to rest, that worth is finally not to be judged in terms of such distinctions but of money" (195–96). Rather, it is Lily's combination of beauty and birth/behavior that is the enabling condition for her continued value to Rosedale, with his "collector's passion for the rare and unattainable" (113), when she has no money and even her beauty is perceived to be fading.

20. Remember, too, James's description of the "caged and dishonored condition" of the spire of Trinity Church in *The American Scene.*

21. Although Africa Hall was not opened until 1936, Osborn was president of the Museum from 1908 to 1936, and the overpowering presence of the Theodore Roosevelt Memorial locates the experience firmly within early-twentieth-century modes of representation.

22. It is for this reason that Lily is unable to pursue the other option repeatedly hinted at in the novel: motherhood. Although her final dream is of Nettie Struther's child lying on her arm (323), Lily's combination of financial need and ethnic selfhood renders marriage and *biological* reproduction impossible. She cannot marry Gryce or Rosedale because to do so would go against her ethnic training. Yet, to marry Selden is equally infeasible, since he lacks the wealth to allow her to pursue the lifestyle to which her breeding has conditioned her.

23. Also see Michaels (*Gold Standard* 217–44) for a powerful reading of the ways in which Lily's "scruples and resistances . . . make her valuable" to collectors like Rosedale (228). Michaels is surely correct to point out that "each gesture of 'resistance' to the market serves only to augment one's value in the market" (228). Nevertheless, his reading neglects those

effects of Lily's "ethnicity" which have been the subject of this essay and fails to differentiate between the various speculative economies to be found in the novel.

Works Cited

Baudrillard, Jean. *Cool Memories*. Trans. Chris Turner. London: Verso, 1990.

Bell, Ian F. A. *Washington Square: Styles of Money*. New York: Twayne, 1993.

Benjamin, Walter. "Thesis on the Philosophy of History." *Illuminations*. Trans. Harry Zohn. London: Fontana, 1992. 245–55.

Bentley, Nancy. *The Ethnography of Manners: Hawthorne, James, Wharton*. Cambridge: Cambridge University Press, 1995.

Clifford, James. "Introduction: Partial Truths." *Writing Culture: The Poetics and Politics of Ethnography*. Ed. James Clifford and George E. Marcus. Berkeley: University of California Press, 1986. 1–26.

Gair, Christopher. " 'The Way Our People Came': Citizenship, Capitalism and Racial Difference in London's] *The Valley of the Moon*." *Studies in the Novel* 25 (1993): 418–35.

Haraway, Donna. "Teddy Bear Patriarchy: Taxidermy in the Garden of Eden, New York City, 1908–36." *Cultures of United States Imperialism*. Ed. Amy Kaplan and Donald E. Pease. Durham: Duke University Press, 1993. 237–91.

Hawthorne, Nathaniel. *The Scarlet Letter*. Oxford: Oxford University Press, 1990.

Howells, William Dean. *The Rise of Silas Lapham*. Harmondsworth: Penguin, 1983.

James, Henry. *The American*. Ed. James W. Tuttleton. New York: Norton, 1978.

———. *The American Scene*. London: Penguin, 1994.

———. "The Jolly Corner." *Selected Tales*. Ed. Peter Messent and Tom Paulin. London: Dent, 1982. 352–94.

———. *Washington Square*. London: Penguin, 1986.

Kaplan, Amy. *The Social Construction of American Realism*. Chicago: University of Chicago Press, 1988.

Lidoff, Joan. "Another Sleeping Beauty: Narcissism in *The House of Mirth*." *American Realism: New Essays*. Ed. Eric J. Sundquist. Baltimore: Johns Hopkins University Press, 1982. 238–58.

Messent, Peter. *New Readings of the American Novel: Narrative Theory and Its Application*. London: Macmillan, 1990.

Michaels, Walter Benn. "Armies and Factories: *A Connecticut Yankee.*" *Mark Twain: A Collection of Critical Essays.* Ed. Eric J. Sundquist. Englewood Cliffs, N.J.: Prentice Hall, 1994. 129–39.

———. *The Gold Standard and the Logic of Naturalism: American Literature at the Turn of the Century.* Berkeley: University of California Press, 1987.

———. "Race Into Culture: A Critical Genealogy of Cultural Identity." *Critical Inquiry* 18 (1992): 655–85.

Papke, Mary E. *Verging on the Abyss: The Social Fiction of Kate Chopin and Edith Wharton.* Westport, Conn.: Greenwood Press, 1990.

Sollors, Werner. "Introduction: The Invention of Ethnicity." *The Invention of Ethnicity.* Ed. Werner Sollors. Oxford: Oxford University Press, 1989. ix–xx.

Trachtenberg, Alan. *The Incorporation of America: Culture and Society in the Gilded Age.* New York: Hill and Wang, 1982.

Veblen, Thorstein. *The Theory of the Leisure Class.* Introduction C. Wright Mills. New York: Mentor, 1953.

Wharton, Edith. *A Backward Glance.* London: Everyman, 1993.

———. *The Custom of the Country.* Oxford: Oxford University Press, 1995.

———. *The House of Mirth.* London: Penguin, 1985.

Wolff, Cynthia Griffin. *A Feast of Words: The Triumph of Edith Wharton.* Oxford: Oxford University Press, 1977.

———. Introduction. *The House of Mirth.* By Edith Wharton. London: Penguin, 1985. vii–xxvi.

Extinction, Taxidermy, Tableaux Vivants

Staging Race and Class in The House of Mirth

JENNIE A. KASSANOFF

◆ ◆ ◆

"But what *is* your story, Lily? I don't believe any one knows it yet." Gerty Farish's question, coming as it does near the end of Edith Wharton's 1905 best-seller *The House of Mirth*, is certainly ironic. In the context of a novel that labors to tell the whole story of Lily Bart, Gerty's question suggests the absence or concealment of the text's central narrative. Lily's response, moreover, is disconcertingly opaque:

> "From the beginning?" Miss Bart gently mimicked her. "Dear Gerty, how little imagination you good people have! Why, the beginning was in my cradle, I suppose—in the way I was brought up, and the things I was taught to care for. Or no—I won't blame anybody for my faults: I'll say it was in my blood, that I got it from some wicked pleasure-loving ancestress, who reacted against the homely virtues of New Amsterdam, and wanted to be back at the court of the Charleses!" (226)

Lily decides that her flaws are not the work of her environment; rather, they are hereditary traits in the blood, passed down from a sybaritic ancestress. Such logic is a prime example of belief in what Laura Otis calls "organic memory"—the idea that "repeated patterns of sensations, whether of the recent or distant past, had left traces in the body, making the individual an epitome of his or her racial history" (3). Indeed, Lily's assumption that she embodies a genealogy responsible for "all of her instinctive resistances, of taste, of training, of blind inherited scruples" reflects a popular Spencerian notion of the day (Wharton, *House* 104). As the writer Forbes Phillips queried in 1906, "Is it not possible that the child may inherit some of his ancestor's memory? That . . . flashes of reminiscence are the sudden awakening . . . of something we have in our blood; . . . the records of an ancestor's past life?" (980). For Wharton, the answer was self-evident: Lily's "ancestral memory" reveals not only her deep racial consciousness but also, more important, her embodiment of race itself.

Walter Benn Michaels, describing the "structural intimacy between nativism and modernism," remarks in *Our America* that "[t]he major writers of the Progressive period—London, Dreiser, Wharton—were comparatively indifferent to questions of both racial and national identity" (2, 8). This essay will argue, however, that Wharton's early fiction is profoundly invested in the imbricated logic of race, class, and national identity. If, on one level, *The House of Mirth* famously documents a woman's disinheritance—from familial money, from maternal support, from timely true love, from political power, and from the comforts of social position—I will suggest that the novel in fact pursues the opposite end. Although Wharton indicates that Lily's status as a twenty-nine-year-old unmarried socialite renders her vulnerable to the whims of what Charlotte Perkins Gilman called "the sexuo-economic relation" (121), she equally insists that her heroine's racial status is reassuringly immutable. Race becomes an essentialist—if deeply problematic—answer to the cultural vulnerabilities of class and gender. Wharton uses Lily's disinheritance to underscore and consolidate the permanence of the character's racial inheritance, reworking the amorphous possibilities of class and gender into a seemingly inviolate teleology of blood. In this sense, *The House of Mirth* highlights the tensions inherent in the now familiar trinity of race, class, and gender: if class and gender have conventionally structured Wharton criticism, race is the missing but historically crucial component complicating progressive interpretations of Wharton's project.

Lily's body becomes a supreme emblem of her race in all the ways race was understood at the turn of the century.[1] As a figure for whiteness, class pedigree, Anglo-Saxon origin, and incipient nativism, Lily articulates a central set of early-twentieth-century patrician anxieties: that the ill-bred, the foreign, and the poor would overwhelm the native elite, that American culture would fall victim to the "vulgar" tastes of the masses, and that the country's oligarchy would fail to reproduce itself and would commit "race suicide."[2] What links these concerns is an implicit belief—held by Wharton and a number of her elite compatriots—in a genealogical conception of American citizenship, one that transformed the contingencies of gendered disadvantage and class decline into an anthropology of racial extinction.

To examine the pervasive and instrumental role of Wharton's racial strategy, this essay will locate *The House of Mirth* within a diverse range of cultural phenomena that together generated the novel's complex discourse of race.[3] Indeed, Wharton's multiform dialogue with the racial questions of her day demonstrates at once her profound investment in the hybridity of American culture and her simultaneous rejection of the country's elastic accommodations. On one level, the multivocality of race in turn-of-the-century American rhetoric made the notion quintessentially useful for Wharton's purposes. If race expansively embraced the changing dimensions of class, family, ethnicity, and nation, it often did so to transform these fluctuating categories into a static vision of the organic, the permanent, and the real. Expediency was central to this strategy. As cultural democratization, class mobility, and ethnic pluralism eroded the elite's belief in the social exclusivity of Darwinian fitness, hereditary distinction increasingly seemed neither permanent nor unique. The patrician rationale behind appeals to race thus underwent a perceptible shift, relying less on nature, with its manifest susceptibility to change excess, and ruin, and more on culture, the rarefied domain of beauty, order, and permanence. Caught on shifting ideological ground, Wharton strategically exploited the meaning that best suited the situation at hand. Thus, she variously insisted that race was natural and hence inimitable, that it was cultural and thus durable, and, ultimately, that it was spiritual and therefore intangible. Because this pliant notion of race could encompass everything from class affiliation and genealogical origin to physical appearance and aesthetic preference, it served as an all-purpose ideological epoxy, fixing disparate and often unpredictable orders of meaning within a seemingly structured, essentialist taxonomy.

This protean approach is evident in *The House of Mirth*, a text that, along with Thomas Dixon's *The Clansman*, captured the popular imagination of 1905. Wharton famously observed that her first New York novel had explored how "a frivolous society can acquire dramatic significance only through what its frivolity destroys" (*Backward Glance* 207). Critics have long assumed that Wharton was targeting her own affluent Knickerbocker set, an interpretation bolstered by her scathing indictment of the elite self-interest and moral cowardice that catalyze Lily's demise. But Wharton's remark equally censures American culture more generally—a culture in which entrenched class distinctions had given way to what her friend Barrett Wendell called "the dangers of democratic tyranny" ("Democracy" 188). In a 1905 letter to Morgan Dix, rector of Trinity Church in New York, Wharton noted that "[s]ocial conditions as they are just now in our new world, where the sudden possession of money has come without inherited obligations, or any traditional sense of solidarity between the classes, is a vast & absorbing field for the novelist" (*Letters* 99). Who are these rich new Americans? Surely they are not Lily's wealthy friends, who, despite their instrumental role in her demise, hardly qualify as the disruptive arrivistes of Wharton's complaint. Rather, the author seems to fault other, less genealogically privileged citizens, whose ascendancy has fostered the culture of materialism and mobility that spells Lily's doom. Because their advantages are bought goods rather than birthright, these Americans have challenged the foundations on which the social hierarchy is based. A potent combination of urbanized labor and robber-baron industry had dealt "a double blow" to the complacent American patriciate (Herman 166). As Arthur Herman points out, elite intellectuals felt themselves doubly besieged: "anarchy and despotism" threatened from below, and "incorporated power and greed" menaced from above (168). Even more perilously, the old stock found itself strangely attracted to the invader's clamorous ways (Kaplan 92–93). Wharton's response to these conditions was adamant: an upstart culture that could not value Lily Bart, she insisted, could itself have no value.

This principle seems to be what Wharton had in mind when she remarked in 1905 that a "handful of vulgar people, bent on spending and enjoying, may seem a negligible factor in the social development of the race, but they become an engine of destruction through the illusions they kill and the generous ardors they turn to despair" (*Uncollected Writings* 110). If vulgarity, like frivolousness, was a symptom of egalitarian leveling, Wharton crucially reinscribed this phenomenon within the context of racial decline. Inherited biogenetic distinctions, she contended, were disappearing in a democratic quagmire of spending and enjoying. As her admired mentor, the Harvard art historian Charles Eliot Norton, observed, "Quantity tells against quality." "Vulgar people," Norton complained, were cultural vandals, eradicating "the common inheritance . . . of thought and experience of the race" and accelerating national deterioration (321–22). "Such groups," Wharton wrote in *The House of Mirth*'s 1936 preface, "always rest on an underpinning of wasted human possibilities" (*Uncollected Writings* 266). Lily personifies this squandered Anglo-Saxon promise. She is caught in a complex web of racial discourses that require at once her apotheosis and her extinction.

I

From its opening moments, when Lawrence Selden encounters Lily in Grand Central Station, *The House of Mirth* meticulously describes its heroine's eugenic superiority: "He led her through the throng of returning holiday-makers, past sallow-faced girls in preposterous hats, and flat-chested women struggling with paper bundles. . . . Was it possible that she belonged to the same race? The dinginess, the crudity of this average section of womanhood made him feel how highly specialized she was" (5). The female throng throws Lily's evolutionary specialization into high relief. Echoing the work of the American neurologist George M. Beard, who had declared in 1881 that "the lower must minister to the higher. . . . Millions perish that hundreds may survive" (302), Selden theorizes that "a great many dull and ugly people must . . . have been sacrificed to produce her" (5). Lily's evolutionary advantages are evident. Her vulnerabilities, however, are equally so. Despite the appearance that Lily belongs to the "same race"—the human race—Wharton will gradually insist that Lily represents an exclusive, albeit imperiled, race, at once superior and fatally overspecialized.

Lily is, in a sense, *over*bred: "She could not figure herself as anywhere but in a drawing-room, diffus ing elegance as a flower sheds perfume" (100). Beard had warned that "development . . . along any one line of . . . race, family, or tribe, in time reaches its limit, beyond which it cannot pass" (300), and this vulnerable perfection is crucial to Wharton's logic. Too refined for her own good, Lily is racially doomed. As Henry Adams would grimly predict in 1919, when "man [is] specialized beyond the hope of further variation, . . . he must be treated as . . . a degraded potential" (*Degradation* 195).

Lily's very survival requires certain choice conditions:

> The dreary limbo of dinginess lay all around and beneath that little illuminated circle in which life reached its finest efflorescence, as the mud and sleet of a winter night enclose a hothouse filled with tropical flowers. All this was in the natural order of things, and the orchid basking in its artificially created atmosphere could round the delicate curves of its petals undisturbed by the ice on the panes. (150)

Lily is a hyperevolved specimen whose purity demands a life sheltered from the encroaching dinginess of American democracy. The hothouse with frosted windows thus perfectly captures her evolutionary dilemma: once breeding has become a rarefied art, akin to the skilled horticulture of lilies and orchids, the well-bred can no longer survive in the chill air of a potentially heterogeneous world.[4]

The hothouse, we know from John Auchard, is the quintessential site of aesthetic decadence—a place "rich in discriminated delicacy, but . . . foster[ing] little or no hardy growth" (1–2). Lily's effete hyperaestheticism therefore reveals Wharton's unexpected place in the discourse most often associated with the flamboyant Oscar Wilde.[5] Indeed, despite her prim persona, Wharton professed the "keenest admiration" for her friend Paul Bourget's *Essais de psychologie contemporaine* (1883), a collection that contained his landmark analysis of decadence (*Uncollected Writings* 213). Bourget described decadence as the inevitable consequence of a stratified culture's capitulation to the forces of anarchy and barbarism. Under such circumstances, he said, the elite inevitably relinquished its commitment to social unity and embraced instead an "aesthetic individualism" (Calinescu 171). The results, for Bourget, were appealing: "Let us indulge in the unusualness of our ideal and form, even though we imprison ourselves in an unvisited solitude. Those who come to us will be truly our brothers, and why sacrifice what is most intimate, special and personal?" (qtd. in Calinescu 171).

Lily dramatically personifies this lonely prisoner. Unwilling to tolerate America's crass compromises, she is prepared to sacrifice herself to the "intimate special and personal"—a sincere gesture that requires the height of artifice. As the French poet and critic Théophile Gautier had asserted in 1868, decadence was the "inevitable idiom of . . . civilizations in which factitious life has replaced natural life," in which art exists for itself alone.[6] Lily is Wharton's answer to these contradictory imperatives: at once personal and artful, intimate and factitious, she is a portrait of American decadence.

Is Lily's hair "ever so slightly brightened by art" (5)? Was it her "streak of sylvan freedom . . . that lent such savour to her artificiality" (13)? Selden's speculations arguably beg the question. The issue for Wharton is not whether Lily is natural or artificial but how nature can be transformed into an acculturated art. Lily's mysterious blend of the sylvan and synthetic captures natural perfection in the realm of aesthetic permanence. She projects what Alan Trachtenberg calls "an official American version of reality"—the natural reconceived by the upper classes and recast as an emphatic rejection of ethnic and racial pluralism (143). In a world transformed by urbanization, immigration, and social mobility, Wharton insists that Lily's racial perfection is not simply natural (and thus presumably vulnerable to loss); rather, Lily is the product of Gilded Age culture—the "privileged domain of refinement, aesthetic sensibility," and continuity (Trachtenberg 143). In this sense, her "art of blushing at the right time" fuses nature and culture in a deeply class-specific way (Wharton, *House* 6): Lily effectively transforms the biological into a culturally engineered aesthetic. Surpassing unaffected beauty, she controls the natural, projecting a decadent vision of racial permanence.[7]

The novel's opening "sight of Miss Lily Bart," motionless in Grand Central Station, dramatically stages this strategy. Standing "apart from the crowd, letting it drift by her to the platform or the street" (3), Lily stresses her stylized distinction. While sallow women hurry through the terminal, itself a symbol of industrial movement and commerce Miss Bart's unmoving presence not only forces Selden to "pause" but also stops anonymous passersby, "for Lily Bart was a figure to arrest even the suburban traveler rushing to his last train" (4). Wharton's choreography suspends Lily in a moment of arrested dynamism: fixed in the first of her many tableaux of racialized stasis, Lily distinguishes herself from the mobile American crowd by performing a fantasy of equilibrium, wholeness, and aesthetic singularity. Having "learned the value of contrast," she is "lifted to a height apart" (47, 116).

Wharton, of course, was not alone in attempting to stage racial perfection by capturing an ideal image of the endangered Anglo-American. As Nancy Bentley has shown, Carl Akeley's 1908 taxidermic displays of African mammals in the American Museum of Natural History in New York are relevant to Wharton's project. Building on Donna Haraway's assertion that the Akeley specimens resist the vulgarity of industrial modernism by representing nature as a permanent totality, Bentley argues that *The House of Mirth* deploys a similar aesthetic, transforming the modern woman's "chaotic subjectivity" into "a social or medical artifact" (192). Despite her innovative approach, however, Bentley's argument serves a somewhat conventional purpose, emphasizing Wharton's preoccupations with gender, class, and authorial agency.[8] Taxidermy's central role in the novel's racial critique remains unexplained.

The art of endowing the natural with "factitious immortality" and the unnatural with the "illusion of . . . life itself," taxidermy engendered a fantasy of plenitude in which eugenic specimens were held in poses of ideal strength, transcending the potential concessions of time (Walton 555, 556). By 1900 a growing number of urban elites shared Theodore Roosevelt's alarm at the "extensive and wasteful slaughter of strange and beautiful forms of wild life" by the "forces of greed, carelessness, and sheer brutality" (Roosevelt, "Conservation" 424, 426; see also Judd 209–22). Fearing the annihilation of the country's "leading species," the director of the New York Zoological Park, William T. Hornaday, urged American hunters to collect "examples of . . . beautiful and interesting animal[s]." "[I]f you must go and kill things," he declared in 1900, at least "save their heads and mount them as atonement for your deeds of blood" (ix, 158). This logic, at once sporting and strangely spiritualized, informs Lily's racial fate. Like the nation's imperiled wildlife, she is a Miranda among Calibans, an innocent creature who requires the staged naturalism of a protective Prospero (Wharton, *House* 135). Indeed, *The House of Mirth* reveals a moment of self-recognition, however subliminal: America's elite had glimpsed the future and realized that they, like Akeley's gorillas, were an endangered species.

Mark Seltzer's observation that "the naturalist art of taxidermy" seems "to hover midway between the tableau vivant and the *nature morte*" offers a provocative correlation in this regard (170). Like the American Museum of Natural History dioramas, the art of tableaux vivants immobilizes the mobile, rendering life still. The real is represented in a stylized simulacrum that fixes nature in an attitude controlled by aesthetic technology. Consider, then, the continuity between Akeley's spectacles and Lily's motionless poses, which culminate in a ballroom tableau of Joshua Reynolds's "Mrs. Lloyd." The logic informing both styles of exhibition reveals a stunning instance of nature's unnaturalness, the decadent preservation of the organic in the service of a perfect but failing racial myth.[9]

If the patrician impulse to glorify racial culture and the taxidermic quest to capture eugenic nature shared a common desire—to secure an American identity impervious to hybridization and change—then, as Stuart Culver notes, such "arresting" displays also ran a significant risk, for "[t]he image of a complete body is also the picture of death or dehumanization" (100). Wharton acknowledged this hazard in the final pages of her 1905 travel narrative, *Italian Backgrounds.* Recalling a Venetian museum where "life-sized mannikins" stiffly displayed costly eighteenth-century apparel, Wharton regards "the very rigidity of their once supple joints" as a poignant "allegory of their latter state"—a sumptuous nobility laid waste by Napoleonic republicanism. "[D]iscarded playthings of the gods," these lifeless aristocrats embody an inanimate fate that threatens Lily's stylized stasis. Like them, she risks becoming a "poor [doll] of destiny," a wooden aristocrat collapsing the distinction between person and thing (213).

The novel's title encodes this anxiety. Taken from Eccelsiastes 7.4—"The heart of the wise is in the house of mourning; but the heart of fools is in the house of mirth" (*New Oxford Annotated Bible*)—the title poses a crucial choice: is the American "house" to be the artificial construction of fools or the racially authentic home of oligarchic mourning? In the final pages of *The Decoration of Houses* (1897), the interior design treatise she wrote with the architect Ogden Codman, Jr., but for which she was largely responsible (Benstock 83–84), Wharton begins to tackle this question:

> Modern civilization has been called a varnished barbarism: a definition that might well be applied to . . . modern decoration.

> Only a return to architectural principles can raise the decoration of houses to the level of the past. Vasari said of the Farnesina palace that it was not built, but really born—*non murato ma veramente nato*; and this phrase is but the expression of an ever-present sense—the sense of interrelation of parts, or unity of the whole. (192)

Scornful of modern American barbarism, Wharton appeals to the principles of the past—a European past in which dwellings were not built but born.[10] Every house, she maintains, is an "organism" whose essential integrity is compromised by the "superficial application of ornament totally independent of structure" (1). This organism, as her biological language suggests, is more than just a house: it is a metaphor for the country's elite and a metonym for the United States at large. "It is a fact recognized by political economists that changes in manners and customs, no matter under what form of government, usually originate with the wealthy or aristocratic minority, and are thence transmitted to other classes," Wharton remarks. "This rule naturally holds good of house-planning" (7). Throughout *Decoration* and later in *The House of Mirth*, Wharton attempts to restore America's "aristocratic minority" to a sense of "interrelation of parts," a sense, that is, of eugenic plenitude, strength, and continuity.

Wharton's repeated analogy between persons and their houses is by now familiar: "The Fullness of Life," an 1893 short story, provides perhaps the best-known example of a woman whose "nature is like a great house full of rooms" (22). In *Decoration*, however, the home operates as the central metaphor in a cautionary tale of democracy. The entrance to America's house, Wharton notes, "should clearly proclaim itself an effectual barrier," preventing the "hordes of the uninvited" from trespassing on hallowed ground (Wharton and Codman 107; Wharton, *House* 87). These "other classes"—immigrants, workers, and middle-class capitalists—are the human equivalents of Wharton's much-deplored decorative "cheap knick-knacks": they are mass-produced human beings, built—not born—to menace the American patriciate by democratically cluttering the national home.[11] Wharton remarks that "[v]ulgarity is always noisier than good breeding, and it is instructive to note how a modern bronze will 'talk down' a delicate Renaissance statuette or bust."[12] Unable to make herself heard amid the many-voiced din of modern America, Wharton uses *Decoration* to talk down the abundant agents of varnished barbarism.

The problem in both *Decoration* and *The House of Mirth* is that of staging racial perfection without sacrificing the privileges of personal specificity. If America's elite was threatened by what Edwin Lawrence Godkin caustically called "chromo-civilization," a "pseudo-culture" that "diffused through the community a kind of smattering of all sorts of knowledge," then blue-blooded Americans were urged to vigilance (202). The ubiquitous chromolithograph—a cheap printed copy of an original work of art—had come to represent a dangerous accessibility that would undermine the exclusivity of upper-class privilege. Wharton thus insists in *Decoration*'s nursery section that teaching a child to distinguish between "a good and a bad painting" is a "civic virtue"—one easily destroyed by popular chromos that confused the hierarchical sensibility by imitating authenticity (Wharton and Codman 175).

For Wharton, such perils were the inevitable consequence of mass production. In an important 1903 essay, she mockingly connected "the vice of reading" to "[t]hat 'diffusion of knowledge' commonly classed with steam-heat and universal suffrage" (*Uncollected Writings* 99). This diffusion, like other dubious emblems of modern progress, had produced the dangerously undiscerning "mechanical reader."[13] "To read is not a virtue; but to read well is an art, an art, that only the born reader can acquire." By contrasting born readers with their mechanical counterparts, Wharton draws a distinction between Americans who inherit culture and those who acquire it artificially. Mechanical readers, she laments, "seem to regard literature as a cable-car that can be 'boarded' only by running; while many a born reader may be found unblushingly loitering in the tea-cup times of stage-coach and posting-chaise" (100). The contrast between an older, more exclusive form of locomotion and modern mass transit is telling: mechanical readers represent the newly mobile citizenry rushing through Grand Central Station in *The House of Mirth*; guided by the capricious "*vox populi*" and given to the "socialistic use of certain formulas," they threaten to propel themselves over and beyond the horse-drawn American patriciate (102, 103). Wharton's political and economic critique is clear: democracy threatens the nation with civic unrest, cultural decline, and even the wholesale redistribution of wealth.

II

Like *The Decoration of Houses*, *The House of Mirth* offers a blueprint to separate the born from the built. Indeed, tableaux vivants perfectly capture the politics of replication and reproduction fundamental to the novel's racial concerns. The "living picture" controversy in New York, fueled by the titillating possibilities of scantily clad performers representing classic works of art, had become a staple of vice debates by the 1890s. In 1894, Susie Kirwin, poseur and design artist, wrote a spirited defense of the entertainment, which, she insisted, offered "rational, wholesome enjoyment" for the whole family. Audiences were amazed, not aroused, by the "wonderfully counterfeited" spectacles. The "human model" became "an inanimate thing, no more than so much paint or canvas or marble" (7).

Kirwin's insistence on the lifelessness of tableaux vivants indicates the fears and fantasies that underwrote the form. If complete mimesis was the longing of realism more generally, an additional anxiety is equally palpable. Tableaux vivants involved a representational shell game in which a person (Lily, in this case) represented a thing (a painting by Reynolds), which in turn represented a person (the original "Mrs. Lloyd"), who then represented a thing (a classical archetype). As we have seen, however, the risk of such sleight of hand is that the person will be confused with the reproducible thing. The fact that Reynolds's portrait is the subject of parlor theatrics at all proves the case in point: tableau vivant, as Henry James made comically clear in his 1899 short story "Paste," was the democratic illusionist's genre of choice. When James's heroine, Charlotte Prime, questions the appropriateness of using her dead aunt's seemingly faux jewels for a tableau of *Ivanhoe*, her friend Mrs. Guy retorts, "*Our* jewels, for historic scenes, don't tell—the real thing falls short. Rowena must have rubies as big as eggs" (459). The real thing always falls short because tableaux deliberately conflate the genuine and the counterfeit. The distinction between paste (sham markers of class status) and pearls (authentic essence) is intentionally reversed: the fake suddenly appears real, while the real seems fake. "Living pictures" played on this possibility: the authentic was displaced, the original was duplicated, and high art was democratized into yet another American commodity.

Lily's famous appearance midway through the text in an elaborately costumed tableau arguably climaxes the Wellington Bry ball and the novel as a whole. The setting is significant. Like Simon Rosedale, the Jewish financier with whom they are repeatedly linked, the "Welly" Brys have made their fortune at the expense of the Knickerbocker elite (121). They are invaders "advancing into a strange country with an insufficient number of scouts" (130). It is no surprise, then, that the Bry gala functions as a journey into the terra incognita of a new, democratic America. The ballroom is immediately marked as a space of illusion—a trompe l'oeil in reverse: "so recent, so rapidly-evoked was the whole *mise-en-scène* that one had to touch the marble columns to learn that they were not of cardboard, to set one's self in one of the damask-and-gold armchairs to be sure it was not painted against the wall." This is not the real America, linked in the novel to the rituals of an elusive European past; instead, this is a strangely improvised country associated with fairy tale and fantasy, a "boundary world between fact and imagination" (132, 133).

The Bry entertainment opens with a series of tableaux "in which the fugitive curves of living flesh . . . have been subdued to plastic harmony without losing the charm of life." Wharton's socialite performers, accommodating themselves to the limitations of theatrical form, effectively become "types." Carry Fisher's "short dark-skinned face," for instance, makes a "typical Goya," while a "young Mrs. Van Alstyne, who showed the frailer Dutch type . . . made a characteristic Vandyck" (133–34). Such classifications participate in the novel's pervasive discourse of racial typology. Rosedale, for example, is earlier described as "a plump rosy man of the blond Jewish type" (14), while Selden has "keenly-modelled dark features which in a land of amorphous types, gave him the air of belonging to a more specialized race" (65). A staple of Victorian vocabulary, *type* indicated a distinct racial ontology of permanent (if often peculiar) genetic characteristics—a way of determining the general by extrapolating from the specific (Cowling 184).

Typology met its logical extreme in the strange composite photography of the eugenicist Francis Galton, whose work is curiously relevant to Wharton's tableaux. By superimposing fractional exposures of individual faces on top of one another, Galton created "portraits" in which distinguishing features faded into a hazy common face. His best work, he claimed, was a composite of the definitive "Jewish type," a synthesis of boys from the London Jews' Free School that captured the Jew's "essence"—his "cold scanning gaze . . . coolly appraising [one] at market value" (243). Galton's work, if nothing else, reveals typology's propensity to erase human specificity in order to mass-produce images of the generic subject. Indeed, if the camera had democratized the formerly elite aesthetic of portraiture, composite photography introduced a new possibility—what Allan Sekula has called an "essentialist physical anthropology of race" (370).

Wharton's familiarity with Galton's enterprise is evident from a 1905 review of Maurice Hewlett's novel *The Fool Errant*. After criticizing Hewlett's previous heroines, who blur "into a kind of composite portrait, while their moral idiosyncrasies fail to leave any impression at all," Wharton praises the present protagonist, whose "certain definiteness of outline [is] marred only by an occasional reversion to type" (*Uncollected Writings* 111). The edges of this critique are sharp, for such typological lapses could hardly be more anathema to Wharton's singular representation of Lily Bart:

> [S]o skillfully had the personality of the actors been subdued to the scenes they figured in that even the least imaginative of the audience must have felt a thrill of contrast when the curtain suddenly parted on a picture which was simply and undisguisedly the portrait of Miss Bart.
>
> Here there could be no mistaking the predominance of personality—the unanimous "Oh!" of the spectators was a tribute, not to the brush-work of Reynolds's "Mrs. Lloyd" but to the flesh and blood loveliness of Lily Bart. . . . it was as though she had stepped, not out of, but into, Reynolds's canvas, banishing the phantom of his dead beauty by the beams of her living grace.

As an astonishingly vibrant portrait of herself, Lily cannot be reduced to type. Indeed, by choosing "a type so like her own that she could embody the person represented without ceasing to be herself," Lily transcends typology altogether: she effectively performs the impossible, subordinating the Galtonian composite to her personal specificity (*House* 134). Unlike her assimilating peers, Lily resists the generic abstraction of "plastic harmony," preserving instead her "flesh-and-blood loveliness." Were she to become the portrait she represents, she would risk losing the eugenic quality that makes her previous tableaux so arresting and racially loaded. She would risk, in short, becoming a mere type—either the equivalent of the racially typologized Jew or what Seltzer describes as "the American *as* typical, standard, and reproducible" (5).

Wharton rescues Lily from these possibilities by stressing the "predominance of personality"—the "serious purity of the central conception" that can "break through the strongest armour of stock formulas."[14] "Undisguisedly" herself, Lily stands in stylized opposition to the generic and the mechanized—a strategy not without risk. Throughout the novel, Wharton implies that Lily is imperiled by the very racial economy she represents—an economy consumed with purity and terrified of sham. Lily's embodiment of the William Jamesian double self—"there were two selves in her, the one she had always known, and a new abhorrent being to which it found itself chained"—crystallizes this vulnerability (148; see W. James 142 and Lears 38). Struggling to define her real self in a world where distinctions between the genuine and the imitative, the natural and the cultural, have all but collapsed, Lily's crisis reveals the instability of race as an ontological category. Indeed, Wharton can only tenuously resolve this problem by shifting the grounds of the debate. To be a real self, she increasingly suggests, is to be realigned with a racial soul—the "slowly-accumulated past [that] lives in the blood" (319). Walter Benn Michaels's contention that race in this period becomes essentially invisible—something spiritually inherited rather than physically acquired ("Souls")—is thus central to Wharton's logic. Hovering over Lily's deathbed, Selden fantasizes that he can distinguish the "sleeping face" from "the real Lily" who was "close to him, yet invisible and inaccessible" (326). Only in her final tableau of death is Lily truly transmogrified into her authentic racial personality—a disembodied soul, at once real and invisible.[15]

III

The overreaching effort to consolidate Lily into an authoritative real self reveals at once the imperiled condition of the oligarchic body and Wharton's insistence on its transcendent possibilities. Part of an endangered species, Lily is not so much a circulating commodity as she is a rare museum piece, desirable precisely because she is out of circulation. Stephen Greenblatt's notion that the museum retains its "mystery" by displaying the masterpiece "in such a way as to imply that no one, not even the nominal owner or donor, can penetrate the zone of light and actually possess the wonderful object" is thus pivotal to Wharton's vision (51–52). As Rosedale eventually realizes, "It was [Lily's] very manner of holding herself aloof that appealed to his collector's passion for the rare and unattainable" (113). Miss Bart is fundamentally—indeed, ontologically—inviolate.

Rosedale's presence in the novel underscores this perfect inaccessibility. If the appearance of the Jewish businessman in a "paternal rôle," "kneeling domestically" before Carry Fisher's daughter, seems to reveal the sympathetic "fireside man" (249), then Lily's eventual rejection of Rosedale's proposals indicates the alarming nature of the Jew's familial persona. Although later scenes appear calculated to make Rosedale less sexual and thus more socially admissible, *The House of Mirth* remains what Elizabeth Ammons calls the story of "the flower of Anglo-Saxon womanhood . . . not ending up married to the invading Jew" (80). Rosedale as father raises the horrifying specter of reproducing with a Jew—indeed, reproducing Jews. The novel's working title, "The Year of the Rose," thus inadvertently reveals one of its central anxieties: were Lily to marry the Jewish millionaire, the country's future might only bring racially degenerating years of the Rosedale.[16]

To prevent this outcome, Wharton commits herself to the iconic preservation of a perfect American museum piece. The Whartonian hothouse becomes a gallery—a decadent house of mourning designed to preserve and exhibit a vanishing species.[17] Like the rare "Americana" lovingly collected by Jefferson Gryce in the opening sequences of the novel, Lily is of interest to the curator, the historian, and the "real collector [who] values a thing for its rarity" (11). The acquisition of antiquarian books, by definition "an unmarketable commodity" (20), is crucial to Lily's status. Susan Stewart's point that the "antiquarian sensibility" presumes "a rupture in historical consciousness" that makes "one's own culture *other*—distant and discontinuous" suggests that Lily is simultaneously the object and the source of antiquarian desire. She is not only a rare, talismanic beauty, but she is also a disenfranchised patrician orphan nostalgically determined to retrieve "an imagined past" (Stewart 142). In this sense, the failure of the Hudson Barts to provide their daughter with "the house not built with the hands but made up of inherited passions and loyalties" marks Lily as the quintessential site of antiquarian loss and nostalgic recuperation (Wharton, *House* 319). In her reawakened desire for aristocratic rootedness, Lily embodies the patrician quest for a "homogenous and uninterrupted culture" (Wharton, *French Ways* 80).

Such impulses reveal Wharton's sympathy with a group of like-minded northeastern intellectuals who, fearing for the country's future, increasingly forged a rhetoric of "racial nativism" (Higham 137). Charles Eliot Norton, writing in 1888, had decried "a predominance of . . . the uneducated and unrefined masses, over . . . the more enlightened and better-instructed few" (321). Under such circumstances, he worried, the republic surely could not survive the melting pot. As the *New York Tribune* editor Whitelaw Reid told a posh gathering of the New England Society in 1903, "We have emphatically and even vociferously made everybody else, from all over the world, at home in our Fathers' house. But as we look around at the variegated throng, do we always feel just as much at home ourselves?" (46).

Voicing a growing sense of racial siege, the Williams College minister John H. Denison declared in 1893, "We have tried to share our freedom with foreigners, only to discover that freedom is not transferable . . . The higher force cannot be dominated by the lower. Nature will not tolerate it; she prefers disintegration and reorganization" (18). The imagined world of the racially uniform New England village was crumbling into what Henry James in 1904 called "a prodigious amalgam, . . . a hotch-potch of racial ingredients" (*Writings* 456). Social Darwinism armed patrician intellectuals with a fitting vocabulary to predict imminent Anglo-Saxon extinction. Denison's warning that old-stock Americans had "entered upon a struggle for survival" and would soon share the fate of "the American Indian and the bison" (17) found its most famous spokesman in Theodore Roosevelt, who urged well-born Americans to resist "race suicide" ("Letter"). Cheap immigrant labor, the president of the Massachusetts Institute of Technology, Francis A. Walker, agreed, had forced America's "native" stock to reduce family size in order to preserve a higher standard of living—a socioeconomic strategy that spelled biological ruin (Higham 143–44). As Henry Adams observed, Kelvin's second law of thermodynamics—the "Law of Entropy"—made the dissipation of America's "vital energies" inevitable (*Degradation* 184–85, 155). Henry's brother Brooks, a sometime guest at Wharton's Berkshire estate, spoke for a generation of Brahmins when he gloomily predicted that "when the waste of energetic material is so great that the martial and imaginative stocks fail to reproduce themselves, disintegration may set in, the civilized population may perish, and a reversion may take place to a primitive form" (x–xi). Fearful for their cultural survival, upper-class nativists could look forward only to eventual reorganization in the wake of imminent racial disintegration.

In 1902, Wharton began writing a novel she would abandon after some seventy pages to begin work on *The House of Mirth.* It was entitled "Disintegration." The story of an ambitious woman who deserts her shabbily genteel husband and their daughter only to win social redemption after marrying an upstart millionaire, "Disintegration" was a dress rehearsal for *The Mother's Recompense* (1925). More fundamentally, however, Wharton's unfinished project outlines the racial concerns that were to dominate *The House of Mirth.*

The narrative charts the spiraling decline of the cuckolded Henry Clephane, whose loyalty to the "family pieties" and the "honourable past," "six or seven generations of upright and gentle living," magnifies the gravity of his wife's betrayal. "To continue the family tradition . . . had been part of his conception of life . . . to have failed in this continuance meant the rending of innumerable fibres with which his own were inwoven" (48–49). Alice Clephane's infidelity strikes a number of chords simultaneously: not only does she sever Henry's unblemished genealogy, but she also does so as a direct result of democratic license. Henry cynically proposes to write a book on the subject:

> It's to be a study of the new privileged class—a study of the effects of wealth without responsibility. Talk of the socialist peril! That's not where the danger lies. The inherent vice of democracy is the creation of a powerful class of which it can make no use—a kind of Frankenstein monster, an engine of social disintegration . . . The place to study [the results] is here and now—here in this huge breeding-place of inequalities that we call a republic, where class-distinctions, instead of growing

> out of the inherent needs of the social organism, are arbitrarily established by a force that works against it! (64)

Railing against counterfeit class distinctions and pining for what Denison called "the Anglo-Saxon organic nation" (26), Clephane becomes Wharton's case study in "the disease" of racial decline ("Disintegration" 64). He is the end of the line, the victim of a culture untethered from its legitimate fixtures of racial demarcation. As his friend George Severance predicts, when South Dakota divorcees outnumber Old New Yorkers, society "will have ceased to exist": "There will be nothing to hold together. You can't found a state on a penal settlement. But before that happens, the social instinct of self-preservation will assert itself: society will not let itself be destroyed by a band of robbers and murderers" (61). "Disintegration" reveals the more extreme edges of Wharton's conservative critique. The invaders of American life are robbers and murderers, threatening to transform a consecrated nation into a penal settlement. The "socialist peril" cannot rival the menace of these democratic impostors—Frankenstein monsters, built, not born, to threaten oligarchic dominion and social cohesion.

If "Disintegration" demonstrates Wharton's share in the abundant gloom of her intellectual milieu, her failure to finish the manuscript indicates an important shift in her thinking. Like a number of contributors to the discourses of racial nativism and aesthetic decadence, Wharton eventually came to believe that Anglo-Saxon extinction, however inevitable, would not take place in the depths of Henry Clephane's demise but at the peak of Lily Bart's brilliant racial achievement. Barrett Wendell's exhilarated 1893 pronouncement that "[t]he songs that live are the swan-songs" speaks to this realignment (*"Stelligeri"* 113). A great culture would vanish only at its aesthetic summit, Wendell insisted, for "[a]rtistic expression is apt to be the final fruit of a society about to wither" (*Literary History* 462). This singular combination of elation and elegy found its most ardent spokesman in George Edward Woodberry, a professor of comparative literature at Columbia University. "Race-history," Woodberry declared in 1903, had always documented the process of Christian sacrifice whereby eugenic peoples, "at the acme of achievement," bequeathed their civilized legacy to their inferiors—what he called the "absorption of aristocracies in democracies" (29, 5). If "a vanquished nation [alone] can civilize its victors," as Wharton's friend Vernon Lee had maintained (45), Woodberry's conclusions were compelling. "[F]or a race, as for an individual," Woodberry rapturously declared, "there is a time to die, and that time, as history discloses it, is the moment of perfection" (4).

Lily Bart fully embodies this paradigm of apotheosis, sacrifice, and extinction. Wharton captures and immobilizes her at the moment of racial perfection, a fate preferable, she implies, to a slow demise in New York's competitive wilderness. Lily's final tableau of death thus transforms her into the period's quintessential museum piece—the perfectly preserved taxidermic specimen. As Selden enters Lily's boardinghouse room, he discovers "a delicate impalpable mask over the living lineaments he had known" (325–26). Lily becomes the site of racial elegy: she incarnates the house of mourning. Despite her social decline, she embodies a decadent fantasy of oligarchic wholeness that, like Akeley's dioramas and the Gryce Americana, preserves an iconic instance of completion and permanence. Wharton's description is rich in the language of eugenic preservationism:

> But at least he *had* loved her . . . and if the moment had been fated to pass from them before they could seize it, he saw that, for both, it had been saved whole out of the ruin of their lives.
>
> It was this moment of love, this fleeting victory over themselves, which had kept them from atrophy and extinction. . . .
>
> He knelt by the bed and bent over her . . . and in the silence there passed between them the word which made all clear.

It is this battle against "the influence of . . . surroundings" (329), now suddenly democratic and accessible, that Wharton wages throughout *The House of Mirth*. Like Roosevelt and Hornaday, she is committed not only to protecting Lily from "atrophy and extinction" but also to the larger project of preserving her "whole out of the ruin of their lives."

This commitment supersedes all others in *The House of Mirth* as it does in the logic of taxidermy. The emphasis on Lily's completeness outweighs the possibility that she might eventually give birth to eugenic offspring. She is more useful dead and stuffed, as it were, than alive. The messy contingencies of motherhood, Wharton seems to suggest, would compromise—indeed, diminish—Lily's status as a racial icon. The longing for an ancestral past with the "power of broadening and deepening the individual existence, of attaching it by mysterious links of kinship to all the mighty sum of human striving," is realized not in the quest for an individual family (Lily, after all, rejects her own stifling kin) but in the desire, in Wharton's vocabulary, for "Family"—for the genealogical continuity that can originate only in the elusive centers "of early pieties" that are born of aristocratic blood (319). Wharton sacrifices her heroine to these values: Lily is to stand for a kinship that must supersede individual, mortal families and instead represent a timeless tableau of racial stasis.

Lily's final hallucination of cradling the infant daughter of the working-class Nettie Struther thus enacts the novel's most fundamental fantasy: Lily appropriates the child of the reformed laboring class as her own, a switch that marks at once working-class acculturation and the mysterious, immaculate reproduction of the elite—what Candace Waid calls Lily's "virgin sacrifice" (47). Indeed, if the novel's conclusion seems to envision class convergence, it does so on oligarchic terms. The striking absence of any proletarian consciousness in Nettie's fawning idolatry of Lily ("Sometimes, when I . . . got to wondering why things were so queerly fixed in the world, I used to remember that *you* were having a lovely time, . . . and that seemed to show there was a kind of justice somewhere" [312–13]) implies that a just world is one governed by a "traditional sense of solidarity between the classes." In such a world, one knows one's place.

Nettie's decision, then, to name her infant daughter "Marry

Anto'nette . . . after the French queen in the play at the Garden—I told George the actress reminded me of you"—satirically captures the dynamics of class emulation and, for Wharton, their racial impossibility (314). The baby's silly name has meaning only in a democratic society that transforms doomed aristocrats into the stuff of cheap melodrama and real nobility into the site of mimetic, mass-produced distortion. *The House of Mirth* will ultimately insist that Lily's racial markers are inimitable. Despite Nettie's maternal ambitions, Wharton reassures us that, in the end, "Marry Anto'nette" will be only a doubly displaced theatrical imitation of the disappearing real thing.

Indeed, if Wharton acknowledges the inevitable Darwinian doom of America's insular elite, she equally envisions a form of cultural production that transcends the mutating mechanics of mere survival. Lily embodies a sacrificial transmission of culture possible only within the most hallowed of museums—the ancient cathedral, the site where preservation becomes veneration and the specimen becomes the relic. Without the untidiness of mating, Lily enacts a purified form of cultural reproduction, mystically incorporating Nettie's baby: "[it was] as though the child entered into her and became part of herself" (319, 316). Like the sacred mother in Henry Adams's famous antimodern critique, Lily embodies "the force that created it all—the Virgin, the Woman—by whose genius 'the stately monuments of superstition' were built."[18] She offers an elegiac answer to the mechanized culture of the dynamo—what Wharton saw as society's "atoms whirling away from each other in some wild centrifugal dance" (*House* 319). In willingly "sacrificing her pleasures to the claims of immemorial tradition," Lily incarnates J.-K. Huysmans's "Christian Venus," the *mater dolorosa* of the "word which made all clear."[19] A plaintive paragon of "spiritual motherhood," she bears the pathos and promise of Anglo-Saxon deliverance. Her "passion of charity for [the] race" in the end engenders the word (Wharton, *Sanctuary* 112)—a word "not . . . for twilight, but for the mo[u]rning" (*House* 324).

Notes

The archival research for this project was funded by a grant from the American Philosophical Society. I am grateful to Lisa Gordis, Martha Hodes, William Sharpe, Herb Sloane, and, in particular, Ross Hamilton for their valuable comments on earlier drafts. This essay is dedicated to the memory of Lora Romero—teacher, scholar, friend.

The quotations from Edith Wharton's "Disintegration" are reprinted by permission of the Estate of Edith Wharton and the Watkins/Loomis Agency.

1. The Progressive Era bears out Thomas Gossett's observation that the ambiguity of the notion of race "made it a powerful tool for the most diverse purposes" (117–18). While nativists, nationalists, and racists grounded campaigns for immigration restriction, segregation, and imperialism in the pseudoscience of eugenics, the Supreme Court's "separate but equal" ruling in *Plessy v. Ferguson* (1896) vested hermeneutic authority in the vagaries of local "custom," forcing New Negro intellectuals to formalize, however problematically, a representative African American (Higham; Solomon; Sundquist 233–49; Gates).

2. These concerns were by no means confined to the upper classes. Fearing immigrant competition, Populists decried "imported pauperized labor" in their 1892 platform, and their horror of mob rule appeared in Ignatius Donneley's *Caesar's Column* (1891; Hofstadter 66–70). The rhetoric of race suicide, moreover, pitted native middle-and working-class Americans against their seemingly more prolific immigrant peers (Gordon 136–58).

3. Arguing that Lily is an example of "dazzling, overdetermined whiteness" (79), Elizabeth Ammons contrasts the color of Lily's skin to Simon Rosedale's "glossy-looking" appearance (Wharton, *House* 14). I will suggest, however, that the logic of race in the novel is far more pervasive, transcending issues of skin and encoding instead a complex semiotics of class, genealogy, ethnicity, and nation.

4. Despairing of America's "gros public," Wharton in 1903 located the patriciate's evolutionary dilemma in the hothouse. "We are the wretched exotics produced in a European glasshouse, the most déplacé & useless class on earth!" (*Letters* 84). While overstating the elite's socioeconomic vulnerability, Wharton nonetheless imagined the glasshouse as a Europeanized alternative to the United States—at once patrician

breeding ground and decadent refuge from the country's emerging identity as the "house of mirth."

5. I have confined my analysis to writers most pertinent to the formation of Wharton's intellectual perspectives. For further discussion of American decadence, see Auchard; Herman; Hoopes; and Williams.

6. Qtd. in Ellis 26. For Wharton on Gautier, see "Eyes" 338, *Uncollected Writings* 191, and *Backward Glance* 330.

7. Wharton champions this "artificial-natural" aesthetic in *Italian Villas and Their Gardens* (1904). Italy's "frank artifice," she argues, outstrips England's "laboured naturalism" by unabashedly replacing nature's "deficiencies, . . . repetitions . . . meannesses and profusions" with a "fixed smile of perennial loveliness" (205, 206).

8. Such concerns have a long history in Wharton criticism. Recent examples include Michaels (*Gold Standard*); Dimock; Showalter; and Kaplan.

9. The notion of a pristine Knickerbocker past was, of course, itself factitious. Wharton recalled a complex pecking order in which New Yorkers of middle-class ancestry were distinguished from those with authentically aristocratic genealogies (*Backward Glance* 10).

10. In an 1896 letter to the *Newport Daily News*, Wharton chided "puerile" disciples of the colonial revival for their pretentiously "original" mansions (*Uncollected Writings* 56). " 'Colonial' architecture," she insisted, was "simply a modest copy of Georgian models" (Wharton and Codman 81–82). Displacing American originality by displacing American origins, Wharton urged a return to the nation's European roots.

11. Wharton and Codman 187. Wharton clarified this connection in 1908, blaming the "chaos of ornament" marring a French church on the ethnically "strange fellowship" of Flemish, Lombard, German, and Spanish artisans who had contributed to its "deluge of detail." Such "profusion—and confusion" of nationalities flouted Wharton's racialized aesthetic of "artistic unity" (*Motor-Flight* 151–52).

12. Wharton and Codman 186. In this sense, the stifling home of Lily's aunt, Mrs. Peniston, underscores patrician decline. Aunt Julia's unseemly replica of the Louvre's "Dying Gladiator" (98), her "ormulu clock" (made of a copper alloy imitating gold), and her derivative "steel engravings of an anecdotic character" all contradict the precepts inculcated in *The Decoration of Houses* (110).

While Wharton's critique of sham furthers what I suggest is a conservative agenda, her conclusions were by no means inevitable. Gustav

Stickley, influential proponent of the Arts and Crafts style, advocated a strikingly similar aesthetic. According to Stickley, however, "closer contact with real things, with real work, with real life," would reconnect Americans to "the common needs of the common people" (qtd. in Orvell 161–62).

13. Wharton embraced twentieth-century technology only insofar as it enhanced personal privacy (Kassanoff 31–32). Her beloved "motor-car," for instance, liberated her "from all the compulsions and contacts of the railway" (*Motor-Flight* 1).

14. *Motor-Flight* 154. The association between personality and racial singularity is evident in Wharton's 1908 description of French visitors to a Paris salon: "the angles of difference have been so rubbed down that personalities are as hard to differentiate as in a group of Orientals" (*Motor-Flight* 188). While personality was not the exclusive domain of the well-born, its "slow but continuous growth" required "space"—a "larger . . . symphonic plan" generally contingent on affluence (*Writing* 48). Indeed, if type found refuge in the "temporary shelter" of the short story, personality thrived in the "slowly built-up monument" of the novel (75, 50).

15. William E. Moddelmog argues that Wharton rejected a property-owning model of personality in favor of the "boundlessness" of depersonalization (353). I suggest, however, that because Wharton's model of selfhood was fundamentally racial—grounded, that is, in the invisible and the inaccessible—such unmarketable boundlessness is entirely compatible with the Whartonian personality.

16. Rosedale's threatening alliance with his charwoman employee Mrs. Haffen (who shares his propensity for blackmail) personifies the double blow to the American patriciate—nouveau riche wealth fueled by intrusive working-class labor.

17. Wharton regretted the democratization of museums in the age of mass tourism. She sharply criticized the "museumised aspect" of Europe's ancient shrines, valuing only the sites that looked "like the house of a great collector who still lives among his treasures" (*Motor-Flight* 150, 154). Merging museum with ancestral home, Wharton reveals her paradoxical desire to preserve the privacy of patrician exclusivity while publicly exhibiting racial distinction.

The Whartonian museum thus monastically conforms to Selden's "republic of the spirit," a place free from "everything—from money, from poverty, from ease and anxiety, from all the material accidents" (68). Lily's reply that Selden's republic is really "a close corporation" echoes the well-publicized comments of the Metropolitan Museum director Louis di Cesnola, who in 1897 ejected a plumber in overalls from the gallery. The museum, Cesnola famously remarked, was "a closed corporation" entitled to regulate conduct within its walls (Levine 185–86).

18. *Education* 387. As the traditional attribute of the Virgin in Christian iconography, the lily symbolizes whiteness, purity, and immortality (Whittlesey 217–18; Hall 192–93). Its conventional association with the Annunciation, moreover, speaks to what Wharton, in an 1891 sonnet, described as the Madonna's "strange presentiment" of "the Light's terrible eclipse." This "foreboding pain," paired with the Virgin's ultimate assurance that "He also rose again," mirrors the dynamic of sacrifice and salvation in *The House of Mirth* ("Botticelli's Madonna").

19. Wharton, *House* 35; Hanson 48. The word functions here as a curiously decadent palimpsest of aestheticized gospel. Bourget's oft-quoted definition of decadent style—the book is sacrificed to the page, the page to the sentence, and the sentence to the "independence of the word"—thus gains numinous resonance in Wharton's novel (Calinescu 170). While a full discussion of Wharton's relation to Christianity and decadence is beyond the scope of this essay, it is worth noting that Lily's ecstatic renunciations at the end of her life bear a striking resemblance to the retreat of Wharton's ancient hermits in *Italian Backgrounds*: "from the strife of the circus factions and the incredible vices and treacheries of civilized life, the disenchanted Christian, aghast at the more than pagan corruption of a converted world, fled into the waste places to wear out his life in penance. The horrors he left behind surpassed anything the desert could show" (66–67). On monasticism and decadence, see Hanson 218–28.

Works Cited

Adams, Brooks. *The Law of Civilization and Decay: An Essay on History*. New York: Macmillan, 1897.

Adams, Henry. *The Degradation of Democratic Dogma*. New York: Macmillan, 1919.

———. *The Education of Henry Adams*. Boston: Houghton, 1918.

Ammons, Elizabeth. "Edith Wharton and Race." *The Cambridge Companion to Edith Wharton*. Ed. Millicent Bell. Cambridge: Cambridge University Press, 1995. 68–86.

Auchard, John. *Silence in Henry James: The Heritage of Symbolism and Decadence.* University Park: Pennsylvania State University Press, 1986.

Beard, George M. *American Nervousness: Its Causes and Consequences.* New York: Putnam's, 1881.

Benstock, Shari. *No Gifts from Chance: A Biography of Edith Wharton.* New York: Scribner's, 1994.

Bentley, Nancy. *The Ethnography of Manners: Hawthorne, James, Wharton.* Cambridge: Cambridge University Press, 1995.

Calinescu, Matei. *Five Faces of Modernity: Modernism, Avant-Garde, Decadence, Kitsch, Postmodernism.* Durham: Duke University Press, 1987.

Cowling, Mary. *The Artist as Anthropologist: The Representation of Type and Character in Victorian Art.* Cambridge: Cambridge University Press, 1989.

Culver, Stuart. "What Manikins Want: *The Wonderful Wizard of Oz* and *The Art of Decorating Dry Goods Windows.*" *Representations* 21 (1988): 97–116.

Denison, John H. "The Survival of the American Type." *Atlantic Monthly* 75 (1895): 16–28.

Dimock, Wai Chee. "Debasing Exchange: Edith Wharton's *The House of Mirth.*" *The House of Mirth.* By Edith Wharton. Ed. Shari Benstock. Boston: Bedford, 1994. 375–90.

Ellis, Havelock. Introduction. *Against the Grain* (A rebours). By J.-K. Huysmans. New York: Illustrated, 1931. 11–49.

Galton, Francis. "Photographic Composites." *Photographic News* 17 Apr. 1885: 243–45.

Gates, Henry Louis, Jr. "The Trope of a New Negro and the Reconstruction of the Image of the Black." *Representations* 24 (1988): 129–55.

Gilman, Charlotte Perkins. *Women and Economics.* 1898. New York: Harper, 1966.

Godkin, Edwin L. "Chromo-civilization." *Nation,* 24 Sept. 1874, pp. 201–2.

Gordon, Linda. *Woman's Body, Woman's Right: A Social History of Birth Control in America.* New York: Penguin, 1977.

Gossett, Thomas F. *Race: The History of an Idea in America.* Dallas: Southern Methodist University Press, 1964.

Greenblatt, Stephen. "Resonance and Wonder." *Exhibiting Cultures: The Poetics and Politics of Museum Display.* Ed. Ivan Karp and Steven D. Lavine. Washington: Smithsonian Institution Press, 1991. 42–56.

Hall, James. *Dictionary of Subjects and Symbols in Art.* Boulder: Westview, 1974.

Hanson, Ellis. *Decadence and Catholicism.* Cambridge, Mass.: Harvard University Press, 1997.

Haraway, Donna. "Teddy Bear Patriarchy: Taxidermy in the Garden of Eden, New York City, 1908–1936." *Cultures of United States Imperialism.*

Ed. Amy Kaplan and Donald E. Pease. Durham: Duke University Press, 1993. 237–91.

Herman, Arthur. *The Idea of Decline in Western History*. New York: Free Press, 1997.

Higham, John. *Strangers in the Land: Patterns of American Nativism, 1860–1925*. 1955. New York: Atheneum, 1981.

Hofstadter, Richard. *The Age of Reform from Bryan to F.D.R.* New York: Vintage, 1955.

Hoopes, James. "The Culture of Progressivism: Croly, Lippman, Brooks, Bourne, and the Idea of American Artistic Decadence." *Clio* 7 (1977): 91–111.

Hornaday, William T. *Taxidermy and Zoological Collecting*. 7th ed. New York: Scribner's, 1900.

James, Henry. *Collected Travel Writings: Great Britain and America*. New York: Library of Amer., 1993.

———. "Paste." 1899. *The Complete Tales of Henry James*. Ed. and introd. Leon Edel. Vol. 10. Philadelphia: Lippincott, 1964. 451–69. 12 vols.

James, William. *The Varieties of Religious Experience*. Cambridge, Mass.: Harvard University Press, 1985.

Judd, Richard W. *Common Lands, Common People: The Origins of Conservation in Northern New England*. Cambridge, Mass.: Harvard University Press, 1997.

Kaplan, Amy. *The Social Construction of American Realism* Chicago: University of Chicago Press, 1988.

Kassanoff, Jennie A. "Corporate Thinking: Edith Wharton's *The Fruit of the Tree*." *Arizona Quarterly* 53.1 (1997): 25–59.

Kirwin, Susie. Letter. *New York Herald* 19 Aug. 1894: sec. 4, 7.

Lears, T. J. Jackson. *No Place of Grace: Antimodernism and the Transformation of American Culture, 1880–1920*. New York: Pantheon, 1981.

Lee, Vernon [Violet Paget]. *Euphorion: Being Studies of the Antique and the Mediaeval in the Renaissance*. Vol. 1. Boston: Roberts, 1884. 2 vols.

Levine, Lawrence W. *Highbrow/Lowbrow: The Emergence of Cultural Hierarchy in America*. Cambridge, Mass.: Harvard University Press, 1988.

Michaels, Walter Benn. *The Gold Standard and the Logic of Naturalism*, Berkeley: University of California Press, 1987.

———. *Our America:Nativism, Modernism, and Pluralism*. Durham: Duke University Press, 1995.

———. "The Souls of White Folk." *Literature and the Body: Essays on Population and Persons*. Ed. Elaine Scarry. Baltimore: Johns Hopkins University Press, 1988. 185–209.

Moddelmog, William E. "Disowning 'Personality': Privacy and Subjectivity in *The House of Mirth.*" *American Literature* 70 (1998): 337–63.

The New Oxford Annotated Bible with Apocrypha. Ed. Herbert G. May and Bruce M. Metzger. New York: Oxford University Press, 1977.

Norton, Charles Eliot, "The Intellectual Life of America," *New Princeton Review* Nov. 1888: 312–24.

Orvell, Miles. *The Real Thing: Imitation and Authenticity in American Culture, 1880–1940.* Chapel Hill: University of North Carolina Press, 1989.

Otis, Laura. *Organic Memory: History and the Body in the Late Nineteenth and Early Twentieth Centuries.* Lincoln: University of Nebraska Press, 1994.

Phillips, Forbes. "Ancestral Memory: A Suggestion." *The Nineteenth Century* June 1906: 977–83.

Reid, Whitelaw. "Speech by the Honorable Whitelaw Reid." *Anniversary Celebration of the New England Society in the City of New York.* New York: Green, 1903. 41–52.

Roosevelt, Theodore. "The Conservation of Wild Life." *The Works of Theodore Roosevelt.* Vol. 12. New York: Scribner's, 1926. 423–31. 20 vols.

———. "A Letter from President Roosevelt on Race Suicide." *American Review of Reviews* May 1907: 550–51.

Sekula, Allan. "The Body and the Archive." *The Contest of Meaning: Critical Histories of Photography.* Ed. Richard Bolton. Cambridge, Mass.: MIT Press, 1992. 342–89.

Seltzer, Mark. *Bodies and Machines.* New York. Routledge, 1992.

Showalter, Elaine. *Sister's Choice: Tradition and Change in American Women's Writing.* Oxford: Clarendon, 1991.

Solomon, Barbara Miller. "The Intellectual Background of the Immigration Restriction Movement in New England." *New England Quarterly* 25 (1952): 47–59.

Stewart, Susan. *On Longing: Narratives of the Miniature, the Gigantic, the Souvenir, the Collection.* Durham, N.C.: Duke University Press, 1993.

Sundquist, Eric J. *To Wake the Nations: Race in the Making of American Literature.* Cambridge, Mass.: Harvard University Press, 1993.

Trachtenberg, Alan. *The Incorporation of America: Culture and Society in the Gilded Age.* New York: Hill, 1982.

Waid, Candace. *Edith Wharton's Letters from the Underworld: Fictions of Women and Writing.* Chapel Hill: University of North Carolina Press, 1991.

Walton, William. "The Artist-Taxidermist and the Great African Hall of the American Museum of Natural History." *Scribner's Magazine* Oct. 1914: 555–58.

Wendell, Barrett. "Democracy." *Literature, Society, and Politics: Selected Essays.* Ed. Robert T. Self. Saint Paul: Colet, 1977. 161–89.

———. *A Literary History of America.* New York: Scribner's, 1900.

———. *"Stelligeri" and Other Essays concerning America.* New York: Scribner's, 1893.

Wharton, Edith. *A Backward Glance.* New York: Appleton-Century, 1934.

———. "Botticelli's Madonna in the Louvre." *Scribner's Magazine* Jan. 1891: 74.

———. "Disintegration." Ts. and ms. Edith Wharton Collection. Beinecke Lib. Yale University, New Haven.

———. "The Eyes." *"The Muse's Tragedy" and Other Stories.* Ed. and introd. Candace Waid. New York: Signet, 1990. 321–41.

———. *French Ways and Their Meaning.* 1919. Lee: Berkshire, 1997.

———. "The Fullness of Life." *"The Muse's Tragedy" and Other Stories.* Ed. and introd. Candace Waid. New York: New York: Signet, 1990. 20–31.

———. *The House of Mirth.* 1905. New York: Penguin, 1985.

———. *Italian Backgrounds.* 1905. Hopewell: Ecco, 1998.

———. *Italian Villas and Their Gardens.* 1904. New York: Da Capo, 1976.

———. *The Letters of Edith Wharton.* Ed. R. W. B. Lewis and Nancy Lewis. New York: Collier, 1988.

———. *A Motor-Flight through France.* 1908. DeKalb: Northern Illinois University Press, 1991.

———. *Sanctuary.* 1903. *"Madame de Treymes" and Others: Four Short Novels by Edith Wharton*, London: Virago, 1984. 85–162.

———. *The Uncollected Writings.* Ed. and introd. Frederick Wegener. Princeton: Princeton University Press, 1996.

———. *The Writing of Fiction.* New York: Scribner's, 1925.

Wharton, Edith, and Ogden Codman, Jr. *The Decoration of Houses.* 1897. New York: Classical America Ser. New York: Norton, 1998.

Whittlesey, E. S. *Symbols and Legends in Western Art.* New York: Scribner's, 1972.

Williams, Sherwood. "The Rise of a New Degeneration: Decadence and Atavism in *Vandover and the Brute.*" *ELH* 57 (1990): 709–36.

Woodberry, George Edward. *The Torch: Eight Lectures on Race Power in Literature Delivered before the Lowell Institute.* 1905. Freeport: Books for Libraries, 1969.

Selected Bibliography

Abbott, Reginald. " 'A Moment's Ornament': Wharton's Lily Bart and Art Nouveau." *Mosaic: A Journal for the Interdisciplinary Study of Literature* 24.2 (1991): 73–91.

Ammons, Elizabeth. "Edith Wharton and the Issue of Race." In *The Cambridge Companion to Edith Wharton*. Ed. Millicent Bell. New York: Cambridge University Press, 1995. 68–86.

———. *Edith Wharton's Argument with America*. Athens: University of Georgia Press, 1980.

Bauer, Dale M. "The Failure of the Republic." In *Feminist Dialogics: A Theory of Failed Community*. Albany: State University of New York Press, 1988. 89–127.

Bazin, Nancy Topping. "The Destruction of Lily Bart: Capitalism, Christianity, and Male Chauvinism." *Denver Quarterly* 7.4 (winter 1983): 97–108.

Beaty, Robin. "Lilies That Fester: Sentimentality in *The House of Mirth*." *College Literature* 14 (1987): 263–75.

Bell, Millicent. *Edith Wharton and Henry James: The Story of Their Friendship*. New York: Braziller, 1965.

Bell, Millicent, ed. *The Cambridge Companion to Edith Wharton*. New York: Cambridge University Press, 1995.

Bendixen, Alfred, and Annette Zilversmit, eds. *Edith Wharton: New Critical Essays*. New York: Garland, 1992.

Benert, Annette Larson. "The Geography of Gender in *The House of Mirth*." *Studies in the Novel* 22 (1990): 26–42.

Benstock, Shari. *No Gifts from Chance: A Biography of Edith Wharton*. New York: Scribner's, 1994.

———. *Women of the Left Bank: Paris, 1900–1940*. Austin: University of Texas Press, 1986.

Benstock, Shari, ed. *The House of Mirth*. Case Studies in Contemporary Criticism. New York: St. Martin's Press, 1994.

Bentley, Nancy. *The Ethnography of Manners: Hawthorne, James, Wharton*. New York: Cambridge University Press, 1995.

Beppu, Keiko. "The Moral Significance of Living Space: The Library and the Kitchen in *The House of Mirth*." *Edith Wharton Review* 14 (1997): 3–7.

Boydston, Jeanne. " 'Grave Endearing Traditions': Edith Wharton and the Domestic Novel." In *Faith of a (Woman) Writer*. Ed. Alice Kessler Harris and William McBrien. New York: Greenwood Press, 1988. 31–40.

Brooks, Kristina. "New Woman ¯allen Woman: The Crisis of Reputation in Turn-of-the-Century Novels by Pauline Hopkins and Edith Wharton." *Legacy* 13 (1996): 92–112.

Clubbe, John. "Interiors and the Interior Life in Edith Wharton's *The House of Mirth*." *Studies in the Novel* 28 (1996): 543–64.

Colquitt, Clare. "Succumbing to the 'Literary Style': Arrested Desire in *The House of Mirth*." *Women's Studies: An Interdisciplinary Journal* 20.2 (1991): 153–62.

Colquitt, Clare, Susan Goodman, and Candace Waid, eds. *A Forward Glance: New Essays on Edith Wharton*. Newark: University of Delaware Press, 1999.

Dawson, Melanie. "Lily Bart's Fractured Alliances and Wharton's Appeal to the Middlebrow Reader." *Essays in Reader-Oriented Theory, Criticism, and Pegagogy* 41 (1999): 1–30.

Dittmar, Linda. "When Privilege Is No Protection: The Woman Artist in *Quicksand* and *The House of Mirth*." In *Writing the Woman Artist: Essays on Poetics, Politics, and Portraiture*. Ed. Suzanne W. Jones. Philadelphia: University of Pennsylvania Press, 1991. 133–54.

Dixon, Roslyn. "Reflecting Vision in *The House of Mirth*." *Twentieth Century Literature* 33.2 (summer 1987): 211–22.

Donovan, Josephine. *After the Fall: The Demeter-Persephone Myth in Wharton, Cather, and Glasgow.* University Park: Pennsylvania State University Press, 1989.

Dwight, Eleanor. *Edith Wharton: An Extraordinary Life: An Illustrated Biography.* New York: Abrams, 1995.

Erlich, Gloria C. "On the Threshold." In *The Sexual Education of Edith Wharton.* Berkeley: University of California Press, 1992. 50–74.

Esch, Deborah. *New Essays on* The House of Mirth. Cambridge: Cambridge University Press, 2001.

Fedorko, Kathy A. *Gender and the Gothic in the Fiction of Edith Wharton.* Tuscaloosa: University of Alabama Press, 1995.

Fetterley, Judith. " 'The Temptation to Be a Beautiful Object': Double Standard and Double Bind in *The House of Mirth.*" *Studies in American Fiction* 5 (1977): 199–211.

Fryer, Judith. *Felicitous Space: The Imaginative Structures of Edith Wharton and Willa Cather.* Chapel Hill: University of North Carolina Press, 1986.

———. "Reading Mrs. Lloyd." In *Edith Wharton: New Critical Essays.* Ed. Alfred Bendixen and Annette Zilversmit. New York: Garland, 1992. 27–53.

Gargano, James W. "*The House of Mirth*: Social Futility and Faith." *American Literature* 44.1 (Mar. 1972): 137–43.

Gerard, Bonnie Lynn. "From Tea to Chloral: Raising the Dead Lily Bart." *Twentieth Century Literature* 44.4 (1998): 409–27.

Gimbel, Wendy. *Edith Wharton: Orphancy and Survival.* New York: Praeger, 1984.

Goodman, Susan. *Edith Wharton's Inner Circle.* Austin: University of Texas Press, 1994.

———. *Edith Wharton's Women: Friends and Rivals.* Hanover, N.H.: University Press of New England, 1990.

Goodwyn, Janet Beer. *Edith Wharton: Traveller in the Land of Letters.* New York: St. Martin's Press, 1990.

Herman, David. "Style-Shifting in Edith Wharton's *The House of Mirth*: A Study in Point of View." *Language and Literature: A Journal of the Poetics and Linguistics Association* 10 (Feb. 2001): 61–77.

Hochman, Barbara. "*The Awakening* and *The House of Mirth*: Plotting Experience and Experiencing Plot." In *The Cambridge Companion to American Realism and Naturalism: Howells to London.* Ed. Donald Pizer. New York: Cambridge University Press, 1995. 211–35.

———. "The Return of the Author: The Realist Writer as a Woman

Onstage." In *Getting at the Author: Reimagining Books and Reading in the Age of American Realism.* Ed. Barbara Hochman. Amherst: University of Massachusetts Press, 2001. 70–92.

———. "The Rewards of Representation: Edith Wharton, Lily Bart and the Writer/Reader Interchange." *Novel: A Forum on Fiction* 24.2 (1991): 147–61.

Howard, Maureen. "*The House of Mirth*: The Bachelor and the Baby." In *The Cambridge Companion to Edith Wharton.* Ed. Millicent Bell. New York: Cambridge University Press, 1995. 137–56.

Howe, Irving. *Edith Wharton: A Collection of Critical Essays.* Twentieth Century Views series. Englewood Cliffs, N.J.: Prentice Hall, 1962.

Hutchinson, Stuart. "From *Daniel Deronda* to *The House of Mirth.*" *Essays in Criticism* 47.4 (1997): 315–42.

Jones, Suzanne W. " 'Secret Sensitiveness,' *The Decoration of Houses*, and Her Fiction." *Journal of Modern Literature* 21.2 (winter 1997–1998): 177–200.

Joslin, Katherine. *Edith Wharton.* Women Writers series. New York: St. Martin's Press, 1991.

Joslin, Katherine, and Alan Price, eds. *Wretched Exotic: Essays on Edith Wharton in Europe.* New York: Peter Lang, 1993.

Karcher, Carolyn L. "Male Vision and Female Revision in James's *The Wings of the Dove* and Wharton's *The House of Mirth.*" *Women's Studies* 10 (1984): 228–44.

Kay, Richard. "Literary Naturalism and the Passive Male: Edith Wharton's Revision of *The House of Mirth.*" *Princeton University Library Chronicle* 56 (1994): 47–72.

Killoran, Helen. *Edith Wharton: Art and Allusion.* Tuscaloosa: University of Alabama Press, 1996.

Lewis, R. W. B. *Edith Wharton: A Biography.* New York: Harper and Row, 1975.

Lindberg, Gary. *Edith Wharton and the Novel of Manners.* Charlottesville: University Press of Virginia, 1975.

Loebel, Thomas. "Beyond Her Self." In *New Essays on* The House of Mirth. Ed. Deborah Esch. Cambridge: Cambridge University Press, 2001. 107–32.

Lubbock, Percy. *Portrait of Edith Wharton.* New York: Appleton-Century, 1947.

McDowell, Margaret B. *Edith Wharton.* Boston: G. K. Hall, 1976.

Michaels, Walter Benn. "Action and Accident: Photography and Writing." In *The Gold Standard and the Logic of Naturalism.* Ed. Walter Benn Michaels. Berkeley: University of California, 1987. 215–44.

Michelson, Bruce. "Edith Wharton's House Divided." *Studies in American Fiction* 12.2 (1984): 199–215.

Moddelmog, William E. "Disowning 'Personality': Privacy and Subjectivity in *The House of Mirth.*" *American Literature* 70 (1998): 337–63.

Montgomery, Maureen E. *Displaying Women: Spectacles of Leisure in Edith Wharton's New York.* New York: Routledge, 1998.

Nettels, Elsa. *Language and Gender in American Fiction: Howells, James, Wharton and Cather.* Charlottesville: University Press of Virginia, 1997.

Nevius, Blake. *Edith Wharton: A Study of Her Fiction.* Berkeley: University of California Press, 1953.

Norris, Margot. "Death by Speculation: Deconstructing *The House of Mirth.*" In *The House of Mirth.* Case Studies in Contemporary Criticism. Ed. Shari Benstock. New York: St. Martin's Press, 1994. 431–46.

Nowlin, Michael. "Edith Wharton and the Matter of Contexts." *Studies in the Novel* 33.2 (2001): 64–78.

Nyquist, Mary. "Determining Influences: Resistance and Mentorship in *The House of Mirth* and the Anglo-American Realist Tradition." In *New Essays on* The House of Mirth. Ed. Deborah Esch. Cambridge: Cambridge University Press, 2001.

Orr, Elaine Neil. "Negotiation Our Text: The Search for Accommodations in Edith Wharton's *The House of Mirth.*" In *Subject to Negotiation: Reading Feminist Criticism and American Women's Fictions.* Ed. Elaine Neil Orr. Charlottesville: University of Virginia Press, 1997. 27–45.

Pickrel, Paul. "Vanity Fair in America: *The House of Mirth* and *Gone with the Wind.*" *American Literature* 59.1 (Mar. 1987): 37–57.

Pizer, Donald. "The Naturalism of Edith Wharton's *The House of Mirth.*" *Twentieth Century Literature* 41.2 (summer 1995): 241–48.

Preston, Claire. *Edith Wharton's Social Register.* New York: St. Martin's Press, 1999.

Price, Alan. "Lily Bart and Carrie Meeber: Cultural Sisters." *American Literary Realism* 13 (1980): 238–48.

Raphael, Lev. "The Classics." In *Edith Wharton's Prisoners of Shame: A New Perspective on Her Neglected Fiction.* Ed. Lev Raphael. New York: St. Martin's Press, 1991. 255–73.

Riegel, Christian. "Rosedale and Anti-Semitism in *The House of Mirth.*" *Studies in American Fiction* 20.2 (1992): 219–24.

Restuccia, Frances L. "The Name of the Lily: Edith Wharton's Feminism(s)." *Contemporary Literature* 28 (1987): 222–38. Repr. in *The House of Mirth.* Case Studies in Contemporary Criticism. Ed. Shari Benstock. New York: St. Martin's Press, 1994. 404–18.

Robinson, Lillian S. "The Traffic in Women: A Cultural Critique of *The House of Mirth*." In *The House of Mirth*. Case Studies in Contemporary Criticism. Ed. Shari Benstock. New York: St. Martin's Press, 1994. 340–58.

Rosk, Nancy von. "Spectacular Homes and Pastoral Theaters: Gender, Urbanity and Domesticity in *The House of Mirth*." *Studies in the Novel* 33.3 (2001): 322–50.

Sapora, Carol Baker. "Female Doubling: The Other Lily Bart in Edith Wharton's *The House of Mirth*." *Papers on Language and Literature* 29.4 (fall 1993): 371–95.

Singley, Carol J. *Edith Wharton: Matters of Mind and Spirit*. New York: Cambridge University Press, 1995.

Steiner, Wendy. "The Causes of Effect: Edith Wharton and the Economics of Ekphrasis." *Poetics Today* 10.2 (1989): 279–97.

Sullivan, Ellie Ragland. "The Daughter's Dilemma: Psychoanalytic Interpretation and Edith Wharton's *The House of Mirth*." In *The House of Mirth*. Case Studies in Contemporary Criticism. Ed. Shari Benstock. New York: St. Martin's Press, 1994. 464–82.

Tillman, Lynne. "A Mole in the House of the Modern." In *New Essays on* The House of Mirth. Ed. Deborah Esch. Cambridge: Cambridge University Press, 2001. 133–58.

Tuttleton, James W., Kristin O. Lauer, and Margaret P. Murray, eds. *Edith Wharton: The Contemporary Reviews*. New York: Cambridge University Press, 1992.

Tyson, Lois. "Beyond Morality: Lily Bart, Lawrence Selden and the Aesthetic Commodity in *The House of Mirth*." *Edith Wharton Review* 9 (1992): 3–10.

Vita-Finzi, Penelope. *Edith Wharton and the Art of Fiction*. London: Pinter, 1990.

Waid, Candace. *Edith Wharton's Letters from the Underworld*. Chapel Hill: University of North Carolina Press, 1991.

Wharton, Edith. *A Backward Glance*. New York: Appleton-Century, 1934.

———. *The House of Mirth*. New York: Scribner's, 1905. Rpt. in *Edith Wharton: Novels*. Ed. R. W. B. Lewis. New York: Library of America, 1985. 1–347.

———. *The Letters of Edith Wharton*. Ed. R. W. B. Lewis and Nancy Lewis. New York: Scribner's, 1988.

———. *The Writing of Fiction*. New York: Scribner's, 1925.

White, Barbara. *Edith Wharton: A Study of the Short Fiction*. New York: Twayne, 1991.

Wiser, William. *The Great Good Place: American Expatriate Women in Paris*. New York: Norton, 1991.

Wolff, Cynthia Griffin. *A Feast of Words: The Triumph of Edith Wharton*. New York: Oxford University Press, 1977.

Wright, Sarah Bird. *Edith Wharton A to Z: The Essential Guide to the Life and Work of Edith Wharton*. New York: Facts on File, 1998.

———. *Edith Wharton's Travel Writing: The Making of a Connoisseur*. New York: St. Martin's Press, 1997.

Yeazell, Ruth Bernard. "The Conspicuous Wasting of Lily Bart." *English Literary History* 59 (1992): 713–34. Repr. in *New Essays on* The House of Mirth. Ed. Deborah Esch. Cambridge: Cambridge University Press, 2001. 15–41.